Handbook of counselling in Britain

Handbook of counselling in Britain

Edited by Windy Dryden, David Charles-Edwards, and Ray Woolfe

Published in association with the British Association for Counselling

TAVISTOCK/ROUTLEDGE

First Published in 1989
by Routledge
11 New Fetter Lane, London EC4P 4EE

Typeset by LaserScript Limited, Mitcham, Surrey
Printed and bound in Great Britain by
Biddles Ltd, Guildford and King's Lynn

British Library Cataloguing in Publication Data

Handbook of counselling in Great Britain.
   1. Great Britain. Counselling
   I. Dryden, Windy II. Charles-Edward, David, *1938–*
   III. Woolfe, Ray IV. British Association For Counselling
   361.3'23'0941

   ISBN 0–415–01327–5

THIS BOOK IS DEDICATED TO
LOUISE
ALISON and ANNA
ADRIENNE, CLARE, and ALEX

Contents

Contents

Figures and tables

Figures

Tables

Contributors

Anne Abel Smith, Research psychologist and Director of Leeming Research Ltd., Nottingham

Diane Bailey, Senior Counsellor, The Open University

Tony Bolger, Senior Lecturer, Department of Applied Social Studies and Social Work, University of Keele

Paul Brown, Director, Marylebone Consultancy Unit, Marylebone Health Centre, London

Jocelyn Chaplin, Psychotherapist in Private Practice, London

David Charles-Edwards, Consultant in Organizational and Individual Development; formerly Executive Officer, British Association for Counselling

Grahame F. Cooper, Training and Consultancy Services, Birmingham

Windy Dryden, Senior Lecturer in Psychology, Goldsmiths' College, University of London

John Foskett, Chaplain, Bethlem Royal and Maudsley Hospitals; former Chair, Association for Pastoral Care and Counselling Division, British Association for Counselling

Patrick Hughes, Guidance Unit, School of Education, University of Reading

Jill Irving, Counsellor in General Practice; Chair, Counselling in Medical Settings Division, British Association for Counselling

Michael Jacobs, Director of Counselling Studies, Department of Adult Education, University of Leicester; Director of Pastoral Care and Counselling, Dioceses of Derby, Lincoln, and Southwell

Colin Lago, Head, Counselling Service, University of Sheffield; former Chair, Association for Student Counselling Division, British Association for Counselling

Michael Megranahan, Manager, Employee Advisory Resource, Control Data Ltd.; Chair, Counselling at Work Division, British Association for Counselling

Tony Milne, Director of Counselling at the Centre for Professional Employment Counselling (CEPEC); formerly first Chair of the Counselling at Work Division of the British Association for Counselling

Barbara Pearce, Director, Counselling and Career Development Unit, University of Leeds

Bernard Ratigan, Principal Adult Psychotherapist, Nottingham Psychotherapy Unit, St Ann's Hospital, Nottingham; formerly Head of the Student Counselling Service, Loughborough University of Technology

Tom Schröder, Department of Psychotherapy, Southern Derbyshire Health Authority

Julia Segal, Research Officer, Action for Research into Multiple Sclerosis

John Sketchley, Consultant to the World Health Organization on HIV/AIDS and Counselling; former National Organizer of Friend

Averil Stedeford, formerly Consultant in Psychological Medicine, Sir Michael Sobell House, Oxfordshire Health Authority

Eddy Street, Clinical Psychologist, Preswylfa Child and Family Centre, Cardiff

Léonie Sugarman, Lecturer in Psychology, Birkbeck College, University of London

Carole Sutton, Senior Lecturer in Psychology, School of Applied Social Sciences and Public Administration, Leicester Polytechnic

Joyce Thompson, Senior Education Manager, West Lambeth Health Authority; Chair, Racism Awareness in Counselling Education Group, British Association for Counselling

Richard Velleman, Lecturer in Psychology, University of Bath; Principal Clinical Psychologist, Bath Health District

Ray Woolfe, School of Education, The Open University; Chair, Counselling Psychology Section, British Psychological Society; formerly Deputy Chair, British Association for Counselling

Preface

Counselling has developed widely in Britain over the past two decades. This is reflected in the employment of people, both in a paid and a voluntary capacity, as counsellors. It is also evidenced in a growth in the number of people, not specifically employed as counsellors, but claiming to employ counselling skills in the course of their work and their day-to-day activities. Looking at these changes, it seemed to us that there was a need for a book which would provide an overview of the main strands underlying the various developments.

The three editors came together through their involvement, in various capacities, in the work of the British Association for Counselling. This organization was established in 1977, the product of a Standing Conference for the Advancement of Counselling, which had existed since 1971. The British Association for Counselling attempts to provide a co-ordinating forum for all the varied activities which go on under the heading of counselling and is widely acknowledged as representing the voice of counselling in Britain.

The book seeks to offer a comprehensive review of the main fields of counselling activity in Britain today, and is published in association with the British Association for Counselling. Clearly, the opinions expressed within each chapter are those of the individual authors and do not necessarily represent the views of the Association.

A book of this kind, with over twenty contributors, inevitably reflects the diversity as well as the coherence of counselling in Britain. Nevertheless, we believe that the book offers, as far as this is possible, a snapshot of the theory and practice underlying the mainstream world of counselling in Britain at the present time. Moreover, because authors were requested to construct their chapters around an organizing framework of 'Principles, Issues, and Future Developments', the book possesses a degree of coherence which otherwise would have been difficult to achieve in a project of this magnitude.

The book is divided into five parts. In the first part, the Introduction, we set the scene by describing the nature and range of counselling as it is practised in Britain today. Then in Chapter 2, Woolfe and Sugarman place counselling in the context of the life cycle, which we see as an important framework in which the work of counsellors with clients of different ages can be viewed. In Part 2, the practice of counselling is described as it occurs in its major arenas, i.e. individual, couples, family and group counselling. In Part 3 various authors consider counselling as it is practised in a wide variety of social settings. Then in Part 4, important thematic topics are highlighted. Here authors consider counselling where the focus ranges from race and gender to questions of sexual orientation, HIV and AIDS, and alcohol and drug problems amongst others. Finally, in Part 5, the book ends by considering issues of evaluation and professionalism.

We have not included detailed information about individuals or agencies offering counselling services or about training courses in counselling as such information frequently changes. However, if you seek current details in these areas you should contact the British Association for Counselling at 37a Sheep Street, Rugby, Warwickshire CV21 3BX.

Windy Dryden
David Charles-Edwards
Ray Woolfe

Abbreviations

ABC   Association of Black Counsellors
APCC   Association for Pastoral Care and Counselling (BAC)
ASC   Association for Student Counselling (BAC)
ASMT   Association of Sexual and Marital Therapists
BAC   British Association for Counselling
BACUP British Association for Cancer United Patients
BPS   British Psychological Society
CAW   Counselling at Work (BAC)
CCDU   Counselling and Career Development Unit (Leeds University)
CEPEC Centre for Professional Employment Counselling
CIE   Counselling in Education (BAC)
CMS   Counselling in Medical Settings (BAC)
CRUSE National Organization for the Widowed and their Children
CVPE   Certificate of Pre-vocational Education
DES   Department of Education and Science
DHA   District Health Authority
EAP   Employee Assistance Programme
FPC   Family Practitioner Committee
ISDD   Institute for the Study of Drug Dependence
MS   Multiple sclerosis
MSC   Manpower Services Commission
NHS   National Health Service
NLP   Neuro-linguistic programming
NMGC   National Marriage Guidance Council (now known as Relate: National Marriage Guidance)
PAPI   Perception and Preference Inventory
PSMF   Personal/Sexual/Marital/Family Counselling (BAC)
SEPI   Society for the Exploration of Psychotherapy Integration
TA   Transactional Analysis
TC   Training Commission

TVEI   Technical and Vocational Education Initiative
WPF   Westminster Pastoral Foundation
YTS   Youth Training Scheme

Part one

Introduction

Chapter one

The nature and range of counselling practice

Ray Woolfe, Windy Dryden, and David Charles-Edwards

Introduction

In this chapter, we aim to provide an introduction to the Handbook which will:

(1) Offer a definition of counselling and discuss its universality.
(2) Ask the question, Is Counselling a Movement? Through this question, we ask whether it is legitimate to regard counselling as a homogeneous, unitary activity.
(3) Examine the nature of counselling by looking at the different theoretical streams which provide the origins of the various activities we now describe as counselling. We do not pretend that this account of schools of thought is comprehensive. Our aim is simply to indicate the heterogeneity of the influences impinging upon counselling.
(4) Identify different categories of people who practise counselling and counselling skills.
(5) Extend this discussion within the context of the British Association for Counselling, the co-ordinating body in the field of counselling in England and Wales.
(6) Focus on the question of how one becomes a client and the facilities available in the public and private (including the voluntary) sectors.
(7) Attempt to pull together all these strands through an overview of the forces likely to influence the world of counselling in the years ahead.

A definition of counselling

There is no copyright or patent on the use of the term counselling. In common parlance, it is frequently presented as a form of advice-giving; a definition legitimated by the practice of well-known dictionaries such as the Concise Oxford (Sykes 1987). The term is now widely employed in this way, not least in the area of finance and business where there can increasingly be found references to such activities as debt counselling or double-glazing counselling. This serves to indicate the magnitude of the task which people involved with counselling still

3

face in explaining its true meaning to the wider world. Counselling is a helping activity and one characteristic of such events is that they often happen spontaneously. Most of us have had the experience of a friend, relative, neighbour or fellow worker suddenly raising with us a personal problem, stressful event, or area of life concern. A standard response is of the 'let's sit down, have a nice cup of tea and talk about it' variety. The person seeking help talks and perhaps even cries. All we have done is to listen, but the simple fact that another person has made the effort to listen uncritically, and tried to understand what it feels like, may itself be cathartic. We have helped that other person. In the process, and whether we realize it or not, we have displayed some of the skills of counselling, such as listening actively to the other person's feelings, focusing on their problem rather than on our own immediate concerns, and being accepting and uncritical.

As we indicated above, a major characteristic of events such as these is that they happen almost spontaneously. In contrast, counselling is a more deliberate activity and in its definition of the term the British Association for Counselling (BAC)[1] spells out the distinction between a planned and a spontaneous event. 'People become engaged in counselling when a person, occupying regularly or temporarily the role of counsellor, offers or agrees explicitly to offer time, attention and respect to another person or persons temporarily in the role of client' (BAC 1985: 1). Key terms within this definition are, first, the notion of 'offers or agrees', and second, the word 'explicitly'. Normally the counsellor is approached by the client. Counselling can only begin, therefore, when the counsellor has agreed to offer his or her services. Sometimes, however, a counsellor may approach another person with an offer to help. In that case counselling only begins when the other person has clearly accepted that offer. In essence what we are involved with here is the subject of boundaries and that is also evident in the use of the term 'explicitly'. According to the British Association for Counselling, this 'is the dividing line between the counselling task and *ad hoc* counselling and is the major safe-guard of the rights of the consumer' (BAC 1985: 2).

This definition of counselling provides a model or framework or reference point around which further discussion about the nature and range of counselling practice can take place. Counselling needs rigorous definition of this sort if it is to avoid the danger of becoming woolly and diffuse. At the same time, the use of such a precise definition raises a number of important issues. These derive primarily from the fact that the activity of counselling is not confined to the work carried out by people formally designated as counsellors. People with a vast variety of titles in both paid and voluntary fields would claim to employ counselling skills, though they would not necessarily define themselves as counsellors. Their work represents an important part of the world of counselling and without it counselling would be a very restricted and exclusive activity. However, to acknowledge such activity as counselling presents us with a potential contradiction: that to do so, we may have to accept that the BAC definition, while providing a basic reference point or ideal, is too narrowly restrictive to encompass all the activity carried out under the heading of people practising counselling skills. It is this difference which is being referred to by the distinction made by the BAC between 'the counselling task' and '*ad hoc* counselling'. In practice, however, the difference is not always easy to draw in every context and we may be faced with a continuum rather than two polarities. A refinement of this problem arises from the fact that counsellor and client may hold other roles in relation to each other. Thus, for example, a manager may have the task of counselling a worker for whom he or she has line management responsibility or a tutor may have the responsibility for counselling a student for whom he or she has a teaching responsibility. The BAC definition attempts to resolve this potential conflict by suggesting that 'clarification of the opportunity offered, in a way that the client can understand, differentiates the counselling task from other mutual responsibilities, in the perception of both client and counsellor' (BAC 1985: 2). However, once again the tidiness of a theoretical definition may not be easy to replicate in the complex and often messy and confusing empirical world in which we all have to live.

The definition of counselling employed by the BAC is helpful and indeed vital if counselling is to develop as a professional field of activity with appropriate ethics and standards. It is something to which all people practising counselling skills should seek to aspire. Nevertheless, at this stage in the historical development of counselling in Britain, a restriction upon any activity calling itself counselling, which did not satisfy the criteria incorporated within this definition, would run the risk of strangling the growing organism in its infancy. In any event, because nobody has any proprietary rights on the term 'counselling', it would be difficult or even impossible to control its use. The reality is that if the definition employed by the British Association is to become widely accepted and acted upon, it will almost certainly happen by argument and persuasion and not through restrictive, formal legislation.

Is counselling a movement?

Readers of this book will not be surprised to find that within its pages there are references to something described as the 'counselling movement'. There are also occasional references, particularly in Pearce's chapter on counselling in professional and organizational development (Chapter 12), to what is referred to as the 'counselling-skills movement'. This frequent usage of the notion of movement reflects the popularity of the term within the wider community of counselling and suggests a commonly held set of beliefs, attitudes, and convictions. To some extent these clearly do exist. All counsellors would subscribe, for example, to the view that their aim or mission is to improve the quality of human life. There are also other values which would command at least widespread lip-service. There is, for example, a widespread belief among counsellors in the human potential for change and development. On the other hand, major differences also exist, some of which are basic and fundamental. Thus, there is no conformity of opinion about whether counselling is the same activity as, or a different activity from, psychotherapy, and if indeed there is a difference, where the boundary lies. Similarly, there are major doctrinal disagreements between such diverse schools of counselling as person-centred, psychodynamic, cognitive, and behavioural. Counsellors operating within each of these paradigms may have a greater sense of identity with each other than they do with the so-called counselling movement as a whole. To find an area of total agreement, it is necessary to adopt a broad lowest common denominator. Indeed, the values and objective outlined above could to some extent be subscribed to by other groups such as doctors, nurses, social workers, or priests whose primary commitment was not to counselling.

In short, in thinking about the nature and range of counselling practice, we need to avoid the danger of reifying something called the counselling movement; that it is to say, treating it as though it were a unitary body which had some kind of objective, real in the world existence akin to a formal organization. The concept of a counselling movement has been addressed by Chester (1985) in discussing the changes which were taking place within what was then the National Marriage Guidance Council during the late 1980s.[2] He refers to the development of the NMGC from a 'marriage movement to service agency'. The difference between the two is defined by saying that 'the former has values to promote and members to affirm them, whilst the latter has objectives to achieve and personnel to implement them' (p. 6). Another way of thinking about this distinction is to say that a movement is something which inspires voluntarily given support, whereas an organization enlists support through more instrumental arrangements with its members.

Applying this sort of definition, it is doubtful whether counselling represents a sufficiently coherent set of values to be described as a movement, though services offered within the field might warrant such a description, particularly if they formed an integral part of an organization whose wider remit was to promote a cause. Examples might include organizations concerned with offering counselling services as part of a wider programme like promoting gay/lesbian rights or greater or more restricted access to abortion, or better care for people with a disability. The development from movement to organization has already been exemplified by the case of the NMGC and another major example is CRUSE. Here we have a body founded as an association concerned with the welfare of widows (i.e. specifically for women), but which has gradually transformed itself into an organization with a wider 'gender neutral' concern with bereavement.

We do not wish to labour this discussion. Terms like movement can never have entirely watertight definitions. Moreover, while in theory, movement and organization may be seen as two polarities, in practice we are inevitably referring to a continuum along which counselling agencies can be located. Our purpose is to indicate that the term is worth unravelling in order to demonstrate that the notion of counselling as a movement, a kind of body of like-minded people harmoniously pursuing the same goals, should not be treated uncritically as though it were some kind of self-evident truth. There is plenty of room for debate about the multifarious patchwork quilt or set of activities that we know of (and love) as counselling and the purpose of this chapter is to articulate both the heterogeneity and the common basis of counselling practice within Great Britain.

The origins of counselling: different schools of thought

A necessary starting-point in this survey of the nature and range of counselling practice is to ask ourselves where counselling comes from. Answering this question is no easy task. Counselling is an activity whose roots are extremely complex. However, a number of key influences can be identified. These include (a) Sigmund Freud and psychoanalysis; (b) the Californian personal growth and humanistic psychology movement of the 1950s and 1960s, of whom Carl Rogers has had the most influence upon counselling practice; (c) more orthodox schools of mainstream psychology out of which have developed a variety of behavioural and cognitive therapies. These have been particularly influential in fields such as sexual dysfunction, alcohol and drug abuse, and social-skills training programmes. In thinking about what each of these influences have contributed to contemporary counselling practice it is important to see each of them as a product of a particular historical age and culture. This is well exemplified by the debate about the relationship between counselling and psychotherapy.

Counselling and psychotherapy

A long-running discussion within counselling circles concerns the boundaries between counselling and psychotherapy. Some people see the two as different terms describing the same sets of activities. Patterson (1974), for example, concludes that there are no essential differences and Truax and Carkhuff (1967) use the terms interchangeably. On the other side of the argument the following points are sometimes made:

(a) that psychotherapy is concerned with personality change whereas counselling is concerned with helping an individual to utilize his or her own coping resources (see Tyler 1967). However, Nelson-Jones (1982) argues that mobilizing coping resources might well be considered as personality change;
(b) that psychotherapy is concerned with people who are in some sense 'neurotic' or psychologically disturbed, whereas counselling is concerned with people who are basically emotionally healthy but who are confronted by a temporary life problem or issue;
(c) that whereas the focus of methodology for the psychotherapist is the nature of the transference[3] between therapist and client, the counsellor is less

7

concerned with this relationship than with helping the client to clarify the issues and develop strategies of management by the counsellor's deployment of a specific set of relatively restricted skills;

(d) that the psychotherapist is concerned with the inner world of the client as opposed to the counsellor's focus on helping the client to resolve external issues which are generating problems;

(e) that the work of the psychotherapist is based on psychoanalytic theory, whereas the counsellor's work is inspired by humanistic approaches;

(f) that psychotherapists tend to work in medical settings, whereas counsellors tend to work in non-medical environments. Thus, the former work with patients and the latter with clients;

(g) that counselling tends to be a shorter-term process than psychotherapy, and vice versa.

In our view, attempts to resolve this issue in terms of some overarching theoretical plan are futile and serve no purpose. Both enterprises lay stress upon the need to value the client as a person, to listen in a non-judgmental and accepting fashion, and to foster the capacity for self-help. If there is a distinction, it lies in more mundane and down-to-earth concerns about the nature of the training, the settings in which people work, and the problems and issues with which they are typically confronted. Moreover, psychotherapy is as much an umbrella term as is counselling and like the latter contains a variety of subgroups. Thus, for example, what is known in 1988 as the Rugby Psychotherapy Conference which will eventually be transformed into the Standing Conference for Psychotherapy has for the past year or so had a number of embryo sections into which members have been asked to locate themselves. These are:

(a) Analytical Analyst;
(b) Analytical Psychotherapy;
(c) Behavioural Psychotherapy;
(d) Family, Marital, and Sexual Therapy;
(e) Humanistic, Eclectic, and Integrative Psychotherapy;
(f) Hypnotherapy and Neuro-linguistic Programming.

This list contains a lot of variety and many areas of sometimes strong disagreement. Members of the behavioural or humanistic sections, for example, would probably find more in common with counsellors of the same ilk than they would with each other or with other categories of psychotherapists.

It follows, therefore, that the two simple terms counselling and psychotherapy hide some complex variations within each category. In exploring these variations, it is necessary to look at their origins in different cultures, traditions and sometimes clearly distinct bodies of scientific knowledge. While contemporary practice reflects a great deal of contamination of ideas across traditions, the fact that they do stem from different traditions is important. They are, therefore, to be seen as social enterprises with their own cultures and values and to understand the modern practices we know as psychotherapy and counselling, it is necessary to trace them back to their cultural roots. It is only through such an analysis that we can properly understand the basis for the similarities and differences which appear to exist between psychotherapy and counselling and between different schools of psychotherapy and counselling.

The psychodynamic school

What we might refer to as the psychodynamic school (Freud, Jung, Adler, and their modern successors such as Klein, Bowlby, and Winnicott) was nurtured in a middle-class, patriarchal, hierarchical, emotionally and relatively sexually repressed medical Central European culture. If its modern manifestations still reflect some of these origins, it is hardly surprising. This is not to say that ideas have not changed or that methods have not developed: to make such an assertion would be absurd. Nevertheless, the notion of a patient rather than a client; of the person being helped lying down rather than being seated (in the psycho-analytical tradition); and of therapy as a long-term process involving transference and regression are important ones in the psychodynamic paradigm. What is important to acknowledge is that such an approach to helping was a product of its age and can appear old-fashioned in a world which emphasizes equality and a less hierarchical, more open relationship between professional and client. Nevertheless, schools of thought are not static and crucial ideas derived from Freud and his successors have been assimilated into, and have become part of, a great deal of contemporary counselling practice. The ideas of the past influencing the present and of personal crisis resulting from unresolved developmental conflicts in the past are familiar to most counsellors, acceptable to many, and acted upon in their counselling practice. A useful basic introduction to these ideas is contained in Jacobs (1985).

Inevitably such an account is simplistic. Just as the perception of counselling or psychotherapy as a unitary movement has been questioned, so the notion of a unitary psychodynamic school is also misleading. Nevertheless, what we can say is that much of what we now know as psychodynamic counselling has roots which go deep into the nineteenth century and that the nature of these origins has an influence upon the definition of the client's problem as perceived by the therapist, upon the kind of therapeutic methodology employed, and upon the nature of the relationship between therapist and client.

Person-centred, non-directive counselling

It may well be that many readers of this book would identify themselves with counselling rather than psychotherapy and might be only too tempted to agree with a point of view which sees much psychodynamic theory and methodology as somewhat outdated. While we have not accepted such a proposition, a majority of readers may still argue that the strongest influence upon their practice derives from the work of Carl Rogers and that his ideas about person-centred counselling, in particular the importance placed upon the core personal conditions of empathy, warmth, and genuineness, have a degree of universal validity. However, we do not accept this view at face value. The philosophy, theory, and methods of Rogerian person-centred counselling are as culturally located and, therefore, subject to exactly the same analysis and questions as the work of Freud and his successors.

Humanistic psychology, of which person-centred counselling is one stream, has been described as a 'third-force' in psychology (see Rowan 1976: 8). Its primary characteristic is seen as its optimistic view of human nature as compared with the more pessimistic, animalistic stance adopted by psychoanalysts and the somewhat deterministic stance of the classical behaviourists. Perhaps the optimism is not surprising given the origins of the humanistic school. The object of person-centred counselling, as seen by Rogers himself, is to help the client 'to become what he/she is capable of becoming' (Rogers 1951), or, to employ an even more well-worn phrase associated with Maslow, to achieve self-actualization (Maslow 1962). These terms have a slightly hollow ring about them in the enterprise economy of the late 1980s in Britain, in which the division between the 'haves' and the 'have nots' is sharply apparent. Striving for self-actualization is easier if one is well-off, well-housed, has a rewarding and secure job, and lives in a pleasant environment than if one is unemployed, poor, ill-housed, and lives in a run-down neighbourhood. Terms like self-actualization simply do not feature in and do not derive from the culture of the 1980s. Where they originated was the leisured, affluent, optimistic world of California in the 1950s and 1960s. For clients with plenty of money and in full employment, the process of moving towards self-actualization was and is a realistic goal. For clients who are unemployed, poor, and homeless, other objectives assume a higher priority. Just as the psychodynamic strand in counselling is a product of a time and place, so the humanistic strand is a product of its culture in the one case 'fin de siècle', Europe and in the other the affluent, utopian world of North America in the 1950s and 1960s.

Of course, just as many of the ideas of the psychodynamic approach have infiltrated into counselling, the process has also worked in reverse. Most psychotherapists, for example, would now work with the client in a seated position rather than lying down, thus acknowledging a more equal relationship between client and counsellor. The humanistic approach has also been influential in undermining the medical emphasis upon labelling, symptoms, and illness categories. Thus, the direction of ideas is both ways. What we are left with is a number of social enterprises which reflect both differences and similarities.

Egan: a bridge between the humanistic and the behavioural approaches

In the same way as the work of Freud has been added to and amended, so has that of the humanistic school. Carkhuff had suggested a fourth core condition, 'concreteness' (Carkhuff 1969), and the modern fashion is to perceive the core conditions as necessary but not sufficient for effective counselling. To be fully effective the core conditions have to be embedded in the practice of specific skills which have been identified and articulated particularly through the work of Egan (1975). Egan is arguably the most frequently quoted writer in the field of counselling at the present time and his work has been a major influence upon a generation of trainers. This is not surprising. Egan, ahead of his time, has succeeded in his work in capturing the emphasis of the enterprise economy of the 1980s on the acquisition of skills as a precondition for changing one's position in life. Awareness by itself is not enough. It is paradoxical that many counsellors who would perceive the behavioural therapies as manipulative and de-humanizing are themselves keen exponents of Egan's work. Yet a close examination of his work reveals that, particularly in its stages two and three, it owes a clear debt to the behavioural approach. Defining goals and specifying behaviours which if rewarded can help to achieve these goals is a clear acknowledgement of the influence of behaviourism.

Rogers's work is also dated in another way. Increasingly there is an interest in short-term, crisis-oriented counselling for which more directive, action-oriented procedures are usually advocated (see Murgatroyd and Woolfe 1982). We would suggest overall, therefore, that the person-centred strand within the world of counselling, though still strong and important, is less absolute than many counsellors might suppose and is itself subject to re-evaluation and change as the world we live in changes. As one of the writers of this chapter has argued elsewhere, counselling is a 'social enterprise' and cannot be divorced from the social, economic, and political environment in which it is practised (Woolfe 1982).

The influence of mainstream psychology

A third major theoretical influence upon counselling has been the world of post-war mainstream psychology, both European and North American. Behaviourism has already been referred to. It is not just a fringe counselling activity or the preserve of a few clinical psychologists. On the contrary, as we have indicated, its influence is deeply enmeshed within the work of probably the most important contemporary writer about training in counselling, Gerard Egan.

A long-standing concern of psychology has been with the development of a scientific methodology, particularly through the use of experimental research; and behaviourism has been both a vehicle for and an output of this concern. Essentially the tradition sees behaviour as the product of learning. People respond to stimuli and the response will, if reinforced, be likely to persist. People can learn to be helpless, for example (Seligman 1975), if a response to a particular stimulus, such as loss, is reinforced by significant others. Eysenck (1976) suggests that we should look at the symptoms of those in need as the product of learned behaviour. Over the past decade, behaviourally oriented

11

workers have broadened the methodology of their work by examining the relationship between the way in which a person evaluates or labels his or her situation and his or her emotional and behavioural reactions to such situations. Thus, for example, a person who labels forthcoming examinations as a potentially catastrophic event is more likely to experience anxiety problems than the person who perceives the event as a challenge.

One school of therapy, inspired by the work of Ellis (1962), has developed out of the viewpoint that behaviour can be changed by encouraging the client to dispute irrational beliefs and thus be taught to think more logically and rationally. This concern with cognition reflects a wider concern with cognitive factors within the world of psychology. It is also part of a debate about the relationship between thinking and emotions (cognition and affect) in the field of therapy. The traditional argument has been that emotions precede cognition and that how people think is dependent upon how they feel. People under stress, for example, may think less clearly than they would otherwise do or may find it more difficult to concentrate. However, the balance of opinion now is that the relationship is more complex and circular and that how people appraise a situation (i.e. how they think about it) may itself be a generator of feelings (see Lazarus 1978). Hence, for example, if you believe that talking to your boss will be difficult, it is likely to generate a host of feelings associated with stress.

The way in which behavioural and cognitive therapies have influenced each other and have become embedded as integral parts of the rich fabric we know as counselling indicates yet again what a heterogeneous field counselling is. Moreover, it indicates that the ideas which influence the practice of counselling are not static, but on the contrary are constantly and quietly in a state of flux. We believe that it is helpful to know whence the modern practices of counselling are derived, both in terms of understanding better the knowledge and ideas upon which the practices are predicated and the cultural beliefs which inspired them. Any therapy can be examined in this way. Thus, for example, Transactional Analysis is influenced both by Freud and by a social-psychological concern with the analysis of social as well as intrapsychic transactions. Similarly, gestalt therapy is seen (Patterson 1986) as deriving from a mixture of gestalt psychology (a concern with configuration and integration), from an existential emphasis on individual responsibility for thoughts, feelings, and actions in the here and now; and from Zen Buddhist concerns with people discovering their true natures.

Readers who seek a more detailed analysis of individual therapies should consult Dryden (1984) and we do not intend to repeat that discussion in this chapter. Our concern is primarily to suggest that the term 'counselling movement' is in fact a considerable over-simplification of a variety of approaches to working with people which have different origins, methods, objectives, and values. While the emphasis today may well be on eclecticism (see Dryden, Chapter 3), a lowest common denominator of what constitutes counselling has to be drawn extremely widely.

Counselling and counselling skills – who counsels?

Counselling is a broad church and this is reflected not just in its variety of therapeutic methods, but also in the structure of its practice – indeed, to some extent the latter is a function of the former. By structure, we refer to the question of who does what, where, and with whom. It is not without significance that the primary co-ordinating body for counselling in Britain is called the British Association for 'Counselling', not 'Counsellors'. This reflects the reality that the world of counselling encapsulates a much greater collection of interests than is represented by people employed as professional counsellors. It is useful, therefore, to attempt to identify groups of workers with an interest in counselling. We have identified five such categories. We have also attempted to describe each category in detail, though the absence of scientific data makes this a somewhat difficult and inevitably tentative exercise.

People whose primary professional training is in counselling and who are employed full-time as counsellors

Within the public sector of employment, this group is relatively limited. Its greatest concentration is among student counsellors in institutions of higher education. In addition, there also exists a significant number of counsellors working in the field of careers guidance. In general, the decline of public-sector employment during the 1980s has affected counselling at least as much as other occupations. For example, a development in the appointment of counsellors in secondary schools which at one point appeared to offer some promise of increasing employment for counsellors proved to be stillborn (see Chapter 9 by Hughes in this volume).

Perhaps as a response to the decline in public-sector employment, many trained counsellors now operate as private consultants. This field has always been strong in parts of London, where psychoanalysis and various fields of psychotherapy have long traditions. However, such therapies tend to be long term and expensive (as is the training which produces such therapists) and on the whole this form of private psychodynamic psychotherapy is not widely available. However, it should be clear that terms such as 'psychotherapist' or 'counsellor' have no copyright attached to them. At the moment, anybody can offer their services by describing themselves in these terms. Increasingly attempts are being made to regulate the field. Thus, the BAC operates an accreditation scheme for counsellors and approved persons are eligible to refer to themselves as BAC Accredited Counsellors. However, it is significant that in 1986 the percentage of BAC members accredited stood at less than 9 per cent (Aldridge 1987). There is no doubt that a very large number of persons throughout the United Kingdom are offering private counselling services and it is extremely unlikely that more than a small proportion of these are accredited.

People whose primary professional training is not in counselling, but who are employed as full-time counsellors

Counselling skills are increasingly being seen as an integral and intrinsic part of wider professional training programmes. These include such diverse occupational groups as nurses, social workers, probation officers, personnel managers, managers, community workers, and psychologists. This has led to a situation in which a number of these professionals now work as counsellors particularly in health-linked fields such as AIDS, pregnancy, contraception and abortion, and alcohol and drug abuse. Some of these professionals have received further specific forms of training in counselling either as a pre-condition for doing the job or voluntarily. In many cases, however, it is likely that the primary professional identification will remain as nurse, doctor, or psychologist rather than as counsellor. Even if further counselling training has been undertaken, it is probably unlikely that many such workers would quality for accreditation. Most would fail to satisfy one of the following three criteria:

(a) participation in personal development activities and training;
(b) the experience of being a client;
(c) receiving appropriate supervision.

People whose primary professional training is not in counselling, and who are not employed as counsellors, but who are employing counselling skills in their work

This category is increasing and counselling skills are now acknowledged as a standard feature of both the initial professional and in-service training programme for a large number of professional groups. Indeed, the wider area of interpersonal and communication skills is also beginning to feature even on undergraduate courses in fields like medicine, psychology, and management. Shillito-Clarke (1987), for example, has described how experiential courses on interpersonal skills have been incorporated into the curriculum of one undergraduate psychology course. It is encouraging to see this development at such an early point in the educational process; for counselling is of course concerned with attitudes and values and with the counsellor's own personal qualities and is not just about the deployment of a mechanical set of skills. It would be only too easy for highly trained professionals to see counselling as a group of skills to be tacked on to their existing repertoire of skills without any recognition that this might involve a basic questioning of the nature of the professional–client relationship. In other words, counselling skills can only be effective if deployed as part of a wider process in which professionals remove their white coats, get rid of the desk in their consulting rooms, and begin to reveal their own feelings to themselves. Were this process not to take place, the end result would be to emasculate clients rather than to empower them.

People whose primary professional training is in counselling, but who practise counselling in a largely voluntary capacity (with perhaps a small amount of part-time paid work)

This cohort is very large and includes, for instance, almost all 'Relate' counsellors. It almost certainly contains an overwhelming proportion of married women. The group is important, not just because it is numerically large but because it contains potentially many of the working counsellors eligible for accreditation. Many Relate counsellors were accredited under the BAC's initial accreditation scheme which ran from 1982 to 1987. In the early stage of the second scheme which began in 1988, Relate counsellors were being rejected because of a failure to satisfy the criterion relating to supervision. However, at the time of writing, there seems some potential for a scheme of peer supervision in dyads or triads which would appear to offer an increase in the amount of supervision at little extra cost.

While Relate probably offers the most thorough training available for volunteers, the work of other agencies should not be ignored. In particular, CRUSE (National Organization for the Widowed and their Children) is important both for the size of its volunteer counselling force and for the quality of its training. However, in addition, there is a vast number of smaller agencies offering much more specific and limited training which also claim to provide counselling services. Examples include rape-crisis centres, centres for unemployed workers, gay-lesbian units, agencies concerned with counselling parents with newly born disabled children, and units concerned with alcohol abuse, drug abuse, and AIDS. While some of these workers may eventually go on to receive more intensive training, it is unlikely that they will form such a fertile recruiting ground for full-time counsellors as Relate: National Marriage Guidance. In a sense, if the concept of a movement in counselling is valid, it is in the many small agencies operating in areas like those above that it resides. In these agencies, workers, both voluntary and professional, are very likely to have a particular ideological commitment to the work of the agency concerned. This whole category of trained volunteers reflects something of the strength and the weakness of counselling in Britain today. It reflects the strength of tapping philanthropic desire to help. It also provides a source of professional counsellors as after some years of largely unpaid experience, many female counsellors begin to seek more consistently paid work as counsellors either in salaried posts or through private consultancy work. In effect they then move out of the category being described here into the first category outlined above. The weakness is that in cost–benefit terms, the training agency gets relatively little in return for the expense of training. In this way, from the agency's point of view there is a big drop-out rate, though from the point of view of the counselling world as a whole the result is a net gain. In effect, some voluntary agencies are providing a hidden subsidy to other organizations and this makes it difficult to produce accurate accounts of the true costs of training counsellors.

People, both professional and voluntary, whose primary commitment is less to counselling than to the notion of community self-help

None of the four groups outlined above is homogeneous and the previously described group, in particular, contains a huge variety of models of training and practice and patterns of voluntary service. However, there is a point on the dimension where this latter group can be said to be less concerned with delivering a counselling service than with providing and supporting helping relationships. The term 'barefoot' counsellors is sometimes attached to this category, though we dislike the term because it seems to imply a set of values which denigrate the importance of the work. Nevertheless, there is no doubt that there exists a vast number of people throughout Britain who do not see themselves primarily as counsellors but who are delivering a variety of basic support and helping skills.

The largest agency within this category (and far larger than any agency in any other category) is undoubtedly the Samaritans, which has always eschewed the notion of counsellor in favour of that of 'befriender'. However, the characteristic of most of the agencies in this sector is that they are small rather than large. Characteristic of them all is their commitment to specific causes such as tenants' rights, the needs of mothers with pre-school children, the problems of wives of prisoners, the difficulties faced by parents with handicapped children and so on. The agency is often local, strongly rooted in its immediate community, and concerned as much with the provision of services for advice, information, and advocacy as with counselling. A lot of community groups fit this description and are not easily placed into conventional accounts of counselling practice. It is worth noting that this community-work tradition may be of more significance in some parts of Britain than in others. A reason why the Scottish Association for Counselling has had less success as a co-ordinating body than the BAC may lie in the powerful community-work tradition in Scotland which has made it more difficult for an umbrella body to operate effectively. In contrast, in England and Wales the professional end of the counselling world has been very effective in directing the energies and resources of the umbrella body (the BAC) to issues such as accreditation of individual counsellors and recognition of training courses which are of major concern to them, but of less concern to the community-work end of the spectrum.

There is a real issue here about power, about the values placed on different kinds of work, and about the energy devoted within bodies like the BAC but also in the world of counselling generally to furthering the needs of groups at different points in the counselling spectrum. Meeting the needs of one group can easily lead to the alienation of others and holding the balance between different sets of needs is not an easy task for the BAC or any other body to perform.

The British Association for Counselling

Examining the BAC in the context of looking at the range of counselling practice is a useful strategy, because here in one organization is to be found a microcosm of the world of counselling in England and Wales. With almost 4,000 individuals and 250 organizational members (BAC 1987a), the organization can be said with some degree of validity to be the co-ordinating body representing the interests of counselling in England and Wales, though there does exist a separate umbrella body for Psychotherapy (the Rugby Psychotherapy Conference). By examining the BAC's structure, we can elicit in a concrete fashion some of the issues which face the wider counselling community. These concern the relationship between professionals and non-professionals; between paid and voluntary counsellors; between counselling in the public and private sectors; and between counsellors and counselling. One of the authors of this chapter, himself a past Executive Officer of the BAC, has described the resolution of these issues as involving the task of reconciling a 'tension between the pulling together spirit and divisiveness'[1]. (Charles-Edwards 1988). Paraphrasing his ideas we can identify a number of sources of tension as between:

(a) those who are employed as counsellors and those who regard counselling or pastoral care as a central component of their work;
(b) those who are paid for their work, whether by salary or fee, and those who work voluntarily;
(c) those who identify strongly with differing theories or schools and consider that other theories are inadequate, if not downright bad, and those who take a more eclectic stance;
(d) those who have undertaken more rather than less in-depth, self-developmental and experiential work, including experience as a client and those who have not; and
(e) those who are radical and have a concern with the social implications of counselling and those who take a more conservative stance by arguing that counselling is concerned with helping the individual to change, not with changing society. We shall return to this issue again before the end of this chapter.

Looking at the organization overall, Charles-Edwards concludes that those with most energy for the BAC have tended to come from among the paid counsellors and consequently the Association's output has been disproportionately geared to counsellors rather than those employing counselling or pastoral care skills in their paid or voluntary work. He suggests that there is a danger within the BAC of fostering the concept that counselling should become highly professionalized, which would involve those not formally trained being squeezed out and de-skilled. He perceives this as a threat to what he describes as the 'ecumenicism of BAC', a word which with some justification could be attributed to the whole field of counselling.

BAC divisions

This ecumenicism becomes apparent if we look at the primary sub-units of the BAC, namely the Divisions (of which there are six) and try to link their membership to the five categories of worker outlined in the previous section of this chapter. Each division consists of a variety of people working in a particular field of activity. The Divisions are entitled: the Association for Pastoral Care and Counselling (APCC); the Association for Student Counselling (ASC); Counselling at Work (CAW); Counselling in Education (CIE); Counselling in Medical Settings (CMS); and Personal/Sexual/Marital/Family Counselling (PSMFC). Of these Divisions, two (ASC and APCC) existed before the BAC was founded in 1977. They then merged into the new organization. Within the public sector, as we have already indicated, counsellors working in the tertiary sector of education contain the largest number of persons whose primary professional training is in counselling and who are employed full-time as counsellors. It is probably the only division of the BAC whose membership is constituted primarily of full-time professional counsellors. This, therefore, is a relatively homogeneous area both in terms of its organizational setting and its high degree of professionalization and the fact that it consists of a clearly defined occupational grouping. The APCC also has a degree of homogeneity, but in this case the common element is religious conviction. A large number of its members are in holy orders and we may presume, therefore, that their primary allegiance is to their ministries rather than to the world of counselling. Needless to say, many ministers are interested neither in BAC nor in the wider world of counselling but are more concerned with the general issue of pastoral care. At the time of writing there is some debate within the APCC about how far it meets the needs of this group. Nevertheless, in public statements made by the APCC, a concern with professional standards is clearly evident and the organization's interest in accreditation is apparent (BAC 1987a: 31).

The other four divisions post-date the foundation of the BAC and in this sense can be seen as a product of the expansion of counselling over the past decade and a half. They are arguably less homogeneous bodies than either the ASC or the APCC, each of which consists of almost a single occupational group. Indeed, Counselling in Medical Settings describes itself as 'a divergent group' (BAC 1987: 35). Members counsel, work, and teach in many areas of the hospital, psychiatric, and primary care services and include nurses and doctors (the third category in the previous section, plus a considerable number of persons in the first, second, and fourth categories). The whole field of counselling as a component part of Primary Health Care offers an enormous and probably the largest single potential area of expansion for the paid employment of counsellors.

Counselling at Work has as its mission statement the concept of the workplace and the use of counselling skills as a way 'to reduce excessive stress and release energy and creativity' (CAWD 1987: backpage). Its membership is probably composed mainly of persons in the third category and this is reflected in its identification of the provision of training workshops in counselling skills as one of its main areas of concern (BAC 1986: 30). A subjective impression from its public statements (BAC 1986; BAC 1987a) is that there is a greater concern with what one can describe as 'spreading the message' than with the professional focus issues like accreditation.

Recent years have witnessed the development of counselling projects within such organizations as the Post Office, Shell, Control Data, British Airways, and some police services. These represent some of the most impressive decisions to resource counselling, as a process which can contribute significantly to organizational as well as individual health and well-being. They represent the broadening of counselling at work from educational and health-care places of work.

Personal/Sexual/Marital/Family Counselling is the largest Division of the BAC (BAC 1987a: 36) and again is a heterogeneous field. It includes a large number of persons practising in the private sector as counsellors or consultants (part of the first category). This may be a reason for a 'continuing preoccupation with . . . specialist accreditation . . . it is the implied recognition of the individual as a professional counsellor that leads to so many counsellors seeking membership of this organization' (BAC 1987a: 37). Our estimate is that the fourth group, which contains the majority of Relate counsellors, is under-represented within this Division.

The sixth Division, Counselling in Education, primarily covers the primary and secondary sectors of education. Though with the decline in the 1980s in the number of persons employed as full-time counsellors, it is the setting rather than the presence of a single occupational group (as in the case of the ASC) which brings this group of people together. As with CAW, its public statements emphasize its concern with group issues, in this case particularly radical ones such as young people and drugs, the treatment of black pupils in schools, and the link between AIDS and child haemophiliacs (BAC 1986: 31). In terms of categories, it consists of a mix of people in the first and third categories.

If we look as these six Divisions and their relation to the six categories, the strong impression is that the interests of the first category is overrepresented in the BAC at the expense of the third and probably also the fourth categories. In effect, professional issues, like accreditation appear to receive the bulk of attention, lending empirical support to the view expressed by Charles-Edwards (1988) about the dominance of the professional sector in defining issues. Professionalization is a complex subject. The desire to codify training, standards, and ethics can and does lead to sharp boundaries being drawn in which insiders and outsiders are clearly delineated. The danger than becomes that those inside develop as their main concern the defence of their own rights, privileges, and powers. This topic has been addressed by writers such as Freire (1972) and Illich (1973) who have referred to welfare and service institutions as being part of the problem of modern society in creating dependency and thus disabling people rather than forming part of the solution. On the other hand, the process of professionalization can be said to defend the interests of people by guaranteeing standards of training, ethics, and practice. Moreover, if counselling is to develop in esteem in the wider community, it seems important to encourage potential employers of counsellors and potential users of the service (clients) to regard some form of accreditation as a mark of competence. In the case of the former group, this is beginning to happen. Unless the world of counselling regulates its own boundaries, others will emerge to do the job and this may not be in the best interests of counsellors or clients. The process of professionalization, therefore, raises many complex issues and dilemmas which are now being faced by counsellors and organizations concerned with counselling. This issue is discussed further in the final chapter of this book.

Finally, it is worth pointing out that like counselling itself, the BAC is a constantly changing organization. The existence of groups active in relation to racial awareness in counselling education and to the potential counselling contribution to creating peace indicates that counselling takes place in the context of wider social forces. The debate between those people who want counselling to be more widely accessible within society and those who place a premium on raising its standards takes place in a changing world in which 'new' items like race and peace have appeared on the agenda.

The structure of provision for counselling – becoming a client

Earlier sections of this chapter have approached the subject of counselling from the perspective of the worker. In this section, we wish to alter the angle of focus by raising the question of what counselling in Britain looks like from the point of view of the client. In particular, we wish to address the question of how one becomes a client. Because the range of provision is, as we have indicated, so great, the number of routes available to becoming a client is also considerable. However, there are two variables which are of particular relevance. The first concerns the fact that the provision of counselling is essentially a problem-resolution service, rather than one concerned with development or prevention. The second is that, by and large, the provision of counselling is a mixed economy containing a private sector in which clients usually but not always pay in addition to a public service available free of charge.

Let us take the former factor first. The idea of counselling as a form of life-enhancing developmental help is still limited in Britain. On the whole, people go to counsellors in Britain because they have a problem and to use the language of Relate, need 'remedial' counselling. The concept of 'remedial' implies that there is something wrong and that the role of counselling is to help the individual to move back into a position of equilibrium. The two largest voluntary counselling organizations, Relate and CRUSE, both developed within this tradition, though the former in particular has now begun to stress its preventive and developmental role, particularly through its educational programme. Other large voluntary organisations like the Samaritans are specifically crisis-orientated. Over and above these large organizations, there exists a veritable myriad of organizations of all shapes and sizes within the voluntary sector, ranging from, at one end of the spectrum, highly professionalized centres like the Westminster Pastoral Foundation where the primary concern is with long-term psychotherapy to, at the other end of the continuum, agencies which are highly local, which usually operate with partly untrained staff, and may be concerned as much with advocacy and social and communal change as with counselling. In the middle, there exist many well established agencies like BACUP (British Association of Cancer United Patients), and the Brook Advisory Centres (for contraceptive and related psychosexual problems) that have specific foci for their work. While agencies like these have increasingly begun to perceive their function as the provision of education for the public in addition to individual crisis management, the tendency generally is still towards problem resolution.

Moving outside the voluntary into the public sector, we find the same problem focus. Children and their families receive counselling from clinical or educational psychologists because they are experiencing some kind of behaviour problem or learning difficulty which has an emotional component. Families or individual members are counselled by social workers and probation officers for a whole variety of reasons; because there is an elderly or disabled relative, because there has been physical or sexual abuse, because the law has been broken, and so on. The common factor is that there is a problem: 'no problem no counselling' is essentially the fact of life in the public sector. If we move from the social welfare into the health sector, the position is not dissimilar. Some General Practitioner practices now offer a counselling service, though the number is as yet limited. Sometimes the counsellor is called a social worker. Very rarely do we come across an agency like the Isis Centre, a National Health Counselling service opened in Oxford in 1970 (Oldfield 1983). Health Visitors (Community Nurses) sometimes provide an exception to the rule that counselling is provided only after some kind of problem or crisis emerges.

Shifting into the educational field, we have seen that the tertiary sector is perhaps the only field in which trained professional counsellors as such are employed as a matter of rule. The corollary of this is that counselling services are widely available to students in establishments of further and higher education (see Breakwell 1987). Interestingly, in Chapter 10 of this book Ratigan discusses how counsellors in this sector have begun to move away from a remedial into a more dynamic developmental role, focusing particularly on organizational change and encouraging systems to adapt in ways which will facilitate the emotional well-being of individuals.

It is clear, then, that people receive counselling from a large variety of sources. Many people who receive counselling will not have sought it or may not even be aware that this is the experience in which they are involved. Many professionals may not consciously be aware that this is the service they are offering. Actually to seek out a service termed counselling is still probably the exception rather than the rule. Where a counsellor and counselling is specifically sought, it is usually for a specific purpose and usually related to a specific problem. These include sorting out a problem marriage, remedying a sexual difficulty in a relationship, coping with an illness like cancer, dealing with an unexpected contingency such as pregnancy or abortion, managing anxiety, reducing levels of anti-social behaviour, defining conflicts about sexual orientation, and so on.

Moving now to the second variable, the economic context, we can see that all this activity takes place in a mixed economy, in which public and private sectors intertwine in complex fashion. Apart from student counsellors, the category we have defined as professionals employing counselling skills in their work, but who are not employed as counsellors (our third category) are employed largely within the public sector. These are the social workers, nurses, doctors, health visitors, probation officers, teachers, and psychologists who still exist in large numbers within the public sector, despite the Thatcherite attack on public services. However, the work of professionals in the private sector should not be ignored and one can think particularly of the growing interest in counselling at work on the part not just of personnel managers, but of people occupying more general managerial roles.

Within this mixed economy, if one is looking specifically for counselling, the private sector is almost certainly the place to look. This sector consists of voluntary agencies like Relate, which asks clients to contribute fees according to their means and inclination and others which offer a free service. However, it also includes individual counsellors or consultants who earn a living from this activity. It is not always easy for the man or woman in the street to locate such help and some kind of information service or register which was readily available in places like Citizens Advice Bureaux and public libraries is highly desirable. Indeed, the BAC is working actively towards the provision of such an information service. As we have already pointed out, the title 'counsellor' or 'psychotherapist' has no copyright attached to it. Anybody can call themselves such and set up in practice. It is not surprising, therefore, that there exists a whole host of fringe activities whose practitioners label themselves in one way or another as counsellors. Because of the decline in the public sector of employment in the 1980s, it is not surprising that many people who might otherwise have been employed there (or who were indeed employed in this sector before the advent of the economics of Thatcherism) have now set up as private consultants. It is necessary for these people to charge fees which will allow them to earn a living; between £12 and £20 per hour is probably not too untypical a figure. Inevitably, however, the cost of therapy, added to the difficulty of locating a counsellor in the first place, means that clients will tend to come from a particular section of society which has the surplus income available for this form of consumption in addition to the general know-how about counselling which motivates them to seek out a counsellor in the first place.

One area where private counsellors may have particular room for expanding their services lies in the growing willingness of large organizations to consider counselling as a vehicle for reducing stress and increasing job satisfaction and performance among the work-force. This is likely to provide a growing source of employment for individual consultants and a vehicle through which individual members of the community can receive counselling without having to pay for it themselves. Reddy (1987) suggests that in-company counselling services pay off in commercial terms and that the number of such schemes is growing though still tiny in number compared with the USA where over 4,000 companies operate 'Employee Assistance Programmes'. Looking ahead more generally, the growth of counselling in the private sector appears likely to continue, which makes it imperative for counsellors to be aware of the implications this has for the availability of counselling across the range of social groups within the community. Similarly, with an impoverished state sector, the role of voluntary agencies is likely to grow more rather than less important, though they are unlikely to find it easy to find the funds necessary for their survival. The future of counselling in the public sector looks more problematic, and while counselling in the area of general medical practice offers great scope for the employment of counsellors, it is difficult to see where the finance will come from to support this kind of development. Unfortunately the more starved of funds the public sector becomes, the more it is likely that the emphasis will remain on counselling as a remedial or crisis rather than as a preventive or developmental service.

Into the 1990s: The shape of things to come

We began this chapter by looking at the definition of counselling adopted by the British Association for Counselling and the difficulty of applying this definition universally across the field. This allowed us to ask whether it was appropriate to perceive counselling as a unified movement. By now it should be clear that we regard such a picture as over-simplified and that the world of counselling contains areas both of commonality and of difference. It also contains both centrifugal (pulling apart) and centripetal forces (pulling together). In the same way as the present world of counselling has evolved from many different streams, we can detect today a variety of different influences at work. As we have already pointed out, nobody has patent rights on the term counselling. That is both a strength and a weakness. It is a weakness because sometimes the term is used in ways in which those committed to counselling find unacceptable. On the other hand, it is a strength because it means that counselling is not a static force but rather is something which is alive and vibrant and in a constant process of evolution.

The boundary with psychotherapy is not the only boundary in which counselling faces zonal disputes. Dictionaries irritatingly continue to define counselling as a form of advice-giving. (Sykes 1987). This confusion is reflected in an inability to differentiate between the two sets of activities. Though established bodies like the National Association of Citizens' Advice Bureaux are aware of the difference, newer bodies are often less cognizant. Thus, for example, a large number of telephone help-lines are springing up at the present time in fields such as drugs, alcohol, suicide, gay/lesbian issues, and AIDS. Unless backed up by a supporting network of helpers, as in an agency like Childline, such services should more properly be described as a form of advice- and information-giving rather than counselling.

However, the use or misuse of the term counselling goes beyond this. There are examples to be found in newspapers of advertisements for debt counsellors or business counsellors. Within the work context more generally, Reddy (1987: 123) describes how comments such as 'I counselled him to ...' are used, when the correct word would be advised. Increasingly, counselling skills have begun to be perceived as an integral aspect of appraisal procedures at work, in which employees have the opportunity to review satisfactions and objectives with their managers. It has also come to be employed as a part of training processes in which employees can evaluate their strengths and weaknesses. Reddy describes how these developments generate potential role conflicts for managers in reconciling their evaluative and controlling responsibilities as line managers with the individual needs of the client/worker. This issue has been addressed by the BAC in its Information Sheet of 'Counselling and Disciplinary Procedures at Work' (BAC 1987b). It is argues there that

> the objectives of counselling and counselling skills ... are compatible with a joint problem solving and non-punitive approach, that should be adopted at the *informal* stages of a disciplinary procedure ... the Association advises strongly that those responsible for negotiating discipline procedures should ... ensure that the word counselling does not appear in the procedure itself. If the procedure is accompanied by a separate code of practice of guidance notes, some reference to counselling skills ... would not, however, necessarily be inappropriate.

The overall question is whether the needs of the individual can be reconciled with the needs of the organization. We are involved here in some complex issues concerning ethics and practice. It would be all too easy, but highly inadvisable, to reject such developments as inconsistent with the principles of counselling. Simply to fall back into the purist philosophy of regarding as counselling only those encounters which take place in the consulting room of the counsellor would be regressive. It would also involve us in disregarding the history of counselling. It seems far better to get involved with industrial and commercial and other large organizations (as in education) in helping them to understand what the philosophy is behind the skills of counselling and assisting them towards using counselling in a responsible fashion. But of course the large organization is only one example of the fact that we live in a wider social world and that counselling is, therefore, not just a personal but a social enterprise. It reflects conflicting values and attitudes derived from this world about which there is often considerable debate. Counselling involves social as well as individual purposes and the values of the former are subject to continuous debate.

This raises the issue of whether counselling becomes a vehicle for empowering individuals or alternatively becomes a means for bolstering an existing social order. This is particularly an issue in a society where the dominant ideological position holds that problems are rooted in individual motivation and attitudes rather than in social and economic causes. Its most celebrated expression is to be found in the 'Get on your bike and look for work' remark, attributed to Normal Tebbit. The danger is that the more that problems are perceived as individual in origin, the more the role of something called counselling is exalted. This has led in education, for example, to the growth of a plethora of courses in fields like interviewing and social and life skills. The assumption is that the individual's failure to get a job is the result of his or her lack of appropriate skills or personal dispositions. There is a real danger here that the counsellor can get sucked into and unknowingly collude with a process in which by a subtle shift of emphasis the problem becomes one of changing so called deviant, awkward, lazy, or under-socialized clients rather than changing society or structures which create problems for individuals in the first place. In this way, counselling can easily become part of the problem rather than part of the solution. The moral is that counselling cannot just perceive itself as existing over and above the social world in which the activity is carried out.

Increasingly, counsellors have begun to acknowledge these dangers and have countered them by encouraging people to examine their personal problems not just alone and out of social context, but in association with others with similar experiences. In this way, Rape Crisis Centres encourage women to explore the nature of the social relations between men and women which generates male violence; or unemployed people can evaluate the social and cultural values of a society that accepts endemic unemployment as an inevitable economic phenomenon; or gay/lesbian men and women can explore the reason for social attitudes towards their particular sexual orientation. It is interesting to note how feminist therapists have seen the danger of counsellors simply helping women to adapt and adjust to the very family system which disadvantages and oppresses them in the first place and thus helping to perpetuate that system.

Counsellors will need to become more sensitive to such issues and to what a distinguished American counselling psychologist has referred to as the 'ahistoricism' which characterizes many of the conventional approaches to counselling. In his view, theories such as Rogers's person-centred therapy, Frankl's logotherapy, psychoanalysis, the reframing therapies such as psychodynamic and Transactional Analysis, Kelly's personal construct psychology, and Gestalt 'operate somewhat egocentrically in that they do not question their own assumptions about reality' (Ivey 1986: 103). He refers particularly to the way in which they unquestioningly separate an individual's problems from their social origins and context. You may or may not agree with this proposition, but what is indisputable is that the theory and practice of counselling is not static and will certainly change and develop in response to the dominant social forces which exist as we move into the 1990s.

Counselling is a complex activity, which is a lot broader than just the work carried out by people with a formal designation as counsellors. It contains the highly professional end, often shading into psychotherapy with its strong interest in issues like accreditation, standards, supervision, and training. Without these groups and these interests, counselling would become a diffuse activity, lacking any theoretical integration. It also contains a vast number of professionals not designated as counsellors who practise counselling skills in their work. Without them, the benefit of counselling would be spread much more thinly on the ground and counselling would possess less public credibility than it has now. It also contains at the other end of the spectrum the community groups who use interpersonal, helping, and counselling skills as a vehicle for developing self-confidence and mutual understanding as a precondition for social change. Without them, counselling would be more inward looking and less progressive in its general orientation towards the need for social change. The measure of whether counselling can ever accurately describe itself as a movement will depend upon its ability to contain all these disparate strands.

Notes

1. The British Association for Counselling is open to all individuals and organizations involved in and concerned about counselling in Britain.
2. NMGC is now known as Relate: National Marriage Guidance.
3. In the words of Storr (1979: 69), 'we do not approach new people as if they were blank sheets, but "transfer" what we have already experienced from the past into the present'. Thus, transference refers to the way in which clients transfer or displace on to the therapist feelings, attitudes, and fantasies which derive from earlier experiences, responses, and relationships.

References

Aldridge, S. (1987) 'The role of accreditation within BAC', *Counselling* 61 (August): 24–8.
BAC (1985) *Counselling: Definition of Terms in Use with Expansion and Rationale*, Rugby: BAC.
——(1986) *Tenth Annual Report 1985–86*, Rugby: BAC.
——(1987a) *Eleventh Annual Report 1986–1987*, Rugby: BAC.
——(1987b) 'Counselling and disciplinary procedures at work', Information Sheet No. 11, Rugby, BAC.
——(1988) *Counselling and Psychotherapy Resources Directory*, Rugby: BAC.
Breakwell, G. M. (1987) 'A survey of student counselling in higher and further education in the United Kingdom', *British Journal of Guidance and Counselling* 15(3): 285–96.
Carkhuff, R. R. (1969) *Helping and Human Relations*, New York: Holt, Rinehart and Winston.
Charles-Edwards, D. M. (1988) 'Counselling, management and BAC', *Counselling* 63 (February): 3–11.
Chester, R. (1985) 'Shaping the future: from marriage movement to service agency', *Marriage Guidance* Autumn: 5–15.

Counselling At Work Division (1987) *Counselling At Work Digest*, Rugby: CAWD.

Dryden, W. (ed.) (1984) *Individual Theory in Britain*, London: Harper & Row.

Egan, G. (1975) *The Skilled Helper: Model, Skills and Methods for Effective Helping*, Monterey, California: Brooks/Cole.

Ellis, A. (1962) *Reason and Emotion in Psychotherapy*, New York: Lyle.

Eysenck, H. J. (ed.) (1976) *Case Studies in Behaviour Therapy*, London: Routledge & Kegan Paul.

Freire, P. (1972) *Pedagogy of the Oppressed*, Harmondsworth: Penguin.

Illich, I. (1973) *Deschooling Society*, Harmondsworth: Penguin.

Ivey, A. E. (1986) *Developmental Therapy*, San Francisco: Jossey-Bass.

Jacobs, M. (1985) *The Presenting Past: An Introduction to Practical-Psychodynamic Counselling*, London: Harper & Row.

Lazarus, R. (1978) 'The stress and coping paradigm', University of California, Berkeley (Mimeo).

Maslow, A. H. (1962) *Towards a Psychology of Being*, Princeton, NJ: Van Nostrand.

Murgatroyd, S. J. and Woolfe, R. (1982) *Coping With Crisis: Understanding and Helping People in Need*, London: Harper & Row.

Nelson-Jones, R. (1982) *The Theory and Practice of Counselling Psychology*, London: Holt, Rinehart and Winston.

Oldfield, S. (1983) *The Counselling Relationship*, London: Routledge & Kegan Paul.

Patterson, C. H. (1974) *Relationship Counseling and Psychotherapy*, New York: Harper & Row.

——(1986) *Theories of Counseling and Psychotherapy*, New York: Harper & Row.

Reddy, M. (1987) *The Manager's Guide to Counselling at Work*, London: Methuen and the British Psychological Society.

Rogers, C. R. (1951) *Client-centred therapy*, London: Constable.

Rowan, J. (1976) *Ordinary & Ecstasy: Humanistic Psychology in Action*, London: Routledge & Kegan Paul.

Seligman, M. E. P. (1975) *Helplessness – On Depression, Development and Death*, San Francisco: W. H. Freeman.

Shillito-Clarke, C. (1987) 'Experiential interpersonal skills in the psychology curriculum: an ounce of practice is worth a pound of theory', *Review of the Counselling Psychology Section of the British Psychological Society* 2(1): 6–10.

Storr, A. (1979) *The Art of Psychotherapy*, London: Secker & Warburg/Heinemann.

Sykes, J. B. (ed.) (1987) *The Concise Oxford Dictionary of Current English*, Oxford: Oxford University Press.

Truax, C. R. and Carkhuff, R. R. (1967) *Towards Effective Counseling and Psychotherapy*, Chicago: Aldine.

Tyler, L. (1967) *The Work of the Counselor*, New York: Appleton-Century-Crofts.

Woolfe, R. (1982) 'Counselling in a world of crisis: towards a sociology of counselling', *International Journal for the Advancement of Counselling* 6: 167–76.

Chapter two

Counselling and the life cycle

Ray Woolfe and Léonie Sugarman

Introduction

The life course of each of us can be thought of as a river. On occasions turbulent, but at other times calm, it flows in a particular general direction whilst deviating here and there from a straight and narrow path. It meets and departs from other rivers or streams along the way, having a momentum of its own whilst both influencing and being influenced by the environment through which it flows. In the counselling encounter the lives of client and counsellor touch each other at a particular point in the life cycle of each. Each will be working, both inside and outside the counselling relationship, implicitly and explicitly, and with varying degrees of ease and success, on his or her developmental tasks – that is, those 'physiological, psychological, and social demands a person must satisfy in order to be judged by others and to judge himself or herself to be a reasonably happy and successful person' (Chickering and Havighurst 1981: 25). Each phase of the life course has its own developmental tasks, the successful achievement of which contributes to personal happiness and to the successful management of later tasks. Failure contributes to unhappiness, social disapproval and/or later difficulties. This view of the life cycle is like a glue which binds together the experience of the helper and the client, and of the disparate concerns raised by clients at different life stages. The client's development tasks will often be the *raison d'être* of counselling.

Change is the basic raw material of counselling. Yet there is only one kind of change that can be said, with certainty, to be experienced by each and every human being and that is the change associated with ageing. It is an inexorable fact of human life that we are born; that the process of ageing begins at the moment of birth; and that sooner or later we die. While we die at different ages, a majority of people, at least in the developed western world, will arrive there by a process of growing through childhood into adolescence, and via early and middle adulthood into old age. Together with gender, race, and class, age is a key defining characteristic of personal and social identity. It is not for nothing that the counsellor, after eliciting the name and address of the client, will then ask the question 'what is your age?' It follows, therefore, that the process of counselling would be enhanced by the existence of a conceptual framework that offers an understanding of the changes associated with ageing. Such a framework is provided by the notion of 'life-cycle development'; a concept which attempts to articulate what happens to individuals as they grow and develop and move through the various periods of life.

Although each individual is unique, there is a developmental framework of predictable stages through which individuals pass as they move through life. At each stage of development there is a need for new knowledge and skills to be acquired. Counselling may be relevant at any stage of development, but particularly at the point of transition from one stage to another, where the potential for stress but also for personal change may be greatest.

Age and personal identity

An individual's personal identity is intimately bound up with the notion of age. It provides a peg on which to hang a notion of who and what we are. Since counsellors are centrally concerned with a client's sense of identity, they are, *ipso facto*, also involved with the variable we know as age. Our sense of age gives us an indication of what is expected of us by others in terms of behaviour, dress, attitudes, relationships, and so on. Some clients may approach a counsellor with an issue which is explicitly age-related: a person may be frightened of growing old; be left with a feeling of loss as children grow up and leave home; or simply experience a vague sense of purposelessness as life passes by. Phrases to describe such states have developed in the vernacular. Thus, we talk of the 'empty nest syndrome', the 'mid-life crisis', or the 'male menopause'; of people being 'old before their time'; or of being 'mutton dressed up as lamb'. All these reflect assumptions about age-related or age-appropriate concerns and behaviours. Other issues which clients bring to counsellors may have a less explicit and more subtle association with age or life stage. Thus, a couple in their mid-forties might seek help with a marital issue concerning one spouse's infidelity. They will almost certainly raise questions about feeling bored with the same partner after sixteen years of marriage and how it feels still to be found sexually attractive. Likewise, parents of a teenager with a mental handicap may feel trapped and helpless that their child will never be able to leave home. They cannot look forward to the freedom from routine parental responsibilities that usually accompanies the later years of life.

There are many more examples and each one provides its own focus for the work of the counsellor. Thus, clients in their early thirties may feel depressed because, unlike their peers, they have not found a steady partner. The task for the counsellor is to explore with the client his or her fantasy about what a person of this age should be doing. Similarly, a twenty-year-old student feels trapped because he or she can not afford to leave home, yet feels that by this age an individual ought to be independent. The counsellor's task once again is to explore with the client the origin of this belief system. In each case the client has implicit and often explicit expectations about what life should be like at a particular point in time. These expectations are reflected in hopes, fears, and fantasies. Through helping clients to explore these grey areas, the counsellor assists them to clarify the origins of their expectations and the extent to which they are realistic.

Age and change

Change is implicit when we talk about the life course. We are not just human beings, we are young, adolescent, middle-aged, or elderly human beings. While our gender and our ethnic and social origins remain with us, we need constantly to engage in a subjective process of re-evaluating what the process of ageing means. While growing older affects us physically, intellectually, and emotionally, we are not always aware of what is happening to us. Often it takes some kind of critical event to teach or remind us that we are living life against a moving backcloth of time and ageing. It may be a major life event such as having a heart attack or becoming a grandparent that draws our age to our attention. Alternatively, small incidents – like being called 'Sir' or 'Madam' for the first time, being turned to for advice, or being offered a seat on a bus by a younger person – can be infused with a personal meaning for our sense of identity which far outstrips their objective significance. Sometimes the realization that we have not, as it were, kept up with the passage of time can be startling, emotionally upsetting, and, perhaps, challenging. This is often associated with the dawning awareness that we are in some way 'out of step' with our peers or with what we assumed our life would be like at a particular age. We might, for example, realize that, unlike us, most of our contemporaries have moved on from their first job and are driving cars, not motor bikes. Chancing upon an old diary, letter, or acquaintance may remind us that we had expected to be doing something quite different 'by now'. Our sense of age and identity is infused with this social component – how we stand in relation to others and to the social norm. We are not, however, always brought up short by these reminders of ageing and of time passing. Perhaps for most of us, most of the time we realize that change is occurring slowly, gradually, and inexorably; and in an approximate kind of way we remain in tune with it. Almost without conscious awareness we adjust our dress, language, behaviour, and attitudes so that what we expect of ourselves is in a rough kind of congruence and harmony with what others expect of us. In this way we avoid setting ourselves unachievable targets and reduce the danger of being disappointed or rejected.

Life events, and marker points

The process of change encompasses a large number of significant life events, some already referred to, which both demand and denote change, and which serve as marker points in an individual's life. Frequently these marker events entail a change in status or role, and may signal to the individual that he or she is either 'on time' or 'off time' with regard to society's norms and expectations (Neugarten 1977). A typical sequence of such events might include going to school, finding a boy/girl friend, leaving school, getting a job, getting married, becoming a parent, gaining greater responsibility at work, retiring, becoming a grandparent. A few events – entering school and retiring, for example – may be closely tied up with age and many more will be consistent with a life stage occurring within an age range of varying breadth.

People may face crises in their lives if such markers or normative events (which typically occur at a particular age or life stage) do not take place, or take place at the 'wrong' time. Thus, for example, a young person may find it impossible to get a good job; a couple may find they are not able to conceive the child they want, whilst another may conceive a child at the 'wrong' time, for example in their early teens, or when the woman has just obtained a new job. Counsellors are not unfamiliar with such cases. They are also familiar with age-related issues such as the client's sense of despair – 'by my age I should have ...', or personal ageism – 'I can't do that at my age.' In all those instances the counsellor may assist the client to understand the source and derivations of such age-related assumptions, and the ways in which these influence current feelings and behaviour. Are these age-related beliefs an accurate expression of reality and of the individual's personal values; or are they the injunctions of society's norms which, with the help of a counsellor, the individual might seek to challenge? More generally, the counsellor can be said to have a role in encouraging clients to examine the stereotype of adulthood and ageing which informs their thinking.

Let us not, however, see age or life stage as a primary factor in all settings. Some life events, termed non-normative events (Baltes *et al.* 1980) can occur, if at all, at any point in the life course. Moving home, undergoing major surgery, and bereavement could all be included in a list of such events. Even with these events, however, their impact may vary according to the point in the client's life at which they occur.

Stage theories of development

Plotting the typical pattern of occurrence of such events across the life course has led to the formulation of a number of stage-based accounts of human development. These theories have a number of implications for the work of the counsellor. They provide circumstantial evidence of the psychological issues being faced by clients. They also provide a reminder about the desirability of seeing an individual client's emotional needs as rooted in an affective and cognitive developmental process which began at birth.

Typically such an approach perceives human life as a series of stages or steps, at each of which the individual is faced with the need to resolve certain 'developmental tasks' (Havighurst 1972) or 'crises' (Erikson 1950). Failure to do this may result in difficulty in moving satisfactorily through later stages. When psychodynamic theories of counselling refer to clients having 'unresolved

31

conflicts', they are describing the way in which just such a failure may create problems for the individual long into the future. Erik Erikson, one of the most influential theorists in this field, suggests that the growth of the ego involves the sequential and cumulative emergence of personal strengths. Although each characteristic may always exist in some form, there is a time when each assumes special importance.

Erikson's work hypothesizes the existence of eight stages and thus eight crises. The first four are rooted in childhood and we have not the space here to do more than simply name them. They are Basic Trust versus Basic Mistrust; Autonomy versus Shame and Doubt; Initiative versus Guilt; and Industry versus Inferiority. They are related to Freud's Oral and Genital and Latency stages of development. The resolution of each crisis leads respectively to the development of Hope, Will, Purpose, and Competence. The fifth stage is concerned with Identity versus Role Confusion and is typically a characteristic of adolescence. This is a phase when the work of the counsellor is concerned with client issues such as sexual identity, autonomy from parents, and developing a coherent set of values. Haley (1973: 47), in discussing the psychiatric techniques of Milton Erickson, says that

> for many adolescents, help from a professional therapist becomes an initiation ceremony, in that it provides a relationship with an outsider whose goal is to help him to achieve independence and maturity. It is one way the culture helps ease the young person out of his tight family organisation and into a marriage and family of his own.

Erikson sees adulthood as containing three stages, each with its own crisis or turning-point: Intimacy versus Isolation; Generativity versus Stagnation; and Ego Integrity versus Despair. The first adult crisis is concerned with the need to establish intimate relationships. This involves a fusing of identity with another person, as, for example, in marriage. This stage is characteristic of the early twenties and its central feature is a mutual search for a shared identity through the development of the ego characteristic of Love. Unless this takes place, it becomes difficult for the individual to move to the next stage, whose crisis involves the need to be creative and to give of oneself to other people; for example to one's children, friends, colleagues, or the community generally. The ego quality that is developed here is that of Care. If this fails to occur, the result is stagnation and self-absorption which makes much harder the overcoming of the final challenge, which involves coming to terms with life as finite and one's one and only life. The successful resolution of the crisis at this stage generates Wisdom. Neugarten (1977) invites us to think about the period of middle age in terms of 'time left to live'. Emotional problems in old age arise if the individual sees life as a chapter of failures and missed opportunities.

This kind of stage theory is helpful to counsellors because it indicates how current crises faced by individuals can reveal flaws in the resolution of earlier crises. In other words, the past is often revealed in the present and the work of the counsellor is directed towards examining the link between the client's past experience and present modes of operating in the world. Gould, another stage theorist, has described adult development as the sequential relinquishment of erroneous assumptions developed as guiding principles during childhood. Thinking about the life cycle in this way helps the counsellor to become clearer about the possible nature and origins of some of the problems with which he or she is characteristically presented. Thus, for example, failure to resolve the so called 'mid-life crisis' (associated with the second of the three adult stages) may invite exploration not just of what has happened to the client in his or her thirties and forties, but also of how the individual's psyche has become rooted and formed at earlier stages. As Gould puts it, the concern of the counsellor is with the emergence, confrontation, and transcendence of childhood consciousness.

It is important not to take this kind of stage theory too literally, as covering every individual and every culture. This would be too mechanical an interpretation of a model which we would describe as a useful guide to our thinking. Normative accounts of human development are written not on tablets of stone, but on the shifting sands of time; and it is somewhat ironic that as interest in such accounts has increased, so their likely accuracy for any one individual has declined. Neugarten and Neugarten (1986) point to the blurring of distinctions between life periods that has occurred in our society and resulted in 'the fluid life cycle' (Hirschhorn 1977). Thus, for many people education and training is no longer confined to childhood and the early adult years, and more people undergo major career changes than ever before. An increasing number of people not only marry, but divorce, remarry, and possibly re-divorce. Women's childbearing years can extend over a quarter of a century or more, and first-time grandparents may be aged from about thirty-five to well over seventy.

The family life cycle

In thinking about the life cycle, it must be remembered that individual development takes place in a social context and in particular within the institution we know as the family. Thus, when we talk about the developmental needs of an individual, we are referring to needs which exist alongside those of other people with whom we have ongoing intimate relationships, many of whom are at different points in the life cycle. Therefore, we would benefit from some kind of transactional model which will take account of this fact; some kind of life cycle of the family, not just of the individual. The framework of the family life-cycle is crucial to an understanding of family counselling outlined by Street in Chapter 5 of this volume. Haley (1973), an influential figure in this field, has suggested that family psychopathology is the result of disruption or dislocation in the unfolding of the life cycle of the family. As in the individual model, families are seen as passing through critical stages, each one involving important developmental tasks. A problem is viewed 'as a developmental impasse which occurs when the family is struggling to negotiate developmental transition' (Bennun 1988: 15).

We do not wish to go through the various stages in detail. They are discussed by Street and in any case are not difficult to imagine. They range from courtship, to marriage, to starting a family, to living with teenagers, to the children leaving home, to the marital couple becoming independent again, to their needing care during old age; and the whole process being repeated. The key point is that at each stage, each member of the family system and each subsystem (such as parents, children, father/daughter, mother/son) have needs which if not resolved will generate problems. A few examples may be helpful. Haley (1973) describes the difficulties frequently encountered by young couples after the birth of their first child. For the woman it often involves being cut off from adult life, and a perceived loss of status, whereas for the man it represents an added dimension to life. Sometimes a mother will attempt to extract maximum meaning from the child-rearing role by unconsciously exaggerating a child's need for her. This then allows her to devote her attention to meeting these needs. The counsellor's task is then to encourage mother–child disengagement by helping the mother to find a more satisfying life of her own. Another common issue found around this time is that of one parent siding with a child against the other parent, the former being described as being 'over-involved' with the child. As the triangular pattern continues the child becomes the vehicle through which the parents communicate with each other. Problems are created when the family becomes locked into rigid patterns of problem-solving and the unproductive expenditure of ever-increasing amounts of energy. The family is then stuck and the unfolding of the life cycle is disrupted. Counselling involves supportively 'unbalancing' the family, so as to force its members from the rigid patterns of communication and interaction in which it has become set (Haley 1980).

Such therapeutic work in the area of family life-cycle development illustrates the value of employing a life-cycle approach in the setting of clinical practice and indicates how the former can inform the latter. In doing so, it highlights the potential of a life-cycle perspective for the counsellor working with an individual client.

Principles of intervention

While there is a great deal more that can be said, and is said in Chapter 5 of this book, about the family life-cycle and the work of the counsellor, our focus in this particular chapter is on the role of the counsellor in the context of the individual life-cycle. So far we have indicated why the concept of the individual life-cycle might be important for counsellors and that without an awareness of its existence, the counsellor is limiting his or her understanding of the client's cognitive and emotional concerns. We have already explored some of the implications of such a perspective for the work of the counsellor. We now intend to look at these in a more systematic fashion, by examining four specific principles of intervention which seem to emanate from the idea of life-cycle counselling: self-empowerment as the goal; life-event or transition processes as the focus; developmental, eclectic counselling as the strategy; and the 'system' as well as the individual as the target.

Goal: Self-empowerment

The assumption of developmental potential throughout life is no stranger to the practice of counselling or the value system of counsellors, but, even so, it does beg the question of what we mean by development – especially in the adult years when self-evident criteria of physical, social, and intellectual maturation may be less apparent. A more subtle or, indeed, a quite different concept of development is needed unless we are simply to say that any change and any life-course pattern constitutes development. The counselling literature is replete with potential candidates for the basis of such a definition. Formulations concerning the nature of the healthy personality permeate the literature on counselling. Discussions of, for example, the 'fully functioning person' (Rogers 1961) or the 'self-actualized person' (Maslow 1962) revolve not around static end-states but rather around dynamic ways of being. Thus, it is more appropriate to talk of the developing rather than the developed person – with an emphasis on process and direction rather than merely outcome.

Hopson and Scally (1980) make a distinction between 'change' and 'development'. While change offers a potential for development, it is not in itself a sufficient condition for development to take place. It is possible, for example for a person to change in a way that inhibits or prevents development. As Hopson and Scally make clear 'for a change to be developmental there needs to be a movement towards a greater realisation of personal potential; namely, acquiring new skills, increasing self awareness and clarifying one's values' (p. 183). Their operational definition of development is based on the notion of the individual becoming more self-empowered, that is 'more proactive, less dependent upon others, valuing the integrity of others as well as themselves, more in charge of themselves and their lives' (p. 183).

Hopson and Scally's concern with promoting as well as describing self-empowerment leads to a definition of the developing person which at the same time provides a set of targets for counsellors. Central to the concept of self-empowerment is the belief that in any situation there are always alternatives, even though none may be desirable; that is, we always have a choice. Self-empowered living involves the ability to identify these alternatives; to choose between them on the basis of personal values, priorities, and commitments; and to act on these choices in order to implement them. A further dimension of self-empowered behaviour is the ability to facilitate the self-empowerment of others, enabling them to live more self-empowered lives.

Hopson and Scally focus on five attributes needed in order to become more self-empowered: awareness, goals, values, life skills, and information. In addition to the more commonly mentioned need for awareness of self and others, there is the need for healthier systems in which to live and work. In talking of goals they do not mean vague or highly abstract aspirations such as the wish to be happy. Rather, they mean specific concrete outcomes – for example, 'I wish to expand my social life' or 'I wish to gain two promotions within the next five years' – which can form the basis of action planning. The specification of goals, whilst being necessary, is not a sufficient indicator of self-empowered behaviour. The goals must be the individual's own goals, consistent with his or her well-considered values. Hopson and Scally describe such goals as commitments. Not all goals would mark the person as more rather than less self-empowered. To be defined as such the values on which the goals are based must be consistent with many of the criteria of self-actualization or maturity. These values centre around self-respect and respect for others; responsibility for self; and the assumption that oneself, others, and systems all have the potential to change.

The notion of counselling which emerges from this analysis, based upon the assumption of life-long change, places an emphasis on the development of generic skills which can be transferred from one situation to another. Thus, for example, a client who has some understanding of the coping process involved in grieving a death would be better able to cope with the loss involved in, say, unemployment or retirement or just growing older and losing one's youth than a client who does not have this understanding. Counselling from this perspective has the goals of encouraging client self-awareness and values clarification, and of teaching creative problem-solving skills. Placing it in a life-cycle framework directs attention at the blocks to client learning that may be found in both the helper's and the client's stereotypes about age, ageing, and age-appropriate behaviours.

Focus: Life events

Life events are processes or transitions as well as markers. Evidence from a number of sources suggests that a fairly typical sequence of responses will tend to follow the onset of a critical life event. Perhaps the best-known example is with regard to the bereavement process of Loss, Searching, Re-finding, Re-loss, Awareness, and Emotional burial (Murray Parkes 1972). Others include the response to major surgery or to job promotion (Parker and Lewis 1981). More generally Hopson (1981; Hopson and Adams 1976) identifies a sequence or cycle of seven phases as typically accompanying a wide range of critical life events, both positive and negative. First is a period of immobilization or shock, a sense of being overwhelmed, unable to plan or think logically. This gives way to a minimization phase where the existence of the change or its impact is denied or at least minimized. Third is a period of self-doubt, frequently showing itself as depression, but possibly through other emotions such as anger or frustration. The next stage is reached as the individual begins to become able to accept the post-transition reality. This is followed by a period of testing as the individual begins to spread his or her wings in this new situation. Next comes a phase of seeking for meaning in the changed way of being, and finally, the transition can be said to be complete when the individual has internalized these new realities and meanings. Chapter 19 of this book, by Averil Stedeford, explores this process in more detail in the specific context of bereavement.

The idea of a cycle contained within the transition sequence emphasizes its inherent potential for growth and provides pointers to the counsellor, who can adapt the style and type of intervention to the client's stage in the process. Progress will not necessarily be smooth. There may be much vacillation between stages, and no definitive units of either time or degree of response can be given to any one phase. The fourth stage (accepting reality) is, however, something of a watershed in that it marks the point at which the individual begins to come to terms with and deal creatively with the change. Supporting, or perhaps sometimes pushing, the client into this confrontation can be a turning-point in the counselling relationship at which the whole emphasis becomes more forward-looking. Of course, timing is of the essence; too early, and the confrontation risks plunging the client further into the depths of depression with no immediate prospect of relief.

The transition cycle, with its emphasis on coping with change and managing loss, is particularly compatible with a life-cycle perspective. Growing up and growing older involve major gains, but also major losses. We are aware of losing our childhood sense of the world as a magical place; we become aware of losing our sense of not having responsibilities for others; we lose our feeling of youthful vigour, energy, and vitality; we experience the loss of children as they leave home; we lose the identity of being a worker when we retire – the list is endless. Each event involves the individual in a process of grief work which, if completed successfully, enables that individual to work through the transition in such a way as to feel emotionally fulfilled and not left with a sense of crisis. In a sense we can say that coping with change involves working through a process of grieving for what is lost.

Strategy: Developmental, eclectic counselling

Counselling from a life-cycle and, hence, a life-events perspective frequently involves helping clients manage transitions. Different counselling interventions may be denoted depending on the stage the client has reached in the transition cycle. Egan's (1986) model of helping – described by Inskipp and Johns (1984) as a model of developmental eclecticism – proposes a sequence of three stages which are compatible with the phases of a transition outlined in the previous section. During the early transition phases of shock, minimization, and self-doubt (depression) the client will need time to allow the fact of the transition to sink in. Self-esteem and the sense of the world as a predictable place may be rocked, particularly if the life event was unpleasant and unexpected. The non-judgemental acceptance which pervades the helper–client relationship during stage 1 of Egan's model is of particular importance here. It is a person-centred, non-directive stage during which the client's goal is self-exploration and the helper's goals are understanding and relationship building. It can counter the range of feelings the client may experience at this stage – panic, urgency to do something, paralysis. 'Look before you leap' could be an aphorism for the work done at this stage.

It is possible for individuals to become stuck in these early phases of a transition – never, for example, coming to terms with the death of.a loved one, the children's departure from the family home, or being dropped from the firm's football team, for example. At some point the client needs to move on from the period of taking stock if the transition is to be an experience from which he or she learns and grows. The skills characterizing stage 1 of Egan's model may need to be supplemented by more forceful, probing interventions. Stage 2 of Egan's model is a more overtly challenging and objective phase during which clients are encouraged to develop new perspectives on their situation; explore unstated or taken-for-granted assumptions, and shift their orientation from what was or is to what might be. If clients are unable of their own volition to move up from the bottom of the depression phase, confrontation or challenging may propel them into the 'recovery' phases of the transition sequence. 'Nothing ventured, nothing gained' might be the adage here. The confronting skills of stage 2 tend to be more risky than the reflective, accepting skills of stage 1, and they need to be used with both tentativeness and careful timing. Also important to remember is the client population for which Egan's model was developed: that is, people who are basically emotionally well but experiencing 'problems in living' rather than as people who are severely emotionally disturbed.

The third and final stage of Egan's model is one of action planning, implementation, and evaluation. It is compatible with the latter phases of the transition cycle, during which clients strive to live and find a meaningful place for themselves in the new post-transition world. It is here that the developmental goal of more self-empowered living is addressed most directly. 'If you don't know where you're going, you'll probably end up somewhere else', the title of David Campbell's (1974) book on life-career planning, captures the assumptions of this stage.

Ivey (1986) considers client development during counselling in a somewhat different way which is explicitly informed by an understanding of human cognitive developmental stages. He sees development as the aim of counselling and psychotherapy: 'Change, growth, creativity, transformation, and evolution are all about development. Staying put, refusing or being unable to change are what development is not' (ibid.: 28). Furthermore, Ivey proposes that the development which occurs in adult clients during therapy recapitulates that of children working through the Piagetian stages: sensori-motor, preoperational, concrete operational, and formal operational. Different therapeutic interventions can promote change and movement at different points through this sequence. Through all this, Ivey sees life, and therapy, as a dynamic process rather than as means to a particular end. Both are about journeys rather than destinations.

Target: Systems as well as individuals

A number of writers in this book point to the responsibility of the counsellor to act as an agent not just of personal change, but also of systems change. This features particularly in Chapter 10 by Ratigan on counselling in the higher-education sector. This view is of particular relevance in a discussion of life-cycle change and counsellor response. The counsellor informed by this perspective will be concerned with prevention as well as cure; in particular with challenging social stereotypes about adulthood in order to demystify them, rather than just responding to adults who arrive with age-related issues to discuss. Institutional change is also an integral notion underlying the goal of empowering clients to take greater control over their own lives. There is a real danger that counselling can become a vehicle for helping people to adjust to social systems which are themselves pathological and may well generate problems for individuals in the first case. It is just such a perspective which has encouraged many feminist therapists to question how far the traditional family is a system in which the rights of women have been abused and whether it is appropriate to help women to adapt to such a situation (see Chapter 14 by Chaplin). Adopting such a perspective has a number of implications for the work of counsellors. At the very least it highlights the desirability of allowing clients to share experiences with each other in groups, so that a conceptual and personal understanding can be reached of how the cognitive and emotional repertoires of individuals are rooted in their social contexts.

Conclusion

We have sought in this chapter to examine the importance of age and life stage in the construction of an individual's personal identity and to illustrate ways in which this knowledge influences the practice of the counsellor. It is unlikely that there will ever be counsellors working in Britain who style themselves primarily as life-cycle counsellors. However, this in no way detracts from the importance of the subject. There can be few counsellors who are unaware of the importance of the life cycle as an issue in their work and our hope is that this discussion has elevated the topic to a more conscious position in their awareness. Our belief is that a greater focus by counsellors on developmental work will reduce the amount of remedial work in which they are currently engaged.

References

Baltes, P. B., Reese, H. W., and Lipsitt L. P. (1980) 'Life span developmental psychology', *Annual Review of Psychology* 31: 65–110.
Bennun, I. (1988) 'Systems theory and family therapy', in E. Street and W. Dryden (eds) *Family Therapy in Britain*, Milton Keynes: Open University Press.
Campbell, D. P. (1974) *If You Don't Know Where You're Going, You'll Probably End Up Somewhere Else*, Niles, Illinois: Argus Communications.

Chickering, A. W. and Havighurst, R. J. (1981) 'The life cycle', in A. W. Chickering *et al.* (eds) *The Modern American College: Responding to the New Realities of Diverse Students and a Changing Society*, San Francisco: Jossey-Bass.

Egan, G. (1986) *The Skilled Helper*, 3rd edn., Monterey, California: Brooks/Cole.

Erikson, E. H. (1950) *Childhood and Society*, New York: Norton.

Gould, R. L. (1978) *Transformations: Growth and Change in Adult Life*, New York: Simon & Schuster.

Haley, J. (1973) *Uncommon Therapy: The Psychiatric Techniques of Milton H. Erickson*, New York: Norton.

——(1980) *Leaving Home*, New York: McGraw Hill.

Havighurst, R. J. (1972) *Developmental Tasks and Education*, 3rd edn (1st edn 1948), New York: David McKay.

Hirschhorn, L. (1977) 'Social policy and the life cycle: a developmental perspective', *Social Service Review* 51: 434–50.

Hopson, B. (1981) 'Response to the papers by Schlossberg, Brammer and Abrego', *Counselling Psychologist* 9(2): 36–9.

——and Adams, J. (1976) 'Towards an understanding of transition: defining some boundaries of transition dynamics', in J. Adams, J. Hayes, and B. Hopson (eds) *Transition: Understanding and Managing Personal Change*, London: Martin Robertson.

——and Scally, M. (1980) 'Change and development in adult life – some implications for helpers', *British Journal of Guidance and Counselling* 8(2): 175-87.

——(1981) *Lifeskills Teaching*, London: McGraw Hill.

Inskipp, F. and Johns, H. (1984) 'Developmental eclecticism: Egan's skills model of helping', in W. Dryden (ed.) *Individual Therapy in Britain*, London: Harper & Row.

Ivey, A. E. (1986) *Developmental Therapy: Theory into Practice*, San Francisco: Jossey-Bass.

Maslow, A. H. (1962) *Towards a Psychology of Being*, Princeton, New Jersey: Van Nostrand.

Murray Parkes, C. (1972) *Bereavement*, London: Tavistock.

Neugarten, B. L. (1977) 'Adult personality: towards a psychology of the life cycle', in L. R. Allman and D. T. Jaffe (eds) *Readings in Adult Psychology: Contemporary Perspectives*, New York: Harper & Row.

——and Neugarten, D. A. (1986) 'Age in the aging society', *Daedalus* 115(1): 31–49.

Parker, C. and Lewis, R. (1981) 'Beyond the Peter Principle: managing successful transitions', *Journal of European Industrial Training* 5(6): 17–21.

Rogers, C. R. (1961) *On Becoming a Person*, London: Constable.

Part two

Arenas

Chapter three

Individual counselling

Windy Dryden

Introduction

Most counselling that takes place in Britain today probably occurs within the one-to-one arena[1] of individual counselling. This applies even, for example, within the National Marriage Guidance Council (NMGC),[2] which specializes in marital and relationship problems. Thus, the latest annual figures from that organization shows 149,000[3] interviews with individuals and 102,500 interviews with couples (NMGC 1987). While it is advantageous for counsellors to follow the general principle of meeting clients' preferences for being seen within a particular counselling arena to enhance the development of a good working alliance, each arena (individual, couple, family, and group counselling) has its advantages and disadvantages. What, then, are the particular therapeutic merits of individual counselling? The author interviewed a number of counsellors whose views on this topic are presented below (see Dryden 1984).

(1) Individual counselling, by its nature, provides clients with a situation of complete confidentiality. It is indicated therefore when it is important for clients to be able to disclose themselves in privacy without fear that others may use such information to their detriment. Some clients are particularly anxious concerning how others, for example in group counselling, would react to their disclosures, and such anxiety precludes their productive participation in that arena. Similarly, clients who otherwise would not disclose 'confidential' material are best suited to individual counselling. As in other situations, transfer to other arenas may be indicated later when such clients are more able and/or willing to disclose themselves to others.
(2) Individual counselling, by its dyadic nature, provides an opportunity for a closer relationship to develop between counsellor and client than may exist when other clients are present. This factor may be particularly important for some clients who have not developed close relationships with significant people in their lives and for whom group counselling, for example, may initially be too threatening.
(3) Individual counselling can be conducted to best match the client's pace of

learning. Thus, it is particularly suited for clients who, due to their present state of mind, or speed of learning, require their counsellor's full individual attention. This is especially important for clients who are quite confused and who would only be distracted by the complexity of interactions that can take place in other therapeutic arenas.

(4) Individual counselling is particularly therapeutic when clients' major problems involve their relationship with themselves rather than their relationships with other people.

(5) Individual counselling may be particularly helpful for clients who wish to differentiate themselves from others – for example, those who have decided to leave a relationship and wish to deal with individual problems that this may involve. Here, however, some conjoint sessions with their partner may also be helpful, particularly in matters of conciliation (Gurman and Kniskern 1978).

(6) Individual counselling may also be the arena of choice for clients who want to explore whether or not they should differentiate themselves from others – for example, those who are unhappy in their marriage but are not sure whether to work to improve the relationship or to leave it. The presence of the other person may unduly inhibit such individuals from exploring the full ramifications of their choice.

(7) It can be helpful for counsellors to vary their therapeutic style with clients in order to minimize the risk of perpetuating the client's problems by providing an inappropriate interactive style. Individual counselling offers counsellors an opportunity to vary their interactive style with clients free from the concern that such variation may adversely affect other clients present.

(8) Individual counselling is particularly beneficial for clients who have profound difficulties sharing therapeutic time with other clients.

(9) Individual counselling may also have therapeutic merits but for negative reasons. Thus, clients may benefit by being seen in individual counselling who may not be helped from working in other arenas. Therefore, clients who may monopolize a counselling group, be too withdrawn within it to benefit from the experience, or who are thought too vulnerable to gain value from family counselling can often be seen in individual counselling with minimal risk.

Principles

It should be noted that individual counsellors in Britain vary according to the theoretical orientation that they bring to the work. While research on the theoretical allegiances of individual counsellors in Britain is needed, it is likely that most work within the psychodynamic tradition (Freudian, Kleinian, Jungian, object relations), the humanistic tradition (person-centred, gestalt, TA) or the cognitive–behavioural tradition (behavioural, cognitive, rational-emotive), or are eclectic and/or integrative in approach (in that they draw upon the principles and methods of some or all of the above traditions).

In this section, however, a 'common factors' approach is adopted and some of the principles are highlighted with which most individual counsellors are likely to agree (Frank 1985).

The relationship in individual counselling

Most counsellors would probably agree that the relationship between client and counsellor is an important therapeutic factor in individual counselling, even though different counsellors may point to different features of this relationship as having particular therapeutic value.

Individual counsellors endeavour to form a relationship with their clients that is characterized by mutual trust and respect, and in which clients feel safe enough to disclose and explore their concerns. When counsellors are experienced by clients as being understanding, genuinely concerned with their welfare, and on their side, then there is a much greater likelihood that clients will benefit from the counselling process than when these experiences are absent (Truax and Carkhuff 1967). In addition, when counsellors are experienced by their clients as either over-involved (intrusive) or under-involved (cold, detached, and withholding) in the counselling process, these factors have been shown to be associated with client harm (Grunebaum 1986). It should be borne in mind, therefore, that counselling can be 'for better or worse' and that what has the power to be healing has also, in less skilled hands, the power to be harmful (Strupp et al. 1977).

While the quality of the relationship between counsellors and clients is likely to be a central feature of individual counselling, it may not always be sufficient for a good outcome. When it is sufficient, what is likely to occur is that clients are helped by their counsellors' empathic understanding, genuine concern, and respect to engage in a fruitful period of emotional release and self-exploration, where they begin to lose their fear of looking within themselves and begin as a result to explore different aspects of themselves and their life situation. It also happens that they begin to view themselves, other people, and the world differently, and begin to move towards accepting themselves as fallible human beings with strengths and weaknesses. They may also begin to identify hidden resources within themselves that they may be able to use spontaneously outside the individual counselling arena to improve relationships and in the service of their personally held goals.

However, other clients may require more active help from their counsellors. Some may require, for example, that their counsellor offer a different perspective within which they can begin to view themselves, others, and the world differently. Yet others may require that their counsellor help them acquire new skills with which they can experiment outside counselling sessions. When these 'additive' ingredients are a feature of effective counselling, however, they are generally rooted in the facilitative qualities of the relationship discussed above.

45

A focus on the whole person

Even when clients bring a specific problem to counselling, their counsellors will offer them an opportunity to widen the focus of exploration to other areas of their life. This is due to the shared view among counsellors that clients are complex 'whole' persons. However, counsellors do not seek to impose their 'wholistic' views on their clients, and if the latter want only to work on a delineated problem their wishes would be respected.

If clients do wish to make use of such invitations to widen the focus of exploration, then the arena of individual counselling is particularly facilitative. In this arena the absence of other clients means that counsellors can offer their full time and attention to their individual clients who are thus encouraged to take an unhurried look at themselves in the total context of their lives.

A focus on the whole person not only means that clients can explore, should they wish to, any aspect of their lives, but also that counsellors should pay attention to different aspects of their client's functioning. They may, however, be constrained by their theoretical perspectives (see section on Issues). While individual counsellors are noted by the emphasis they place on clients' feelings, they may also focus on their clients' thoughts and attitudes, behaviours and skills, images, dreams and fantasies, relationships[4] (with other people and with the counsellor), sensations and physiological responses (if they have the requisite skills and knowledge). Such a focus also means that counsellors should neither lose sight of the interconnections among these different aspects of client functioning nor of the fact that the person is more than the sum of his or her parts.

This focus on clients as whole persons and on their different but interconnecting modes of functioning can be more easily undertaken in individual counselling than in other arenas where (a) the presence of other clients may emphasize the relationship between the client and others, and (b) time constraints may restrict the focus of exploration to a smaller number of modes of client functioning.

Explanatory frameworks and tasks

A preoccupation of some research into counselling has been to pit one approach or method against another to determine which is more effective. Apart from a number of client problems that are not often the focus of intervention by counsellors in Britain (for example agoraphobia, obsessive-compulsive disorders)[5], it appears that different counselling approaches yield comparable results (Luborsky *et al.* 1975). One reason for this equivalence is that relationship variables are common across different counselling approaches, although it is also likely that clients find value in a diverse range of these approaches.

Frank (1985) has noted that each approach to counselling involves an explanatory framework (a conceptual scheme that provides an explanation for clients' concerns and for what is considered therapeutic) and a set of *tasks* (in which both clients – inside and outside the counselling room – and counsellors – inside the counselling room – engage in the service of clients' goals). In rational-emotive counselling, for example, the explanatory framework centres on the important role that irrational beliefs play in explaining clients' concerns and the tasks dictate that counsellors should help clients to identify, challenge, and change (through thought and deed) these irrational beliefs in the counselling session and that clients should practise this same sequence both within and between counselling sessions.

It is likely that in effective individual counselling, counsellors and clients agree (albeit most often at an implicit level) (a) on an understanding of the clients' problems, and (b) to undertake to carry our their respective tasks in the service of clients' goals. The degree to which each participant accommodates to the other's view of the client's concerns is unknown but it is probable that the client is more likely to adopt and work within the counsellor's explanatory framework than vice versa. It is difficult, thus, to imagine a psychodynamic counsellor, for example, agreeing with a client that the latter's relationship concerns are explained by a lack of social skills and even less likely that such a counsellor would actually teach the client these skills (although psychodynamic counsellors may well refer clients to other counsellors for social skills training).

Extending this argument, ineffective counselling may occur when counsellor and client fail to agree to use a similar explanatory framework. Thus, using the above example, if the client maintains his or her stance that their problem is due to a lack of social skills and the counsellor considers it to be explained by the client's conflict with authority figures, then unless one accommodates to the view of the other or the two arrive at an explanation that somehow encompasses both viewpoints, progress is not likely to occur.

Similarly, progress may be hindered in the realm of tasks. Thus, for example, clients may not understand the tasks they are asked to perform and/or how these relate to their goals, or they may not be able or willing to carry them out. Counsellors, on the other hand, may not be skilful at carrying out their own tasks and/ or may not succeed in helping their clients to engage productively in their tasks.

Some counsellors deliberately set out to educate their clients in their explanatory framework and the tasks recommended by their approach to counselling, while other counsellors do not do this. In the latter case, the client is likely to learn about this implicitly. One person who went to consult a person-centred counsellor, for example, was puzzled at first regarding what she was expected to do as a client, but came to realize that her role was 'to talk about my feelings'. She soon experienced some benefit from counselling and her puzzlement ended. In the scheme employed here, at first she did not know the nature of her tasks but came to see that she was expected to engage in the task of 'talking about feelings'. The benefit she experienced led her to understand[6] one aspect of her counselling's explanatory framework; 'talking about feelings is therapeutic'. This encouraged her to continue to engage more deeply in this helpful process.

There is an important connection between 'explanatory framework', 'task', and 'relationship' variables. A good counselling relationship may help the client and counsellor to share a similar explanatory framework and an agreed set of tasks but it is not a sufficient condition for this to occur. One client remarked that he found his counsellor very understanding and concerned with his development, but claimed that he needed more active help than 'just talking'. 'I needed explicit help to change my behaviour in the real world but she didn't give me this.' On the other hand, a client may agree with the counsellor's explanatory framework and agree to perform the tasks implicit in the counselling approach but may not benefit from the process because a good working relationship has not been developed. Thus, for example, the client may not experience his or her counsellor as understanding or may feel judged negatively by the helper.

To summarize, effective individual counselling probably involves the development of a good relationship between counsellor and client, a shared agreement to employ a useful explanatory framework concerning the client's problems and what is therapeutic and successful execution of helpful mutually agreed tasks.

The process of individual counselling

While it should again be remembered that individual counsellors bring different orientations to their work, it is likely that most practitioners would concur with the view that counselling is a process and that different interventions are more salient at different points in this process. Since space does not permit a thorough examination of this viewpoint from different theoretical perspectives, I will illustrate this principle with reference to the work of Gerard Egan (1986), whose impact on the work of individuals' counsellors in Britain has been noteworthy (Inskipp and Johns 1984).

Egan's view is that counselling is a developmental process and that different counsellor skills are needed at different stages in the process.[7] He further notes that the success of this developmental process depends on the extent to which the client experiences the counsellor as offering high levels of the core relationship conditions discussed earlier.

Given the above, in the early stage of the process counsellors strive to develop a good working relationship with their clients and to help them to explore their concerns in increasingly concrete and clear terms. Then clients are helped to develop new perspectives that form the basis for later constructive action. In the next stage, counsellors help their clients to set and commit themselves to goals based on the emerging new perspective of the previous stage. Finally, counsellors encourage their clients to achieve their goals by helping them to (a) develop a range of strategies for action; (b) evaluate and choose among these strategies; (c) formulate action plans, and (d) implement these new strategies in appropriate areas of their lives.

While Egan outlines specific skills[8] that counsellors require to help them to carry out the tasks of each stage, counsellors who employ such a developmental model may use a broader range of skills than those discussed by Egan in the service of each stage's tasks. Whether counsellors are competent at using skills at each stage will depend partly on their training experiences (and partly on their personal inclinations and temperament). Indeed, it follows from this model that counsellor training programmes need to train their students in a broad range of skills if they are to help their clients across the entire developmental cycle of counselling.

Issues

At present the British counselling literature does not include much substantive debate on vital issues pertaining to individual counselling. As such the discussion in this section will centre on two issues that the author considers to be important and worthy of public debate. First, the issue concerning the relationship between individual counselling and other counselling arenas will be discussed. While counsellors work predominantly in individual counselling, they may also work in other arenas and thus need to consider both the limitations of individual counselling and the pros and cons of clients moving among different arenas. The second issue concerns the differences among various approaches to individual counselling. The differences often centre on practical principles and rarely receive a public airing in Britain since most counsellors interact with colleagues who share their therapeutic orientation. Thus, this issue will be presented 'as if' such a debate were to occur. This debate would help counsellors to appreciate the differences among different counsellors' approaches – an appreciation which is necessary if counsellors are to explore the possibilities and limitations of eclecticism and integration (to be discussed in the final section of the chapter).

Relationship with other counselling arenas

As was noted in the previous section, counselling can take place in a number of arenas (individual, couple, family, and group). One question that emerges here concerns which arena is appropriate for which clients at which stage of the counselling process. In order to answer this question an appreciation of the contraindications (as well as the particular therapeutic merits) of individual counselling is necessary. The following points again emerged from the author's discussion with a number of counsellors (see Dryden 1984).

Contraindications for individual counselling

(1) Individual counselling may be contraindicated for clients who are likely to become overly dependent on the counsellor, particularly when such dependency becomes so intense as to lead to client determination. Such

clients may be more appropriately helped in group counselling where such intense dependency is less likely to develop due to the fact that the counsellor has to relate to several other people.

(2) Individual counselling, by its dyadic nature, can involve a close interpersonal encounter between client and counsellor and as such may be contraindicated for some clients who may find such a degree of intimacy or the prospect of such intimacy unduly threatening and where the likelihood of overcoming this is poor.

(3) Individual counselling may be contraindicated for clients who find this arena *too* comfortable. Based on the idea that personal change is often best facilitated in situations where there is an optimal level of arousal, individual counselling may not provide enough challenge for such clients. In this context, Ravid (1969) found that it may be unproductive to offer individual counselling to clients who have had much previous individual counselling but still require therapeutic help.

(4) Individual counselling may not be appropriate for clients for whom other arenas are deemed to have greater therapeutic value. Clients who are shy, retiring, and afraid to take risks, for example, are more likely to benefit from group counselling (if they can be encouraged to join such a group) than from the less risky situation of individual counselling. In addition, partners who can productively use the conjoint situation of couple counselling often benefit more from this arena than from working in individual counselling. This is particularly true when they have both committed themselves to remain in and to improve their relationship.

Having outlined some indications and contraindications for individual counselling, I should like to stress that these are guidelines and not relevant in all cases. Perhaps the best way of determining whether a client will benefit or not from this arena is in fact for counsellors to work with their clients in individual counselling and to monitor their response to it, although a 'reception' or initial interview should aim to establish which of the available arenas is best for that client.

Movement among counselling arenas

Once the counsellor and client have decided to work in individual counselling, this does not mean that the client will remain within it throughout counselling. Thus, a client may be first seen in individual counselling and then join a counselling group once their intrapsychic concerns have largely been dealt with and their interpersonal concerns have come more to the fore. Indeed, some clients may be seen in individual counselling and group counselling conjointly. This can be valuable when clients need to work on a one-to-one basis and discuss at length their personal reactions to their experiences in the group.[9]

Should a client's individual counsellor also be his or her counsellor in another arena? Since initially clients in group counselling are generally strangers to each other, this issue can largely be explored and decided on the basis of the client's feelings and opinions alone. However, when movement from individual counselling is being considered, it is often inadvisable for the client's individual counsellor to act as counsellor to the convened couple or family. One reason for this is due to the fact that the counsellor–client dyad has a history, the content of which is unknown to the other partner or family members. The latter may feel, as a result, that the counsellor may have a stronger alliance with the client than with them and the development of a productive counselling relationship among participants in the couple or family counselling arena may thus be inhibited.[10] The longer the client has worked in individual counselling, the more likely it is that this will be an issue for the other client(s). Also, given that the client's partner or other family members are part of the client's everyday world, the client may find sharing the counsellor in the new arena much more difficult than he or she would with strangers in group counselling.

In addition, issues of confidentiality may add to this tension. If a counsellor has been working with a woman in individual counselling, he or she is bound to keep confidential material that has arisen in that arena. If the counsellor then were to see the woman and her husband in couple counselling, then the husband will know that the counsellor cannot disclose this material and may feel the three-person alliance to be unbalanced against him. Such issues need to be kept firmly in mind when discussing movement among counselling arenas with clients.

Different emphases among differing approaches to individual counselling

In the first section of this chapter, some general principles were outlined about individual counselling that arise from taking a 'common factors' approach (Frank 1985). However, it is important not to deny that there are differences among the various approaches to individual counselling that are currently practised in Britain. These differences may make it difficult for counsellors with diverse orientations to communicate effectively with one another unless these differences are understood and, if possible, accepted. Applicants to training courses, in particular, need to be made aware of understanding these differences if they are to make informed decisions concerning their choices for initial counsellor training. In addition, if the field is to move towards an integrative or eclectic position, an appreciation of the different emphases in the major counselling traditions will facilitate the exploration of the possibilities and limits of integration and eclecticism in individual counselling. This will be considered more fully in the final section.

Modality focus

Although it was argued earlier that many counsellors adopt a whole-person focus in their work, various counselling approaches place differential emphasis on the seven modalities of human functioning outlined in the section on 'Principles' (i.e. behaviour, affect, sensation, imagery, cognition, interpersonal relationships, and physiological functioning). Thus, humanistic approaches to counselling focus particularly on affect, phenomenally based cognitions about self, and interpersonal relationships; psychodynamic approaches do not place a direct focus on any of the modalities but look for the existence of unconscious conflict as it is manifested in the modalities; while cognitive–behavioural approaches tend to emphasize cognition, imagery, and behaviour while considering affect to be the product of cognitive processes.

Image of relationship

The major traditions within counselling tend to consider the relationship between counsellor and client in different ways. Psychodynamic approaches view the counsellor–client relationship as an 'as if' one where the emphasis is on perceptual, affective, and interactional distortions; where, for example, the client unconsciously views and relates to the counsellor 'as if' the latter were a significant person, usually from the client's past. The 'real' relationship between counsellor and client is considered to be important but as a backdrop enabling the counsellor and client to stand back and reflect on the meaning of the client's distortions.

In the humanistic approaches (and particularly so in person-centred counselling) the emphasis is on the real, present relationship between counsellor and client which is seen as the major vehicle for therapeutic change. The important curative factor in the person-centred approach is the client's experience of the counsellor as a person in his or her own right who is understanding and genuinely concerned for the development of the client. The focus on the 'as if' quality of the relationship is consequently played down.

In cognitive–behavioural approaches, the relationship between counsellor and client is regarded as a real present-centred relationship which serves as a facilitative backdrop to the successful execution of a set of important therapeutic tasks. Such counsellors are likely to view themselves primarily as educators whose major role is to help clients acquire cognitive and behavioural skills that they then practice between counselling sessions.

Time and space focus

Counsellors from the major traditions also differ concerning the focus they place on issues of time and space in engaging their clients in exploration in counselling. With respect to *time* counsellors may facilitate clients' exploration of their past, present, and/or future. With respect to *space*, some counsellors may place a greater emphasis on interaction within the counselling relationship, while others may focus more on clients' lives outside of the counselling sessions.

Psychodynamic counsellors tend to view clients' functioning in terms of the latters' past experiences and encourage them to understand that their present and future aspirations are coloured by their past. In addition, they tend to seek clues to their clients' current relationship difficulties in terms of the clients' relationship with their counsellors (the transference relationship). When the transference relationship is manifest, this is then linked to clients' past and present relationships outside the counselling arena. This dual focus is well expressed in the title of Jacobs's (1986) book on psychodynamic counselling, *The Presenting Past*.

Person-centred counsellors (who probably represent the majority of humanistic counsellors) tend to work in the time and space frames determined by their clients. Thus, they weave between the present, past, and future time frames and between the 'in here' and 'out there' space frames. Gestalt counsellors, on the other hand, tend to emphasize the 'here and now' space and time frames in their work and endeavour to help the focus on these frames as far as possible.

Cognitive–behavioural counsellors tend to work within the present and future time frames and focus more on their clients' outside experiences than on their experiences within the counselling room, although the latter focus is not neglected when it becomes salient.

At present, counsellor training programmes tend to be based on one of the major traditions as listed above. Whether this will continue in the future depends on the extent to which counsellors can explore how far eclectic and integrative counselling is possible. This exploration, as has been noted, will include discussion about the issues raised in this portion of the present chapter.

Future developments

Eclecticism and integration

It is likely that in future individual counsellors will become increasingly interested in exploring the prospects and possibilities of eclecticism and integration. Eclecticism defines the practice of counsellors who claim to choose what appears to be best from diverse counselling systems, sources, and styles. Eclectics often state a dislike for working within a single orientation, select from two or more theories, and believe that no present theory is adequate to explain or predict all of the phenomena that counsellors observe (Norcross 1986).

Integration, on the other hand, refers to the process of incorporating parts into a whole and stresses the formulation of a perspective on counselling that emphasizes common factors within a generally accepted overarching framework. Integrationists, like eclectics, are disenchanted with a single theoretical approach to counselling but are more preoccupied than eclectics with integrating the endeavours of counsellors from disparate schools.

There are signs that the trend away from single counselling systems is beginning to get underway in Britain; for example, there exists a growing UK network of members of the Society for the Exploration of Psychotherapy

Integration (SEPI). However, a caution is in order at this point. To call oneself an eclectic or an integrationist reveals nothing about one's mode of practice. These terms may be fashionable but it is important that they do not obscure undisciplined practice. Indeed, eclectics, for example, are often perceived as muddle-headed individuals who are too sloppy or lazy to develop a sound set of theoretical principles to guide their work. It may be that for the development of a mature eclecticism or integrationism in individual counselling to occur practitioners need to have either (a) sound initial training in one theoretical approach to counselling while being exposed to the merits of other approaches, or (b) a sound training in one eclectic or integrative approach of counselling – for example, that based on Egan's (1986) work. However, such developments will also be enhanced by a much-needed growth in more advanced training courses in counselling (in both the public and private educational sectors) where experienced practitioners might come together to explore the possibilities of eclecticism and integration.

What are the issues that such individuals might explore in such forums? These could include the development of: (a) a set of common principles, couched in acceptable language, that could form the basis of further exploration; (b) a matrix of modalities of client functioning that would facilitate comprehensiveness in individual counselling. Lazarus (1981) has outlined one such matrix that was referred to earlier in this chapter for example, behaviour, affect, sensation, imagery, cognition, interpersonal relationships, and physiological functioning); (c) salient dimensions of client variability to enable counsellors to consider how they might vary their practice in response to such client variability. Beutler (1983), for example, has argued that symptom complexity, level of client reactance (to therapeutic influence), and style of defence constitute important dimensions along which clients vary and which merit a differential counsellor response. To this list might be added an understanding of clients' learning styles and how they may warrant modifications in counselling approach; (d) a schema for counsellor decision-making allied to a taxonomy of salient dimensions of client variability that would help practitioners make decisions concerning, for example, variations in interactional style, modifications in the therapeutic alliance, and selection among a set of counselling methods and techniques. It is apparent that putting these points together in a consistent and productive manner constitutes an immense task, but I predict that exploration in this area will be along these lines out of which counsellors will discover the advantages and disadvantages of eclectic and integrative practice.

Individual counselling is a particularly appropriate arena in which the development of these ideas can be explored. Thus, for example, if counsellors are going to consider how to vary their approach to clients across the counselling process then this is best done, at least initially, in the arena of individual counselling where practitioners do not have to consider the impact that such variation might have on other clients present.

Specialized versus generalized counselling

Most individual counsellors working in Britain today are likely to be generalists but with one or more particular specialisms. They are trained (within the constraints of particular counselling orientations) to offer general counselling to clients with a range of concerns and difficulties, but in the course of their work may come to specialize in working with a particular group of clients. As shown elsewhere in this volume, working with particular client groups involves a detailed knowledge of the specific concerns and issues that face these groups. However, to what extent does working with particular client groups involve modification of one's general counselling approach? There is a need to translate careful delineation of particular clients' problems and issues into the development of specific counselling interventions targeted for use with these clients and I predict that this is one area in which individual counselling will develop in the future. If the development can be harnessed to those in the area of eclecticism/integration, then the likelihood that a personalized counselling approach will be offered to clients who have specialized needs (with regard to their concerns) and individual needs (with respect to their learning styles, and so on) will be increased.

Addressing the 'plastic bubble' effect

Critics of individual counselling have argued that there is a danger that a kind of 'plastic bubble' surrounds work that is done in this counselling arena, in that the work may become isolated from the realities of the client's life. While I have shown that movement among different counselling arenas can (and, some would argue, should) occur to obviate this effect, what can the counsellor do to weaken the boundary between individual counselling and the client's everyday life? I foresee that individual counsellors will increasingly grapple with this problem, especially as issues of accountability and effectiveness with respect to counselling in general and individual counselling in particular come more to the fore in British society. It is likely, then, that individual counsellors will experiment with modifications in their approach, such as (a) incorporating interventions that *specifically* address the generalization issue (i.e. how clients can specifically use their counselling- inspired gains in their daily lives), and (b) utilizing interventions that treat absent significant others 'as if' they were present. Bennun's (1985) description of doing marital counselling when only one partner is present is a good example of this latter trend.

Conclusion

To what extent these and other developments in individual counselling will occur depends on the willingness of counsellors to (a) adopt an experimental attitude to their work; (b) read widely the literature on counselling (including that from

North America where, in the author's view, most creative developments still seem to originate); and (c) learn from each other's innovations.

Given the great strides that counselling in Britain has made in the 1980s, the future prospects for individual counselling look most promising.

Notes

1. In this chapter I use the word 'arena' to refer to the setting of individual, couple, family, and group counselling.
2. Now called Relate: National Marriage Guidance.
3. Of which 104,000 were with women.
4. In individual counselling, *direct* exploration of the client's relationship style is only possible by examining the counsellor–client relationship. This arena, then, does not permit *direct* exploration of the client's interpersonal patterns as manifest with significant others (as can be done in couple and family counselling) and strangers (as can be done in group counselling).
5. Clients with these problems are more likely to be referred to clinical psychologists.
6. It should again be borne in mind that such understandings as outlined in this example are implicit.
7. Egan's developmental model should be seen as a flexible guide for intervention rather than as a rigid approach that should necessarily be used with all clients (cf. Egan 1986).
8. For a fuller discussion of these skills see Egan (1986).
9. It should be noted, however, that some counsellors argue that the conjoint use of individual and group counselling inhibits clients from dealing with their experiences of the group in the group.
10. This phenomenon can also occur in group counselling but is much less likely to be an inhibiting factor on the ensuing group process.

References

Bennun, I. (1985) 'Unilateral marital therapy', in W. Dryden (ed.) *Marital Therapy in Britain, Volume 2: Special Areas*, London: Harper & Row.

Beutler, L. E. (1983) *Eclectic Psychotherapy: A Systematic Approach*, New York: Pergamon.

Dryden, W. (1984) 'Therapeutic arenas', in W. Dryden (ed.) *Individual Therapy in Britain*, London: Harper & Row.

Egan, G. (1986). *The Skilled Helper: A Systematic Approach to Effective Helping*, 3rd. edn, Monterey, CA: Brooks/Cole.

Frank, J. D. (1985) 'Therapeutic components shared by all psychotherapies', in M. J. Mahoney and A. Freeman (eds) *Cognition and Psychotherapy*, New York: Plenum.

Grunebaum, H. (1986) 'Harmful psychotherapy experience', *American Journal of Psychotherapy* 40(2): 165–76.

Gurman, A. S., and Kniskern, D. P. (1978) 'Research in marital and family therapy', in S. L. Garfield and A. E. Bergin (eds) *Handbook of Psychotherapy and Behavior*

Change, (2nd edn), New York: Wiley.

Inskipp, F. and Johns, H. (1984) 'Developmental eclecticism: Egan's skills model of helping', in W. Dryden (ed.) *Individual Therapy in Britain*, London: Harper & Row.

Jacobs, M. (1986) *The Presenting Past*, London: Harper & Row.

Lazarus, A. A. (1981) *The Practice of Multimodal Therapy*, New York: McGraw-Hill.

Luborsky, L., Singer, B., and Luborsky, L. (1975) 'Comparative studies of psychotherapy: is it true that "everyone has won and all must have prizes"?', *Archives of General Psychiatry* 32: 995–1008.

NMGC (1987). *The Annual Review of the National Marriage Guidance Council*, Rugby: NMGC.

Norcross, J. L. (1986) 'Eclectic psychotherapy: an introduction and overview', in J. C. Norcross (ed.) *Handbook of Eclectic Psychotherapy*, New York: Brunner/Mazel.

Ravid, R. (1969) 'Effect of group therapy on long-term individual therapy', *Dissertation Abstracts International* 30: 2427B.

Strupp, H. H., Hadley, S. W., and Gomes-Schwartz, B. (1977) *Psychotherapy for Better or Worse: The Problem of Negative Effects*, New York: Aronson.

Truax, C. B. and Carkhuff, R. R. (1967) *Toward Effective Counseling and Psychotherapy: Training and Practice*, Chicago: Aldine.

Chapter four

Couples counselling

Thomas Schröder

Introduction

The first English-language account of couple therapy was published less than 60 years ago. Since then there has been a conceptual shift from regarding the concerns of marital partners as an obstacle to individual therapeutic work towards viewing counselling of couples as one valid and important option among others. In Britain this development has been underlined by the foundation of the National Marriage Guidance Council* (which was a direct consequence of the rapid growth in the marriage-counselling movement) in 1947 and of the Family Discussion Bureau (today the Institute of Marital Studies) in 1948. While, as will be discussed below, there are various ways of helping couples, it is conjoint work (where both partners are seen together) which is most clearly distinguished from other forms of counselling and much of the following discussion will pertain to this modality.

Although this chapter will attempt to present an integrative view, there are two biases which need to be declared. First, my own clinical orientation is psychodynamic, and it would be surprising (and somewhat disconcerting) if this had not influenced my views. Second, although a recent review of the field (Gurman *et al.* 1986) asserted that 'marital therapy (is) now viewed by most clinicians as a subspecialty of family therapy', couples counselling will be treated here as an endeavour in its own right which is different from family counselling. The reason lies partly in the historically separate development of both forms of therapeutic work, but also, more to the point, in a theoretical distinction between the various modes of counselling which can be described as follows. Conjoint marital counselling differs from other counselling approaches in terms of the nature of the initial relationships. Whereas in individual and group counselling the development of the important relationships (between counsellor and client as well as between group members) can be observed from the start, in conjoint counselling the strongest initial relationship in the room is pre-established and independent of the counsellor. On the one hand, this state of affairs affords opportunities for the counsellor to disengage and to observe the couple's interaction directly. On the other hand, it may be experienced as quite disorientating, as interactional pressures are exerted which derive from the couple's joint history and therefore may not be made comprehensible by counsellors referring to their internal experience. Thus far, the situation is identical to that encountered in family counselling. The crucial difference lies in the fact that in marital work counsellors cannot make an alliance with one partner without necessarily excluding and isolating the other, whereas in family work they may 'join' (make an alliance with) a sub-system, leaving other family members to support each other. Working with a co-therapist mitigates but does not eliminate this special feature of counselling couples.

Much of the literature concerning helping couples with their relationship problems makes reference to 'marital therapy' or similar terms, raising the question as to whether one might usefully distinguish between couple counselling and marital therapy. As in other areas of counselling the answer will differ according to the context in which the work is carried out (for example, 'voluntary' vs. 'professional' or 'caring' vs. 'curative') and to the theoretical model followed. For the purposes of this chapter no distinction is drawn between marital counselling and therapy, although it should be borne in mind that couple counselling, like any other therapeutic activity, can be practised at various levels of depth and sophistication.

While the vast majority of couples coming for help are heterosexual and married, the basic principles of couple counselling apply equally to unmarried and homosexual pairs, and terms like 'spouse', 'partner', 'marital counselling', or 'couple work' will be used interchangeably and taken to apply generally. This is not to deny that, for instance, gay couples face special issues arising, among other reasons, from their minority status. However, the commonalities between dyadic relationships far outweigh such special features, a fact which is acknowledged in the practice of most agencies offering help to couples.

Principles

Settings

Today, a spectrum of agencies offering couple counselling exists in Britain. This ranges from specialist services, such as those of Relate or the Institute of Marital Studies, through more general counselling agencies, which offer help to couples as one among several options, to Social Services and health care settings in which the primary focus may well be on individual symptoms or family problems rather than on marital issues. To which of these agencies a couple presents will largely depend on their own view of the problem and their initiatives.

The decision to seek counselling help for marital problems does not come easily to most couples and typically indicates that the informal social resources – such as friends, families of origin, and so on – available to both partners have already been drawn upon without effecting the desired help. (For a discussion of the informal and formal aspects of a 'help-seeking career', see Brannen and

Collard 1982.) However, if the couple are clear about the source of their troubles, they are likely to seek out or be referred to a specialist service. Otherwise, they may seek clarification and referral from their General Practitioner or some other person trusted to know (for example, clergy) or contact a generalist service for advice. In either case the couple counsellor can draw on an initial understanding that what is required is marital work and can act in a context sympathetic to this approach.

The situation is somewhat different in agencies which do not see marital work as their primary concern. Couples will have presented there because they did not construe problems as lying within their relationship and the marital counselling comes about either as an adjunct to other interventions (for example, dealing with a child's problems) or because the focus on one partner's psychological or somatic symptoms has not been fruitful. Some of the problems arising from this in the counselling process are discussed below, but in addition couple counsellors may be faced with the task of justifying their approach to sceptical colleagues or of convincing somewhat bewildered referrers.

Diagnostic criteria

Once the couple have made their way through the various stages of seeking help and are established as presenting with a joint problem between them rather than with individual difficulties, the question arises as to which form of help is most appropriate for them. There are five basic options: the couple can be engaged in individual work (where partners are seen separately by different counsellors); or in collaborative counselling (where partners are seen separately by different counsellors who communicate with each other about the couple); they may be seen in concurrent mode (i.e. separately by the same counsellor); or conjointly by one or two counsellors; or they may be assigned together with other couples to conjoint groupwork.

The choice between these options might well be based on theoretical considerations. Grunebaum *et al.* (1969) suggest a three-stage model for diagnosis and treatment planning. First, they seek to establish whether the couple are committed to working on the marital difficulties. If not (for instance, if the partners come to the decision that they wish to end their relationship rather than seek to improve it), they recommend individual or collaborative work. For those couples who are committed to tackling their joint problems, the second diagnostic question concerns the locus of symptoms. If there are serious difficulties outside as well as inside the relationship, the authors favour concurrent counselling which affords the opportunity of working on different individual problems as well as on couple issues. If most of the difficulties arise from within the relationship, the final question concerns chronicity. For those couples whose problems are acute and relatively recent, the recommendation would be for conjoint work whereas couples with long-standing, chronic problems are considered to benefit from groupwork.

While to my knowledge there is no empirical support for this model, it has practical appeal and it furthermore meshes well with developmental concepts. From the vantage point of individual development one would ask if partners (who, at least from a dynamic viewpoint, one assumes had chosen each other because of a shared level of immaturity) had progressed enough in their own individuation to be able to tolerate the complications of conjoint counselling, especially the triangular relationship arising in work with a single counsellor. Looking at the development of the couple, one would ask if – regardless of whether they had formally contracted a marriage or not – both had actually progressed beyond the 'premarital' or 'courtship' phase with its inherent denial of interdependency and were thus committed to work conjointly on shared problems; or whether – at the other end of the spectrum – their relationship had come to the end of its life and was in fact 'emotionally dead', thus precluding the option of useful conjoint work.

So far, the available evidence from empirical research is too sketchy to form a coherent basis for decisions in treatment planning. However, there are indications that individual counselling for marital problems may well be an ineffective strategy (for the empirical evidence see Gurman *et al.* 1986; for a dissenting clinical view see Bennun 1985). The decision between the various options will in reality often be made on the basis of practical considerations such as available resources or skills and personal preferences of the counsellor. Furthermore, many practitioners will feel free to mix modes; for instance by contracting some concurrent individual sessions with a couple seen in conjoint counselling if the partners become temporarily too preoccupied with their own individual needs to focus on their relationship.

A conceptual framework for conjoint counselling

Considering the variety of conceptual approaches – some of which are discussed below – currently used by marital counsellors and therapists, it may seem artificial (if not pretentious) to attempt the presentation of a single, integrated frame of reference. However, I do believe that there is enough common ground between the various schools of thought in their practice of working with couples to allow us to construct such a framework without losing or obscuring what is of value in their differences. The relatively short history of the field has helped to avoid the establishment of entrenched positions and one might thus broadly characterize the current situation as one of diversity of theory and convergence of practice.

The following framework, which is partly informed by Ables and Brandsma's (1977) exposition, is built around the sequence: Forming a working alliance → Agreeing a therapeutic contract → Making therapeutic interventions. In marital counselling, where working alliances tend to be more difficult to maintain than, for example, in individual work, this sequence may need to be worked through repeatedly by the counsellor having to focus on repairing the working alliance with one partner and restating the contract before being able to proceed with interventions.

Alliance issues

The importance of establishing a good working alliance for the successful outcome of any therapeutic endeavour is perhaps the best documented of all process variables, even though definitions vary. What is discussed here rests on the premiss that the working alliance consists of an understanding that there is a joint therapeutic task to be done by counsellors(s) and clients, that to carry out this task requires an atmosphere of trust, and that the potential social aspects of the relationship will have to be set aside for the benefit of the task. Other issues often connected with the alliance, such as establishing joint goals, are dealt with below in the section on contracting.

The process of establishing, maintaining, and, if necessary, repairing the working alliance is well familiar from individual counselling. Indeed, some ascribe a major therapeutic influence to the gradual disillusionment and adjustment to reality brought about by repeated minor alliance breakdowns and repairs. However, the maintenance of an alliance is nowhere as central to the counselling process as in conjoint couples' work, especially if there is only one counsellor involved. From a developmental point of view one might argue that it is the difficult and often traumatic transition from two-person to three-person relationships (where the latter entail all the new potential for rivalry, jealousy, competition, and exclusion which the former lack) which is reawakened in the counselling room; and, indeed, some couples experience marital problems in connection with the birth of the first child, which raises similar issues (see Clulow 1982). From the counsellors' perspective it is the sheer difficulty of trying to relate to two people at the same time – often in the face of determined efforts by one or both partners to form a dyadic relationship – which makes for the challenge and the special opportunities in triadic couple work.

While experienced counsellors will have a number of means at their disposal to mitigate the stresses of a triadic relationship (such as disengaging from the couple, addressing them jointly, balancing attention given to each partner), the fact remains that the quality of the alliance is based on subjective experience – equal time for both partners may be satisfactory for one, but not feel anything like enough for the other. Ultimately, what is required of both spouses is the capacity to set aside their own needs temporarily in order to have those of their partner attended to. In successful marital counselling this achievement will serve the couple well in the future. If either partner cannot tolerate the temporary deprivation entailed in triadic work, they fulfil one of the exclusion criteria for this form of counselling.

Contracting

After the establishment of a satisfactory working alliance with both partners, the agreement of a therapeutic contract becomes possible. Explicit contracts tend to promote a feeling of security but may foster dependence; agreements which are left largely implicit underline the client's competence and autonomy but may be confusing and anxiety-provoking. Finding the right balance will depend on the clients as well as on the personal style of the counsellor; however, if the terms are not even clear in the counsellor's mind they are unlikely to have been successfully established with the couple.

It may seem trivial to restate the central premiss, namely that the work in hand is couple counselling and that the focus is therefore primarily between the partners rather than with either one of them. However, it is surprising how easily this basic principle can be 'forgotten' under the pressures of the counselling session, and it may well be helpful for the counsellor to be able to refer back to an explicit agreement when trying to refocus a couple on their primary task.

Some counsellors routinely state at the outset of the work what they see as the responsibilities of the parties involved; others rely on the fact that their conduct within the session makes their assumptions sufficiently clear. What is important is that deviations from the counselling framework do not go unchallenged. If, for instance, the couple start acting as if it were the counsellor's role to decide who was right and who was wrong in one of their arguments, a comment or demonstration that this is not in the range of the counsellor's responsibilities, but that adopting a neutral stance is, will prevent the session from becoming a mere repetition of the partners' domestic quarrels.

Time-limited couple counselling is becoming more widely practised, especially in professional settings, and trial periods of a few weeks are popular. Practical reasons, such as the lengths of waiting-lists, are probably as responsible for this trend as clinical experience or research demonstrating the efficacy of briefer contracts. While it is to be welcomed that counselling is thus made available to a wider range of clients, there is a more disturbing aspect in that gross average treatment lengths (which tend to lie somewhere between five and six sessions) drawn from a great number of disparate cases are sometimes regarded as normative figures prescribing the 'ideal' number of sessions for every couple. As with other features covered by the contract, what matters is that decisions are not made as a matter of routine but with the interests of the specific clients in mind.

Interventions

The following paragraphs will list some of the main areas of intervention available to the couple counsellor. It would be regrettable, however, if this created the impression that couple counselling could proceed in a technological fashion, delivering packaged interventions to the clients once the ground has been cleared by alliance-building and contracting. Couple counselling, in my view, is primarily about listening to the client couple's leading concerns, and interventions are of use only if they speak to those concerns.

Formulation Naturally, couples will present to their counsellor(s) with their own ideas as to what their difficulties are about. Frequently, partners' views will differ considerably as both are convinced that problems would all but disappear if only it were possible to persuade the other to be more reasonable. While the couple's formulation will inevitably be restricted (if they had gained a comprehensive understanding they would already have successfully dealt with their problems by themselves), it is nevertheless based on their personal experience. The counsellor's task is therefore not one of discounting or replacing the views of the couple on the nature of their predicament, but rather (as in any other form of counselling) one of adding a different perspective or meaning.

Inevitably, counsellors' formulations of problems will depend upon their theoretical backgrounds, but there are some common principles. One of these concerns an understanding that the actions of the couple are interdependent and that their disparate views may well represent two different angles on the same cycle of events (system-orientated counsellors would say that the couple punctuate the same sequence differently). Hence a husband (for the purpose of an example, it could equally be the wife) might claim that trouble always starts when his wife takes to going out at night. As a result he becomes concerned, starts questioning her when she comes home, but is met with what he feels to be indifference. He therefore takes issue with her when she plans to go out next and, in the face of her reluctance to listen, is moved to make his point more forcefully. Rather than considering his wishes she absents herself even more frequently and a major row which has been building over weeks finally erupts. If only she would show more consideration none of this need ever happen. His wife for her part might say that things go quite smoothly until her husband has one of his jealous turns. He then starts persecuting her with unreasonable questions and generally makes the atmosphere at home so miserable that she goes out to let him simmer down. However, far from becoming calmer, he seems to positively take pleasure in getting at her and, try as she may to get out of his way to avoid a row, it finally erupts. If only he could get a grip on himself none of this need ever happen.

If the counsellor can successfully convey to the couple that their own disparate stories are representing different angles on the same interactional sequence to which both contribute and which both escalate with ever more determined efforts to pursue what they think would resolve the conflict (while attributing sinister motivation to their partner), a major step towards a better understanding of their problems has been achieved. It is then dependent on the counsellor's theoretical persuasion whether the formulation is left there or elaborated in terms of the links between the collusive pattern and the partner's experiences in their families of origin, or of the maladaptive beliefs the partners hold, or of the costs and benefits they see themselves as accruing in the relationship.

Another widely shared principle in formulating a couple's problems is the acknowledgement of natural stresses arising from different stages in the couple's life cycle (a concept popularized by Sheehy 1976). It is far from obvious to many couples coming for help that quite normal and predictable events such as setting up house together, coping with the first baby, supporting ailing parents, having children at the adolescent stage, seeing the last child leave home, or dealing with the changes brought about by retirement, require adjustments from both partners which may well lead to the emergence of conflicts which could hitherto be contained. The same, of course, holds true for unexpected changes such as redundancy. If, for instance, a couple had operated a division of labour by which one partner would go out to paid work and the other concentrate on the household, the working partner's loss of job – be it through retirement or redundancy – and consequent re-entry into the domestic sphere (hanging about in the kitchen all day) will threaten both their identities and make it even harder to cope with the greatly increased hours of forced togetherness. Having their attention drawn to life-cycle issues will often come as great relief to a couple as it 'normalizes' their distress and diminishes guilt feelings.

In the literature on marital difficulties several attempts to classify couples into recurring types can be found. Most of these supposedly stable matchings, especially the so-called 'obsessive/hysterical marriage' has at one time attracted wider attention. In practice, couple typologies have little to contribute to the formulation of a particular case. Their value may rather lie in allowing counsellors faced with difficult couples to recognize aspects of their own clients in these descriptions and by reassuring them that they are not alone in their struggles.

Interpretation Not all counsellors would say that they are using interpretations in their work, especially if they understand the term as being restricted to statements which are intended to 'make the unconscious conscious'. However, if the word is used in a wider sense, probably most counsellors would recognize interpretations as an aspect of their own practice. One might view them as explanatory statements which are related to the process of formulation in that the counsellor's understanding of the couple's problem is conveyed in a piecemeal fashion. Which part of the formulation is thus communicated may depend on the particular aspect of their problem which the clients are demonstrating at the moment, or on their counsellor's sense as to what they are currently 'ready to hear', i.e. what they can admit to themselves or to each other.

Apart from conveying what the counsellor understands already, interpretations can serve to enhance or modify the formulation if they are used as hypotheses about the couple's difficulties which need to be explored and which can be confirmed, discarded, or reformulated. Taking this point of view one might almost say that the counselling process has come to an end when the complete formulation has been elicited and communicated by the counsellor and understood by the couple; however, there is probably no end to improving formulations, so indications as to when to end counselling will have to be sought from elsewhere.

Aiding communication Difficulties in communicating are one of the most visible signs of marital distress and many couples will describe their problems in this fashion when they first come for help. As the ways in which partners fail to talk to each other are readily observable in the counselling room, communication appears as a fruitful area in which to concentrate the therapeutic work. It should be borne in mind, however, that 'communication difficulties' is largely a descriptive rather than an explanatory concept. The question of the 'why' rather than the 'how' of miscommunication becomes relevant as soon as the counsellor's efforts to help the couple to talk more effectively fail to meet with success. At this point it often emerges that partners respond to each other not on the basis of the current interaction but according to a pre-established 'set' originating from an earlier phase in the couple's joint history or from previous relationships – especially those in their families of origin. Dicks (1967) first drew attention to the phenomenon of partners being initially attracted but ultimately repelled by seeing a disavowed aspect of themselves represented in their spouses.

If such internal obstacles can be dealt with, a whole spectrum of ways of promoting effective communication is open to the counsellor, ranging from active techniques, such as inviting the partners to role play each other in an argument, to relying on the counsellor's listening stance to serve as a model for the couple. It is also worth taking note of the extent to which partners try to make use of the counsellor to channel their communications as a measure of how much the couple are used to talking to each other directly and how much they tend to involve third parties.

Aiding negotiation In order to make use of the opportunities which counselling affords, it is essential for the couple to give up a combative mode of being with each other and to adopt a negotiating stance instead. In the long run this stance will be important in helping them to resolve their day-to-day conflicts if they decide to stay together, or to effect a separation in which the damaging consequences are minimized. Relinquishing a combative mode does not mean that spouses are required to forget about their dissatisfactions. On the contrary, in order to be able to negotiate with each other as to how and how far both their needs can be met, it is important that both partners accept responsibility not only for having been part of the problems but also for contributing towards their solution. This requires both to become aware of their needs and wants and to express them in specific terms which can be met by their partner. Thus, 'you never take my wishes into account and I am not going to stand for it any longer' may be useful ammunition in marital fighting; something like 'I want you to ask me before you accept an invitation for both of us, because I feel put down if you don't' is more useful in starting a joint negotiation.

Although the couple will bring current conflicts which may well be resolved during the course of counselling, the actual issues are mainly of value as examples demonstrating how to negotiate, since the couple cannot hope to begin to cover all possible areas of differences in the counselling work. Some couples may find it initially helpful to write down their agreements, but the practice of detailed behavioural contracting with reward or penalty points attached to a list of desired or unwanted actions is probably rare today. In any case it is probably better to use ways of negotiating which the clients are likely to carry on using once their counselling has finished.

If adopting a negotiating stance were easy, couples would do so without coming to counselling. Apart from a backlog of unaired grievances, partners have often come to a point where neither will make the first step. To help them to shift into a more constructive mode requires tact and patience of their counsellor and often takes considerable time.

Termination While most aspects of couple counselling have been extensively written about, its termination is a curiously neglected topic. Even though the literature on individual counselling is hardly overflowing with writings on endings, its lack in relation to marital work seems too glaring an omission to explain it solely out of the universal reluctance to dealing with such particularly painful areas as separation and loss. Perhaps it is the fact that couple counselling concerns itself by definition with the threatened break-up of an attachment that was once, however briefly, experienced as good and satisfying which makes the breaking of the therapeutic bond such a taboo subject.

It is to be hoped that the reticence shown by writers is not matched by a similar avoidance on the part of the counsellors. The tasks around termination are similar to those in individual counselling; namely for the counsellor fully to hand back and for the couple fully to accept the previously shared responsibilities of observing, reflecting on, and if necessary changing their conduct, while acknowledging that the counselling relationship was important and will be lost, but has now become unnecessary. Complications are similar to those arising in individual work as well, for instance in that the approaching ending may be heralded by the couple relapsing into ways of interacting which previously had long been overcome.

What is perhaps unique to the termination of marital counselling is the necessary withdrawal of the couple from a three- (or four-) person relationship back into the dyad, leaving them with the question as to how much they are in future going to make use of third parties in order to regulate the distance between them.

Issues

Areas of debate

Even though the practice of couple counselling shows evidence of many unifying features, there are, of course, areas about which opinion is divided. Some of these issues which give rise to current debate within the field are discussed below.

Different theoretical approaches

Theoretical differences are important despite the tendency among many counsellors and therapists to embrace the label 'eclectic'. For the field as a whole, a true integration needs well elaborated theoretical positions to draw on; for individual counsellors a secure internal framework is a vital prerequisite for assimilating new and different ideas.

Theoretical views of couple counselling can be differentiated according to the main therapeutic persuasions, which in turn draw on theories of dyadic relationships, varying widely in their sophistication and elaboration. In fact, as I have argued elsewhere (Schröder 1985), the relative importance conceptually afforded to the couple provides the central criterion by which to distinguish the various schools of thought. These can therefore be located on a continuum: on the one end we would find cognitive approaches, such as rational-emotive therapy, focusing on the individual's maladaptive cognitions which may be changed without reference to a partner. Further along we would find the client-centred view of spouses aiming for individual congruence to provide optimum conditions for personal growth for each other. Next on the spectrum we would locate behavioural approaches which concentrate on the interaction between the couple, making individual satisfaction contingent on the partner's response. Yet further along we would find the psychodynamic view of the couple as a psychic entity with shared phantasies and collusive defences derived from the 'fit' of their individual histories (for an elaboration see Willi 1982). Systemic approaches which emphasize the couple's role as a sub-system of families and wider social contexts would be placed right at this end of the continuum.

With this model in mind, we can understand theoretical differences as deriving from different ways of looking at couples. Not surprisingly, altering the angle of vision affords a different vista; a useful fact to bear in mind when our familiar outlook does not allow us to see the problems of particular clients clearly.

Co-therapy

Whether to use one or two counsellors in the conjoint work with couples is a theoretically and practically controversial question. There seems to be little empirical evidence that foursomes in marital counselling result in greater therapeutic benefits, but it is likely that most studies do not take account of differential client groups. Many counsellors like the idea of working in pairs but are restricted by the pressure of waiting-lists and the shortage of available co-workers. This frequently precludes setting up a stable counselling partnership, which would maximize therapeutic potential, and as a result regular co-therapy in conjoint couples counselling is often confined to specialist settings.

Practical constraints apart, the question remains if co-therapy should be regarded as the modality of choice. As mentioned above, establishing a working alliance is easier in a foursome than in triadic work. Another factor in the decision may be found in the theoretical persuasion of the counsellor:

— From a social learning point of view the opportunity for modelling presented by counselling in pairs is as obvious as the danger of unwittingly presenting to the clients an example of a dysfunctional partnership. Sophisticated behavioural counsellors might therefore be expected to prefer co-working.
— From a systemic point of view the additional worker would probably be better employed as a live supervisor in the room or behind a one-way

screen. Counsellors who are grounded in this approach might therefore see little value in working with a co-therapist.

— From a psychodynamic viewpoint, the mirroring of the client couple's conflicts by the counsellor couple is an important source of information and the containment of one pair's anxiety by the other a powerful therapeutic factor (for an illustration of these issues see Skynner 1979). The danger lies in the possibility that co-workers who are unaware of enduring conflicts among themselves may well end up working them out through their clients – to the detriment of the latter. However, if proper space for reflection can be made, the richness and flexibility of interaction which co-therapy allows makes it the preferred mode of working for psychodynamic counsellors.

It would be regrettable if increasing scarcity of resources and pressures towards cost effectiveness were to marginalize co-working in conjoint counselling. However, in reality it will probably be of most importance with more difficult clients and in settings which are invested in training, research, or theory development.

'Convening' a couple

This term, taken from the vocabulary of family counselling, is meant to describe a situation in which the counsellor has made a unilateral decision that conjoint work would be appropriate and proceeds to persuade the couple accordingly. If one takes a strategic perspective on the helping process (such as for instance Haley 1976), and therefore sees all interventions as directive and designed to persuade, there is only the technical problem of circumventing possible reluctances. From other points of view it seems ethically questionable to impose a focus which the couple did not choose.

At the diagnostic stage a recommendation for conjoint work when only one partner has presented with problems, however well founded theoretically, may well convey the message that the counsellor places greater value on the relationship than on individual needs. Feminist writers have been particularly alert to the possibility that couple counselling may present yet another instance where women's needs for individual space and attention are discounted in favour of concentrating on marriages which generally afford greater psychological protection to men.

There is a strand of opinion recommending convening a couple when individual work has become stuck, especially if there is evidence that the partner at home in some way 'sabotages' therapeutic gains. The resulting problems for the working alliance are formidable and, practical circumstances allowing, it may well be better to bring in a co-therapist or have the couple work taken on by a different counsellor.

Wider applications

Preventative work with couples

Within the health services the current trend towards prevention and education is unmistakeable if still comparatively weak. Within the counselling field, Relate (formerly the National Marriage Guidance Council) has shown considerable commitment to educative work, but otherwise, prevention is still a largely untapped area in Britain.

Preventative efforts have been brought to bear at various points in the life cycle of the couple, each resulting in a clearly discernible area of work such as relationship education in schools, marriage preparation, preparation for parenthood, and marriage enrichment. However, the only consistent effort has been in the field of marriage preparation, which derived much of its impetus from the Church. Marriage enrichment, while gaining ground in North America, is still in its infancy in Britain and there may well be cultural obstacles, such as widespread reservations to discuss intimate relationships, which will check its development here.

Common to preventative work is its emphasis on the non-pathological, ordinary aspects of couple relationships. This can present a difficulty for counsellors who are trained to direct their attention towards the dysfunctional aspects of their clients' interactions, even though they may include information-giving and education in their counselling work. It has therefore been argued that preventative work requires an educational rather than a counselling background. However, counsellors can draw on their knowledge and experience of human development and, given adequate preparation themselves, may find prevention a welcome addition to working with distressed couples.

Conciliation and divorce counselling

Conciliation, meaning the structured arbitration of a dispute between couples (usually following separation or divorce), is a fast-growing area. Once exclusively the domain of the Probation Service, the field has over the past ten years witnessed the emergence of a number of specialized agencies which can be affiliated to an umbrella organization since 1983. The boundaries to family counselling are diffuse as children are often involved in the conciliation process.

Different models of practice have emerged, ranging from strictly task-centred mediation to counselling which includes the exploration of interpersonal conflicts and established patterns. Common to all is the emphasis on conciliation rather than reconciliation – that is to say, the acceptance of the couple's decision to break up and the attempt to deal with the consequences of this decision in a non-adversarial manner which is normally precluded by the legal system.

Divorce counselling is an altogether wider area which includes therapeutic goals such as emotionally supporting the partners through their breakup and preparing them for new relationships. While one might argue that this would be well within the brief of traditional couple counselling, it seems that clients prefer to discuss the end of their marriage in a setting different to those which are commonly held to be devoted to 'marriage mending'.

The possible savings to the Legal Aid budget effected by the avoidance of protracted legal battles have been cited as a compelling reason for increased funding of conciliation and divorce-counselling services. However, it appears that the ideological stigma attached to supporting services which expressedly do not aim to keep couples together may in the long run outweigh such rational considerations.

Future developments

The future of counselling couples cannot be separated from developments in the entire therapeutic field. There is, however, one feature which distinguishes marital work: the voluntary sector is very strongly represented and is probably dominant in terms of number of cases seen. Arguably, this has led to a relative neglect of couple counselling in professional settings – one or two specialist establishments notwithstanding. This has been more than offset by the vigorous growth of work in the voluntary sector (which has the advantage of preventing couples from being defined as 'patients' or 'official' clients with all the potential for a pathological 'career' which such labelling entails). Such growth will inevitably lead to voluntary agencies becoming more professional – as already evidenced by Relate's transition from 'social movement' to 'service agency' – increasing their expertise and ultimately charging market rates for their services.

Training opportunities in couple counselling are in Britain mainly provided by Relate: National Marriage Guidance. Its link- up with the Institute of Marital Studies is an excellent example of a broad-based voluntary organization drawing on the expertise of a specialist professional agency and has had beneficial spin-offs for the probation service and other social work agencies. It would be desirable if other approaches could draw on similar specialized centres and if couple work took a more prominent role in the training of helping professions.

One area deserving more sustained attention is that of conjoint couples groups. Perhaps counsellors are overawed by the logistics of setting up such ventures or by the complex interplay of dyadic and group relationships. In any case, the therapeutic opportunities afforded to couples who are able to combine individual and relationship work warrant more widespread interest in this neglected field.

Both the voluntary and the professional sector are currently under the same pressure towards increased cost effectiveness. At worst, this presages a trend towards high turnover / low intensity counselling carried out by inexpert workers briefly trained in 'core skills'. At best, it would engender a more widespread interest in clinically meaningful evaluation and in briefer, focused approaches to couple counselling. However, proficiency in brief work demands training and experience beyond that required in ordinary counselling and proper evaluation needs time and energy. Given the prevailing climate, it will take the combined efforts of both sectors to keep developments being guided by a search for quality rather than by expediency.

References

Ables, B. S. and Brandsma, J. M. (1977) *Therapy for Couples*, San Francisco: Jossey-Bass.

Bennun, I. (1985) 'Unilateral marital therapy', in W. Dryden (ed.) *Marital Therapy in Britain*, Vol. 2, London: Harper & Row.

Brannen, J. and Collard, J. (1982) *Marriages in Trouble*, London: Tavistock.

Clulow, C. F. (1982) *To Have and to Hold*, Aberdeen: Aberdeen University Press.

Dicks, H. V. (1967) *Marital Tensions*, London: Routledge & Kegan Paul.

Grunebaum, H., Christ, J., and Neiberg, N. (1969) 'Diagnosis and treatment planning for couples', *International Journal of Group Psychotherapy* 19: 185–202.

Gurman, A. S., Kniskern, D. P., and Pinsof, W. M. (1986) 'Research on the process and outcome of marital and family therapy', in S. L. Garfield and A. E. Bergin (eds) *Handbook of Psychotherapy and Behavior Change*, 3rd edn, New York: Wiley.

Haley, J. (1976) *Problem-Solving Therapy*, San Francisco: Jossey-Bass.

Schröder, T. A. (1985) 'A psychodynamic practitioner's point of view', in W. Dryden (ed.) *Marital Therapy in Britain*, Vol. 1, London: Harper & Row.

Sheehy, G. (1976) *Passages: Predictable Crises of Adult Life*, New York: Dutton.

Skynner, R. (1979) 'Postscript to: the family therapist as family scapegoat', *Journal of Family Therapy*, 1: 20–2.

Willi, J. (1982) *Couples in Collusion*, New York: Aronson.

*Now called Relate: National Marriage Guidance

Chapter five

Family counselling

Eddy Street

Introduction

Families and their functioning always seem to be at the centre of any discussion about the social ills of society and how 'care' should be administered by the community. It appears as if the family is perceived as both the cause of, and the solution to, a great many problems. Even though it has been evident for some time that the family is the main socializing agent of a community, it is only in more recent decades that the family has warranted it's own 'theory', 'policy', or even a special kind of counselling. Following the Second World War a new emphasis was placed on the importance of family life for, although there is no formal 'family policy' in Britain, the majority of our legal, financial, and social legislation has been based on the notion of the 'normal' nuclear family. These policies rest on the view that the family is the basic social unit in society and that, apart from educational provision, the state should work to uphold the sanctity of the family and should not in normal circumstances intervene in its functioning. Given this major emphasis on the way in which our society and its provisions have been constructed it is not surprising that many professional workers who are involved in dispensing a vast range of welfare and care services find themselves offering help and advice to families. It is not the purpose of this chapter to discuss the differences between family therapy and family counselling; they have a natural overlapping field of interest and are separated perhaps by degrees of disturbance, techniques, and professional attitudes.

We can regard the topic of family counselling as covering such situations as a health visitor discussing with young parents how they might help their 6-month-old child to adopt a different sleep pattern; or an educational psychologist talking to a divorced mother about her 15-year-old son who persistently plays truant; or a community nurse listening to the problems of caring for a demented elderly lady looked after by her married daughter; or a psychiatric nurse suggesting to a wife of a depressive man some management strategies for dealing with him and her children; or a General Practitioner talking to an elderly couple who care for their 29-year-old chronically mentally ill son. In essence, all these situations involve the care of one generation by another and sometimes that care is dispensed co-operatively by two or more adults and sometimes it is dispensed by one adult alone. Whatever the practicalities of the situation it does involve one person at one time (but not all the time) being able to deal with his or her own needs in such a way that the needs of another are met. Naturally, these circumstances create reactions in the care-giver, the person who is receiving the care, and those other people who are intimately involved in this care-giving situation. Family counselling can, therefore, occur in a multitude of settings but it will always involve these same central elements.

Principles

Guiding theoretical principles of family counselling

Individuals and the family life-cycle

Human development is interactional, i.e. it is a process in which the behaviour of one person is meshed with the behaviour of another (Lerner and Spanier 1978). It also cannot merely be confined to that time of life known as childhood, but has to be seen as a life-long process (Lidz 1976). Not only do adults affect the development of a child but, by virtue of the reciprocity of interaction, a child affects the development of adults. From this it is a small step to note how adults, within the context of their relationships, affect the development of each other. Development, therefore, is a process that occurs throughout life and is of essence relationship bound.

Central to this view of the life-embracing and interactive nature of development is the concept of the developmental task. These are tasks which face all individuals at particular stages of the life cycle. They are tasks which have to be dealt with so that the next set of tasks on the path of development can be approached. As the 'family' is the principal primary group for the majority of people in western culture, it represents the principal context in which individuals face developmental tasks. Families are composed of individuals as well as couples; they are composed of children as well as parents. The task of family life itself is to balance the need of individuals, of the marriage, of adults, of children, in such a way that there is a blending together allowing the needs of all to be met more or less simultaneously. When this occurs then the tasks facing the individuals and the family present as enjoyable experiences rather than as problems, and there is then the time and emotional energy to confront and adaptively deal with any unforeseen or unfortunate event that may occur.

At a general historical and cultural level, we all face similar life tasks, and it therefore becomes possible to map out those issues that a family may have to face throughout the life of its individual members. Street (1985) has outlined the tasks that face the individual, the marital pair both as a couple and as parents at different stages of the life cycle. Each set of tasks is different but it is possible for each to be met in a manner which is synchronized with the other sets of tasks.

Family life is therefore characterized by the balancing of the differing needs and these needs, by virtue of the way in which life changes, will be altering and modifying over time.

The influence of past and present behaviour

In facing the tasks that arise for themselves, individuals and families use two types of information to set about problem-solving. They use the historical information they have about how they, as members of a particular family, set about dealing with life's issues. They also make use of information that they acquire in the here-and-now. Obviously these types of information are dynamically related.

Historical influences are principally concerned with the developing notion of the 'self'. As children we all acquire a sense of who we are through our relationship with our parents. We develop our view of ourself in terms of the relationships that are constructed for us in our families of origin. This view, based on modern psychoanalytic thinking (Pincus and Dare 1978), conceives of the developing child drawing upon expectations of family relationships as the prototype for all other relationships, particularly those that are made in the construction of adult families. The set of relationship patterns that is established internally when we are children becomes the templates that we use when we are adults. Elements of these templates will refer not only to adult relationships but also to parenting relationship, i.e. the relationships we construct with our children. Hence a process occurs of 'transgenerational transmission' in which an individual's sense of self is embedded in the history of his or her family (Boszormenyi-Nagy and Spark 1973). Some families are so dominated by their history that they need intensive therapy to allow them to begin to live in the present.

In the ongoing hurly-burly of daily family life, family members will be attempting to do their best to maximize pleasant events in their world and to minimize unpleasant events. In order to decide what is pleasant or unpleasant they will be using their current awareness as well as the view of events handed down historically. Once the decision of the pleasantness or unpleasantness of events is determined, individuals then act in a way that the behaviourists have well described (Patterson 1975). Thus behaviour can be increased or decreased by the effects of positive and negative reinforcement. A considerable amount of family behaviour can therefore be considered to be contingency based. It has to be remembered, however, that the determinants of what is considered a positive or negative contingency are historically determined. To an outsider some interaction that occurs in families may be considered to be definitely noxious, for example persistent outbursts of anger; but for the individuals concerned, definitions of 'love' may involve someone being frequently very angry. As our sense of worth and lovableness is determined by our past learning history, then we will seek out experiences that reinforce that sense of self even though, to someone else, they may appear to be negative. The way in which present behaviour is construed and then put to use is therefore an important element in the way in which families establish their particular way of interacting.

The family as an open system

As the family is a social unit there is a need to conceive of its operation in terms of activity as a social group. Workers with families have tended to base their view on General Systems Theory (Kerr 1981). This holds that the family is a functioning operational system comprising of interrelated parts, all of which combine to influence its total functioning. It naturally still considers the individual but events are studied within the context in which they occur with attention being placed on connections and relationships rather than on individual characteristics. The family is seen as being composed of 'subsystems', such as individuals, the parental subsystem, the sibling subsystem, men and women subsystems (fathers and sons, mothers and daughters), with each subsystem contributing to the functioning of the total family system. Some subsystems are hierarchically related in that the efficient operation of one determines the operation of another; in particular, an efficient parental system determines whether the children (sibling) system functions appropriately. It has been argued (Street 1985) that the marital subsystem is hierarchically related to the parental subsystem, for the marital pair will need to have a 'good enough' marriage in order for them to function as 'good enough' parents. Families need a means to cope with change and they differ in the extent to which they are able to adapt and accommodate to changing circumstances. Some will remain rigid, with both their internal and external boundaries and their rules of behaviour remaining the same, even though the situation demands an alteration. Other families are so loose in their boundaries and have so few rules of relating that they deal with the world in a chaotic fashion and, consequently, there is permanent change where stability would be of assistance (Olson *et al.* 1983). In order for the family to begin to accommodate to life's events, there needs to be communication both between and within subsystems. Communication is the means by which family members develop a collective view of the tasks that face them. The boundaries of a family, in fact, define the flow of communication within that system. Thus, if communication is not occurring, the boundaries are inevitably rigid and impermeable so that individuals or other subsystems are isolated. When communication is excessive but unheard, it merely becomes 'noise' in the system. In these circumstances boundaries fail to differentiate between subsystems: in this case confusion reigns for family members as they are unsure of which subsystem they belong to; and they may even be confused as to the nature of their identity as the boundary between self and others is unclear. This has been termed an 'undifferentiated ego mass' by Bowen (1979) and indicates a serious distortion of communication that may require help of a special nature so that it can be unravelled.

A feature of the functioning of systems is feedback, which is the process whereby a system takes information from itself in order to determine the next event. Feedback therefore involves a system using its own activity to determine what its next activity should be. This briefly outlines what is termed circular causality or circularity, which views the origin or development of family behaviour as arising from the interactions between the various subsystems of the family itself. This is particularly important when considering family problems, for the origin and particularly the maintenance of problems can be viewed in terms of circularity. The emphasis is therefore on mutual causality. Since each part of the family system continually influences all the other parts, the focus is on the overall pattern of relationships rather than just one element of those relationships; and issues of 'blame' in the family therefore change when one adopts the view of circular causality.

The counsellor as part of the system

As the family is a social group that is continually in interaction with its immediate social environment, at various points in time, different individuals and groups from the world at large will be incorporated into its system. This certainly occurs when a counsellor meets with family members to discuss difficulties they may be facing. The manner of this process takes as its context the 'definition' of the problem. The majority of counsellors will come from agencies that, in the eye of the public world, will have a clear definition of the problem. Thus, for example, a family being asked to see a psychiatrist is quite likely to assume that this is because someone is to be seen as psychiatrically ill and they the family may be antagonistic to this. In some contexts the family may willingly accept the agency's definition of the problem, but in other contexts, the family will attempt to have its definition of the problem accepted by the counsellor. Within the 'counselling system', interaction in the initial stages of contact occurs in the mutual search for a common definition.

As there is this mutual search for a definition of the problem that is addressed through counselling, it is possible that the activities of the counsellor may not always assist the family by intervention. The offer of counselling always implies that an input from outside the family is needed. As the counsellor is incorporated into the system then it may be that the family believes it can only deal with its difficulties if its members are involved with a counsellor. In other circumstances the family can pressurize or manipulate the counsellor to adopt its definition of the problem and this can result in the maintenance of a difficulty with nothing changing. Thus, for example, parents of a mentally handicapped adult can persuade a community nurse that they need constant visiting because of the nature of their child's handicap, and even though the nurse has a different view of the handicap; the constant visiting reinforces the parents' perception and does not effect changes through the counselling process. The counsellor in these circumstances is offering 'more of the same' (Watzlawick *et al.* 1974) in a fashion that does not assist the change process.

As counsellors can be incorporated into systems in unhelpful ways it is important that the position of counsellor is maintained such that it can be helpful to all concerned. This position of being both a member of a system and an 'objective' outsider can be easy under some circumstances, but in others, the counsellor will need to make use of colleagues and seek the advice of consultants to ensure that the appropriate stance *vis-à-vis* the family is maintained.

Practical principles of family counselling

Assessing the situation

In assessing the situation prior to embarking on the direction of counselling, counsellors need to be aware of three important facets of the family situation. First, the counsellor requires an awareness of the life-cycle issues that are confronting the family. Different families have different histories and these influence the issues that the family faces through life. Issues that face a married couple, for example, may be different if one of the partners was married previously. The age of the parents when a handicapped child was born to them may also be very relevant to how they face the task that lies in front of them. This example also illustrates how the counsellor, in many circumstances, will need an appreciation of how the future could unfold for a particular family. In the above example, a younger couple may, at some point in the future, consider what would happen if they had another child, whilst an older couple will have to consider a different set of future tasks. By bringing to the fore the issues as part of the life cycle, it allows the family to face the problems they have within the context of their own situation; this allows for the family to experience the counselling situation as a personal one for themselves. Workers who offer family counselling often find that many of the problems they meet involve primarily dealing with life-cycle issues and the adaptations that are necessary for a particular family's situation.

Second, the counsellor will need to acquire an understanding of the meaning that the family holds of their difficulty. In many situations the family will have an erroneous perception of the meaning of particular acts. They may believe, for example, that elderly people with dementia can be in more control of their behaviour than they are in fact capable of. Similarly, young parents often ascribe intentionality to an infant's spontaneous behaviour when it is not developmentally possible for the child to commit those acts in an intentional way. In another situation, there will be no 'right' or 'wrong' understanding of the behaviour and there may in fact be several explanations. Thus, for example, an 8-year-old boy's misbehaviour may be considered to be due to his poor relationship with his stepfather and to the poor discipline offered by both parents. In this case the counsellor will seek to clarify the exact meaning the family has of the behaviour and indeed whether or not there are any conflicting views held by different family members. It is important for the counsellor to establish the ideology of the family with regard to the difficulty it faces. This ideology may also include notions of who is and who is not willing to help the family.

The third important facet of the family situation that the counsellor needs to establish is the interactive sequence in which the problem behaviour is embedded. It needs to be remembered that what is defined as the 'problem' is in fact only one element of the family's interaction and that the events both prior to and following the 'problem' are just as much causal to the distress everyone feels as the actual difficulty itself. The counsellor therefore needs to establish how each family member thinks, feels, and acts before and after the problem appears. Different types of difficulties will necessitate differing emphasis on the 'before' and 'after' in the interactive sequence. Hence, when a child misbehaves there is reason to look at the events which led up to the misbehaviour, for in this case the misbehaviour may be construed as being contingent on behavioural acts, say, between the parents. In the case of an adult with a brain injury the problem behaviour itself – for example, sudden memory lapses – may not be the consequence of any discernible event but the reaction of family members to the lapses, i.e. actions which become contingent on the problem itself are the focus of the counsellor's concern. In the stream of interactive behaviour that occurs within each and every family the counsellor has to assist the family in determining an appropriate punctuation for its members' behaviour, for as interactions are construed within terms of their circularity, it is an arbitrary decision as to what will be perceived as being the 'beginning' or 'end' of any series of interactive events. It is this process of mutually constructing a beneficial punctuation of interaction that, in an important way, marks out the family counselling approach from other approaches.

Constructive aims

The general aims for the family counsellor are to assist the family in forming a realistic view of the task that faces them, then assisting them in constructing a strategy to deal with the task and of then supporting them whilst it is ongoing. In order to meet this general aim the counsellor should ask four questions, the answers to which will guide the content of the counselling process.

(1) **Does the family have information on which to base an appropriate view of the task?** In many situations family members will be operating on insufficient knowledge about the difficulty that faces them. It is the counsellor's task to ensure that their knowledge in appropriate. In the case of someone suffering from schizophrenia some family members may believe that delusive thoughts can be argued away by reason, and every time a delusion is expressed, they may become angry and spend a good deal of time trying to discuss the reality of the situation. Some of the most effective programmes for helping families with a member suffering from schizophrenia involve an education phase (Birchwood and Smith 1987). Family members are sometimes given prepared leaflets and talks so that they are aware of the problem with which they are dealing. Many young families are quite ignorant about the behaviour of infants and young

children and need help to become aware of this. Similarly, most families do not have appropriate notions of the likely course of chronic physical illnesses and the way in which treatment will affect them (Nichols 1987). Subsidiary questions that the counsellor will need to ask are 'Is the manner in which the information is imparted effective for a problem of this nature?' and 'Do family members have a view of the problem that is flexible enough to accept new information that could result in them changing their behaviour?'. The answers to these questions may affect the direction that counselling will take for particular families. Some families will be found to have considerable difficulty in recognizing and assimilating new information; such may be the problems of these families that they will need help of a psychotherapeutic nature as opposed to the approaches of counselling.

(2) **Is the communication in the family clear and open or does it need to be clarified?** Much of the behaviour that takes place within families is based upon how each person interprets the behaviour of the other family members. When a difficulty or a crisis emerges, a situation is created which is not typical for the family; in that sense it is 'new'. Under these circumstances, any one person's acts may convey messages which are not appropriately received or understood by others. It is important to appreciate that this type of communication may or may not be verbal. The counsellor's task is to ensure that each family member, as far as possible, is able to appreciate the nature of the communication that he or she is making so that other family members can be clear about the way in which the communication affects themselves. In doing this the counsellor will be unravelling the 'ideology' of the family that surrounds the particular problem they are facing. The meaning that each family member places on the acts of each other and of themselves needs to be discovered. Once this has been done the counsellor can set about the task of ensuring that the communication (both verbal and non-verbal) that takes place is clearly understood as it is intended.

(3) **Is it possible to specify the needs of everyone in the family?** Even though a difficulty presents itself primarily through one person, each family member is affected by it. The family task therefore is to deal with the particular difficulty whilst ensuring that the needs of all other family members are being met. The task for the individual is to ensure that his or her personal needs are met in a way appropriate to family functioning as well as him/herself. It is in this situation that the counsellor joins with the family in helping its members to balance the needs of all. When families face difficulties it is often found that some members feel they have to put their own needs too much to one side to meet the needs of the person encountering the difficulty; or alternatively, in some families anger occurs because a member is perceived as just 'looking after him/herself' when there is a task to be met by all. The changing closeness that a family needs

in order to deal with the tasks constitutes a major feature of the dynamics of family life. All families need to be in permanent negotiation regarding what has been termed family 'cohesion' (Olson *et al*, 1983). The counsellor's task is therefore to be able to bring to discussion what each individual feels that they need themselves in order that they can deal with the task that faces them generally. In some situations the counsellor will need to use knowledge of child development to be sure that the needs of the children are clearly understood by all.

In this part of the counselling process the family is being assisted to be aware of the way personal needs affect the solving of a problem. Thus, for example, a married daughter who is caring for her ageing parent may require her husband to deal with particular aspects of their children's care, and this couple may need the help of their brothers and sisters to offer respite care, so they may be relieved occasionally. In this case, if the daughter requires help from her brother, it naturally introduces into the counselling situation how the needs of the brother are to be seen and met. He may for example have certain perceptions and feelings about how his mother is being cared for which may affect the ease with which he can assist his sister; and these then become elements to the general family situation that need to be taken into account.

(4) **What negotiations for adaptations to change need to be made?** Once the family has acquired a clearer idea of the task that faces its members and how this task affects their particular family, it may become apparent that some changes will be required. Such changes in behaviour in any one member will obviously have implications for others. The family will need to investigate the alternative paths of change in order to become aware of the implications of each action. The process takes the form of family members saying 'If I do this then what will you do?', or 'If you do that then I would think...', or 'What will happen if we decide to do...?'. The counsellor can help the family during this process by holding on to an overall view of the task, so that the discussion that takes place does not lose its context. It may well be that the counsellor will suggest possible alternatives as the family considers the changes that could be made. It should be remembered that not all counselling situations involve a change in behaviour: many merely involve the opening of awareness, the acceptance of what is happening, and, in these situations, using the availability of the counsellor's support. Murgatroyd and Woolfe (1985) have listed the tasks that counsellor's have when they assist a family coping with a crisis.

The answering of these broad questions frames the activity of the counsellor. Not only does this apply to the overall counselling process which may occur over many sessions, but it also outlines what needs to occur moment by moment. In order to assist each individual in the family the counsellor needs to hold on to a view of the family as a single entity. In order to assist the family as a whole the counsellor needs to hold on to a view of each person functioning in his or her own particular way and requiring respect for his or her own individuality. It is the balancing of these paradoxical positions that represents the personal challenge to the family counsellor.

Issues

Within any field of counselling, particular activities seem to draw attention to the ideology, ethics, and practice of the counsellor. In family counselling, workers are very sensitive about questions regarding the 'identity' of the client. Can the client be regarded as the family unit alone or are separate people within that unit all individual clients? There are occasions when counsellors need to be mindful of the position and role of individuals in the family; this is especially the case with children and to some extent with women. At the core of this issue is the debate concerning the tenability of holding on to a view of the family as a unit or whether the needs of particular individuals have to take priority. In order to review the ethical, ideological, and practical issues concerned with this debate three areas will be surveyed.

Meeting the needs of children: involvement with families that neglect and abuse

The incidence of non-incidental injury to children and child sexual abuse has been revealed as being much more extensive than was previously considered. There is clearly a need for families who are faced with such situations to be offered help. Such is the complexity of the emotional and interpersonal factors of such cases that it is beyond the scope of this chapter to detail the varieties of assistance that families could require. However, at some point in their contact with a helping agency a worker may be offering help of a counselling nature to such a family. It may well be that through the counselling process a family reveals the presence of abuse, and a counsellor therefore needs to be very clear about the issues of confidentiality that these cases raise. An essential principle vigorously held within counselling is that of the confidentiality between client and counsellor. The counsellor in the first instance will have to determine who is the client – is it the child or is it the family? Clearly counsellors cannot allow themselves to be placed in positions where the dilemma of who is the client has not been satisfactorily resolved and cannot be resolved. Knowledge of abuse often involves the prospect of a child being removed from a family. To make decisions concerning whether or not a child should be taken from a family because his or her development is being seriously affected is not something that the counsellor offering assistance to a family can take into account during counselling. Sometimes also, the family may be legally obliged to be involved in particular agencies and it could be that a form of counselling is offered to them: under these circumstances the clients cannot be considered to be voluntary, and this places the counsellor in particular difficulties. Often information acquired about the abuse during 'counselling' could have a bearing on the management of the case by the agency. Clearly, when clients cannot be deemed to be presenting themselves for counselling solely as a result of their own motivation, then the issue of control in counselling is brought to the fore.

To deal with some of these dilemmas there certainly needs to be an appropriate definition of roles worked out by the agencies and the professionals concerned. This would make it clear to the workers and family alike as to who has responsibility for what and the rules of discussion that frame different worker/family interactions. Issues connected with the care of children raise a variety of complex questions and they can only be adequately addressed by the worker embarking on counselling being well prepared for any situation in which the ethics of counselling may be called into dispute. This issue has been discussed by Bentovim and Jacobs (1988) and Dale *et al.* (1983) with regard to child abuse; and Ainley (1984) has considered the implications of offering help to clients under legal orders.

Divorce and conciliation

The increase in divorce in society has resulted in many children beginning life in one family and then continuing it in a family that has changed its composition by divorce and remarriage. There is evidence that children who maintain contacts with both natural parents in a non-conflictual context are well-adjusted. There is a trend for divorce courts to suggest that children can be cared for by one parent even though both natural parents hold 'joint custody'. A situation is therefore created of attempting elements of co-operative parenting between adults whose marital relationship has broken down and for whom there potentially exists residual hostility and mutual distrust. It can often happen that difficulties ensue not only in the usually traumatic immediate pre- and post-divorce period but also for a considerable time following this. Parents individually will often seek someone in a counselling role in order to recruit him or her in a conflict between them and their previous partners concerning issues usually related to their children. The counsellor is therefore faced with a situation in which past family conflicts affect the present-day functioning of a system which can no longer be considered to be a family but which still requires co-operation over particular tasks. There are several dangers in undertaking this conciliation role; as the issue invariably concerns children there are strong pressures to place the children in the 'power' positions, i.e. to imply that, as children, they have a definite choice about this particular problem – for example, how often they will visit their father – and that these choices can be acted upon in a rational way. Although the amount of say children have in these issues varies with their age, the counsellor needs to operate on the premiss that the task at hand is to move towards a negotiated balance of everyone's needs and, in this respect, the views of children have to be regarded within the context of the development-enhancing maintenance of generational boundaries. A second danger is to be 'recruited' on one parent's side; and this again brings to the fore the need for the counsellor to make clear to the clients the ethics on which his or her practice is based. In the case of the above example, the counsellor may need to inform the mother that the father has the right as a natural parent to see his children: not only is this an ethic that determines how the counsellor behaves, it is in fact the reality of the situation. The third danger in this type of 'family' counselling is the attempt to deal with 'old' issues through the means of the here-and-now problem. In any divorce there are naturally many unresolved issues between the partners: it has to be assumed that the couple decided on separation as a means of dealing with all those issues between them that did not seem to be resolvable within the marriage. In the post-divorce period elements of these issues may become 'replayed' through the negotiations that need to occur about arrangements for the children. It is important for the counsellor to convey to each parent that he or she has an appreciation of the situation that led to the person adopting the attitude being taken, but it is then important to move on to discuss the present problem purely in the context of the new 'family' situation, i.e. a family separated by divorce. If this is borne in mind it then becomes possible to deal with the here-and-now interaction in such a way that a negotiated solution is found that is acceptable to all.

Women in families

It is now viewed that sexual inequality is a major source of conflict and distress in families. The roles that women are given in families are seen as systematically according them less status and power than men and hence their lives are less satisfying. It is typically the case that, in families where sacrifices have to be made in order to provide an appropriate level of care for a family member, women are those who make and are usually required to make, those sacrifices. It can therefore be argued that family counselling on whatever issue often merely supports the unequal role of women and does little to change the basic inequality that exists. It has been argued (Hare-Mustin 1978; Goldner 1985) that sexual inequality has been ignored in family work because of the dominance of systems theory as an explanatory account of family structure and functioning. This theory views systems as organizing themselves hierarchically; and by adopting a particular historical view of the family, namely that of the 1950s, the family was seen as a haven and sexual inequality was perceived as a harmonious complementary arrangement in which men and women presided over separate but equal worlds. Indeed, it has been held that healthy functioning is maintained by men and women residing in their stereotypical roles. There are some who suggest that the helper to the family can often play a role in 'pathologizing' women's position (Williams and Watson 1988).

Clearly, the counsellor must be aware of the context in which the modern family operates. That political and social context is one in which questions of power and sexual inequality are very much to the fore. The external world will therefore have some very important influences on how the family members will perceive their role and how they will attempt to negotiate the meeting of their needs. The issue is whether or not the counsellor should foster the process of thinking about sexual inequality or whether he or she should allow the family to deal with it in their own way, knowing that some may choose the usual sexual stereotypes. Families require of their counsellor genuineness concerning the principles on which practice is based and these principles should very easily be capable of being put into operation through the process of counselling. If during counselling, for example, it transpires that violence has occurred between partners the counsellor could inform them that this is unacceptable and that, if it continues, then particular types of advice would be given and action taken to prevent its recurrence. One cannot assume that any decision or issue is more the province of one person rather than another because of the power of that person in the family. The counsellor should start from the basis that equal power-sharing occurs at every moment through the counselling process and that the family's reaction to this will determine whether any issues of sexual inequalities become a part of the context of the counselling.

Future developments

At the core of family counselling is a dilemma that faces the counsellor about the view held concerning the relationship between the individual and the family. On the one hand there is the view that the individual is so much a part of the family and that the individual's behaviour is so influenced by the activities of the family that, at all times, one should view the unit to be helped as the 'family' (Haley 1976). Alternatively, there are those who view the links between the individual and the family as being of varying strengths under particular conditions (Holmes 1985). These workers are therefore able to discuss the indications and contra-indications of family counselling, determining it as being appropriate in some circumstances but not others.

That there are these two ways of considering family counselling has naturally led to developments in different directions though paradoxically eventually these developments pose identical problems for counsellors. For those who do not overly stress the 'systems' aspect but emphasize the family *per se*, the developments initially lie in ensuring that family issues are given due weight when individual presents with any type of stress or difficulty (Orford 1987). An example of this is provided by Bunn and Clarke (1979), who demonstrated that just one session of counselling with relatives of seriously ill people focusing on the expression of fears and the provision of information reduced high levels of anxieties. Clearly, the ability to offer even a minimal amount of family counselling at a time of crises will have considerable beneficial effects.

The counselling of the family, however, is not limited merely to crises as there are a growing number of other areas in which the skills and knowledge of family counselling can be applied. Thus, for example, the last decade has seen significant changes in attitude, support, and responsibility towards children and teenagers with handicaps and disabilities, encouraging living in ordinary family environments rather than in large institutions. This particularly affects the many foster and adoptive families who have to be recruited to help move some of these children out of inappropriate care. These families have to adjust to a new member with very particular and special needs and often they will encounter their own doubts and insecurities as well as the doubts and scepticism from their wider social network (British Agencies of Adoption and Fostering 1985). As the need for more substitute families increases, the preparation and support the new family will require will be considerable: an important family counselling input will clearly be necessary for this group. Such work is likely to increase in the years to come.

Another direction of development springs from a growing awareness of the need for preventive-type interventions, particularly with regard to the problems that can arise from parenting young children. In the USA a number of programmes designed for 'family enrichment' have been put into operation (Mace 1983). In the United Kingdom there has been a growth in the use of behavioural approaches to children's problems. These have been heavily based on the 'triadic model' (Herbert 1978), which involves the worker developing a relationship with the carer of the child rather than with the child. The development of this particular approach has necessitated the use of counselling skills in the process of assisting the parenting relationship. De'Ath (1983) has argued that the health, education, and social services devote little attention to equipping people with knowledge to anticipate problems or the skills to solve or manage them. Instead, families are required to identify themselves through a problem, casting them in an inadequate or passive role rather than as people able to specify some of their immediate needs, and seeking ways in which to meet those needs. If such arguments are accepted, which seems to be happening slowly, then clearly this is an area in which family counsellors will have a major contribution to make. One specific aspect of this developing field will certainly be in 'family centres' which offer particular resources to their communities. These do challenge the notion of 'treatment' sessions and discreet activities with individual children and families (Phelan 1983; Hasler 1984). Many centres are exploring ways of working with all local families, both separately and in groups, and in a mixture of supportive, preventive, and interventionist ways (De'Ath 1985).

Apart from being involved in the direct provision of services in such centres, family counsellors may find that the needs of the families they see lead them into involvement with community action and wider political considerations. De'Ath (1988) has argued that those workers assisting with families cannot avoid becoming involved in issues of social policy. Naturally, counsellors always need to be mindful of their role as well as being aware of the limits of counselling *per se*, but certainly here is a 'growth' area for family counsellors in which the question of the boundaries of counselling as an activity will clearly be raised.

The other view of family counselling places stress on the system's properties of the family as a social group. This view holds that the family systems perspective is a total orientation and that it is possible and indeed desirable to hold this view and practise its skills across all situations. Taken from this perspective, the developments in family counselling are indeed wide ranging and cover numerous situations in which 'counselling' could be possible. Stated another way, the development proposed by this view is that family counselling is not the response to a particular situation (the family), but is in fact a school of counselling based on an understanding of human systems. This approach then leads on to a focus on the interface between the systems of the families and the organizations/agencies with which they have to deal. Counsellors can then become actively involved in the problems that are posed by the attentions given to a family by a particular public agency. This move in focus shifts the assumption that it is the family that is the problem. The family may have great difficulties but the greatest of them all can be the unhelpful attentions of professional helpers. Carpenter (1987) and Dimmock and Dungworth (1985), for example, have illustrated how it is possible to effect some change in the 'problem' by involving a number of the family's social networks (professional and non- professional) in discussions about how to assist with the family. This is an attempt to apply the notion 'working with the system' in a wider sense and to use the understanding of this wider context for the benefits of particular individuals.

Following on from this approach has been the development of workers offering a variety of forms of 'counselling' (though it rarely is known as that) to agencies and organizations themselves. Street (1981), for example, has described an approach to consulting with the staff group of children's homes by using many of the principles outlined in this chapter. Similarly, Dowling and Osborne (1985) have described a variety of ways in which workers can assist families and schools to deal mutually with children that present with problems. These developments again take the counsellor out of the counselling room and one-to-one relationship and clearly place him or her in the wider social context – a context in which the influence of 'political' issues in their broadest sense are felt. Workers from the 'orientation' viewpoint are therefore willing to involve themselves in complex organizational issues as they believe that their perspective of the system can assist the individual's performance in a wide range of activities not necessarily related directly to the family. Indeed it may well be that some workers from this perspective cease to apply their skills to care-giving organizations and become active with organizations that are ultimately concerned with typical business and financial goals.

Both conceptions of 'family' counselling contain dilemmas and dangers in the manner in which they may develop. There can readily be a shift from counselling to advocacy and from this to other forms of social intervention. As always, counsellors need to keep in the forefronts of their minds the ethics and values that they hold and consider these in conjunction with the variety of roles they may be required to perform. As with all new developments, ultimately the question is raised how counselling is to be defined and practised.

Conclusion

It is, of course, a truism to say that we are all part of a family. Families provide the context in which we attempt to meet our needs, which are by their very nature relational. Given the extent that our families, however composed, have such an influence on our adjustment to the wider world, it is little wonder that many of the problems and worries of life are based within its confines as well as it offering the solution to many difficult situations. The problems that families present and the potential for care and support they offer are enormous. No worker, regardless of discipline or theoretical persuasion, can avoid the ways in which families can affect and influence particular circumstances. It would seem necessary for all workers to have some understanding of family processes and functioning. Our thinking has for too long been dominated by a view of human distress as being the product of processes internal to the individual. It is important for all workers to have an appreciation of the forces and influences of the family on the individual and, in particular, it is essential that workers come to be able to tap the potential of these forces for the well-being of all. It is, therefore, essential that counsellors who in any way deal with families have knowledge of the systems' properties of families so that they may make interventions based on an awareness of the family as a whole. There is now a considerable body of knowledge concerning family functioning and all counsellors should be able to draw upon this. If we neglect the power of families we do so at our peril; if we can tap its tremendous resources we make available to our clients a natural means of care and support of infinite possibilities.

References

Ainley, M. (1984) 'Family therapy in probation practice', in A. Treacher and J. Carpenter, (eds) *Using Family Therapy*, London: Blackwells.

Bentovim, A. and Jacobs, B. (1988) 'Children's needs and family therapy. The case of abuse', in E. Street and W. Dryden (eds) *Family Therapy in Britain*, Milton Keynes: Open University Press.

Birchwood, M. and Smith. J. (1987) 'Schizophrenia and the family', in J. Orford (ed.) *Coping with Disorder in the Family*, London: Croom Helm.

Boszormenyi-Nagy, I. and Spark, G. (1973) *Invisible Loyalties*, New York: Harper and Row.

Bowen, M. (1979) *Family Therapy in Clinical Practice*, New York: Jason Aronson.

British Agencies of Adoption and Fostering (1985) 'Whose handicap? Finding new families for children with mental handicaps' (video), London: BAAF.

Bunn, T. A. and Clarke, A. U. (1979) 'Crisis intervention: an experimental study of the effects of a brief period of counselling on the anxiety of relatives of seriously injured or ill hospital patients', *British Journal of Medical Psychology* 52: 191–5.

Carpenter, J. (1987) 'Some reflections on the state of family therapy in the UK, *Journal of Family Therapy* 9: 217–29.

Dale, P., Morrison, T., Davies, M., Noyes, P., and Roberts, W. (1983) 'A family therapy approach to child abuse: countering resistance, *Journal of Family Therapy* 5: 117–45.

De'Ath, E. (1983) 'Teaching parental skills', *Journal of Family Therapy* 5: 321–36.

——(1985) *Self-Help and Family Centre: A Current Initiative in Helping the Community to Care*, London: National Children's Bureau.

——(1988) 'Families and their differing needs', in E. Street and W. Dryden (eds) *Family Therapy in Britain*, Milton Keynes: Open University Press.

Dimmock, B. and Dungworth, D. (1985) 'Beyond the family: using network meetings with statutory child care cases', *Journal of Family Therapy* 7: 45–68.

Dowling, E. and Osborne, E. (1985) *The Family and the School: A Joint Systems Approach to Children*, London: Routledge & Kegan Paul.

Goldner, V. (1985) 'Feminism and family therapy, *Family Process* 24: 31–47.

Hare-Mustin, R. T. (1978) 'A feminist approach to family therapy', *Family Process* 17 181–94.

Haley, J. (1976) *Problem Solving Therapy*, San Francisco: Jossey-Bass.

Hasler, J. (1984) *Family Centres: Different Expressions – Same Principles*, London: The Children's Society.

Herbert, M. (1978) *Conduct Disorders of Childhood and Adolescence: A Behavioural Approach to Assessment and Treatment*, Chichester: Wiley.

Holmes, J. (1985) 'Family and individual therapy: comparisons and contrasts, *British Journal of Psychiatry*, 147: 668–76.

Kerr, M. (1981) 'Family systems theory and therapy', in A. Gurman and D. Kniskern (eds) *Handbook of Family Therapy*, New York: Brunner/Mazel.

Lerner, R. M. and Spanier, G. B. (1978) *Child Influences on Marital and Family Interaction: A Life Span Perspective*, New York: Academic Press.

Lidz, T. (1976) *The Person: His and Her Development Throughout the Life Cycle*, New York: Basic Books.

Mace, D. (1983) *Prevention in Family Services: Approaches to Wellness*, Beverley Hills, California: Sage.

Murgatroyd, S. and Woolfe, R. (1985) *Helping Families in Distress: An Introduction to Family Focused Helping*, London: Harper & Row.

Nichols, K. A. (1987) 'Chronic Physical disorder in adults', in J. Orford (ed.) *Coping with Disorder in the Family*, London: Croom Helm.

Olson, D. H., McCubbin, H. I., Barnes, H., Larsen, A., Muxen, M., and Wilson, M. (1983) *Families: What Makes them Work*, Beverley Hills, California: Sage.

Orford, J. (1987) 'Integration: a general account of families coping with disorder', in J. Orford (ed.) *Coping with Disorder in the Family*, London: Croom Helm.

Patterson, G. (1975) *Families: Application of Social Learning to Family Life*, Champaign, Illinois: Research Press.

Phelan, J. (1983) *Family Centres: A Study*, London: The Children's Society.

Pincus, L. and Dare, C. (1978) *Secrets in the Family*, London: Faber & Faber.

Street, E. (1981) 'The family therapist and staff group consultancy', *Journal of Family Therapy* 3: 187–99.

——(1985) 'From child-focused problems to marital issues', in W. Dryden (ed) *Marital Therapy in Britain, Vol. 2, Special Areas*, London: Harper & Row.

Watzlawick, P., Weakland, J., and Fisch, R. (1974) *Change: Principles of Problem Formation and Problem Resolution*, New York: Norton.

Williams, J. and Watson, G. (1988) 'Sexual inequality, family life and family therapy', in E. Street and W. Dryden (eds) *Family Therapy in Britain*, Milton Keynes: Open University Press.

Chapter six

Counselling in groups

Bernard Ratigan

Introduction

Aristotle wrote that man is a social animal. Yet the lay person's view of counselling is that it is in essence an individual activity, or, more properly, dyadic: client and counsellor. Although therapy and counselling emerged as individualist disciplines, since the Second World War there has been an enormous growth in the use of group methodologies in a variety of settings. The range is wide and includes formal, long-term groups designed to help bring about major changes in members' functioning, brief but intensive encounter groups to skill training and staff support groups, and groups with a focus on helping members solve, resolve, or accept problems, make adjustments, or cope with trauma. Group counselling covers a wide gamut.

This chapter surveys the major theoretical and clinical perspectives underpinning various forms of group counselling. It includes some descriptive material to illustrate the nature of the counselling process as it can occur in group settings. Issues in group counselling are considered, including the goals of the group, inclusion and exclusion factors, the role of the group counsellor, the 'work' of group members, the development of different types of group over time, how change actually occurs in groups, the limitations of the various types of groups, and effective leadership profiles. There follows a review of the different purposes for which counselling and counselling skills are used in groups and an attempt to identify the different types of group settings where counselling has a part to play. The chapter concludes with a consideration of likely future developments. These include questions to do with training, the increasing use and appropriateness of group counselling, and the convergence of methodologies.

Principles

All the major theoretical approaches to individual counselling and therapy are represented and practised in group counselling. This chapter takes as the primary differences between counselling and psychotherapy the following: length of time over which the group meets, the depth at which the members' material is treated, the use of the transference, and the purposes for which the group is convened. A pragmatic distinction is preferred in which counselling emphasizes work with non-patient groups, is of shorter duration, with little or no explicit use of the transference and where there is a greater degree of task orientation. Throughout the chapter, though, these distinctions will be continually blurred and the literature of psychotherapy and counselling equally utilized.

The history of group counselling is not extensive and has developed rapidly in the second half of the twentieth century. During the Second World War attempts had been made to develop group treatments for soldiers which led to important work at the National Training Laboratory at Bethel, Maine in the USA and the Tavistock Clinic and Tavistock Institute in London. The application of psychoanalytic insights to group processes provides one of the major perspectives in group counselling (Foulkes and Anthony 1957). The work of Carl Rogers is also of great significance in the development of group counselling. From his work with individual clients important ideas evolved about the nature of human development and the necessary conditions for growth and change which have profoundly affected group counselling. Humanistic psychology has a strong base in group methodologies, as for example with gestalt, bioenergetics, psychodrama, and encounter groups.

Group counselling offers a fundamentally different experience to the client from that of individual one-to-one counselling. In his masterly work, Yalom (1986) identified eleven factors which distinguish the curative factors operating in group counselling and provide a background to all its forms:

(1) The instillation of hope is central to all forms of psychological therapy, and to religion and medicine.
(2) Universality: one of the most significant learnings by members of groups is that they are not alone either in their experience or concerns.
(3) Imparting of information: although in the beginning group members often expect that, as in school, they will be taught facts, they come to realize that this is of relatively small importance.
(4) Altruism: group membership often releases within participants previously hidden or forgotten capacities for helping others.
(5) The corrective recapitulation of the primary family group: groups can help members to work through and in some ways heal hurts sustained in earlier life.
(6) Development of socializing techniques: participation in a group provides the opportunity of learning, and practising, different ways of relating to others in a live setting.
(7) Imitative behaviour: by watching others' behaviour and listening to them, group members can discover their own distinctive personal styles.
(8) Interpersonal learning: through interacting with others, members are often able to grow and change. Groups provide an opportunity for both emotional and cognitive understanding.

(9) Group cohesiveness is the result of all the forces acting on the members to remain in a group and is not a curative factor *per se* but a necessary precondition for effective change.

(10) Catharsis and ventilation of feelings are not in themselves sufficient for change, but both can be a significant part of the process and can therefore also be curative factors.

(11) Existential factors such as the need to take responsibility oneself, the fact of individual isolation, contingency, the inevitability of mortality, and the capriciousness of existence are all themes which are often more easily tackled in group settings rather than in individual therapy.

In one of the most significant pieces of large-scale research in this field, Yalom established what members of groups themselves saw as the most helpful factors. In order of importance they were:

(1) discovering and accepting previously unknown or unacceptable parts of myself;

(2) being able to say what was bothering me instead of holding it all in;

(3) other members honestly telling me what they think of me;

(4) learning how to express my feelings;

(5) the group's teaching me about the type of impression I make on others;

(6) expressing negative and/or positive feelings towards another member;

(7) learning that I must take ultimate responsibility for the way I live my life no matter how much guidance and support I get from others;

(8) learning how I come across to others;

(9) seeing that others could reveal embarrassing information and take other risks and benefit from it helped me to do the same; and

(10) feeling more trustful of groups and other people.

Applications

There are a wide variety of types of groups in existence ranging from those in clinical settings offering long slow treatment to educational and management training settings with short lives and focused agendas. Historically, the group-analytic movement established a model of groupwork in which a group of strangers would come together on a weekly or twice-weekly basis, often over a period of years, with the leader (or conductor) acting as group analyst. The conductor would usually only comment on the group process in so far as it revealed the transference material emerging in the free associations of the group members (or patients) about themselves, the other members, and, especially, the leader. It will be seen that such groups are derived from the psychoanalytic ideas of Freud and the theory underpinning them owes much to the work of the Kleinian analyst, Bion (1961).

In contradistinction to analytic groups are those derived from the person-centred work of Carl Rogers, who eschewed the deterministic ideas of Freud and instead emphasized the importance of the personal encounter between client and therapist in both individual and group settings. From using these ideas in small-scale encounter groups in the 1960s, Rogers and his associates have extended the concept of group counselling through to much larger gatherings of people from widely diverse ethnic, racial, and language backgrounds. Some of the most exciting developments in groupwork ideas and practice in the 1980s demonstrated the power of person-centred theories to facilitate communication between people otherwise separated by conventional barriers of nationality, class, sexual orientation, gender, race, and language.

Psychology and education combined to produce a range of group methods which employ theories based upon cognitive–behavioural and social-learning approaches. One of the increasingly widely practised forms of groupwork is assertiveness training. Although there are a variety of models in existence the unifying ideas behind them is that individuals working together in a group with a leader are systematically trained to develop skills which will help them in their relationships with others. There is considerable emphasis on participants identifying situations in their own lives in which they are not assertive – that is, in which they are passive or aggressive. By enacting these scenes with tuition from the leader and the active support and encouragement of the other group members standing in as significant others in the participant's life, skills are acquired (Dickson 1982).

Assertiveness training is of particular interest because it includes within it a number of older methodologies, for example instruction and psychodrama. When groupwork ideas were first being contemplated in the years before and during the Second World War group leaders would sometimes give lectures on aspects of mental health. This practice has now dwindled with the realization that the kinds of changes being worked for in group approaches need something more powerful than information and instruction. Psychodrama has a long and distinguished history. Originating with Moreno's theatre of the mind, it owes not a little to Freud's psychoanalytic ideas, especially with regard to the importance of dreams, but it has become widely disseminated in most forms of groupwork, training, and education through the practice of roleplay. There does, of course, exist the pure form of psychodrama with its own training and applications. It is an especially potent form of group counselling because of its immediacy, the role of the director (*sic*), and its capacity for getting at traumatic material in the group members' lives, current and past (Blatner 1973).

Among some of the most significant changes that have taken place in western society this century have been those in the relationships between men and women. The women's movement is essentially founded upon ideas that have been arrived at in groups. Single sex groupings are not, of course, new. Indeed, throughout much of human history boys and girls have been educated and trained in single-sex groups and much human activity is carried out separately. What is especially interesting in terms of group counselling is that both women's and men's groups are now regularly convened to develop and raise consciousness and to give their members the context and the possibility of exploring issues that are hard or impossible in mixed settings. Inevitably, one of the perennial issues in single-sex counselling groups is the emotional and sexual emotions between members. This century has begun to see the recognition of the complexity and range of human sexuality and sexual orientation. Well-run groups provide safety for people to explore the often painful parts of themselves which may have lain unrecognized or hidden for years and sometimes decades. Such exploration can have the most profound implications not only for the group member but also for his or her partner, parents, children, and friends.

As has already been mentioned, group therapy really began to take shape during the Second World War as part of the treatment given to those suffering neurotic disorders. It is in other total and neo-total institutions that group counselling has grown, if not flourished. In the prison system, for example, there has been some recognition of the power of groups as a therapeutic agent of change. Two particular modalities are worthy of special note. Psychoanalytically derived groupwork methods are used to treat some of the most disturbed and disturbing prisoners (Cox 1978). Methods derived from psychodrama are also practised in work with prisoners. Again, the focus on drama seems to give such methods a special significance and power. Although there are very few psychiatric prisons in Britain, there seems to be a great need to expand groupwork treatments to make them available on a much wider basis.

Groups, then, have an increasingly important impact on the treatment of the emotionally disturbed and ill. Even in organically orientated psychiatric units there is recognition of the importance of establishing a therapeutic milieu, even if this proves difficult in practice (Whiteley and Gordon 1979). Therapeutic communities all have at their centre group therapy and out-patient groups are becoming more widely available (Hinshelwood and Manning 1979; Kennard and Roberts 1983). The particular orientations vary and can include psychoanalytic, person-centred, and a whole range of action approaches like gestalt and Transactional Analysis. Another important development is the range of self-help groups in the community. Examples abound: groups for alcohol and other substance users, for those with eating disorders, for the bereaved, for the recovering mentally ill, for those with HIV/AIDS, and many others. An interesting example of the application of group therapy with insulin-dependent diabetics is reported by Aveline et al. (1985). Although some of these groups would eschew notions of leadership on ideological grounds, they are, of course, subject to many of the same dynamics and processes as more formally convened groups with trained, professional leaders. Indeed, it is clear that as in any other form of therapy the important distinction is not between the professional and the amateur but between the more effective and less effective leader.

Lastly, groups are used extensively in training both for the therapeutic and for the other helping professions such as social work, education, and management. It is increasingly recognized that the formation of people for such professions requires more than cognitive learning and specialist skills. The power of the group can be utilized to show beginners the need for personal knowledge which, paradoxically, is often best acquired in interaction with others. The painful process of change and the acquisition of personal insight and sensitivity is often enhanced and made more powerful by the exposure to the group experience.

Issues

Goals of the group

Counselling groups are convened for many purposes although it is important that they are convened for a purpose. What the group is for will condition how the group is conducted, led, or facilitated. Group counsellors have themselves to understand for what reasons a group is convened so that they can make explicit to the participants the reasons for convening the group. Of course, stated and actual goals can diverge considerably and once groups begin they develop a life, culture, and personality of their own which is as much likely to fluctuate as is any human being.

The role of the leaders

Group counsellors have important but often subsidiary roles when compared with their individual colleagues. The work starts with the conception of the group, when it is called into being and for what purpose the group is convened.

Group counsellors have many important housekeeping and boundary-holding functions. They need, in particular, to ensure that the potential client population is aware of the availability of the group. There are key questions about selection: is the group appropriate for all those who would wish to join? – what are the criteria for selection?; what is the optimum size of the group, the maximum and the minimum?; over what period of time will the group meet and how frequently?; how long will sessions be?; once started is it open so that new members may join as some leave, or is it closed?; where will the group meet?; are there rules about the participants meeting outside sessions and what is to happen if the rule is infringed?; what are the rules about confidentiality?; what supervision arrangements do group counsellors need to support their work? This list is not exhaustive and the reader is referred to Whitaker (1985) for an extended discussion of these and related issues.

The work of the counsellor includes many external functions which, though of apparently small significance, do much to ensure an efficiently and carefully run group with a good therapeutic culture.

Once the group has begun, the work of the counsellor will vary depending on his or her primary theoretical orientation, the purposes for which the group is convened, and the particular point it has reached in its developmental natural history. In all groups, though, counsellors will pay particular attention to both what is said and not said, to helping the group stay in the here-and-now and to boundary matters like time, breaks, and endings. Two important concepts of relevance are holding and leverage. Holding refers to that special quality of relationship that a leader has with the group which parallels that of the good parent able to communicate to the infant and child that they are valued unconditionally. Through reliability and a non-retaliatory stance the leader can help to create and sustain a productive therapeutic atmosphere. By applying the principle of leverage the effective leader can identify just how much force to apply where and for how long to maximize change. It is a skill acquired with experience and from making mistakes.

There are a variety of special elective techniques available to the group counsellor. These can take the form of interventions, which help participants focus on aspects which are causing difficulties or are being neglected or even ignored. Games and simulations, creative therapeutic techniques, role play, psychodrama, and methods drawn from gestalt psychology can be powerfully utilized. One particularly useful tool is the Johari window (Luft 1966), which can help participants to begin to understand that there are aspects of themselves known only to themselves, some that are shared with others, and some that are not known.

Another special technique is the use of written reports. After each session the counsellors write an account of what they have observed. This provides an opportunity for the participants to relive the session, for insights and changes to be underscored and emphasized, for learning to be reinforced, and can help the members see that the group is an orderly process with direction leading to gains (Yalom *et al*. 1975; Aveline 1986). It is usual for the reports to be written by the leaders immediately after each session and posted to group members. Participants often report a range of emotions about the reports which, of course, can become an important part of the group process.

Groups are complicated and subfused with complex interactions. Two leaders are almost always better than one. They provide support for each other, they are able to adopt differing roles in the group at different times, one perhaps more active than the other, and they are able to offer to the group and each other differing perspectives of what is going on. For mixed-gender groups it is particularly helpful if the leaders are of different genders: many issues relating to male–female relationships, to parents, and sexuality can thus be given greater prominence.

The final issue facing group leaders is that of supervision. The powerful forces at work in any therapeutic relationship are, of course, multiplied many times over in a group. It goes without saying that group leaders must themselves have embraced the training tripos of theoretical instruction, a personal experience of group membership, and of doing supervised work. Supervision is necessary from the moment the group is conceived and called into being. One of the advantages of having two leaders is that peer supervision is much easier to arrange. Some kind of supervision is, however, essential both for the well-being of the group and the leaders.

The work of group members

The 'work' of participants in counselling groups will vary with the purpose of the group. One of the unifying concepts throughout most group modalities, especially those derived from analytic, interpersonal/existential, and person-centred ideas, is that of remaining in the here-and-now. This means trying to say what they are experiencing in the present moment. This is especially difficult for most neophyte group participants and requires considerable effort, as many human interactions avoid this.

The basic ground rule for group members is: uninhibited conversation. This is the group equivalent of free associating in individual counselling and therapy. It is an encouragement for continued communication in the face of antagonism. Conflict, both within and between members, is one of the distinctive features of most forms of group counselling. The asymmetry of the power relationship between counsellor and client in one-to-one work is transformed in group counselling, so that in groups clients can often more quickly experience and express angry or fearful feelings towards leaders. A member who attacks a leader may be a spokesperson for others and the public character of the occasion tends to ensure that retaliation will not take place. Further, in individual work, the only source of information is the counsellor; in a group, the other members also serve as sources of feedback, as models, and as guides.

The expression of anger can be a particularly useful medium of learning, growth, and healing, especially with those clients who have been traumatized, have never learned how to express their anger adequately, or have become skilled at converting it into depression or some psychosomatic condition. Members' anger with one another, and with the leaders, is often an important turning-point both for the individuals concerned and for the group's development as a therapeutic vehicle for change. Although painful, being angry with one another is often a way of saying 'I am taking you seriously', and even 'you are important to me.' For those group participants who experience themselves as more or less unimportant, to be able to get close to saying these words can be profoundly significant.

Group members tend to discover that in many ways they are more similar to each other than they expected. Behind the masks of everyday life, of surface coping, even the most seemingly well- adjusted group members will usually have undercurrents to explore. Sullivan's one genus-postulate, 'everyone is much more simply human than otherwise', although conceived in the context of individual psychotherapy, seems even more apt in the context of groups.

The distortions that group members have of themselves, other members, and leaders provide one of the richest sources of material for productive work in a group. The distortions are, of course, a result of the life experiences of the participants and Frank (1974) has identified two, mirror and transference reactions, that are especially common, important, and useful. Mirror reactions are those where group members tend to detect and disapprove of traits in someone else that they deny in themselves. In the group they can be helped to see them as their own. Transference reactions occur when members inappropriately transfer on to or put into other participants or the leaders those feelings which are, or more usually were, appropriate to others in their lives. Through the process of the 'reflective loop' members can be helped to see and work through their distortions and difficulties over and over again. Members of groups come to demonstrate what Frank has called their 'assumptive world'. Instead of merely talking about their life and concerns they become them and so demonstrate them in the group. In the group they create the relationships and the difficulties which they experience in the outside world. The group can then become a workshop or laboratory where steps towards change can be taken with the powerful support of the other group members and leaders.

How groups develop over time

Counselling groups, like all other forms of life, have a natural history: a beginning, a middle, and an end. Early sessions are often characterized by hesitancy, fear, dependency, difficulties in staying in the here-and-now, and high expectations. It is a time for building group norms that emphasize the importance of openness and sharing but not too much too soon. Sometimes it is more useful if participants are able to hold back on what seems very pressing until a sufficient degree of trust has been built up. Likewise, confrontations, although important and often therapeutic in effect, are often the characteristic of the more established, safer atmosphere of the mature group. In these matters there is usually a tension between the need to disclose and the fear of disclosure: done too soon and a fragile therapeutic alliance can be destroyed; left too late, and an anti-therapeutic culture may preclude any real sharing and be very difficult to shift.

In more mature groups, participants are gradually able to free themselves of inhibitions and resistances to talking openly, more able to stay in the present, more able to give and receive feedback and to exercise autonomy both within and outside the group. There is also an increasing ability to risk doing the things, being the person they wish and sharing words and feelings which are hard to express but which are necessary for change and growth.

In counselling groups derived from cognitive, behavioural, gestalt, and psychodramatic modalities, the development is much more determined by the leader. In all forms of groups, however, there comes a moment which, if seized, can result in sharp changes of attitude or behaviour. One of the Greek words for time, *kairos*, better expresses the power of the auspicious moment. It is very much a feature of counselling in groups and links this kind of work with drama and ritual.

All groups have to face issues to do with ending. Even in long, open groups in which members stay as long as they need, there are endings. Most counselling groups are of fixed length and a well run, mature group will be helped to face the questions of ending well in advance of it actually happening. It is a time for reflection on the gains made, the insights, the sense of belonging, the good and the bad times shared. It is also a time for sadness, loss, anger, and frustration. The well-run group will be helped to face these issues and to work through them. As in individual work, breaks and endings will generate many, often lost or repressed, memories of other losses experienced by group members in the past. Members will be surprised at the powerful feelings encountered and, with skilful help, be able to speak of them and work through the pain of the losses.

How change occurs

There are a variety of factors at work in counselling groups which facilitate, and inhibit, change. Participants come to see themselves more fully and are able to try out new ways of being and relating to others and thinking about themselves and their worlds. In the safety of the group they are offered space and time which can provide the context in which these changes can occur. It is a complex (and not fully understood) nexus of factors which allows both the participant to experience the safety necessary for the change to begin to occur and the anxiety or tension which is the spur to move towards change (Yalom *et al.* 1977; Bloch and Crouch 1985). Developments, learning, insight, and growth occur in an episodic rather than linear manner. Merely being in the group is clearly not sufficient for change to occur; involvement in other processes, such as risking saying what one is feeling, sharing secrets, giving and receiving feedback, catharsis, confrontation, modelling, and the corrective emotional experience are all important. An important process in group counselling is the reflective loop of doing, looking back on what was done, and then understanding. As groups mature, members often take over this function from leaders.

Limitations of counselling groups

Group counselling provides a therapeutic and learning environment where many human problems can be worked on with good effect. People for whom a one-to-one helping relationship is essential, will not benefit from groups. Those who will probably not do well in groups are those suffering from psychotic illness and severe depression, those who can only see their difficulties in physical terms, the paranoid who are overly suspicious, the narcissistic who need all the attention for themselves, and the schizoid who are too cut off from other people. Once people have been helped to move from these categories, groupwork can often provide an important and potent ingredient in their return to well-being. In essence, groups are more for interpersonal rather than intrapersonal development.

It is also often difficult to persuade potential participants that a group really is the most useful option and not a second best to individual therapy. The culture of individualism in our society is often strongly embodied in those with difficulties, especially interpersonal difficulties.

The power and flexibility of group counselling is that it can be used to help participants over a whole range of concerns. There are very few people who could not benefit from group counselling which can provide a forum for open and genuine communication.

Future developments

Human beings are born into group life and need other people for physical and emotional nourishment, sustenance, and hope. Although the history of counselling has emphasized work with individuals, it is becoming clear that groups will become more significant. There are many reasons for this. It appears that not only are groups somewhat more economic but they can sometimes provide a more effective form of help than one-to-one work. The empirical work to establish this, although fraught with many methodological difficulties because of the complexities of what goes on in groups, is yet to be fully undertaken (Bednar 1970).

What is clear from observation is that in a group a client is able not only to describe difficulties, but, when they are of an interpersonal nature or have an interpersonal dimension, they can also demonstrate them. Groups are good at mobilizing a range of sources of help, not least other group members. Apart from the boundary and housekeeping functions of the leaders, group members can be helped to become peer therapists to each other. The acts of sharing and being of assistance to others in the group is well documented as giving great benefit to the participants (Yalom 1986).

As our society becomes more fragmented and individuals experience the trauma of alienation, there is an increasing need for the use of psychological techniques to help construct what so-called simple or primitive societies did naturally through social structures and rituals. We need to be able to help ourselves create mechanisms which provide safe space and dedicated time to ensure our physical, emotional, and spiritual well-being and growth. In a society which is rapidly changing, where individuals and families are often separated, where there are conflicting values, goals, and identities on offer, counselling in groups can assist in bringing people to, and keeping them at, a psychologically healthy state. One of the most simple, yet profound, satisfactions reported by group members is that of 'just being together'.

It is possible to discern powerful centrifugal forces in our society which make contact between people harder to make and to sustain. Urbanization, changing patterns of marriage and family life, the increasing specialization of function, and the acceleration of the speed at which life is led are perhaps the more important factors at work. They all have negative effects in that they emphasize the instrumental nature of much human interaction. Yet there seems to be an insatiable thirst for contact between human beings. It is against this background that the work of Carl Rogers and the person-centred school has much to contribute. Rogers extended the concept and practice of group counselling from its origins in small-scale clinical and educational settings to events encompassing many hundreds of people from different cultures speaking a variety of languages (Rogers 1980).

Although it may seem fanciful or wishful thinking, the principles embodied in group counselling can be seen as offering one, perhaps one of the few, ways in which conflict between people of different genders, nations, classes, races, and so on can be helped towards resolution without resort to violence. In the context of the group, human beings can be helped to encounter each other as persons, in what Buber has called the 'I–thou' relationship. In the group setting, participants can, in principle, begin to explore what lies behind these categories, what reality is for the human beings actually present in the room, what their assumptive worlds are, and begin to challenge some of the distortions which impede free communication between people and have such disastrous human consequences. Is it really true, for example, that you cannot take someone who reads the *Sun* or the *Guardian* seriously or is it really not possible for you to like someone who is a Catholic or a Protestant? The powerful and primitive forces at work in all human interactions can, in a well-run group, be experienced, understood, contained, and, perhaps, modified. To take but one example, perhaps the single most important issue facing the human race at the end of the twentieth century, the threat of nuclear war, can be understood in terms of group processes. Mechanisms such as scapegoating, splitting, denial, projection, and many others are all powerfully at work in the microcosm of the group and in the macrocosm of the relations between states. Perhaps exposure to group processes may help to save our world by helping group members see that what is happening in the group also happens outside the group in relations between people and states (Temperley 1987). It is perhaps significant that just before he died Carl Rogers had been working in the USSR on groups to bring world leaders together.

The convergence of group-counselling methodologies

Predicting the future in any field of human endeavour is foolhardy, but at the moment, the dominant ideologies in group counselling are person-centred, psychoanalytic, cognitive–behavioural, and a miscellany of humanistic approaches. The impression is that outside the major training institutes there is a considerable degree of pragmatic eclecticism with, perhaps, a predominance of post-Rogerian person-centred approaches, often stiffened with aspects of Yalom's existential ideas, sometimes with episodes of psychodrama, gestalt, games, and simulations; and the whole being held together with a theory owing not a little to the seminal work of the group analysts.

Whilst the protagonists of the different modalities might well stake claims for doctrinal purity, increasingly the future could well see a merging of approaches. This might come about by practitioners themselves being confronted by intractable group situations which show their existing formulations and practices to be inadequate. The process of convergence may also be accelerated by increasing numbers of training programmes through which both novices and more experienced practitioners progress. It is not unusual for group leaders to have been exposed, for example, to psychodramatic, person-centred, gestalt, psychoanalytic, and bioenergetics trainings. This osmotic process will inevitably affect group counselling; whether this is an enrichment remains to be seen.

Although some research has been undertaken on the effectiveness of one approach as against others and the suitability of approaches for different groups and purposes, much still remains to be done and the field is wide open.

Conclusion

This chapter has reviewed group counselling in Britain as it appears to one practitioner who has been heavily influenced by person-centred, existential, and psychoanalytic notions. Others with differing orientations would, doubtless, have produced a different picture. What is clear is that group counselling has come a very long way in the last 40 years and that it has an exciting and potentially productive future ahead. It is likely to become not only much more important in counselling, but also prominent within society as a resource for personal development in, for example, education, community development, religion, and at work, as well as in clinical settings.

References

Aveline, M. O. (1986) 'The use of written reports in a brief group psychotherapy training', *International Journal of Group Psychotherapy* 36(3): 477–82.
——McCulloch, D. K., and Tattersall, R. B. (1985) 'The practice of group psychotherapy with adult insulin-dependent diabetics', *Diabetic Medicine* 2: 275–82.
Bednar, R. L. (1970) 'Group psychotherapy research variables', *International Journal of Group Psychotherapy* 20: 146–52.
Bion, W. R. (1961) *Experiences in Groups*, London: Tavistock.
Blatner, H. A. (1973) *Acting-In: Practical Applications of Psychodramatic Method*, New York: Springer.
Bloch, S. and Crouch, E. (1985) *Therapeutic Factors in Group Psychotherapy*, Oxford: Oxford University Press.
Cox, M. (1978) *Structuring the Therapeutic Process*, Oxford: Pergamon Press.
Dickson, A. (1982) *A Woman in Your Own Right*, London: Quartet.
Foulkes, S. H. and Anthony, E. J. (1957) *Group Psychotherapy: The Psychoanalytical Approach*, London: Penguin Books.
Frank, J. (1974) *Persuasion and Healing*, revised edn, New York: Schocken Books.
Hinshelwood, R. D. and Manning, N. (eds) (1979) *Therapeutic Communities*, London: Routledge & Kegan Paul.
Kennard, D. and Roberts, J. (1983) *An Introduction to Therapeutic Communities*, London: Routledge & Kegan Paul.

Luft, J. (1966) *Group Processes: An Introduction to Group Dynamics*, Palo Alto, California: National Press.

Rogers, C. R. (1980) *A Way of Being*, Boston: Houghton, Mifflin.

Temperley, J. (1987) 'Why "Psycho-analysts for the prevention of nuclear war"?', *Psycho-analysts for the Prevention of Nuclear War Newsletter* 5: 12–17.

Whitaker, D. S. (1985) *Using Groups to Help People*, London: Routledge & Kegan Paul.

Whiteley, J. S. and Gordon, J. (1979) *Group Approaches in Psychiatry*, London: Routledge & Kegan Paul.

Yalom, I. D. (1986) *The Theory and Practice of Group Psychotherapy*, third edn, New York: Basic Books.

——Bond, G., Bloch, S., Zimmerman, E., and Friedman, L. (1977) 'The impact of a weekend group experience on individual therapy', *Archives of General Psychiatry* 34: 399–415.

——Brown, S., and Bloch, S. (1975) 'The written summary as a group psychotherapy technique', *Archives of General Psychiatry* 32: 605–13.

Part three

Settings

Chapter seven

Counselling in the Personal Social Services

Carole Sutton

Aspects of the historical background

The development of 'social casework'

The origins of counselling are far older than those of the Personal Social Services, and are lost in the mists of time. They are grounded, as Halmos (1965) suggests, in the experiences of comforting the distressed, sharing the grief of the bereaved, and offering a listening ear to the perplexed. Throughout recorded history, and doubtless before, the 'wise men' and 'wise women', the 'elders' and the 'spiritual leaders' of the group or community were, and to some extent still are, the counsellors.

The Personal Social Services in Britain developed from the philanthropic and voluntary services for the poor, the weak, and the vulnerable – which were an extension of the work of the churches in nineteenth-century Britain. Gradually these responsibilities, especially for children, became too complex and too expensive for voluntary organizations, even well-developed ones like Dr Barnardo's (the Dr has now been dropped), to carry out on a national scale, and the twentieth century saw the gradual passing, via statute, of responsibility from the voluntary to the local authority sector.

Alongside these developments, the fragmented efforts of the voluntary charitable and philanthropic groups of the nineteenth century were gradually brought together and co-ordinated in the Charities Organisation Society, and many groups who came under this umbrella are still known as 'voluntary organizations'.

In due course, 'statutory' work expanded greatly and became more complex and exacting. Hence, the demand of workers in those fields arose for 'training'. Workers were developing practice in the Children's Departments and in the Probation Service, and at the same time special workers were seeking to help people in the fields of physical and mental health. These were all complex areas of work, and inevitably those who sought to train workers for them looked to existing contemporary writers and practitioners in, for example, the fields of psychiatry.

Thus, two major strands which contributed to training for working with people in the early and middle years of this century were religious philanthropy and psychoanalysis. The former is illustrated by the contributions of the court missionaries towards the development of the Probation Service, and the latter by Freudian psychoanalytic theory which was adopted as a cornerstone of much work with people and families in difficulty.

Out of this complexity developed an activity called 'social casework'. This was unapologetically individualistic, tended to see individual or family difficulties in terms of underlying pathology, and, in its most extreme form, saw a series of casework/counselling sessions as their only solution. During these sessions, the caseworker might seek to promote 'insight' on the part of the client(s) upon why he or she was experiencing problems. This was a reflection of the prevailing Freudian theory particularly influential in the early and middle years of this century (cf Freud 1922).

Concern for the client was undoubtedly central, however, despite these debatable theoretical underpinnings. An influential text which reflected elements of both Christian concern and psychoanalytic theory was *The Casework Relationship*, by Felix Biestek, SJ, published in 1957.

Principles

Principles underpinning casework: precursors of counselling

Biestek's (1957) text set out a number of principles which caseworkers should observe. These were:

(1) *Individualization*: this principle highlighted the uniqueness of each person whom the worker encountered.
(2) *Purposeful expression of feelings*: this highlighted the value of allowing and enabling people to acknowledge in a supportive setting feelings of which they may or may not have been aware. These were often socially unacceptable feelings, anger, jealousy, hatred, but the release of which *freed* the person to live in more constructive ways.
(3) *Controlled emotional involvement*: this principle reminded the caseworker that it is inappropriate to identify too strongly with one person at the expense of others, or to involve him or herself too closely with a single issue or perspective.
(4) *Acceptance*: this principle confirmed the importance of dealing with people seeking help exactly as they are, whatever their strengths and weaknesses, and of affirming their innate dignity and worth.
(5) *The non-judgemental attitude*: this is linked with acceptance; the worker does not seek to assign guilt or innocence but recognizes that there may be limits to the extent to which *actions* are acceptable.
(6) *Client self-determination*: this principle reminded caseworkers that they

should avoid giving advice, but should enable those with whom they worked to explore the decisions which were right for them.

(7) *Confidentiality*: this principle enjoined caseworkers to raise the issue of confidentiality or, if need be, limitations thereto.

While there have been many developments in counselling since 1957, and some of the basic assumptions have been questioned by, for example, Jordan (1987), Biestek remains a founding father of social casework and a major contributor to modern counselling theory and practice.

The impact of humanistic psychology upon counselling in social work

Practice based upon such principles took place, however, within a Freudian theoretical framework. The study of child development and of family and marital relationships took place within a matrix of psychoanalytic theory: this meant that Freudian psychosexual developmental stages – oral, anal, oedipal and so on – were invoked to try to understand difficulties which arose in, for example, fostering and adoption work. Similarly, great attention was directed to *feelings* within individual, marital, and family counselling: if only personal relationships could be sufficiently explored, and associated or suppressed feelings released, then the resulting insight would effect a 'cure'.

Freudian theory was, and to some extent still is, extremely influential within the field of counselling in the Personal Social Services. Its influence is declining, however, as humanistic psychology, arising largely from the work of Rogers (1951) and Maslow (1954), and strengthened by the 'personal growth' movement, has redressed the emphasis upon pathology in social work and other fields.

This movement was strengthened by the major review of studies published by Truax and Carkhuff (1967) entitled, *Toward Effective Counseling and Psychotherapy*. The evidence from this review indicated that people who were helpful counsellors were characterized by certain personality features: 'genuineness, empathy and non possessive warmth'.

Humanistic psychology, and the associated 'client-centred approach', have been important parts of the psychology syllabus taught to social workers (Sutton and Davies 1986). Such an approach particularly informs work where an element of counselling is involved. While some have questioned the value of this 'therapeutic diad', there is no evidence known to me which has seriously undermined its vital contribution.

As time has passed, many developments have affected the nature of social work. The Seebohm Report (*Report of the Committee* 1968) led to the setting up of the 'generic' model of practice in the 1970s, whereby social workers were trained in, and expected to practise, skills needed by the many groups whom they were employed to serve: children and families, elderly people, young offenders, people with a mental handicap, and people who are mentally ill, whether in the residential sector or in the community. All these groups need social workers with particular knowledge bases, as well as well-practised counselling skills.

The demands placed upon social workers, and thus upon their training, have intensified. The majority work within a complex statutory framework, and changes within the law, as well as the pressures brought to bear by different interest groups, have meant constant and increasing demands for services and skills.

Issues: Counselling in social work: Some aspects of the present position

The community social work – counselling continuum

The Barclay Report (*Social Workers: Their Role and Tasks* 1982) sought to bring clarity to a confused situation when it defined these roles and tasks in the following way:

(1) 'to plan, establish, maintain and evaluate the provision of social care;
(2) to provide face-to-face communication between clients and social workers: the generic name of this is counselling'.

The Report later spells out the meaning which the authors attach to the word 'counselling':

> we use the word to cover a range of activities in which an attempt is made to understand the meaning of some event or state of being to an individual, and to plan, with the person or people concerned, how to manage the emotional or practical realities which face them. Such work is always part of assessment and may be a large or small part of meetings between client and social worker.

Before examining counselling further, it is important to draw brief attention to the tension which can exist between this counselling role and the other role delineated by the Barclay Report: that of planning, maintaining, and evaluating the provision of social care. This latter represents a recognition of the need for social workers to listen to the voices of people in the community upon important *issues* and to try to empower those whom they seek to serve. It encompasses such work as advocacy on behalf of clients, the support of self-help groups such as tenants' associations, and community development.

The two roles are not easily compatible, and the perspectives of those who identify with one or the other are not easily reconciled. Counselling may be seen by some at the community-work end of the spectrum as addressing 'private sorrows' when, in their view, the true origins of those sorrows are such 'public issues' as poverty, unemployment, and racial discrimination. In my experience, practitioners need skills from both perspectives and each group has much to learn from the other: community-development workers can learn from counsellors about skills of positive relationship and trust building, while counsellors can learn to see how their practice is located within larger social, economic, and political systems.

110

The impact of increasing statutory pressures

Social workers who are employed in local authority Social Services Departments constitute the majority; the estimates quoted by the Barclay Report (1982) suggested that there was then approximately one such field social worker for every 3,200 members of the population – compared with one General Practitioner for every 2,100 and one police constable for every 550 members respectively. The first duty of such social workers is discharging their statutory responsibilities towards children, young offenders, and those with mental illnesses or handicaps.

Their work, however, is also changing. Whereas it used to be possible, and appropriate, for local authority social workers to engage in fairly intensive work with families, for example to support those experiencing problems with young people, there is an increasing trend towards 'gate-keeping'. This refers to the necessity, because of shortage of resources, of holding the gate against the large number of referrals which could be made, because of the impossibility of providing the resources and meeting demand.

Nevertheless, it seems likely that it is the social workers in the Social Services Departments who will continue to constitute the main thrust of the profession, because of their ever-intensifying statutory responsibilities. As issues such as child abuse and child sexual abuse become ever more acknowledged and acute, so their work will need to be informed by an ever stronger component of counselling and communication skills.

Some principles characterizing contemporary practice

The reliance upon 'client-centred' counselling as a core skill

The case that social workers need counselling skills is broadly accepted. The nature of the changing tasks of social workers means, however, that these skills can seldom be practised in their 'pure' form; they are far more likely to constitute a way of working with people, an orientation of respect and empathy towards them, rather than an end in themselves. Counselling skills are therefore likely to *underpin* practice in many Social Services Departments.

The model of counselling taught to counsellors is most likely to be the client-centred or Rogerian one. Sutton and Davies (1986), in an investigation of the teaching of psychology on forty social work courses in Britain, found that the average number of hours allocated to the total psychology syllabus was 64; and of these 3.75 hours were devoted to the teaching of client-centred and non-directive approaches. (The next highest allocation of time, 2.4 hours, was to behavioural therapy.)

The attractions of the client-centred approach are apparent: it has a sound empirical base, it is positive in orientation, and it stresses the potential for growth and development within people. Social workers are likely to draw upon the approach differentially, however: for some, it will be the main vehicle of work in, for instance, helping a client to decide whether or not to place a child for adoption; for others, it will underpin skills of family therapy; and yet others will practise it but simply call it 'good interviewing'.

Further, a well-trained social worker would readily recognize the need to draw upon different approaches within the same interview. Thus, for example, a worker discussing welfare rights entitlement who sees the distress on a client's face would swiftly move from 'interviewing' to 'counselling' and back again, as time and circumstances permitted.

The concept of the worker/counsellor as having a repertoire

As we have seen above, however, it is likely that a social worker employed within the Social Services context will be trained in, and expected to draw upon, an extensive repertoire of additional skills, knowledge, and resources. These will include awareness of his or her statutory responsibilities, knowledge of voluntary means of help, such as specialist agencies for those with particular needs, as well as personal knowledge of community support-groups. The wider the repertoire of knowledge of and contacts with well-tried resources, personal and financial, the better.

This repertoire of knowledge and skill will have to become more extensive. Social workers are likely to be called upon to support special groups of, for example, women who have experienced violence or rape, or victims of racial attack; and as research proliferates upon effective ways of handling problems such as depression and anxiety, so social workers will need to update their counselling-based skills to accommodate this new knowledge.

Recognition of the importance of evaluation of practice

Only gradually, because of the pressure of other demands, are social workers recognizing the importance of evaluating their work and being taught how to do so in quantitative as well as qualitative ways. I have suggested elsewhere (Sutton 1987a) that the goal-attainment approach lends itself very readily to the evaluation of counselling: the same is true of social work. Skills of evaluation of practice were taught on only about two-thirds of the forty courses investigated by Sutton and Davies (1986). Rather than criticize those courses which do not teach such skills, it seems important to recognize the major contribution of those which do.

Differing levels of contribution of counselling to social work practice (see Figure 7.1)

If skills of counselling underpin practice within social work, then it follows that there are a range of interactions in which social workers typically take part which contain a greater or lesser degree of traditional client-centred work. Figure 7.1 shows, in schematic form, the range of such interactions.

112

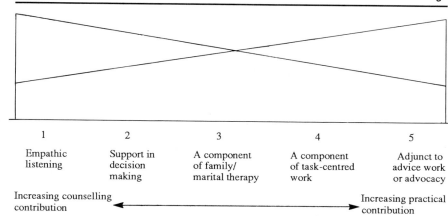

1	2	3	4	5
Empathic listening	Support in decision making	A component of family/ marital therapy	A component of task-centred work	Adjunct to advice work or advocacy

Increasing counselling contribution ←——————————————→ Increasing practical contribution

Fig. 7.1 Differing levels of contribution of counselling to social work practice

(1) *Counselling as empathic listening* is perhaps the form closest to what might be called 'classical or 'client-centred' counselling'. The clearest example of this form is the work of the counsellor who supports those bereaved by death or other loss. As I have indicated above, however, such work would not be routinely accepted as a referral by over-stretched Social Services teams, although some hospital-based social workers are employed in front-line crisis work after road accidents and other major disasters.

(2) *Counselling as support in decision-making* is again near to traditional 'client-centred' work, in that the social worker seeks to support the person concerned in clarifying the implications of, and arriving at a decision in some important aspect of life. Examples are the elderly person who has to decide whether or not to give up his or her home; the adopted person who wonders whether to try to trace his or her natural parents; and the pregnant woman who is undecided as to whether or not to seek an abortion. In each instance, the social worker will seek to clarify and discuss the issues, not to give advice.

(3) *Counselling as a component of family or marital therapy.* Here, counselling will form one important strand of the social worker's effort to enable a family to voice some of the tensions they are experiencing, and to communicate positively. There is good evidence, for example Birchler (1979), that the very act of communicating feelings and fears is, of itself, therapeutic to families in distress. This can be enhanced by basic counselling skills: sensitive listening, the showing of respect, and empathy for each person in distress.

(4) *Counselling as a component of a 'task-centred' approach.* Social workers are familiar with 'task-centred' work. This term, devised by Reid and Epstein (1972), refers to the breaking down of complex situations, such as the difficulties encountered by families with many disadvantages, into manageable tasks: for example, enabling a family to clear rent arrears, to

113

apply for their financial entitlement, and to seek medical help or legal help. Such 'working agreements' are not achieved without relationship-making and trust-building skills, which, in my view, are identical with those of counsellors. Counselling skills thus underpin practice in task-centred work.

(5) *Counselling as an adjunct to advice, advocacy, or statutory work*. Here too counselling skills underpin social work practice, although some would claim that 'counselling' in these contexts is indistinguishable from 'skilled interviewing'. Social workers, for example, draw upon counselling skills when they are employed in welfare-rights agencies: they know that some people, perhaps the elderly, may have real difficulty in disclosing the extent of their need, and unless their trust can be gained, they may never speak of this. The gaining of trust, through empathic listening, is thus a crucial part of welfare-rights work, as well as of advocacy – that is, when the worker, in representing the case of a client to another agency, seeks to understand the point of view of, for example, the local housing department.

Similarly, a parent who is seeking to place a child in, or to remove a child from, local authority care needs calm and respectful behaviour, both verbal and non-verbal, from a social worker – all the more so if the issue is contentious. The process of conveying respect for, and a personal commitment to, people for whom one may have to say painful or unwelcome things can have an effect which, in the long term, may prove constructive: to convey disrespect will *certainly* be damaging.

Thus, in all these situations, from the 'purest' to the most practical, counselling skills have an integral role in social work practice.

Issues concerning the training of social workers in counselling

Here I shall consider three issues: the 'model' of counselling taught, and the inadequacy of the humanistic 'client- centred' model as a universal approach; the necessity that, in certain situations, the social worker shall make clear that he or she is accountable to an agency and may be bound by statute; and the increasing demands of a range of groups for their particular needs to be recognized and addressed in the counselling curriculum.

The first issue touches upon a matter which I have discussed elsewhere (Sutton 1979). Some counsellors who are employed as such, i.e. in counselling centres, may be trained primarily within the humanistic 'client-centred' framework. Whatever the admirable features of this approach, and whatever its empirical strength as a foundation for the various fields shown in Figure 7.1, it is just not *robust* enough to address the complexity of the issues which confront social workers.

Young conduct-disordered children do not reliably 'grow out of' their difficult behaviour, but may become young offenders (Robins 1966); people with alcohol-related difficulties do not reliably 'grow out of' heavy drinking; and men who beat their wives do not seem to 'grow out of' doing so. However valuable the client-centred approach may be as a starting-point, a far stronger theoretical base, together with a repertoire of knowledge and skills, is needed after this first stage of relationship building.

Concerning the worker's accountability to an agency, and the importance of making this clear to clients, it is vital that he or she should have a very sound knowledge of the law, the agency's position *vis-à-vis* the law, together with a clear understanding of the statutory powers and legal responsibilities implicit in the role of social worker. While these powers and responsibilities may not need to be spelled out at the very first meeting, counselling is not being practised when the legal implications of a person's circumstances are not made clear, or when he or she manifestly does not understand what is being said. Unless the meeting is 'on the level', so to speak, it cannot *be* counselling.

The third issue is that of the increasing number of groups who seek specialist inputs on courses of social work training, and who ask, appropriately, that the particular needs of those whom they represent shall feature in the counselling (and other parts of the) curriculum. Thus, physically disabled people, mentally handicapped people, partially sighted people, those from a range of ethnic minority groups, one parent families – all these and more seek representation. Such pressures are entirely fitting but in a typical Certificate of Qualification in Social Work (CQSW) course of two years, each year lasting about 42 weeks of which half is rightly spent in practice settings, where can training pertaining to so many groups be accommodated?

The model of counselling within social work (and other settings) which, as I have suggested elsewhere (Sutton 1979; 1987a), may meet some of these specifications, has several stages. First, the worker/counsellor will have been *selected* with the evidence from Truax and Carkhuff (1967) in mind; he or she is thus likely both to make a respecting and empathic relationship with clients and to 'start where the client is'. The second stage is that of negotiating, agreeing, and writing down goals for work together with the people concerned; these have to take account of any statutory considerations, as well as of the fact that all work takes place within a larger system. The third stage is that of working towards the goals previously negotiated with clients, drawing on a range of specialist knowledge, skills, and resources. Such knowledge will include that pertaining to the specialist groups referred to above. The fourth stage is that of evaluating, with those concerned, how far the previously agreed goals have been attained. Such goals may have been renegotiated in the light of reality factors, but this 'goal-attainment approach' can readily accommodate such renegotiation.

It is hoped that this approach accommodates the essential features of counselling as shown by the empirical research; but it goes further in *offering a structure for shared work* to social worker and client, and in allowing for the evaluation of that work. It makes great demands of social workers that they be clear about what they are trying to achieve, and it imposes upon them the responsibility for continually extending their knowledge and skills. The goal-attainment approach is thus initially very demanding but then very supportive to those who employ it, since the agreed goals are available, in written form, from the earliest meetings as a focus for work.

Ethical issues accompanying counselling and social work

The ethics accompanying the practice of social work become ever more complex. It is undeniable that social workers carry great responsibilities, but they also have great powers, and there are many groups challenging these powers and the way they are, or are not, used.

On one hand, for example, there are serious concerns about the neglect of some social workers to remove vulnerable children from unsatisfactory situations; on the other, there are opposite concerns about social workers' alleged over-readiness to remove a child from situations judged to be dangerous. The legal and ethical tightrope which social workers tread is of the greatest fragility; whichever way they act they are certain to be criticized. It is my personal wish to support them in both their counselling and statutory roles.

Even in their more specifically focused counselling roles there are complex issues involved. It is known that social workers keep records concerning people with whom they work, as do many counsellors. Should not clients have the right to know what is being said or written about them? Since the passing of the Access to Personal Files Act 1987 the clients of social workers have the right to see much of what is recorded about them. General Practitioners do not typically keep open records of consultations: should social workers and counsellors lead the way?

Other ethical issues are raised by a range of groups in the community; people who belong to groups with particular identities or special needs ask where among the ranks of social workers and counsellors are those people with expertise in these fields? Can, for example, a non-Asian social worker/counsellor work appropriately with people from an Asian background? These questions demand answers.

Future developments: Possible future developments in aspects of counselling within the Personal Social Services

We are in a situation, then, of increasing demands upon social workers: different interest and pressure groups call for more attention to their particular needs; researchers in a range of disciplines call for more awareness of, and practice based upon, their findings; and the general public calls for greater openness and greater accountability.

In all this, social workers are underresourced and undertrained. They are, in my experience, committed people, highly motivated and enthusiastic to learn, but so wide is the curriculum, so short the time available, and so varied their roles in the field that it is extremely hard to educate and train them beyond a basic level of competence.

Plans to extend the present two-year training course to three, to allow for greater specialization, have recently been rejected by central government. Efforts to enhance training are however persisting. It is very difficult to anticipate how events will turn out, but I shall briefly consider below some of the possible future developments in social work in relation to counselling.

Increasing demands for specialist counselling skills

Because social workers carry statutory responsibilities, it is virtually certain that in the future the tasks which will have first call upon their time will be the discharge of statutory duties. Many social workers regret this increasing 'social control' element of their work, and wish they could spend their time in, for example, preventive work, community social work, and community development, and in combating the evils which contribute so much to the misery of their clients: unemployment, poverty, and discrimination.

It has to be recognized, however, that within their statutory roles social workers are being called upon to deal with fields of practice which were scarcely recognized as little as five years ago. Skills of intervening in situations where child abuse has been reported or is suspected are increasingly in demand, and these, as I have suggested above, are underpinned by communication and counselling skills. Similarly, the demand for training in counselling the victims of child abuse and child sexual abuse is growing, and is likely to grow further.

To summarize, it seems probable that within training for mainstream field social work, increasing emphasis will be laid upon counselling and communication skills for special areas of statutory practice.

The development of post-qualifying courses

As groups of people with common cause increase, and as they rightly look for their needs to be recognized by the Personal Social Services, so it is likely that workers with a common basic training, but specialized post-qualifying training, will be appointed. Attempts, albeit inadequate, are being made to recruit more candidates from a range of ethnic minority groups, and components on anti-racist and anti-sexist work are likely to feature in the central core of any new social work/counselling curriculum; but post-qualifying courses will be needed in addition. Other groups, such as disabled people, one-parent families, those who care for mentally handicapped children, and elderly relatives may feel themselves inadequately represented; to address the needs of these and other groups, post-qualification courses are likely to be the only answer.

Thus, for example, it may be that the core counselling-skills will be seen as all that can be offered in relation to people suffering from AIDS, and to those people's relatives. If social workers find themselves, after qualifying, working in close contact with AIDS victims, either directly or through such avenues as the care of the children of AIDS sufferers, then those workers will need special teaching and training for those special responsibilities.

The increased use of 'contracts' within counselling

There is considerable evidence from a range of settings of the usefulness of the 'contract' within social work practice. Hazel (1980), for example, in a major study in Kent, found that it was possible to place almost 200 disturbed and delinquent adolescents who were unable to remain in their own homes with foster parents. Of these, 70 per cent later met the criteria for 'success'. Written contracts were devised between the foster parents, the social workers and the young people concerned, which set out very carefully the rights and responsibilities of all those concerned. The evidence indicated that these contracts helped clarify expectations and reduce misunderstandings; they contributed greatly to the success of this pioneering British study.

Workers in other fields advocate the introduction of the contract to clarify the aims of the work between client and helper. Rosenhan and Seligman (1984), writing of research into the broad field of counselling and psychotherapy, wrote,

> Many therapists arrive at an agreement with client, not only regarding the goals of treatment, but also how long treatment will last. That agreement is put in the form of a contract and serves to remind each party of their aims and obligations.
>
> (Rosenhan and Seligman 1984: 632–3)

The practice of writing a contract is increasingly used in research (Sutton 1987b) with good effects, and while there is only limited evidence from well-designed research studies, it seems likely that the fact that lawyers have, by trial and error, arrived at a situation where the contract is an automatic accompaniment to a transaction gives it considerable prima-facie validity.

The contract implies mutually binding responsibilities and can set out goals and commitments in a way which both minimizes ambiguities and also makes the counselling situation one of greater equality. The move is *away* from what might be called formal counselling, and *towards* the 'genuineness' found by Truax and Carkhuff (1967) to be such a valuable feature of counselling which was beneficial. In such a setting two people meet as *people*, with different roles and tasks, it is true, and where status differences are recognized, but not emphasized. If this argument is correct, not only will social workers in a counselling role be trained in devising, and helping their clients to devise, agreements between, say, teenager and parent, or between a husband and wife who are having marital difficulties, but they will be encouraged to develop contracts between themselves and their clients. A notable feature of these is likely to be a statement of the goals which worker and client will seek to reach together. (Nelson-Jones 1982; Sutton 1987a).

Increased readiness to evaluate their counselling

A contractual approach to counselling has many advantages: first, it is ethical, in that it engages the client from the outset in clarifying expectations; second, it

form of treatment is no longer the doctor's prescription, but the client's experience of counselling.

Nevertheless, the advent of counselling has contributed to changes in medical practice which are making the distinction less clear: doctors are increasingly recognizing the value of treating patients as participants or co-workers, sharing responsibility for their own states of health and illness management. This is particularly true of those practitioners consciously committed to the concept of holistic medicine, and it is also evident in any setting where psychosomatic hypotheses are entertained (Pietroni 1986).

In several ways, therefore, counselling and medical forms of treatment are drawing closer together and becoming increasingly intertwined. However, while influencing medical thinking and practice, counselling has also succeeded in maintaining a separate identity within medical settings. This is a considerable achievement, given its relatively recent recognition in Britain in the context of a long-established medical tradition.

The current situation

In the early 1980s, the Counselling in Medical Settings Division (CMS) of the British Association for Counselling (BAC) noted the apparent increase in counsellors operating within general practice, but at the same time pointed out the lack of evidence to substantiate this. Two initiatives arose in consequence: first, the establishment of a working party which existed from 1982–4 and led to the publication in 1985 of two authoritative booklets (Hurd and Rowland 1985; Irving and Heath 1985); and second, a project to map counselling within the National Health Service (NHS) but outside primary care (Breakwell 1987). In addition, in 1986, a survey on counselling in general practice was organized by CMS through the Family Practitioner Committees (FPCs) as a contribution to a Department of Health and Social Security review.

In 1977 fifty schemes were found attached to general practice surgeries in England and Wales involving about seventy counsellors with marriage guidance training (Heisler 1979). The BAC survey in 1986 revealed that twenty-eight Family Practitioner Committees had been approached by general practitioners interested in employing counsellors in their practices. However, it is likely that this was an understatement of demand because, as one administrator pointed out, 'since counsellors cannot be reimbursed, general practitioners are unlikely to approach the FPC with a view to employing a counsellor'.

Nevertheless, after a slow beginning by a small number of pioneering FPCs, a growing number of FPCs are including counsellors amongst the range of ancillary or practice staff who qualify for payment under the Statement of Fees and Allowances, and the Royal College of General Practitioners' (1987) response to the Green Paper on Primary Health Care welcomed the development. It is to be hoped, therefore, that the long-standing controversy over payment to counsellors will be fully resolved with the adoption of a standard procedure.

Where non-primary care settings are concerned, counselling services are available in several health districts. The advent of AIDS (see Chapter 22 by Sketchley) has also promoted the growth of counselling facilities with both a specific and a non-specific focus (Bor *et al.* 1988).

One pioneer venture worthy of mention is the Isis Centre in Oxford which, although managed by the Psychiatric Unit of the Health Authority, has independent premises and accepts self-referrals. This initiative is beyond the scope of this chapter because it provides counselling outside the context of medicine; nevertheless it is mentioned as an important development which has become well respected and established but, surprisingly given its success, has not been replicated elsewhere.

Principles: Distinctive features

The counsellors

There is considerable diversity amongst personnel who practise counselling in medical settings: they include both counsellors with specific training, and other professionals like nurses and occupational therapists who regard counselling as an important part of their role. Breakwell (1987) found that within thirty-nine District Health Authorities (DHAs) the job responsibilities of 31.6 per cent of staff in ten professional categories were considered by their managers to include counselling, although counselling actually featured in job descriptions in only 9.4 per cent of cases. No other context in which counselling takes place, for example educational or occupational settings, contains such a comparable variety of professional groups, each with its own philosophy and approach to the subject.

Furthermore, the counsellor practising in a medical setting is operating as part of a team – either a carefully selected primary-care team or the more loosely knit group of medical, nursing, and other professional staff contributing to a patient's care within a hospital environment. The counsellor and the colleague making the referral do not necessarily share the same expectations and hopes for its outcome – for example, a patient may be referred to a counsellor for reassurance about AIDS, when in reality such reassurance is inappropriate or premature; or the referring colleague may not expect the counsellor to have sufficient medical knowledge to be able to discuss with the patient his treatment and its implications (Bor *et al.* 1988).

Where various professionals are able to offer counselling, the potential benefit to the client is clearly substantial because of the availability of help from several sources. This benefit may however be jeopardized if the widely differing views cannot be drawn together into a common understanding of the nature and aims of counselling practice. An example of the disparity which exists is the way in which definitions of counselling amongst professional groups in the medical sector range from listening attentively through to disciplinary censure. Indeed, to an extent the meaning of the word 'counselling' is becoming distorted through its association by some health-care staff with the disciplinary procedures of their management – for example, the following quotation was recently observed: 'they were counselled and they deserved it' (BAC 1987). This is not meant to imply that counselling has no role within management, nor that some managers do not practise it appropriately and well. It is an indication, however, of the diverse perceptions which exist as to the nature and purpose of counselling amongst the management and staff of different groups.

If consensus is to be achieved as to the real nature of counselling, two developments are necessary. First, standardization of training amongst those engaged in counselling; and second, the spreading of understanding of its true principles to all professional colleagues who are likely to refer patients. Breakwell (1987) found that only 31 per cent of the thirty-nine District Health Authorities who completed her questionnaire were able to specify a budget allocation for counselling training, and the few who could gave percentages ranging from 0.14 per cent to approximately 8 per cent of their total training budgets. At the moment, therefore, one barrier against the further education of colleagues is the disinclination of DHAs to support and finance staff training.

The client's experience

Oldfield (1983) points out how the tendency of a person in distress to adopt a sick role and to expect another person to effect a cure is not a strategy which promotes mental health, because it encourages passivity and the abdication of responsibility. However, in medical settings counsellors commonly encounter what are essentially non-medical problems presented in this traditional way. Indeed, it is one of the challenges facing such counsellors to enable the client to review his or her reliance upon the illness model, as a priority first step in the helping process.

In some hospital settings every patient undergoing a certain procedure or treatment (for example HIV screening, mastectomy) is referred for counselling as a matter of course. While this ensures that all patients are given the opportunity to have counselling, not all will see this facility as relevant or necessary. Moreover, as Bor *et al.* (1988) point out, it is unrealistic to perceive and advocate specialist counselling as *invariably* beneficial – at least in the short term – in view of the distress that can accompany the process of change.

When should referral take place and counselling begin? At diagnosis? Pre- or post-surgery? When all physical measures have failed? After a period of adjustment? Clearly this depends upon such factors as the urgency of treatment, whether alternative methods of treatment are available, and whether there is a shortage of time as in the case of pregnancy and terminal illness. There is no point on the time-scale of diagnosis and treatment when it is consistently appropriate that a referral for counselling should be made. Perhaps a system which encourages patients to self-refer would allow each individual to decide when counselling help would personally be most advantageous. As Cooper (1983) emphasizes in relation to post-abortion counselling, 'the first principle should be to offer counselling at a time and a location which is going to be of most benefit to the *patient*' (original emphasis).

In essence, the practice of counselling in medical settings is similar to its practice in other settings. What is different, however, is how the process begins. The client is more likely to have been referred by others than self-referred, and more likely inappropriately to have adopted a sick role. Thus, the tasks of changing expectations, defining boundaries and clarifying objectives are perhaps harder in medical than in non-medical settings.

Sally, for example, was a young girl about to be married. She was repeatedly consulting the doctor about a variety of 'illnesses' – tiredness, back pain, headaches, and so on – which proved negative on investigation. A referral for counselling revealed the incidence of rape at the age of 14. A client like this, who is seeking treatment for physical effects, may require skilled help in the first instance to reach an awareness that these effects are, in reality, emotions finding an outlet through the body. Once this has been recognized during what is in effect a preparatory stage, there is little distinction between medical and other contexts in the principles and techniques of counselling which are subsequently applied.

Range of problems

Disease is a familiar concept to all. The dis-ease of distress is less obvious and less understood. However, disease and dis-ease are often linked – for example, physical treatment such as mastectomy may have severe emotional implications. A distinctive characteristic of counselling in medical settings is that it permits the two concepts to combine in promoting both physical and emotional well being.

The range of problems dealt with in medical counselling tends to be wider than in other settings, since both medical and non-medical concerns are recognized and seen as appropriate. Cohen and Halpern (1978), for example, describe how the problems addressed by their practice counsellor include economic and legal difficulties amongst the working age-group, and fears of loneliness and death amongst the elderly. There is a distinction, however, between primary care and other NHS settings: Wyld (1981) found that all referrals from general practitioners to counsellors related to 'life problems' of a psycho-social nature; in contrast, the issues which arise in hospital or clinical settings are inclined to be more specific and related directly to disease or surgery.

The official advocacy of counselling is inconsistent (perhaps inevitably at this stage, given its relatively recent, somewhat fitful recognition in Britain): counselling is legally obligatory before an abortion can take place, and a DHSS guideline suggests that it should be offered to all those requesting HIV antibody screening. However, there is no legal requirement before plastic surgery or a vasectomy are undergone, although the effects of these on the patient and his or her family may be similarly acute and far-reaching.

Breakthroughs in medical knowledge not only increase the options available to the patient, but they intensify the ramifications of the choices made. This is especially the case in hospitals where treatment tends to be more interventionist and irrevocable than within general practice. At the same time the 'informed consent' issue and the (increasingly) less authoritarian stance of the consultant are putting the onus of the decision-making back on to the patient (Faulder 1985).

The move towards seeing the patient as a participant in his or her own treatment has opened up the question of 'informed choice'. As Pendleton *et al.* (1984) point out, the patient can only make an informed choice if he or she has a full understanding of the illness and the treatment being proposed.

How can counselling help the patient who finds him or herself an active participant in the management of the illness? By assisting the patient to reflect upon his or her situation, pertinent feelings, and attitudes, it aids the patient's understanding and acceptance; and by giving him or her the opportunity to explore and clarify the options available, it assists the patient's own decision-making. Furthermore, in combination, greater understanding and sharing in the treatment decisions tend to increase not only commitment to but compliance with the programme chosen.

Demand and supply

As Oldfield (1983) points out, it is commonly accepted that between a quarter and a third of all patients visiting their general practitioners are suffering from emotional distress rather than from a physical condition. Nevertheless, there is a wide discrepancy between the recognized need for counselling, and the services which are actually available. As an example, approximately 500 clients a week attend the Westminster Pastoral Foundation (WPF) in London for counselling. This is a registered charity and a charge is made. Research has found that the clients are comparable on several social and psychiatric factors to those attending Guy's Hospital psychiatric out-patient clinic, and it is concluded from this that the WPF is providing a service to those whose needs are not being met at present within NHS psychiatric facilities (Caccia and Watson 1987).

Why should such a discrepancy exist? First, with regard to general practice, the size of case-loads and limited surgery time all serve to prohibit doctors being able to offer counselling explicitly on a frequent or regular basis. However, training in counselling skills is increasingly recognized as central to the work of general practitioners in their interactions with both patients and colleagues in the primary-care team. Second, although an increasing number of practices are arranging counsellor attachments, it is likely that others hold back from so doing. As Rowland and Irving (1984) point out, there is no formal way in which general practitioners are advised of the range of activities and theories unique to counselling, or the best way of incorporating the services of a counsellor into their practices.

With regard to hospital settings, Haslett (1985) points out how the need for counselling, though recognized, can be difficult to meet appropriately within the present procedures for hospitalization. With specific reference to hysterectomy patients, she writes:

> Some gynaecological ward sisters and hospital medical personnel are excellent at foreseeing and fulfilling this need while the woman is actually in hospital. Unfortunately, they are, by definition of their hospital post, rarely available for approach before admission or after discharge – times when counselling is most required.

Moreover, with the advent of AIDS, counselling is being sought not only by the emotionally or physically unwell, but by the 'worried well'. This group – clients who perceive themselves to be at risk – is currently the largest group requesting counselling from the specialist services which are available for AIDS patients (Bor *et al.* 1988).

What kind of objectives or goals are being identified by those engaged in counselling in these settings? In some circumstances a principal initial aim may be to help the client become aware of the possibility that his or her symptom has a psychological cause, when he or she is expecting a response more akin to the 'illness model'.

Sometimes the need may be for the client to come to terms with traumatic circumstances – for example, news of a terminal condition or the recommendation of disfiguring surgery. In other cases the patient's overriding need may be to acquire knowledge with which to give 'informed' consent or make an 'informed choice'. These are instances in which counselling has a complementary role, but there are instances, too, when all medical and surgical forms of treatment have failed, and counselling must be offered in isolation. Here the goal may go beyond acceptance, to the changing of perception and attitude towards the illness itself. Perhaps more commonly, however, emotional and practical aspects are interwoven – for example, pregnancy counselling aims to help the woman reach the right decision by both exploring her feelings and discussing the implications of the available options.

Advice-giving is usually regarded as incompatible with the true nature of counselling. However, although Breakwell (1987) found that nurses generally chose a non-directive definition of counselling, doctors and personnel staff within the DHA she studied tended to see counselling in terms of problem-solving and advice-giving. This is a further example of the different perspectives which characterize counselling in medical settings, and suggest different approaches from different professional groups to the situations illustrated above.

Issues

Personnel

Within medical and nursing practice, hygiene is universally acknowledged as essential to good care. The ability to counsel has taken a similar course within some professional perspectives. Wyld (1981) identifies the professional groups mainly responsible for providing counselling services in primary-care settings as social workers, clinical psychologists, psychotherapists, and marriage counsellors. Yet other professional groups like health visitors, physiotherapists, and occupational therapists all stress the importance of counselling to their roles (Sadlo 1981; Abel Smith 1983).

But what does counselling *mean* to each of these professional groups? Not surprisingly, Breakwell (1987) revealed a wide range of definitions. There is considerable confusion about what *is* and what *is not* counselling; and this uncertainty amongst the practitioners themselves must colour the perceptions of clients. The issue of what constitutes counselling needs urgent attention and clarification. There is a distinction between the everyday use of certain skills, such as listening skills, essential to good practice, and the formal dialogue and interaction which characterizes the more intensive counselling relationship. Our starting definition assumes that the counsellor does have a clear model of the internal world of the individual, in exactly the same way that the doctor has a model of physiological functioning.

Breakwell (1987) found that amongst the thirty-nine District Health Authorities who responded fully to her survey, only clinical psychologists were expected by management to have counselling qualifications prior to their engagement. However, several professional groups other than clinical psychologists were identified as having counselling included in their job responsibilities. It would appear that some in-service training of a multidisciplinary nature was being provided for these groups, but this training tended to be both short and voluntary. At the same time, the limited funds allocated for counselling training (a maximum of approximately 8 per cent of any total training budget) did not suggest that it was seen as a priority by the Authorities surveyed.

In contrast, and not surprisingly, it is the view of the Counselling in Medical Settings Division of BAC that practising counsellors should have undertaken intensive training of either a general or specialist nature. Similarly, other professional staff would be encouraged to complement any counselling component in their basic training by taking advantage of the courses which are available. Clearly, however, there are risks in recommending counselling training as a standard requirement. 'Attempted training of individuals selected by profession and coerced into training by senior staff usually leads to failure and resentment' (Cooper 1983). If appropriate training is to take place within non-primary care settings, however, it will depend largely upon the support of

DHAs and their willingness not only to identify the most suitable staff, but also to make the funds and the time available for those staff to undergo the training required.

Once trained, however, does the counsellor face a conflict of roles? How does he or she fit into the medical team of the hospital or general practice? Although the doctor or consultant making the referral retains primary clinical responsibility for the patient, he or she does not intervene in the counselling process, and cannot therefore exercise continuing authority where this form of treatment is concerned. The counsellor may be party to one of the dilemmas of the concept of 'shared care'.

Another allied difficulty is the question of confidentiality. What are the expectations of the referrer and the counsellor for the supply of feedback information? To what extent does the patient interpret the phrase 'in confidence' to include the doctor or consultant? Once the relationship between doctor and patient has been opened up to include a third party, whose responsibility should it be to set the new boundaries?

The general view of the importance of supervision and support is widely upheld within medical settings. Grey (1987) describes, in relation to AIDS counselling, how counsellors can feel isolated even when they are operating as part of a team, if they alone bear the weight of a client's distress. Indeed, 'caring for the carers' becomes particularly essential because the prevalence of ill-health and disease tends to arouse deep emotion in those striving to help.

Professional health-care staff who undertake counselling as part of their job do so without any formal support system other than perhaps one for their own professional group. If they presented or were overtly recognized as counsellors, it would be easier for them to set up and maintain a system which was adequate to their needs.

However, although in many cases the onus of setting up a support system or mutual-supervision agreement will remain with the individual, some professional groups are becoming increasingly aware of the need to provide such help for their members. In 1984 for example, the Royal College of Nursing advocated the appointment of a counsellor in every district, and their counselling service, CHAT, was subsequently founded for their nurses. Moreover, the development of such a service is being increasingly recommended as a resource for all health-care staff on a multi-disciplinary basis.

Evaluation

Two issues surround the question of the evaluation of counselling practice: is it necessary?; and how can it be done? The view shared by many health professionals, reflected in the literature, is that counselling is 'generally beneficial'. One might argue that this is sufficient evaluation, and certainly 'generally beneficial' things rarely lend themselves easily to substantiation. Marsh and Barr (1975), Cohen and Halpern (1978), and Martin and Mitchell

(1983) provide examples of attempts at evaluation which, though positive, were essentially dependent upon subjective assessments, either by the clients or the counsellors themselves. The doubtful validity of such assessments is illustrated by the discrepancy reported by Corney (1981: 166) in the clients' and counsellors' perceptions of the service given within a general practice setting: 'The social workers over-estimated the helpfulness of their interventions for almost every category of problem, and felt that their involvements had changed their clients' lives and relationships much more than the clients did.'

However, in a climate of competing resources, it is essential that more objective ways are found to assess the effectiveness of counselling and to justify its continued support. Some studies have attempted to do this by exploring whether or not counselling is cost-effective. Maguire *et al.* (1982), for example, reported considerable savings to the NHS through the earlier recognition and treatment of psychiatric problems in counselled mastectomy patients versus a control group.

Other researchers have looked for changes in clients' use of medical services or a reduction in the number of drugs prescribed (Anderson and Hasler 1979; Waydenfeld and Waydenfeld 1980; Ashurst and Ward 1983). The results have either been inconclusive, or open to doubt because of intrinsic limitations in the research methodology (Brown and Abel Smith 1985).

Whether evaluation studies concentrate upon outcomes, cost-effectiveness, or a combination of the two, problems arise not only in selecting appropriate outcome measures but also in establishing suitable control groups for comparison. Earll and Kincey (1982) undertook a controlled trial study, but to date these are rare in evaluations of counselling practice within the medical context in Britain. Their research concerned behavioural treatment by a clinical psychologist, but their criteria for assessment could be applied more widely. These included both objective criteria based upon the uptake of NHS facilities as noted in practice records, and subjective ratings of emotional distress, satisfaction, and control, using information obtained during follow-up interviews and then applied to specific scales.

Further, similar methods of evaluation need to be explored if counselling is to retain the credibility which it is rapidly gaining, and which many health professionals intuitively feel it deserves. (See Chapter 24 by Bolger for a full discussion of evaluation in counselling.)

Future developments

After a slow beginning, counselling in medical settings would appear to be on the verge of expansion: at last the question of payment, which has inhibited the development of counselling throughout the NHS, is beginning to be resolved. At the same time, awareness of the extent of the AIDS risk and the need to allocate funds specifically for AIDS counselling are likely to further the development of specialist counselling facilities for other illness groups.

However, one area of uncertainty arises from the familiar dilemma of competing resources. The rapid development in medical knowledge and the corresponding application of new technology are creating a climate of increasing financial demands, within which the need for counselling facilities may not be seen as a priority. Moreover, in spite of the general consensus that counselling is beneficial, there is insufficient evidence to date with which to present a strong case for employing counsellors in preference to other professional staff whose method and purpose of working are more clearly understood. More evaluation needs to be done, with particular reference to the cost-effectiveness of counselling within the medical context.

The interest in counselling amongst a wide variety of professional groups is indicative of the perceived value of counselling skills. At the same time, however, there is considerable diversity in defining the processes and purposes of counselling. Standardization of training and practice through a system of accreditation will help to draw together the different philosophies and approaches which currently prevent a common understanding and presentation. One effect of this 'demystifying' exercise should be to promote the engagement and use of counsellors by others in the medical hierarchy or team.

It is likely, however, that one impetus for development will come from the lay public. As more people become familiar with the concept or experience of counselling, the demand for facilities will grow. This may lead to a more open referral system: for example, one in which a person who feels his or her problem is essentially of an emotional origin can consult a counsellor rather than a doctor in the first instance. By this means there would be much less need to adopt a sick role and to present the passport of a physical symptom in order to 'qualify' for help. Moreover, as general practices are encouraged to become more competitive and the perceived value of counselling grows, the counsellor may – by popular request – become an essential member of the primary-care team.

Most of all, however, it is the growing co-operation and sharing of goals between medical personnel and counsellors, allowing them to work together – with the patient – to restore well-being, which forecasts the success of counselling not only as an alternative but as a complementary form of treatment.

References

Abel Smith, A. E. (1983) 'Parental and Professional Perceptions re. the Care of a Handicapped Child', unpublished MA Thesis, University of Nottingham.
Anderson, S. and Hasler, J. C. (1979) 'Counselling in general practice' *Journal of the Royal College of General Practitioners* 29: 352–6.
Ashurst, P. M. and Ward, D. F. (1983) 'An evaluation of counselling in general practice', in *Final Report of the Leverhulme Counselling Project*, unpublished.
Bor, R., Miller, R., and Perry, L. (1988) 'Aids counselling: clinical application and development of services', *British Journal of Guidance and Counselling* 16: 11–20.
Breakwell, G. M. (1987) 'Mapping Counselling in the non-primary sector of the NHS', Report for the British Association for Counselling.

British Association for Counselling (1987) 'Counselling and disciplinary procedures at work', Information Sheet 11.

Brown, P. T. and Abel Smith, A. E. (1985) 'Counselling in medical settings', *British Journal of guidance and Counselling*, 13(1): 75–88.

Caccia, J. and Watson, J. P. (1987) 'A counselling centre and psychiatric out-patient clinic: a comparison', *Bulletin of the Royal College of Psychiatrists* 11 (June): 182–4.

Cohen, J. and Halpern, A. (1978) 'A practice counsellor', *Journal of the Royal College of General Practitioners* 28: 481–4.

Cooper, G. (1983) 'Post-abortion counselling', *Nursing Mirror*, Midwifery Forum, 8 August, 24, Supplement.

Corney, R. H. (1981) 'Client perspectives in a general practice attachment', *British Journal of Social Work* 11: 159–70.

Earll, L. and Kincey, J. (1982) 'Clinical psychology in general practice: a controlled trial evaluation', *Journal of the Royal College of General Practitioners* 32 (January): 32–7.

Faulder, C. (1985) *Whose Body is it? The Troubling Issue of Informed Consent*, London: Virago Press.

Grey, A. (1987) 'Aids: a counselling response', *Counselling* 59 (February): 4–11.

Haslett, S. (1985) 'Hysterectomy counselling', *Nursing Mirror* 161 (16): 45–6.

Heisler, J. (1979) 'Marriage counsellors in medical settings', *Marriage Guidance* 18(5): 153–62.

Hurd, J. and Rowland, N. (1985) *Counselling in General Practice: A Guide for Counsellors*, Oxford: British Association for Counselling.

Irving J. and Heath, V. (1985) *Counselling in General Practice: A Guide for General Practitioners*, Oxford: British Association for Counselling.

Maguire, P., Pentol, A., Allen, D., Tait, A., Brooke, M., and Sellwood, R. (1982) 'Cost of counselling women who undergo mastectomy', *British Medical Journal* 284 (26 June): 1933–5.

Marsh, G. N. and Barr, J. (1975) 'Marriage guidance counselling in group practice', *Journal of the Royal College of General Practitioners* 25: 73–5.

Martin, E. and Mitchell, H. (1983) 'A counsellor in general practice: a one-year survey', *Journal of the Royal College of General Practitioners* 33: 366–7.

Oldfield, S. (1983) *The Counselling Relationship: A Study of the Client's Experience*, London: Routledge & Kegan Paul.

Pendleton, D., Schofield, T., Tate, P., and Havelock, P. (1984) *The Consultation: An Approach to Learning and Teaching*, Oxford: Oxford University Press.

Pietroni, P. (1986) *Holistic Living: A Guide to Self-Care*, Guernsey: Dent.

Rowland, N. and Irving, J. (1984) 'Towards a rationalization of counselling in general practice', *Journal of the Royal College of General Practitioners* December: 686–7.

Royal College of General Practitioners (1987) *The Front Line of the Health Service: College Response to Primary Health Care – An Agenda for Discussion*, Report from General Practice 25: 21.

Sadlo, G. (1981) 'Counselling: the role of the community occupational therapist with physically disabled clients', *Occupational Therapy* December: 395–6.

Waydenfeld, D. and Waydenfeld, S.W. (1980) 'Counselling in general practice', *Journal of the Royal College of General Practitioners* 30: 671–7.

Wyld, K. L. (1981) 'Counselling in general practice: a review', *British Journal of Guidance and Counselling* 9(2): 129–41.

Chapter nine

Counselling in education (primary and secondary)

Patrick Hughes

Beginnings

Guidance

Though a counselling movement can be said to have begun in Britain in the mid-1960s, the role and status of counselling in British schools cannot be understood except in relation to a longer-established tradition directed at meeting vocational and personal as well as more specific scholastic needs of pupils. The word which came to identify enlightened educational thinking and practice in this respect was guidance, and its principles and progress in the first half of this century are admirably summarized in the 1955 *Year Book of Education*. In addition to providing a comprehensive account of the scope of guidance and of the meaning of the word in Britain, this symposium of views also re-emphasized the need for a more broadly based view of guidance than had existed in practice until then. In essence this conceived of the provision of professional psychological help and support as the prerogative of every child rather than as a service reserved only for children with special kinds of problem (backwardness, behavioural difficulties, delinquency).

Counselling

The objectives of the counselling movement in this respect did not differ essentially from this earlier tradition and from one point of view represented the continuation of long-standing attempts to democratize and humanize the school. The movement, partly because of its emphasis on the work of Carl Rogers and the active collaboration of eminent figures in the counselling movement from the USA in its initial stages, was popularly construed to be North American in origin. The philosophy of client-centred counselling, however, fitted in well with the existent pupil-centred tradition and with the aspirations of teachers and other educationists in Britain committed to the personal and social development of young people. The counselling movement in fact has been seen as the first major attempt in British schools since the establishment of the Child Study movement to meet this gap in awareness and provision in the school system (Hughes 1971) and as perhaps the single most influential factor in altering fixed attitudes towards the role of helping agencies outside the school, the role of the teacher within the school, and the responsibility of the school itself in the development of the whole child.

The School Counsellor

In more practical terms, however, this new development differed in several important respects from what had gone before. The most obvious manifestation of this was the inauguration of a new role of School Counsellor for the secondary school, where increased attention to the psychological well-being and healthy development of young people in an age of rapid change and heightened stress was seen as an urgent need. Primary education was not directly included, as primary schools in Britain had a much better record in caring for the whole child and in maintaining relationships with home and community. In the long term, however, the more radical departure was the *de facto* acceptance that school personnel trained under educational auspices (and not, for example, under medical supervision) were capable of coping with emotional and motivational aspects of pupils' lives in ways which resembled methods common to well-established types of psychotherapy.

Wider implications

The implications of these enterprising innovations were far-reaching. Counselling was introduced as an acceptable and respectable activity for school personnel. Potentially, this represented an extension of responsibility and work methods well beyond the traditional role of the school teacher, and presaged the arrival of a much more broadly based use of counselling skills. In essence, of course, this applied to the primary as much as to the secondary school, though it is only recently that the literature has made reference to counselling in primary education (Sisterson 1983) and included discussion of the actual use of basic counselling skills, in preference to more formal didactic methods, to promote aspects of children's personal and social well-being (David and Charlton 1988).

Contrary views

In terms of practice, the attempt to introduce full-time counsellors into secondary schools had limited success. At the beginning, LEAs with few exceptions were not enthusiastic about the experiment, many teachers were distrustful and sometimes openly hostile, universities and other institutions were slow to follow the lead of Reading and Keele, the universities which set up the first training courses, and the Department of Education and Science, while in general sympathetic to promising experiments, did not actively promote the idea in schools. Even when, eventually, a number of other institutions of higher education had introduced extended programmes of training, only a small number of schools actually appointed counsellors to their staffs. Often such appointments were made on an *ad hoc* basis by individual heads of schools who in some cases appointed candidates without training. The responsibilities of the role were not always clearly defined and the types of activities which came to occupy the working life of those appointed as school counsellors developed with the job. In the very early days, some counsellors for example attempted to work in a manner similar to that of a therapist in private practice, centring exclusively on counselling sessions with individuals and maintaining a distance between themselves and other staff and activities in the school. This mode of working did not survive for long. It tended to exacerbate suspicion and misunderstanding from other members of staff, isolate the counsellor from recognition and support, and heighten counsellor stress related to such issues as timetabling and confidentiality. Other tasks also came to be seen by both counsellors and schools as both an important and appropriate part of a counsellor's responsibilities. The role, then, fairly soon became a diversified one, including, in addition to individual counselling with self-referred and teacher-referred pupils, such activities as liaison with outside agencies and with personnel in the school's pastoral care system, home–school liaison and liaison with feeder primary schools, agent-of-change functions including training in guidance and counselling skills and objectives (Daws 1976).

Developments in pastoral care

While some of the negative attitudes towards counselling in schools ameliorated as the concept of counselling became better understood and more acceptable, the progress of the counsellor model was overshadowed by the somewhat precipitate transformation of an older, amateur, and relatively underdeveloped system within British schools which purported to address itself to the personal, as distinct from the scholastic, needs of pupils. The skeletal structure was already present in the form of house systems established in the 1960s on public-school lines in many of the new comprehensive schools, but, as the challenges and stresses of reorganization and social and economic change increased, pastoral-care posts over and above subject-department posts were created and pastoral-care structures of some kind were established in virtually all comprehensive schools. By the 1980s these pastoral-care systems had expanded to include considerable attention to the form tutor's caring role, active tutorial work (Button 1975) being one of the best-known attempts to systematize this aspect of the teacher's participation in what has come to be known as the pastoral curriculum.

In 1983 the National Association for Pastoral Care in Education was inaugurated, amid considerable enthusiasm and with strong support from a large number of teachers throughout England and Wales. A new journal, *Pastoral Care*, was launched at the same time. Though closely following contemporary school practice and making use of the phrase 'pastoral care' rather than the term 'guidance', its contents can be seen from one point of view as a continuation in more modern form of attitudes and principles which came to characterize enlightened educational thinking in the second quarter of this century. Research interests and approaches conveyed by the work of writers particularly associated with the promotion of pastoral care in the 1980s (Lang and Marland 1985) are reminiscent of these earlier workers and resemble those espoused by the major contributors to the 1955 *Year Book of Education*.

Summary

After a period, therefore, of some 25 years of review and innovation aimed at finding viable ways of meeting the welfare needs of pupils, pastoral care has emerged as the official repository of the secondary school's role in the promotion and delivery of services and programmes concerned with social and personal development. Those committed to the advancement of counselling, a key way of facilitating such development, must work with and within this system. In the primary school, the term 'pastoral care' is not in common use, as the practice of care has been seen as inseparable from child-centred education. It is easier, therefore, to see counselling at the primary level as a natural extension of the caring school.

Principles

Pastoral care, teaching, and counselling

The place of pastoral-care systems and, in particular, their relationship to the academic structures of the school, has come under scrutiny in more recent years. A strongly held view insists that the academic and the pastoral cannot be separated and that every teacher is, in fact, a pastoral worker. This is very like one of the arguments put forward in the 1960s for not having school counsellors and is reflected in the tendency among some writers to apply the term counselling globally to a wide range of activities (for example, assessment, modification of teaching methods, policy-making) which may or may not include direct discussions with a pupil (Galloway 1981). The view, however, which seems more in tune with the practice of counselling as it has actually developed in schools is that which sees the school's responsibility for the development and betterment of the pupil as divisible into overlapping but distinct areas of activity concerned respectively with the academic, the disciplinary, and the pastoral aspects of the work of the school (Best *et al.* 1983). Similarly, counselling, while sharing in the philosophical commitment of pastoral care and guidance to 'the personal welfare of the child as an individual human being' (Best *et al.* 1983: 275), can be differentiated from other approaches within the pastoral curriculum, and as Best and others conclude, needs to be separated from other teaching and disciplinary aspects of the school's role often included within the brief of pastoral-care workers.

Counselling

Pastoral care at present seems largely concerned with organization, planning, analysis, evaluation, and often discipline. Counselling tends to be invoked at those points in the day-to-day life of schools where problems, needs, and conflicts of a personal kind appear or threaten to emerge. These are wide-ranging and varied. More common problem areas reported by school counsellors include:

> Bullying, friendship fractures, relationships with parents, discipline/ disruption problems in lessons, identity crises, attendance problems, relationships with staff, difficulty in coping with expectations of parents/ teachers, peers, victims of aggressive behaviour, social isolation, under-functioning, school refusal, family breakdown, low self-esteem, social deprivation, sexual problems, overdoses, suicidal feelings, being in the wrong group for a subject, help in making decisions, self-image, learning difficulties, depression, future unemployment worries, anxiety, coping with work, dealing with their own aggression, study skills, examination anxiety, feelings of alienation with their school programmes, difficulty in adapting to a new school, boredom, sense of rejection, child abuse.
>
> (James 1983: 3–4)

Each particular situation is never quite the same as the last one of its kind, and it is impossible to predict what type of problem will next face a counsellor or other member of staff committed to the personal and social welfare of the pupil as an individual human being. It is also more difficult to translate values and intentions (for example, to be accepting and genuine) into practice in the mêlée of school life than in the relative isolation of the consulting room. It is not surprising, then, that responses to such problems have been varied and sometimes confused. In spite of these difficulties, it now seems possible to discern a number of working principles which have evolved primarily from the practical experience of pastoral-care staff, in particular school counsellors. In the remainder of this section I shall first attempt to articulate these developing principles, and then give some examples to illustrate the way in which they have come to inform good practice.

Working principles

The first principle is a simple one, hardly one might think worthy of mention – always respond. It has a particular meaning for counsellors in that the importance of a statement or action by a client is determined not only by its apparent gravity or triviality in the circumstances in which it occurs but by what it means for him

138

or her. Until you begin to interact with the other person, therefore, you are not in a position to evaluate its significance.

The next principle is communication. Highly desirable in many settings, it is a vital necessity in this one. From a counselling point of view, communication is a shared activity involving both helper and client, and a counselling approach in schools can often be distinguished from other types of approach by this characteristic. In broader terms, however, a counsellor's success and continued credibility in a school context is critically dependent on the way in which he or she communicates with others during, after, and before direct interventions in, for example, presenting problems of the kind referred to above. 'Others' include pupils, the head, staff in general and pastoral staff in particular, and, in the community, workers in key helping agencies. Again, in these cases the kind of communication required is open dialogue without recourse to dissimulation or hidden agendas.

Such communication at first sight might seem contrary to the next general principle which is the maintenance of confidentiality where disclosures are made on the understanding that they will not be divulged without permission. Effective counsellors, while generally resolute on this point, are equally convinced that bringing hidden material into the open is in most cases beneficial, provided those they wish to help agree to do so. It is in this latter respect that counsellors differ most notably from other members of staff.

Though these three principles are fairly broad in scope, adherence to them is seen as indispensable for credibility and success in occupying a counselling role in schools. Other working principles are more directly related to the counselling process itself. Respect or regard for the pupil as a person in his or her own right is perhaps the most fundamental of these. It is characterized by an unconditional acceptance of the individual, free from patronizing or paternalistic attitudes and from the sentimental do-gooding with which pastoral care is sometimes identified. In practice, counsellors have found this an essential prerequisite of the kind of relationship they wish to establish with young people. It is notable, however, that competent school counsellors, while accepting and trying to understand the pupil in this way, maintain at the same time a degree of personal detachment. He or she does not get emotionally involved in either the problem presented or in the feelings accompanying it. To sum up these two principles, the counsellor is seen and needs to be seen as someone who stands outside the argument while standing firmly at the side of the young person.

The last of these principles of critical importance to the conduct of successful dialogue with a pupil is listening, an inherent aspect of the two-way communication. It is a principle of overriding importance in individual counselling as, without it, it is not possible to register, much less respond to, the client's view. In a school context, counsellors have found it both desirable and necessary to extend its application to those others, parent, tutor, and so on, who might be involved on any particular occasion.

Examples

The following cases drawn from the experience of counsellors and other school staff may help to illustrate the way in which counselling principles are brought into school practice.

> Mandy, a second former, in one of her good phases, in which she is pleasant, helpful, and working well, suddenly tells her form teacher that all is well at home and that her mother and her little brother are coming back home. The following week, she is uncooperative and bad-tempered again, in tears, slamming doors, throwing books on the floor. Mum apparently is not returning after all and Dad has brought in a new 'Auntie'.

This example draws attention to the caring role of the teacher, in this case clearly a key figure whose support and influence may be of very great significance in Mandy's development. It underlines the importance of two of the broad aims of pastoral care, prevention and support, and also shows how the teacher in this case is already reflecting some basic characteristics of a counselling approach – listening and accepting. In addition, a counselling approach may be conveyed to a pupil in other ways than face-to-face conversation. By paying attention to what Mandy told her in the first place, by responding later to Mandy's angry outbursts and misdemeanours with firmness, detachment, and patience, and by continuing to show uncompromising acceptance of her as a person, the teacher is in practice subscribing to the basic principles which have been applied to the process of conducting a counselling dialogue. Maintaining an approach of this kind, however, can be very demanding, and genuine communication with other members of staff, in particular pastoral care staff and management, and with appropriate outside agency staff where possible, is highly desirable. Good communication in this sense is invariably found to operate in schools where counselling is valued.

> David, bright fourth former, has a good relationship with his mother with whom he lives in a council flat. His parents separated when he was seven. Mother is still young, in her mid-30s. Father, who lives in the neighbourhood, is finding it hard to cope with life so David sees him rarely. During an interview in school in which the careers teacher allows the discussion to develop at a personal level, David reveals that when he goes into the sixth form he intends to make arrangements to live on his own so that he can allow his mother to live her own life without interference from him. He has not mentioned this to his mother. The possible difficulties in carrying out his intention worry him, but he intends to think them through for himself.

This example underlines the importance of having personnel in schools who can understand how useful counselling can be and when it should be used. A school counsellor with appropriate training and experience should be able to enter into a counselling dialogue with David and enable him to explore the situation and his feelings about it more fully. If presented with this problem, he or she would not hesitate to allocate one or more sessions for this purpose, possibly a joint session for both David and his mother, and, if necessary, a follow-up visit at some time during the year. Whether David could be helped or not in the absence of a school counsellor would depend on (1) the recognition accorded in the school to counselling, in particular to the principles specifically relating to the conduct of a counselling interview, and (2) the availability of the time and competence among existing pastoral-care staff to engage in a type of dialogue which depends for its success on counselling skills.

> In a small group run by a teacher-counsellor, five 'difficult' fourth-form pupils are encouraged to express themselves openly and come to terms with their own feelings. One class teacher quizzes two of them about what is happening in the group and another teacher addresses the counsellor in an aggressive manner, demanding to know what this is all about.

While this example illustrates the degree of anxiety and antagonism sometimes engendered among teachers by counsellors, it also stresses the importance of communication before and during as well as after an event. An incident of the kind reported above took place in a school where a genuine dialogue between the teacher-counsellor and other school staff had not yet been established. It would be unlikely to occur in a school where good lines of communication had been established and where staff closely involved with the pupils concerned were consulted beforehand and made aware of the counsellor's intentions. Had this been done in the case of our example, suspicion and lack of trust would not have assumed such proportions. The principle of confidentiality, in particular, often the focus of conflict between those who teach and those who counsel, would already have been put in perspective. The pupils would understand the meaning of confidentiality and its limits, and other staff members would know beforehand what the counsellor was or was not prepared to discuss with them.

> Karen's mother telephones the school counsellor to complain that her daughter has been unjustly treated by one of the teachers. No food is to be eaten in classrooms. Towards the end of break Karen has just arrived in the room and started talking to two other girls already there when the Head of the Year enters, sees several empty crisp packets and other evidence of food consumption on the floor. He reprimands Karen and the others and orders them to clear up the mess. They refuse saying that they didn't create the mess in the first place. The teacher gets very angry and tells them to report for detention until they decide to apologize. At the counsellor's suggestion the mother comes to the school with Karen to talk about the incident. Karen, according to her mother, did not have anything to do with it but is frightened of the teacher and is now saying that she doesn't like school.

During the conversation the mother finds an opportunity to talk privately to the counsellor and tells her that Karen was sexually abused and has been seeing a social worker for some time for counselling to help her over her mistrust of authoritative men. The Year Head, with the mother's reluctant permission, is told about the abuse, but refuses to budge from the stand he has taken. An approach is then made to the Head, who, having investigated the situation further, takes the mother's part, dismisses detention and need for apology, and proposes further involvement of the school and other helping agencies with Karen's case.

In this case the Head of Year felt his authority had been undermined, but did not, in fact, direct his irritation at the counsellor who in the 2 years she had been in post had made it clear that she conceived of her role as listener and mediator, not a judge of teacher- or client-behaviour.

This difficult and time-consuming case was handled well throughout. Success, however, was not fortuitous, but depended to a considerable extent on the establishment by the counsellor over several years before of a comprehensible role in the school and community and a reputation for being able to cope with school situations in general as well as counselling in particular. The psychological climate of communication as well as the ability to conduct interviews according to counselling principles played an important part in helping Karen's mother and Karen to work through confused ideas and feelings about authority and the role of the school, and in enabling a healthier and more realistic relationship to develop between home and school.

Even from these few examples, it should be evident that living by these principles demands a high level of personal competence and resilience in coping with the anxiety, anger, compassion, and many other powerful feelings frequently engendered on these occasions. It is not surprising, then, that training and the provision of support will be of vital importance in determining the provision and quality of work of this kind.

Issues

How is counselling to be distinguished from other types of intervention? What knowledge and skills are involved? How can people best be trained for a counselling role? These are only some of the many and varied questions that arise wherever counselling is undertaken. While some of these questions are shared across settings, particular issues become of special importance where counselling takes place within an institutional context. The school is perhaps the most complex of all settings, where a large number of factors such as age, parental involvement, religion, and ethnic origin are often associated at a publicly visible level with interventions of a counselling kind. In addition, publicly (and politically) declared aims and the legal and professional responsibilities imposed on school staff are not always reconcilable with either the goal of self-direction and individual free choice or with the developmental readiness of pupils. The issues which seem of greatest importance for counselling in schools in Britain today fall roughly under three broad areas concerned respectively with attitudes and values, identity, and resources and priorities.

Attitudes and values

One of the most difficult issues from the point of view of practice centres round the conflicts which can arise or seem to arise between the authority of the teacher and the psychological welfare of the pupil. The growth of pastoral-care systems has not diminished such conflicts, for pastoral care developed from a tradition of authority and control. Its recent expansion in organization and staffing was closely linked with stressful changes in schools during this period – comprehensive reorganization, the creation of new posts of responsibility, and other major developments such as mixed-ability teaching and the raising of the school-leaving age. As some of the foremost writers on pastoral care have argued, its rapid development was primarily 'a consciously evolved device for managing a potentially explosive situation which enables the teacher to remain in control' (Best *et al*. 1977: 131). Some examples of the 'pastoral curriculum' have indeed been identified by those committed to a counselling philosophy as being 'more about expropriating counselling for the purposes of minimizing personal growth than they are about self-actualization' (Murgatroyd 1983: 6). Counselling, in contrast, is basically concerned with enabling clients to take control of their own lives.

This distinction between a controlling aim and an enabling one is a critical one, not only from the standpoint of values and goals, but also from that of practice. In what manner should one approach the task of talking with a pupil about those forms of behaviour or experiences of events which deviate from institutional or social norms and expectations? How can it be certain that in opting for a counselling position one is acting in a way which is truly client-centred, non-judgemental, accepting? The primacy of pastoral care's social-control function and the tradition of paternalism which a number of contemporary writers see as inhering in pastoral-care practices (Best *et al*. 1977; Follet 1986) would inevitably lead to a different type of response from that developed within counselling, and to a quite different view of the kind of helping relationship one seeks to establish with a pupil.

In practical terms this divergence often gives rise to situations in which the adoption of a counselling stance is perceived as a threat to school discipline, to the authority of senior pastoral-care staff, and even to the academic aims of the school. In a similar manner, neutral, non-judgemental acceptance may appear as weakness, and the observance of confidentiality as the withholding of information of a possibly subversive or potentially damaging kind. Such perceptions are encouraged by the re-emergence of competitive élitist attitudes, simplistic beliefs in the value of 'traditional' methods of teaching, and a tough-minded no-nonsense approach to the problems and needs of young people. The task of explaining and maintaining principles and standards in counselling can be both demanding and frustrating in a school, community, or political climate in which such views are pronounced.

Identity

Role diffusion

In the 1960s counselling was clearly differentiated from teaching and indeed from psychotherapy. In the intervening years these distinctions have been gradually eroded so that the term 'counsellor' no longer needs 'to be restricted to those who see their main role as counselling' (Bolger 1982: 14). These changes, on the whole, have been healthy ones and have led to a decrease in some of the fears underlying defensive attitudes towards counselling. On the negative side, however, this diffusion of the counsellor role has been associated with a conceptual confusion between teaching and counselling and with subsequent identity problems for counsellor-teachers, constantly required to switch between teacher–pupil and counsellor–client types of relationship. As Best and others point out, even in those happy situations where mutual respect, tolerance, and concern have been established between teacher and pupil, the nature of the teacher's role and 'the kind of relationship which actually exists between the teacher and pupil in most classrooms is clearly one of authority, dominance and externally-imposed control, and those who advocate that carers should also be teachers of those for whom they care have not given adequate thought to the implications of this fact' (Best *et al*. 1983: 278).

Conflicting philosophies and concepts

Those occupying a counselling role in schools today are also faced with the task of reconciling opposing philosophies and attitudes, not only between a counselling approach and other approaches but also within counselling itself. Though counselling as a concept and as an activity is better understood and accepted, the role difficulties associated with its practice in a school context have, if anything, intensified. Commitment to the principle of self-direction and to the pre-eminent importance of interpersonal relationships may easily come into conflict with the organizational emphasis and controlling element in pastoral care. Increasing demands for evaluation and accountability and the corresponding pressures in teaching, for action rather than insight and instruction rather than self-directed learning, also represent potential areas of friction and uncertainty.

Within counselling, divisions of a rather similar kind are present in the antithesis between experiential and skills-based approaches. Models of the latter kind, though sometimes presented as eclectic systems, rely heavily on principles derived from the experimental analysis of individual and social behaviour. Their emphasis on logical and systematic routines which make complex processes seem easy to understand and handle, and on performance-based criteria which are clearly describable and measurable make them attractive in today's educational climate. They have been widely applied in a variety of forms in many kinds of human training and treatment situations as well as counselling (Hollin and Trower 1986), and are particularly popular in careers education and counselling where many excellent skills-training programmes suitable for use in schools have been produced by, for example, the National Institute for Careers Education and Counselling (NICEC), the Careers and Counselling Development Unit (CCDU), or the Careers Research and Advisory Centre (CRAC).

Models, however, which rely heavily on behavioural analysis and structure are not so readily applicable in human situations of an irrational or contradictory kind, situations which, like those described earlier in this chapter, do not fit neatly into predetermined behaviours or categories. Feelings, intentions, and conflict are very much part of everyday life in schools, and many of those engaged in counselling continue to be influenced by psychodynamic models which focus on internal experience, feeling, insight, and motivation (for example, gestalt therapy, Transactional Analysis, rational-emotive therapy, psychoanalytic psychotherapy).

Those working as counsellors in schools today, therefore, have to deal with not only a vast and ever-expanding range of concepts and strategies but with contradictory philosophies and methods. Such apparent contradictions and competing sources give rise to major issues of identity not only at a theoretical level but in other important areas, for example, that of training. In daily practice, counsellors are required to cope with such a diverse and divided knowledge-base at the same time as they are seeking to establish a secure self-image and a reputation for common sense and consistency.

Resources and priorities

In this current atmosphere, the process of listening, patiently talking things through, and paying attention to personal meanings as well as overt behaviour are unlikely to be accorded high priority in the allocation of time and money. This low evaluation is already apparent from the fact that counselling, though now tacitly accepted, has not been formally recognized within the British school system, where relatively few schools (no primary schools and probably less than 10 per cent of all secondary schools) employ counsellors. At the same time, further financial cut-backs combined with a reversion to narrower views of the nature of pupil progress and the school's function are likely to lead to reductions in the time available for all welfare work, including counselling.

Current emphases in pastoral care

The observance of counselling principles and the quality of work done is even more closely linked into current emphases and attitudes within pastoral care. The new journal, *Pastoral Care*, while providing many excellent contributions on curriculum analysis and evaluation, change, and innovation at a systems level, has so far had relatively little to say about what actually happens or what could happen in psychological terms in counselling-type dialogues, or about, for example, the knowledge, skills, and time required by teachers in coping with the personal welfare of pupils. With few exceptions (schools in Devon are a striking example), little consideration has been given to possible ways of making use of the understanding and skills in counselling and guidance acquired in one year full-time courses by a substantial number of highly motivated teachers over a 20-year period. Even more surprisingly, those most closely associated with the current promotion of pastoral care exhibit little interest in this source of training, though they acknowledge the existence of major gaps in the skills possessed by pastoral-care workers and agree that training is urgently required (Lang and Marland 1985). It is somewhat ironic that, partly as a spin-off from such developments and from attempts by the British Association for Counselling to arrive at a nationally agreed accreditation scheme, the full-time courses which have been the major source of training available for teaching staff are likely to come under pressure to increase the number of hours at present devoted to counselling supervision – a trend resembling recent upgrading of the role of counsellors in mental health in the USA (Gazda *et al.* 1987).

Future developments

It is difficult to predict the future of counselling in schools, not least because it is tied to a more broadly based system – pastoral care – which itself is the subject of much debate and speculation (Lang and Marland 1985). While counselling, however, may not have acquired the status and role accorded to it in some other countries, the earlier antipathy towards it has altered considerably, the attitudes of heads and of school staffs have become more accepting (Best *et al* 1981; Rees 1982, 1983), and it can now be said that counselling is widely recognized as a relevant and legitimate activity for schools. It is, therefore, more feasible than it was to make some educational guesses about the future of counselling – how it might develop, and what steps can be taken to enable progress to be made.

Need for understanding

School counselling does not take place in a vacuum. To be successful, much greater knowledge, understanding, and support are required from educational administrators, from those who represent pastoral care, and from school staffs in general. They will need to know something of the nature of the processes and skills involved in counselling and of how different levels of knowledge and skills may be required according to the nature and demands of the helping task. Those members of staff involved in counselling, whether as a school counsellor or in the course of other duties, must, for example, be able to notice when counselling is or is not appropriate and to distinguish between counselling work at different levels. Hamblin, for example, draws a distinction between specialist, immediate, or intermediate levels (Hamblin 1974). To make such judgements and to handle such situations requires training. Writers on pastoral care and pastoral-care staff are unlikely to take this urgent requirement seriously enough until they begin to appreciate 'the possibility that there may be special skills and experience that can help children directly but which require a level of expertise which cannot be expected as part of the general professional training of the teacher' (Nicol 1987: 660). Teachers without extra training are less likely to move beyond instinctive reaction to informed response.

The examples and discussion under 'Principles' give some idea of how wide-ranging this 'expertise' can be, including not only counselling but human-relationship skills applicable to a broader spectrum of settings and problems. In addition, skills of this kind are required in those teaching and tutorial situations in which Self is the focus of learning, and will be in increasing demand as social and life-skills training comes to play an increasing part in the curriculum. They are at a premium in courses which link school and industry (such as the Technical and Vocational Education Initiative – TVEI) and in many contemporary settings where the ability to communicate across psychological and social boundaries – cultures, subjects, social classes, professions, school/home – can be of critical importance.

Need for training

It must become increasingly obvious, first, that training on a massive scale is urgently needed, and second, that such an aggregate of needs and tasks should not continue to be dealt with, as they frequently seem to be, on an *ad hoc* basis. Hopefully, some attention to counselling and pastoral care may soon be incorporated into initial training for all teachers, and continuing in-service training provided on a more systematic basis for pastoral-care staffs in particular. Training in greater depth is essential for the more complex interventions involved in counselling work with some pupils, in liaison work, and in the selection and provision of treatment and training programmes based on an increasing number of alternative therapy and counselling approaches. These latter have included, for example, cognitive–behavioural, psychoanalytic, gestalt, rational-emotive, Transactional Analysis, and an expanding eclecticism that has also begun to include exercises drawn from a variety of sources including psychological humanistic education and experiential groupwork, directed at promoting psychological growth and awareness (Nelson-Jones 1986).

Need for systematic planning

If we accept the relevance and desirability of the knowledge, competencies, and skills required to cope with demands of this kind at both an organizational and a training level, questions arise about how these can be actualized. Interestingly, the idea that school counsellors with proper training and time should be appointed to every secondary school is again being proposed, this time against the background of a better informed profession and a more searching analysis of the welfare needs of schools (Best *et al.* 1983). The Scottish Central Committee on Guidance which recently arrived at this conclusion associated the role not only with a counselling service available to all pupils but with 'a consultancy service for teachers together with staff development in counselling' (Scottish Central Committee on Guidance 1986: 8). It is a most powerful statement of the view that counselling is an inherent aspect of a good school's function, requiring systematic planning and co-ordination. It might also be pointed out, of course, that a quite different situation could develop, either by design or by default, in which schools would revert again to a more restricted concept of their function, and rely more and more on external agencies and mental health workers based outside to provide services of this kind for young people and other school personnel.

Current resources

These suggestions as to what should be done are neither extravagant nor starry-eyed, as many able and committed people have been working over a very considerable period of time towards these objectives, and virtually every point mentioned can already be found in a successful form somewhere in the system. Impressive examples of understanding and support from both management and staff can be found at both school and county levels. Schools can be identified in which counselling has not been left to chance but has been carefully organized and integrated into the total curricular provision. There are school counsellors, some with a full-time counsellor role, others with a part-teacher/part-counsellor role, working successfully within supportive frameworks of this kind. In contrast with an earlier tendency to focus exclusively on work with individual pupils, sometimes in isolation from the rest of the school, these counsellors are much more involved in the group life of the school, often showing a high degree of awareness of community dynamics and considerable skill in handling interpersonal situations. Full-time training courses or equivalent part-time courses have been available since 1965 in universities, polytechnics, or colleges of higher education. Training programmes of this nature, whose content and methods are derived from an impressive literature, research, and practice in counselling and human relations, continue to offer a high standard of theoretical and practical training in counselling, incorporating supervised placements in schools and helping agencies and often including familiarization with community mental health issues and practice. The tradition of research and enquiry associated with counsellor training from its beginnings in Britain could be of considerable value in current attempts to establish research objectives and methodology in pastoral care (Lang and Marland 1985). Many short-term training inputs with an emphasis on the acquisition of basic counselling skills have also become increasingly available on a local basis.

Looking ahead, therefore, may be construed as a question of how to make maximum use of the resources currently available and to extend these to include all schools. An enquiry at national level into the training needs of all workers in pastoral care and guidance is perhaps overdue. If undertaken, it would be imperative to include in it a systematic analysis of the ways in which counselling is needed and used within the school as an educational and caring community.

References

Best, R., Jarvis, C., and Ribbins, P. (1977) 'Pastoral care: concept and process', *British Journal of Educational Studies* 25(2): 124–35.

Best, R., Jarvis, C., Oddy, D., and Ribbins, P. (1981) 'Teacher attitudes to the school counsellor: a reappraisal', *British Journal of Guidance and Counselling*, 9(2): 159–71.

Best, R., Ribbins, P., Jarvis, C., with Oddy, D. (1983) *Education and Care*, London: Heinemann.

Bolger, A. W. (ed.) (1982) *Counselling in Britain*, London: Batsford Academic and Educational Ltd.

Button, L, (1975) *Developmental Group Work with Adolescents*, London: Hodder & Stoughton.

David, K. and Charlton, A. (1988) *The Caring Role of the Primary School*, London: Macmillan.

Daws, P. (1976) *Early Days*, Cambridge: Hobsons Press.

Follet, J. (1986) 'The concept of pastoral care: a genealogical analysis', *Pastoral Care* 4(1): 3–11.

Galloway, D. (1981) *Teaching and Counselling: Pastoral Care in Primary and Secondary Schools*, London: Longman.

Gazda, G. M., Childers, W. C., and Brooks, D. K., Jr. (1987) *Foundations of Counseling and Human Services*, New York: McGraw Hill.

Hamblin, D. H. (1974) *The Teacher and Counselling*, Oxford: Blackwell.

Hollin, C. R. and Trower, P. (1986) *Handbook of Social Skills Training*, Vol. 1, Oxford: Pergamon.

Hughes, P. M. (1971) *Guidance and Counselling in Schools*, Oxford: Pergamon.

James, J. (1983) 'School counselling in Devon 1983', *Counselling in Education Newsletter* August: 2–4.

Lang, P. and Marland, M. (1985) *New Directions in Pastoral Care*, Oxford: Blackwell.

Murgatroyd, S. (1983) 'Counselling at a time of change and development', *Journal of the Education Section of the British Psychological Society* 7(2): 5–9.

Nelson-Jones, R. (1986) 'Relationship skills training in school: some fieldwork observations', *British Journal of Guidance and Counselling*, 14(3): 292–305.

Nicol, A. R. (1987) 'Psychotherapy and the school: an update', *Journal of Child Psychology and Psychiatry* 28(5): 657–65.

Rees, B. (1982) 'Teachers' attitudes to guidance and counselling', *The Counsellor* 3(5): 2–12.

——(1983) 'Heads' attitudes to school counsellors and careers teachers', *The Counsellor*, 3(7): 13–23.

Scottish Central Committee on Guidance (The Report of the) (1986) 'More than feelings of concern', *Guidance and Scottish Secondary Schools*, Dundee College of Education.

Sisterson, D. (1983) 'Counselling in the primary school', *Journal of the Education Section of the British Psychological Society*, 7(2): 10–15.

Chapter ten

Counselling in higher education

Bernard Ratigan

Introduction

The focus of this chapter is on counselling work undertaken in university, polytechnic, and colleges of higher education in Britain. Although a close relationship between student and teacher has been one of the characteristics of British higher education since the Middle Ages, it is only in the second half of the twentieth century that this tradition of pastoral care has become an area of professional concern and practice. As the ancient universities were originally religious foundations it was axiomatic that students were *in statu pupillari* and the dons *in loco parentis*. Even now, after all the growth and changes since the Second World War, many teachers in higher education still consider the moral (*sic*) welfare or their students of great importance. Despite the advent of professionals in student health, counselling, and careers guidance, it is still tutors, in both academic and residential settings, who are mostly seen as the chief providers of pastoral care. This contrasts markedly with other European traditions where the distance between professor and student is much greater than in Britain.

From the pioneer work at Leicester, London (Malleson 1965), and at Keele (Newsome *et al.* 1973) Universities through to the proliferation of sophisticated multidisciplinary student services teams in many polytechnics, there is a continuing thread of development. In the late 1960s and throughout the 1970s many higher-education institutions set up counselling services in response to pressure from both academic staff and student unions. The increased number of university places and the establishing of polytechnics led to a gradual expansion in student-counselling services. Typically, the pre-Robbins university or college student was educated in a small, intimate learning environment: a thousand students would have been a large institution. The typical higher-education student of the 1990s will not be in a university but in a polytechnic which will be perhaps ten times larger than the pre-Robbins university. He or she will be taught in large groups and be faced with, necessarily, a relatively impersonal relationship with tutors, and will often be faced with a large variety of course choices. The nature of knowledge itself has become more specialized, with an emphasis on assessment; it is instrumental rather than affective, and more vocationally orientated. Teachers are under much greater pressure, especially in universities but increasingly in polytechnics, to be less involved with students, no matter how ideologically committed they are to maintaining the personal dimension in their work. There is pressure to keep a distance, especially because of the demands of continuous assessment, and professional and institutional factors which reward fecundity in research and the raising of money for research. First-year students are frequently told by their academic mentors that 'my door is always open', but the fact that they will rarely be in their offices is less frequently mentioned. The pressure on teachers is such that contact with students is increasingly rare other than in the context of formal lecturing and academic-tutoring settings.

The Open University is the largest educational institution in Britain and has, perhaps, moved furthest to recognizing the counselling needs of students and the responsibilities of tutorial staff for counselling. All its foundation students have allocated to them a Tutor/Counsellor. Although much of what they do with students is termed 'educational counselling', and appears to be a formalization of the well-understood role of personal tutor rather than counselling in the more widely recognized manner in higher education, the Open University has set a clear lead at both the level of institutional policy and practice that counselling is necessary for students.

Notwithstanding this growth in helping agencies in higher education, there persists in British society a form of secular Calvinism which emphasizes the value of independence, and the character-building value of surmounting personal difficulties without recourse to outside, especially professional, sources of help. This, taken with the residual Anglo-Saxon pragmatic scepticism of ideologies such as psychoanalysis, which are seen as dangerously foreign and weakening, has restricted the rate of growth of formal student counselling services. Although all sectors of education have been under great financial pressure because of government policies in the 1980s, any understanding of the processes and vicissitudes of counselling must take into account the wider cultural and historical factors that are at work. It should also be recognized that in any organization and especially one that is itself under threat, many personal agendas can be focused on the issues surrounding the establishment, expansion, or cutting of a counselling service (Pashley 1976).

Against this background a new profession, or semi-profession, according to Crowther (1984), has arisen: student counsellors. They can be seen as having three main functions:

(1) to act as specialist sources of help and/or referral for students experiencing learning, social, relationship, and developmental, as well as more severe psychological or psychiatric, problems;
(2) providing consultation and training for academic, administrative, and residential staff; and

(3) to be a channel between the lived experience of the institution's students and staff and the policy-makers with particular reference to institutional practice and staff training.

Principles

The role of counselling theory in counselling

The major theoretical approaches in counselling are all represented in student counselling. Two in particular are influential: person-centred therapy associated with the work of Rogers (1969) and psychoanalytic therapy derived from Freud, Jung, Klein, and Winnicott (Noonan 1983). Cognitive and behavioural methodologies make their mark also especially in groupwork both in some curriculum activities (Woolfe *et al.* 1987) as well as in clinical work.

Training courses on student counselling tend to adopt one particular theoretical perspective. Thus, for example, one of the longest and most highly regarded training courses in student counselling, that offered by the University of London Department of Extra Mural Studies, is firmly based on psychoanalytic ideas which embrace both the understanding of individual as well as organizational psychodynamics and psychopathology (Noonan 1986). Many other training courses are informed by person-centred philosophy and psychology.

Notwithstanding the theoretical models used in training courses, much of the actual practice of counselling is eclectic and pragmatic. Whilst most student counsellors owe a primary affiliation to either a person-centred, psychoanalytic, or cognitive–behavioural model and this affiliation conditions the form of the clinical work undertaken, the impression is strong that the variety of human problems facing a general-purpose counsellor working in an educational institution indicates that more than a passing acquaintance with all three modalities is necessary for effective work with clients. Unfortunately, or perhaps fortunately, clients rarely come in neat theoretical or clinical categories.

In terms of training for student counselling it seems essential that trainees have a thorough grounding in one theoretical perspective in which they feel profoundly at home and in which they will be able to grow and develop their clinical skills. Beyond this they must also be able to work with students who have needs that can best be met by the application of other theoretical perspectives. Only in the largest institutions and cities are student counsellors likely to have the luxury of referral facilities for all the specialist needs they encounter in their clients. Referral for specialist help is often further complicated by constraints imposed by students living away from home and the constant interruptions of vacations which impose severe practical difficulties. Adolescent and early-adult student crises need a relatively rapid response to requests for help and it is rare that these crises are outside the competence of the professional student counsellor. A measure of theoretical and clinical flexibility is therefore required in student counselling, not only to deal with the range of clients but also with

153

colleagues. Of particular importance among the latter are the medical profession with its own language and rituals. Counsellors need to be able to talk with both primary-care physicians and psychiatrists in a way which allows for both the strengths and limitations of the medical model and in which counsellors do not lose their integrity.

Counselling practice

One useful way of viewing the work of counsellors in higher education is in terms of a three-fold division between their remedial, preventive, and developmental roles.

The remedial role

The remedial function is well known and understood. The counsellor is operating, usually on a one-to-one basis, with clients who have sought help or been referred with a range of difficulties. Examples of these problems can, of course, cover the whole gamut of human existence, but there are some important clusters around such areas as learning difficulties, separation and loss, eating disorders, social and interpersonal relationships, and substance abuse. This is not the place for an extended discussion of counselling methods in higher education (Hunter-Brown 1979; Walker 1979): some vignettes, however, illustrate the range of work undertaken with individuals and how counsellors are often part of a range of helping agencies.

Assistance with disabling anxieties A student was referred by his tutor who had noticed that despite high marks in his school-leaving examinations and his course-work marks at college he was unable to handle the stress of formal examinations. The counsellor, using a cognitive–behavioral model, helped the student devise a structured study pattern, constructed a cognitive rehearsal of the phobic situation, taught him a method of autonomic relaxation, and systematically desensitized him. There was considerable liaison with both the college medical service, in case he needed to take the examinations there or anxiolytic medication was indicated, and with his tutor, who provided much needed moral support. Six sessions. **Outcome**: student took examination with other candidates and passed adequately.

Low social/interpersonal skills A student was visited by his tutor whilst on industrial placement. The firm's training officer told the student and the tutor that, whilst the student was clearly academically able, his poor social skills were stopping much useful learning taking place. The training officer indicated that in her opinion counselling was indicated. The student felt very wounded by what he saw as an attack.

Although the student booked the appointment to see the counsellor he was very hostile when he was seen for assessment. He was offered individual sessions, which he reluctantly accepted. During these he was able to express, first, his anger and subsequently his feelings of hopelessness. He was later offered a place in a social-skills group (eight 2-hour sessions). In this group, run on social-learning principles, he, together with nine other students, was systematically taught a range of basic social and interpersonal skills which he had not hitherto acquired. **Outcome**: enough improvement in his interpersonal skills such that he was offered a job in the same firm.

Intrapersonal difficulties A student, having started and dropped out of two first-degree courses, was offered a third chance at a polytechnic. In his second term there he again experienced the depression that had plagued him since his childhood. During a vacation, whilst at home, he overdosed and was referred to the student counselling service by the consultant liaison psychiatrist who assessed him in the accident and emergency unit. On his return to polytechnic he was seen daily for two weeks and then started on twice-weekly psychodynamic psychotherapy for 6 months followed by once weekly for a further year. During this time he managed to pass both his first- and second-year examinations. During his final year he was seen only very occasionally at moments of crisis for single sessions. **Outcome**: on graduation he obtained a good degree, went on to do research, and subsequently became a university lecturer.

Study difficulties A student apprentice from an automobile manufacturer had previously been a pupil at a high-powered independent school at which he had never developed autonomous learning-skills. Both at work and at university, his tutors experienced him as very demanding and became frustrated at his continual requests for help and reassurance with assignments. He was referred by his industrial tutor to the student counselling service, where, after a thorough history had been taken from him, he was offered and accepted a contract of ten sessions to work with a counsellor to help him with his dependency difficulties. Subsequent to this he was also offered systematic study-skills help in a group. **Outcome:** became somewhat more independent and passed his course.

Bereavement/loss A second-year student was referred by his hall-of-residence warden because he had become withdrawn and morose. From being a promising lively young man with student-union ambitions, he had ceased to mix with others and spent many hours laying on his bed listening to loud, aggressive music. Attempts to reach him by friends, cleaners, and the resident tutors met either with blank looks or uncharacteristic and frightening outbursts of anger. After many days of gentle persuasion by the warden, who himself was in consultation with the student counselling service to help him handle and cope with the crisis, the student agreed to go and seek help for himself. On assessment, he revealed that his best friend at home had been killed in a motor-bike accident during the previous vacation. He was offered weekly counselling, during which he was able to work through the grief he felt and acknowledge the guilt he felt about his friend's death and his own survival.

The preventative role

The Association for Student Counselling's view of this aspect of the role of the counsellor in higher education is instructive:

The counsellor's position affords him a particular perspective and because of this he often has insights into the institution's life which are denied to others. It is not infrequently the case that an institution through its procedures and practices can cause or exacerbate a person's difficulties. If these can be remedied at the institutional level then it is likely that much individual suffering will be prevented.

(ASC, undated).

All organizations have both formal and informal power structures, decision-making processes, and information systems. The counsellor needs to have a good knowledge of all these to be able to work effectively. At the formal level he or she will be part of a management system which will not only establish counselling and ancillary posts but also allocate resources, both physical plant and budgetary. The head of a counselling service will also be a part of the government of the institution by membership of committees, which will also affect the practice of counselling in the university, polytechnic, or college. One important skill of the counsellor, then, is to be able to relate the material gathered in the consulting room to the wider institution's decision-making processes. In the day-by-day work of a counselling service, patterns and lacunae will continually emerge. The counsellor's task is to translate these into information for the benefit of the institution and to have the political know-how either to effect change or get resources, or both. One of the most important conduits for the preventive work of the counsellor is by participation in the institution's academic and administrative staff training and development programmes. In some institutions it may, of course, be necessary for the counsellor to work to bring such a programme into existence. It is clearly inappropriate for a counselling service to attempt to do all such preventive work itself. A more realistic model is for the counselling service to see itself as a midwife, bringing initiatives to institutional birth and then handing them on to others to rear.

Additional to the institutional aspect of the preventive role, counselling services will be engaged in organizing a range of groups, workshops, and courses which will prepare students for the various tasks and skills they will need. By acting in this preventive mode, counsellors are proactively working to stop students becoming clients.

For a counselling service to accept or seek a role definition as a 'non-academic' service is to deny itself a key role as a change agency. Counsellors in higher education are part of the educational process; they are as much 'academic related' as libraries and computer centres. The preventive aspect of the role of the counsellor is further discussed in the 'issues' section below.

The developmental role

Counsellors working in educational institutions are educators to the extent that they contribute to the education and development of students and staff. A counselling service is a potential resource for all those who want or need to develop some aspect of themself either personally or professionally. It is clear that the rapid expansion and increasing fragmentation of knowledge has led to a multiplicity of courses that leave many students with a thirst for integrative, personal-growth experiences. Opportunities to reflect on personal development and to gain skills in interpersonal relations are widely appreciated – if they are advertised and run in a professional manner. It is often the case that students entering professions with a counselling or helping-skills element – and this means most from management to medicine – want the experience of being in training and group-relations workshops. Such experiences are increasingly seen as helping to produce graduates with more insight into themselves and others and more able to hear what others are saying.

Academic and other staff in higher-educational institutions also have personal-development needs. Counselling services can make important contributions to answering these needs by providing contributions in the form of personal-effectiveness workshops especially designed for staff in such areas as assertiveness skills, time management, and career development. By such work counsellors make important contributions to improving the mental health of institutions.

Study and learning difficulties

The complex relationship between effective study and the development of the whole person is well known. The bases of the most serious study difficulties encountered by students is rooted in earlier experiences and relationships, sometimes as far back as infancy (Hazell 1982; Salzberger-Wittenberg *et al.* 1983). The transition from compulsory to non-compulsory educational settings can sometimes provoke or reveal profound difficulties in students. Student counsellors are more than study-skills technicians and will always be alert to the whole person, of which the current difficulties are but a part. In the range of acceptable presenting problems, study difficulties are often much easier to artic- ulate than others that are more dangerous or threatening to the student's identity. Transition to higher education has become one of the important rites of passage in our society. 'Leaving school' for work, training or further/higher education has come to have many resonances of 'growing up' and moving into a more inde- pendent style of life. One of the major differences between school and college is the relationship between the student and the teacher. The transition has much to do with autonomy and the symbolic establishment of a (more) seemingly independent existence and an individual identity independent from the family. The student is not a pupil. The opportunity which higher education gives for sometimes quite profound personal and social identity transformations in students provides counsellors working in this area with some of their most stimulating work.

Unfortunately the very processes that are at work helping pupils to become autonomous students can sometimes help perpetuate patterns of learning and living which militate against both academic and interpersonal success in higher education. Because of the pressure to get into higher education, school teachers can sometimes encourage a teacher-centred approach to learning – the pupil leans or relies upon the teacher for motivation. This extrinsic pressure can be seen as encouraging anaclitic learning where the pupil or student leans on or is over-dependent on the teacher and unable to work autonomously. Of course, in adolescence a healthy rebellion ensures that most pupils do establish independent learning patterns, if only to establish themselves as persons. For those who do not, entry into educational programmes with an implicit model of student autonomy can be a painful and occasionally disastrous experience. Tutors can sometimes become frustrated and 'write off' students who are over-reliant – often labelling them negatively. Counsellors have an important role with both students experiencing learning difficulties and with their academic teachers in helping both to come to more productive understandings of the complexities underlying study problems. For a tutor to label a student as 'too demanding' or a student to explain his or her difficulties in terms of 'laziness' is just too easy. Part of the skill of the counsellor in such situations is to be able to translate their understandings of the dynamics underlying such labellings into a way that empowers both tutors and students.

Teachers in higher education can be encouraged to spell out their assumptions about just what are the appropriate or necessary learning skills for the courses for which they are responsible. Ideally, every course needs to have a study-skills orientation at its outset so that all students are formally helped to acquire the necessary skills. The Open University has set such a standard in this area which is gradually filtering into the rest of higher and further education. Counsellors have an important role in encouraging and disseminating examples of good practice. Student counselling services can also be centres for learning skill acquisition (Main 1980; Raaheim and Wankowski 1981) and, perhaps, providers of central courses for students who have special needs or who do not wish to reveal their deficiencies to their academic tutors. Student counselling services can also hold databases of materials in this area for academic colleagues to use and to which they can contribute.

Professional counsellors are not, in the first instance, teachers but there can be much fruitful interchange if they are able to co-operate with academic tutors in running study-skills workshops. This will ensure that (1) the skills of the counsellor are efficiently disseminated; (2) students will develop effective study skills at the outset of their studies and hopefully have less need to present themselves for individual crisis counselling; and (3) the counsellor will have more reserves of energy for those who really do need expert help which can either be provided individually or in specially convened groups.

Group counselling

To emphasize the developmental and preventive roles of student counsellors, some group interventions are illustrated below:

Orientation

Through the process of anticipatory socialization it is clear that human beings are almost always able to cope more effectively with a transition, and especially a potentially traumatic one, if they are cognitively and emotionally prepared. Orientation groups can be general, as in all the new students entering into an institution, or specific, for example with overseas students (Zwingmann and Gunn 1983).

Study skills

As with orientation groups, workshops to prepare students systematically for the appropriate study techniques can be either provided centrally by student counselling services (Thorne 1979) or by individual departments running bespoke workshops for their own students and courses.

Speciality workshops for particular categories, such as research students (Wilson 1980), or difficulties, such as exam phobics or those unskilled in seminar work, are useful.

Vocational counselling

The move to groupwork counselling methods in careers-guidance work has been significant. Examples of such groups include: life planning, decision-making, interviewing and other interpersonal skills, and groups helping with application procedures.

Stress management

Behavioural and cognitive group-interventions include classes in autonomic relaxation skills, time management, assertiveness, and other interpersonal skills (Priestley *et al.* 1978).

Self-help groups

There are many examples of counselling initiatives in the formation, maintenance, and development of groups of students with particular goals. Examples include: peer counselling, ethnic groupings, gender-based groups, and sexual-minority groups.

Training groups

Student-union officials, especially for those with welfare/casework responsibilities, can be given basic counselling training as well as other skills in time management and assertiveness.

Clinical groups

There are many opportunities for the use of relatively short-term group therapies, mainly of a behavioural–cognitive nature. Examples of these include social and interpersonal skills, assertiveness skills, study and examination skills, and eating disorders. More discursive analytic-type groups are much more difficult to convene and maintain because of the high turnover of student clients, their age, the vacations being very disruptive, the problems of group members meeting each other outside the clinical context, and the length of time it takes to select a viable collection of clients to constitute a group (but see Crighton 1979; Cox 1983).

Issues

Confidentiality and relationships with third parties

There are a number of special issues for a counsellor working in higher education. When a counsellor works for an organization the question of confidentiality is always highlighted. In higher education one of the major sources of difficulty is the relationship between the client, the counsellor, and the institution. Tutors who take an active interest in the welfare of their students, even to the extent of referring them to a counsellor, sometimes have difficulty in accepting that they do not have 'a right to know' both whether the student has sought help and/or the nature of the transaction with the counsellor. Another delicate question concerns whether or not a particular student *is* a client. Sometimes the anxieties generated in tutors and peers by a student experiencing difficulties can be so great that counsellors can expect to be under heavy pressure to 'do something'. In these circumstances it is always important for a counsellor to be able to help the individuals concerned understand what is going on. It also points to the value, if not necessity, for there being more than one counsellor in a service so that there can be a division of responsibility during crises.

Counsellors need to have tried and tested policies and practices for the times when the in-service work interacts with the wider life of the institution, especially for crisis management. The role of ancillary, especially reception, staff is also clearly of great importance, as it is they who often have to hold crises until counsellors become available. The closest link will probably be with the medical and nursing staff, and it will be particularly beneficial if there can be weekly term-time meetings between doctors and counsellors to ensure that patients/clients are well managed. Other important professional links will likely be with careers advisors, chaplains, and student-union welfare staff. With all these colleagues it is important not only to have good working relationships but a clear understanding of the nature and boundary of these relationships.

Although all students in higher education are technically adults, student counselling services can sometimes be contacted by parents, especially at times of crisis. This can pose a threat to the sacrosanct nature of the counselling relationship. In an obviously anxious state about their (usually late-adolescent) offspring, they will sometimes attempt to insist on knowing whether or not their son or daughter is a client or that both the fact and material of their telephone call are kept secret. Generally, it seems in the best interests of the client if his or her counsellor is not involved in speaking with third parties once work has commenced, and, further, that parents should be firmly but gently told that their concern will be reported to their client children. Antitherapeutic and unhealthy misalliances can then be kept to a minimum.

Work-load

How much work should a counsellor in higher education be doing? One of the problems facing the counsellor is that the demand for direct one-to-one work is almost insatiable. It is general for contracts of employment to indicate a 35-hour, 5-day week with 6 weeks annual holiday. To avoid burnout, experience has taught that to attempt to do more than 18–20 clinical hours per week is unwise and, ultimately, unsafe (Hope 1985). There must be time for all the other essential tasks – receiving and making referrals, writing case notes, preparing and participating in case conferences, scientific reading and writing, staff training and development – and, simply, walking about the institution and meeting and talking with people. Although there will be problems with confidentiality, and the counsellor must be clear what can and cannot be discussed, there are considerable benefits to be gained from being known and seen about, even if only occasionally. There are very few roles in a large institution like a university or polytechnic which are as privileged as that of the counsellor, in that all, from the 'humblest' to the 'highest', should be able to feel that they can be sure of a safe response. It is, of course, essential that counsellors have clear time/space boundaries so that they can feel refreshed and secure in themselves.

Institutional pressures on the counsellor

One of the special problems, or opportunities, facing a counselling service in any institution, but especially large and complex ones like universities and polytechnics, is that the many primitive and potentially destructive forces may be experienced as focused on them (Noonan 1986). Many unrealistic expectations may be put upon counsellors, especially about their capacity to effect change in their clients. There needs to be constant vigilance so that these projections, and sometimes introjections, are carefully understood, interpreted, and explained. Otherwise there is an ever-present risk of the counsellors being seduced into a dangerous delusional state, seeing themselves as saviours of the institution or, in another variant, the only ones who really care. At a time of economic stringency it can be very easy for counsellors to be somewhat over-optimistic in making claims for their own competence.

Pragmatically, counsellors in institutions have to consider very carefully just how much work they can do and then set out the criteria on which they will take on clients and for how long. Further, matters such as publicity and advertising need to be carefully monitored so that counselling services are not swamped with work and potential clients given unrealistic expectations of help being available.

The counsellor and institutional policy and practice

As long as counsellors saw themselves as marginal to the central concerns and processes of educational institutions, much valuable information and skill remained locked up in their consulting rooms. There was a reluctance, from both counsellors and their academic and administrative colleagues, to venture out into what were perceived by many counsellors as dangerous waters. The widening of the role of the counsellor, perhaps linked with the increasing use of organizational development models and concepts derived from psychoanalytic theory (de Board 1978), and the conscious search for organizational and financial efficiency has led to the recognition of the valuable skills and information in the counsellor.

The Association for Student Counselling's three-fold definition of the role of the counsellor in terms of remedial, preventive, and developmental work has been widely adopted in higher education in the UK. Of the three components, the first has always occupied student counsellors in that they have devoted most of their professional effort to one-to-one counselling. In recent years the remedial has become increasingly seen and labelled as psychotherapeutic. This may be partly a defensive response on the part of professional student counsellors to distinguish what they see themselves doing from that done by tutors. It may be related to the initial training of student counsellors. Students, in their increasingly enthusiastic use of counselling services, are perhaps heralding wider attitude shifts in British society and a weakening, to some extent, of the Protestant ethic of not asking for help (Knight 1986). Perhaps because of the inherent conservatism in all educational institutions, both of the other roles – the preventive and the developmental – have been slower to take hold and gain institutional recognition. Perhaps also student counsellors have been somewhat reluctant to face up to their institutional responsibilities, sheltering behind their large case-loads.

Student counsellors are in a very privileged position in educational institutions. By virtue of their role they are the recipients of a procession of individual clients who daily present them with information not only about their life experiences but also with the impact of institutional processes and other developments on the members of the institution – both students and staff members.

To illustrate how counsellors can translate their clinical experience into ways which help their institutions function less destructively, two vignettes are given. They show how counsellors need to look beneath the presenting individual problems and have a grasp of organizational dynamics so that they can understand and set about helping to change pathological processes.

Vignette A

A student-counselling-service team became aware that it was helping a substantial number of overseas students who were presenting a variety of difficulties. Operating on the remedial model, for some years the counsellors treated the problems in isolation in terms of individual psychopathologies reacting to socio-cultural changes. A thorough review of the college's treatment of its overseas students was proposed by the student counselling service, which led to the formation of a high-powered committee for the welfare of overseas students which in turn led to major institutional changes.

The student counselling service then had a mechanism to work for the introduction of the following changes:

(1) upwardly revise language entry-requirements and to introduce a similar regulation for research students;
(2) establish an integrated programme for foreign students consisting of a co-ordinated series of events, including a substantial pre-sessional course, orientation sessions, an official-welcome reception, settling-in and special study-skills workshops, extra language-tuition, excursions, and re-entry workshops; and
(3) staff training workshops for those involved with overseas students.

Vignette B

Over a number of years a student counselling service had become aware that a course which had very high entry-requirements was losing some of its most able students. As all students prematurely terminating their studies or failing examinations were systematically offered a counselling session the counsellors were able to build up a qualitative understanding of the individual student reactions to the processes going on in the course.

This was fed back to the academic staff of the departments concerned and, over some years, this led to many hours of informal discussions and to tutors taking part in the academic-staff training and development programme. As a result of the discussions and the training a modified selection procedure, thorough orientation of the students, and a more effective personal-tutoring system were introduced.

The responsibility of counsellors for systems change is increasingly acknowledged (Jones 1987). It is clear to both academic and administrative managers in institutions of higher education that counsellors are both an important source of information on how the institution is actually functioning and have some of the most potent skills in bringing about change.

Where a properly organized professional student counselling service exists it will be in contact with about a tenth of the student population annually, and in a typical UK university or polytechnic, that will mean between 600 and 800 students. This will give counsellors an unrivalled reservoir of knowledge about institutional processes, ranging from the experience of selection, induction, and orientation to matters concerning styles of teaching and the impact of assessment procedures.

The role of the counsellor

Any consideration of counselling in higher education has to address a definitional question. It is possible to discern a spectrum of role definitions ranging from the exclusivist which confines counselling to what goes on in the consulting room of the accredited counsellor (usually practising psychodynamic counselling and/or psychotherapy) through to an inclusivist view which sees all non-academic but professional contacts between students and tutors in an educational institution as counselling. In between these is a role definition which sees the attitude of the tutor as being more or less counselling-orientated. Such a tutor has a fundamental respect for the student as a person, understands the concept of boundary, and attempts to help students in need by getting them to understand themselves and mobilize their own resources. This middle position also sees the professional counsellor as giving a high priority to providing training and support for those tutors with a counselling orientation as they go about their everyday work in the institution. The professional counsellor has, of course, a strong commitment to providing direct clinical services for those students who are self-referring or referred by others such as medical, careers, and welfare-rights personnel and by tutors who are able to acknowledge that the student needs greater expertise than they can provide. Partly on the model of the barefoot therapist (Southgate and Randall 1978), tutors who do their work of teaching and tutoring and are open to the needs of students inevitably find themselves in counselling relationships with them. For this model to work there are a number of requirements to be met and other implications:

(1) there needs to be a policy decision to set up a counselling service on this model;
(2) sufficient individuals from across the institution need to identify themselves or be identified to be able to fulfil this role;
(3) training is essential;
(4) on-going consultative support/supervision is necessary; and
(5) the system needs caretaking.

There are a number of models for training tutors in counselling skills (Ratigan 1986). The initial training is not time-consuming and is all the more effective if it is part of an integrated, coherent, institution-wide staff training and development programme, which will imbue the whole tutor-training effort with more credibility. One of the most useful models is where a student counselling service can contribute to an effective academic staff training and development programme. Such a programme can act as a conduit for transferring the insights and skills of the counsellors into the wider institution.

Future developments

The role of student counselling in the 1990s

There are important forces at work in British society which provide the bases for considering the future of counselling in higher education. Because of the impact of government policies, student counselling, like all other aspects of higher education, is at a crossroads as it moves into the last decade of the century. There is growing professional unease about the actual practice of counselling in this sector as well as external pressures to change and become more accountable.

Student counselling services in Britain have grown up in a somewhat piecemeal manner. They have often been called into existence as a result of shifting alliances between groups of academic and administrative staff and student-union officials. The services have tended to occupy marginal positions in institutions with counsellors often spending most, if not all, of their time seeing clients rather than being involved in institutional processes and politics. By the end of the 1980s there was a strong current running through all institutions of higher education which asked of all activities: are they giving value for money and, more crucially, are they necessary? For a long time the peripheral positioning of many student counselling services kept them out of the management's, and especially the accountant's, gaze, save at moments of acute financial crisis or when extra staffing or resources were being sought. The changed agenda now brings into focus many important issues regarding appraisal and evaluation against a background of permanent questioning about value for money (Breakwell 1987).

It has long been recognized that the special circumstances central to all forms of casework based upon the interaction of one human being with another pose risks and dangers for both client and counsellor. Supervision is an essential component of the helping process. It acts as a safeguard for all concerned and helps to ensure good levels of practice. There will be a growing tendency for institutions to demand performance reviews not only of academic and scientific workers but also of their student-service personnel. As far as student counsellors are concerned there will be both quantitative and qualitative dimensions to these evaluation procedures. It will no longer be possible for counsellors to hide behind their relative peripheral obscurity claiming to be above such matters because of the need to preserve confidentiality. Numbers do not need to have names attached to them. Institutions will want to know what their counsellors are doing: how many clients, how many sessions per client, course affiliations, gender distributions, treatment outcomes.

Wise managers will want to begin to frame institutional policies for their counselling services. To do this they will need quantitative information. They will also want qualitative indicators such as student and staff perceptions of the counselling service role and practice. Those counsellors who have embraced the peripheral role, perhaps often thinking that they had no choice, will need to develop proactive ways in which they can help their institutions understand the somewhat arcane world they inhabit professionally, especially as it is practised in higher education with all its idiosyncratic rituals, understandings, and pressures. Perhaps the most important understanding is that it often takes time for change to occur. Not to move in this direction risks the weakening of the provision of counselling services that already exists. It will be important, then, for student counsellors themselves to take the initiative and draw attention to the importance of their work not only for the individuals helped but also for the health and welfare of the whole institution. Student counsellors have to recognize, however, that their services, no matter how well justified on economic grounds, are ultimately based on a moral imperative that sees such provision as important because it is an expression of the belief that human beings matter.

There are two major models facing student counselling services in the 1990s: havens for the walking wounded or centres for educational and personal development. There are many forces at work in favour of the former and only a few for the latter. Given the shrinking resources available, and the pressures on individual staff and students, it is not surprising that many counsellors see themselves usefully occupied in seemingly endless one-to-one sessions. The challenge being posed in this chapter is to counsellors to consider adopting a model in which they are more strategically and selectively involved in the political life of their institutions. Although lacking the immediacy and the drama of individual work, it may well lead to more powerful long-term results and, arguably, will benefit more students.

References

Association for Student Counselling (undated) *The Role of the Counsellor*, Rugby: British Association for Counselling.

Breakwell, G. M., (1987) 'The evaluation of student counselling: a review of the literature 1962–86', *British Journal of Guidance and Counselling* 15(2): 131–9.

Cox, J. L. (1983) 'Group psychotherapy for university students: progress and problems', *British Journal of Guidance and Counselling* 11(1): 91–8.

Crighton, J. L. (1979) 'Group work with students', in A. Wilkinson (ed.) *Student Health Practice*, London: Pitman Medical.

Crowther, R. H. (1984) 'Is student counselling a profession?', *British Journal of Guidance and Counselling* 12(2): 124–31.

de Board, R. (1978) *The Psychoanalysis of Organizations*, London: Tavistock Publications.

Hazell, J. (1982) 'The unconscious significance of some motivational blockages in students at university', *British Journal of Guidance and Counselling* 10(1): 62–73.

Hope, D. A. L. (1985) 'Counsellor stress, and burnout', unpublished MA dissertation, University of Reading.

Hunter-Brown, I. (1979) 'Psychoanalytically orientated psychotherapy', in A. Wilkinson (ed.) *Student Health Practice*, London: Pitman Medical.

Jones, E. (1987) 'Counselling in the 1990s', *Association for Student Counselling Newsletter*, June: 1–3.

Knight, L. (1986) *Talking to a Stranger*, London: Fontana.

Main, A. (1980) *Encouraging Effective Learning*, Edinburgh: Scottish Academic Press.

Malleson, N. B. (1965) *A Handbook of British Student Health Services*, London: Pitman Medical.

Newsome, A., Thorne, B. J., and Wyld, K. L. (1973) *Student Counselling in Practice*, London: London University Press.

Noonan, E. (1983) *Counselling Young People*, London: Methuen.

——(1986) 'The impact of the institution on psychotherapy', *Psychoanalytic Psychotherapy* 2(2): 121–30.

Pashley, B. W. (1976) 'The life (and death?) of a student counselling service', *British Journal of Guidance and Counselling* 4(1): 49–58.

Priestley, P., McGuire, J., Flegg, D., Hemsley, V., and Welham, D. (1978) *Social Skills and Personal Problem Solving: A Handbook of Methods*, London: Tavistock Publications.

Raaheim, K. and Wankowski, J. A. (1981) *Helping Students to Learn at University*, Bergen: Sigma Forlag.

Ratigan, B. J. (1986) 'Counsellors and staff development: models of tutor training in tertiary educational settings', *British Journal of Guidance and Counselling* 14(2): 190–3.

Rogers, C. R. (1969) *Freedom to Learn: A View of What Education Might Become*, Columbus, Ohio: Charles E. Merrill.

Salzberger-Wittenberg, I., Henry, G., and Osborne, E. (1983) *The Emotional Experience of Learning and Teaching*, London: Routledge & Kegan Paul.

Southgate, J. and Randall, R. (1978) *The Barefoot Psychoanalyst*, London: Association of Karen Horney Psychoanalytic Counsellors.

Thorne, B. J. (1979) 'The study-skills workshop', *British Journal of Guidance and Counselling* 7(1): 101–6.

Walker, J. (1979) 'Student counselling services', in A. Wilkinson (ed.) *Student Health Practice*, London: Pitman Medical.

Wilson, A. (1980) 'Group sessions for postgraduate students', *British Journal of Guidance and Counselling* 8(2): 237–40.

Woolfe, R., Murgatroyd, S., and Rhys, S. (1987) *Guidance and Counselling in Adult and Continuing Education*, Milton Keynes: Open University Press.

Zwingmann, C. A. A. and Gunn, D. G. (1983) *Uprooting and Health: Psycho-social Problems of Students from Abroad*, Geneva: Division of Mental Health, World Health Organization.

Chapter eleven

Counselling in the workplace

Michael Megranahan

Introduction

The earliest example of helping services in the workplace is the welfare department. The welfare department can be traced back to the early 1900s, where employers encouraged mature employees (often managers) to 'look after' the welfare of their employees. Whilst welfare departments continue to exist, mainly in larger organizations, they tend to be seen as a legacy of an earlier time. The actual term 'welfare' has been described as having connotations of charity, something which can be regarded as a handicap (Orlans and Shipley 1983).

It was from the welfare department that the personnel department evolved and employees still tend to regard the personnel department as the place where help for problems can be found. However, fewer and fewer personnel specialists today see welfare as part of their role. Personnel has assumed more of a management function in recent years and the people in this role, whilst sympathetic to employee problems, tend to regard these as secondary to business issues.

The occupational health department within organizations has often indirectly provided a form of counselling service. Ask any occupational health nurse about the mental health of the organization's employees and you will receive a comprehensive picture. However, as Orlans (1986) has reported, occupational-health nurses are rarely trained in counselling. In her survey of thirty-five large UK organizations, thirty-two with occupational-health departments, none of the nurses had undergone extensive counselling training and only a few had been on short counselling-skills training courses. Where employees identify a specific in-house resource to be appropriate to discuss problems, they will use such a resource. This clearly leaves the untrained recipient in a difficult position.

Other examples of counselling services within the workplace have been identified by earlier studies. In 1971 the British Institute of Management conducted a survey of 200 firms in the UK enquiring about their provisions for health care. Some 62 per cent offered regular medical checks for some of their managers at set intervals, and 5 per cent offered personal counselling services. The survey did not enlarge on what personal counselling entailed but is indicative of some early initiatives in this area. Industrial chaplains may also fulfil a counselling role and in the mid-1970s, Prentice (1976) reported there to be 150 full-time and 450 part-time chaplains.

In 1974 Shell Chemicals introduced an in-company counselling service for 3,000 employees in Cheshire. The year 1975 saw liaison between MIND and Plessey, and the subsequent provision of an external counselling-service. This later became known as 'Stress at Work', a group of people who continue to provide external counselling-services to businesses in the Northampton area. Other examples of companies employing a full-time counsellor include Times Newspapers, Shell International, some hospitals and police forces, and a number of trade unions such as the Royal College of Nurses. The first employee-assistance programmes (one type of counselling service for employees: see p. 181–2) in the UK were established in 1981 in Control Data's EAP and Singer Link-Miles. Another similar programme has since started in the Post Office. Additional *ad hoc* external counselling-services are provided by a variety of consultancies and academic institutions such as Sheffield University.

In 1977 the Standing Conference for the Advancement of Counselling, the forerunner of the British Association for Counselling (BAC) published the first book that discussed the need for and application of counselling at work (Watts 1977). Matters have not progressed very far since this time in terms of the acceptance and application of counselling in the workplace. Although many more examples of the use of counselling in the workplace exist than those given above, the main influence for introducing and keeping services of this kind appears to be historical, i.e. we have had this service for some time so let us retain it; head-office directives, i.e. we have the service in the States so why not in the UK; or someone in a senior position within a company who believes in the value of counselling and is prepared to push for it. It is only slowly that organizations are recognising the need for and benefits of counselling, and subsequently meeting this need.

Issues

There are a number of issues that concern counselling in the workplace. These relate to (a) the counsellor's ability to be effective; (b) confusion as to what constitutes counselling; and (c) factors that prohibit the potential for the progress of counselling in the workplace. The following discussion covers the traditional concerns associated with counselling in organizations, for example confidentiality; and examines the reasons and issues surrounding the limited use of counselling within organizations.

The use of counselling skills in the workplace

Whilst the development of workplace counselling services has been slow there has been a growth in counselling-skills training, primarily for managers and supervisors. This activity has greatly increased the acceptance of the term counselling in the workplace, but at the same time has led to confusion and controversy as to where counselling skills stop and counselling begins. Where counselling skills are being acquired for a specific purpose, such as general communication-skills, interviewing skills, performance-appraisal interviews and so on, then counselling-skills courses should enhance the manager's skills.

However, where managers' expectations on completion of a short skills training course lead them to regard themselves as counsellors, consequently equipped to deal with employees' personal concerns, problems are likely to emerge. The manager may fail to recognize the point at which referral of an employee is necessary, and the potential damage that can be done to both the manager and employee if the discussion begins to get out of the manager's depth. This failure may be attributed to two sources: first, the manager wanting or believing that he or she should personally help the employee resolve the problem, thereby disregarding any guidance given on the training course; and/or second, the training course failing to provide any guidance in this area and subsequent support.

If these two factors are adequately dealt with, the manager should also have the skills and knowledge to make an effective referral. Training should also have helped the manager to know how to identify and assess the appropriate resource for his referral. The consideration of ways in which a referral network can be established and validated is also important and an area that is very neglected.

Managers who are properly trained and clear about their objectives for the training should be clear about the limitations of their counselling in their role. Counselling-skills training can be beneficial to the employee and organization where managers recognize (or are confronted with) an employee with a problem, talk constructively and sensitively to the employee, and either help the employee manage his or her problem or are able to make an effective referral to a trained counsellor.

A relationship of this kind, between the manager (or any other employee – it should not be regarded exclusively as a managerial role) with counselling skills and counselling resources, keeps the boundaries between the two areas distinct, and enables good practice to take place. To achieve this the quality of counselling-skills training-courses needs to be high and it also needs to recognize the environment within which the manager is required to work. For the latter, for instance, the course should deal with issues of confidentiality, contracting, and record-keeping, what to do if the working environment is open plan, and how to recognize problems before they become unmanageable.

Counselling-skills courses can provide an excellent skills base for people but they often fail to consider the person's work environment and the need for consistency in applying counselling skills. Also, counselling skills should be moulded into the person's existing style. If these issues are not considered on the course and the manager's style or behaviour changes as a result of the course, employees may be suspicious and the counselling skills undermined.

Another major issue that needs to be addressed is how to help employers determine which counselling-skills courses are appropriate for their needs. Employers need to be clear about their own objectives and the context in which the person they send on the course is required to use the skills. Trainers who do not help an employer in this way are failing in their responsibility to the employer, the participant, and the employee who will be at the receiving end. Guidance is needed in order to provide employers with the confidence to train staff in the use of counselling skills, understand how and where the skills may be best used, and be prepared to support the use of these skills in a workplace environment.

Confidentiality

Where a person is in the role of counsellor, whether it be the employee's manager, or a professional counsellor working within the organization or providing external resources, the issue of confidentiality needs to be looked at from two perspectives: first, as a manager (or person fulfilling a counselling role), and second, as a counsellor.

Some organizations and managers find it difficult to accept that an employee would want to speak to someone in confidence. This may suggest an insecurity on the part of the third party (i.e. manager or organization) or a mistrust of how the content of interviews will be used. It is up to the person in the role of counsellor to reassure and educate the third party of the nature of this confidence. Reassurance will also be needed for employees who are also likely to be suspicious. Such a process will need to be ongoing for all parties as different issues arise. Without the principle of confidentiality and reassurance of it, a counselling service is not likely to succeed or be respected.

Differences are likely to exist in the extent to which confidentiality will apply. A manager in the counselling role, for instance, has a responsibility to the organization as well as to the employee, and the boundary between the two needs to be clear. Consequently, if a manager is told in an interview by an employee that the latter has been stealing from the company and the employee feels unable to disclose the matter personally, the manager is likely to feel that it is necessary to take some kind of action. The employee should be informed what this action will be and the reasons why it is being taken. If at all possible the manager should let the employee know that action will be necessary before the employee informs him or her of this type of problem, thereby preventing the need for a trust to be seen to be betrayed, the employee feeling cheated and the manager feeling guilty. However, an employee who discusses with a manager his marital problems (before referral, if appropriate) and whose job performance is unaffected should expect this to go no further than the interview. No-one else needs to know.

The counsellor, on the other hand, either working within the organization or a resource to it, may adopt a different approach, recognizing the employee's need to tell someone and desire to resolve the problem. This should involve discussing the employee's options. The counsellor may either not inform the organization, choosing to work with the employee to deal with the problem, or adopt a similar position to that described for a manager. This does not make the counsellor's responsibility to the organization any less than the manager's. The way of dealing with the issue is different, a difference consistent with the bounds of confidentiality within which each should be expected to work. The only time when confidentiality will be broken by a counsellor is when clients are a potential danger to themselves or others. (This is consistent with the BAC's Code of Ethics.) However, some other codes of ethics may prevent a counsellor from taking this type of action.

Conflict of interests (individual versus employer) and hence confidentiality are often put forward as reasons why counselling cannot function effectively within an organization. These aspects are put forward by both counsellors and organizations. Conflicts will occur and pressure will be put on counsellors to breach confidentiality, but only where the boundaries have not been clearly drawn or where misunderstanding exists. There is a responsibility on both parties (employer and counsellor) to negotiate where this boundary should exist, and if this is unacceptable to either party, one or other of them is not ready to provide or receive counselling services in the workplace.

Evaluation

This single phrase has been for a long time the stumbling-block for progress of counselling services in the workplace. Organizations want to see a quantifiable return for their investment and counselling is no different. Evaluation is easier when a valued employee has a problem which is affecting work performance and the situation has become 'public'. If counselling is able to help such employees and restore them to their former health, then there may be public acknowledgement of the benefits provided by counselling. Examples of this kind are insufficient to make a lasting impact and suggest a crisis perspective of counselling. This detracts from the preventive role that counselling can and does play where help can be accessed early.

Data are available to demonstrate the need for preventive counselling, including, for example, Goldsmith (1982), who suggested the cost to the UK of stress-related absence from work to be approximately £3,000 million per annum. The number of divorces and the extent of alcohol abuse in Britain also add up to a significant cost to industry. Employers do not appreciate that employees are a frail resource whose mental health can affect the organization's productivity and morale. Communicating this message is both difficult and frustrating. Many employers still do not recognize that their employees work within a stressful environment and therefore need support, and many managers still adhere to the attitude of 'if the weak can't make it, then we don't want them' – this despite considerable research evidence demonstrating the adverse affects of stress for the organization as well as for individuals (for example, Cooper 1983; Aroba and James 1987).

Attitudes are changing slowly but it will continue to be a lengthy process. Some organizations may have a culture or a senior employee who is more receptive to the introduction of counselling, and here the issue of evaluation is secondary to the values associated with helping employees. Where this ethos is not present the counsellor is likely to be hitting his or her head against a brick wall and should perhaps direct his or her energies elsewhere. For these organizations, even a neat and valid equation (which does not exist despite years of research in the USA to find one) demonstrating the value of investment in counselling would not be persuasive enough.

Counselling does help an organization by protecting and maintaining what should be its most valuable resource, its employees. This can be seen in areas of reduced absenteeism and staff turnover, improved morale and communications, fewer accidents, and insurance claims. The University of Manchester Institute of Science and Technology (UMIST) is currently engaged in a research project examining these very issues. Until this and other work is complete, counsellors must work hard to convince others of their effectiveness through practical demonstrations.

Introducing counselling services: anticipating and dealing with the responses of management and trade unions

In addition to the need for counselling to be able to demonstrate through evaluation that it is an effective resource that organizations should actively consider, counsellors need to be proactive in promoting and consolidating their services. To achieve this there are potentially three groups within any organization that the counsellor needs to focus on: managers, trade unions, and employees. Each group will have its own perspective of a counselling service that includes both positive and negative elements. This section will focus on managers and trade unions, and employees will be discussed in the section on 'Principles'.

Counsellors often fail to recognize the unique viewpoint of each group and fail to anticipate the problems put forward by each group, consequently finding it difficult to overcome them. It is useful to look at the needs of each group since they illustrate many of the issues that counselling in the workplace raises for these groups, issues that need to be addressed and overcome for counselling to be effective and successful in this context.

Managers

Managers and supervisors react to the introduction of a counsellor in many different ways. A few may respond positively, seeing the counsellor as an ally in helping employees, some of whom may have had problems for years but have remained out of the reach of management. However, the general response is usually one of hostility or suspicion.

Managers often see the counsellor as a soft option for employees with consequent disruption to the manager's disciplinary control over the workforce. Managers may for instance suspect that employees will use the counsellor as a protection against action for poor performance, claiming that this is due to emotional or alcohol problems and that disciplinary action should be excused. Other managers will deny the existence of problems; regard the counsellor's remit as dealing only with people who have serious emotional problems, and therefore refuse to admit that employees with such problems could be working for them successfully.

Some managers will consider the care of their employees to be their sole responsibility and see the introduction of a counsellor as an indication of failure. Still other managers will regard themselves as counsellors or amateur psychologists who have been 'counselling' for years and are therefore providing all the help that employees require.

The counsellor needs to show that he or she is not, nor likely to be, anti-management. The counsellor has a separate and distinct area of responsibility and authority that does not infringe into the manager's area. Counsellors that fail to recognize and observe boundaries of this type will quickly find their role untenable. The counsellor may make recommendations to management about work practices or policies but the final decision about what actually happens in the workplace stays with the manager.

A counsellor can enhance the manager's role and this needs to be highlighted. A counsellor can increase the time of the manager and free emotional energy by dealing with employees' personal problems. The manager's responsibility is to make sure that employees work to their fullest ability in order to increase productivity and reduce costs. Managers' commitment both to their staff as people and to their effectiveness in their work will, if they are enlightened, mean that they will be concerned that the staff are adequately supported if, for example, they are struggling to come to terms with a bereavement or a broken marriage. However, they may not have the time or skills to become their counsellors, nor will it be appropriate in role terms. The counsellor can relieve the manager of this task and enable the manager to focus on job performance, instituting disciplinary action where required, uncomplicated by delving into personal problem areas.

Managers may be reluctant to take disciplinary action where it is known that an employee has a personal problem, preferring merely to refer the employee to the counsellor. It is important that in-company counsellors and managers understand the neutral role of the counsellor in this context and the beneficial outcome of a manager drawing a firm line when an employee's job performance is unsatisfactory. Motivation for change often follows clear limit-setting by managers. Counsellors for their part should recognize this need and that effective integration of disciplinary action and counselling is possible and beneficial.

The counsellor also needs to help the manager recognize that the counsellor is there as a resource for themselves. Counsellors need to remember that their role is neutral and that managers also have problems. Indeed, their stress levels are often especially acute. However, a manager may need additional encouragement to seek help, and to see such a request in terms of strength and not weakness.

Gaining support from management

Self referrals are likely to be the most frequent type of contact a counsellor will have with employees, and these will increase with time. The help and trust of management also needs to be enlisted in order to ensure that the service is used effectively for the good of the individual and organization. This can be done by making training available to managers and supervisors. The counsellor is able to involve the manager in the process of getting an employee appropriate help. Formal training sessions that advise the manager of the counsellor's role, types of indicators that suggest that an employee has a problem linked to documentation of any poor job performance, ways in which managers can approach employees without causing them to become defensive, and methods of referral to the counsellor – all are very crucial to a successful and supported counselling service.

No referrals should be mandatory from management, but the manager is in a position, if job performance is suffering, to continue normal disciplinary actions if the employee does not seek help and job performance does not improve. Managers should be encouraged to consider that the option of counselling intervention may pay dividends, before disciplinary action is instigated, although this may not always be possible, especially in cases of what is classified as gross misconduct. Equally, if the manager knows that the employee is experiencing personal problems that do not affect job performance, the manager may recommend seeing the counsellor but would have no recourse to disciplinary action. The counsellor should also make it clear that feedback following management referrals is likely to be limited at best. The employee can however be encouraged to inform his or her manager, without revealing details, that contact has been made.

Informal contacts between the counsellor and employees at all levels are also important. Being visible in a low-key way that does not distract people from their tasks or lead them to feel that they have been singled out is helpful in reducing stigma and increasing confidence in a counselling service.

The counsellor should also endeavour to keep in touch with upper management. This serves two purposes. First, it enables the counsellor to inform management, whilst maintaining confidentiality, of his or her activities. This is an important and ongoing educative role. Managers change and if the counsellor does not work to inform new people of the value of the counsellor's role, then it is likely that the role will lose visibility and credibility. Counsellors also have a unique opportunity to assess information from all levels of the organization and feed back appropriate strategies and ideas for constructive change. Managers are only likely to be receptive to this type of input concerning organizational change when the service has shown that it is organizationally effective, for instance in reducing absenteeism and labour turnover.

Second, the counsellor, in turn, should also be prepared to answer questions from senior management concerning the service (whilst maintaining confidentiality) and respond to particular requests for help and assistance with specific employees or organizational problems. An employee may, for instance, refuse to see a counsellor and consequently the manager will need help and guidance on the best way to help the employee; or a group of employees may, on account of operational reasons, need to be retrained and resistance to these changes is envisaged. The counsellor may be asked to play a facilitating role to enable the change to take place more smoothly.

The counsellor must also, where an employee has given permission, be prepared to advise management of that employee's progress towards resolving a problem.

Working with trade unions

The response of union representatives to the introduction of a counsellor is likely to be the same as that of managers; some will be receptive, others suspicious and hostile. Perhaps the single most crucial question that the counsellor will need to overcome with the trade union is one of trust.

Where a counsellor is employed by the company he or she needs to demonstrate loyalty to employees' interests and needs as well as to the company's need to maintain productivity. Where a counsellor's role overlaps with existing in-company functions such as personnel, occupational health, or trade union, the union may be particularly suspicious of the company's motives. This is especially true in the case of broad-brush employee-assistance programmes (see p. 181–2). Questions may be asked about the recording and storing of information and whether it is being transferred on to personnel files. As there should be no occasions when a counsellor would transfer any information, this should be made clear by the counsellor.

Another concern is where the trade union sees the counselling service as another fad, or an attempt to erode union power, especially where there is a history of management trying to introduce different schemes for employees. Such suspicions are likely to be reinforced if the union has not been involved in introducing the service.

To help overcome some of the possible problems, trade-union representatives should be invited to the same training sessions that the managers are attending. This enables each group to see that neither is being told something the other is not. Discussion at the end of these types of training sessions also encourages co-operation for the good of the employee who subsequently seeks help once the service is up and running.

The counsellor should also work with any services offered by the trade union and not attempt to circumvent union policies and procedures. Employees may prefer to consult with a counsellor rather than the union but employees should always be encouraged to explore this route first where it is appropriate to do so. In much the same way the counsellor needs to work to foster understanding from management so the counsellor should do the same with union leaders. Doing this reduces the opportunity for misunderstanding and the counselling service being caught in the middle of management–union disagreements. The counselling service must be seen to be neutral.

Principles

Introducing the service to employees

The problems that employees either bring to the workplace or experience within it are many and varied. It is not possible for an individual to remain unaffected at work by problems based in the home or vice versa. This invasion will and does occur, no matter how great the effort by the individual to prevent it taking place or being detected.

Just as the problems each person is likely to experience are varied, so are the associated emotional responses and visible manifestations which alert others to the existence of a problem:

— depression may occur some months after an employee has experienced a bereavement of someone close to him or her;
— anxiety may pervade all aspects of a person's life on hearing that redundancies are to be made;
— anger may be evident in an employee who has received a poor performance-appraisal;
— an employee who exhibits a pattern of Monday and Friday absences may be exhibiting signs of an alcohol problem;
— a person who is irritable and moody with colleagues may be experiencing relationship difficulties at home;
— periods of sickness which fall into a regular pattern may be associated with specific and recurring aspects in the employee's job which are stressful and with which the employee cannot cope – for example, departmental meetings, presentations, deadlines.

The response to an employee experiencing problems of any kind can be made at two distinct levels: first, by someone within the workplace trained in counselling skills – for example, line or personnel manager; and second, by a designated and trained counsellor. Ideally, both levels should exist and this is the case in some organizations. The employee may seek out help or help may be offered and/or extended. Where an employee's job performance begins to be affected, it falls within the scope of the organization to intervene and offer the opportunity of help and assistance to the employee. If this is not done or the help is rejected, then the organization needs to make a decision concerning the acceptability of the specific circumstances and look at other options – for example, discipline, time off, reduced duties, and so on.

There are a number of general principles which apply to any workplace counselling system:

(1) Any counselling service needs to have the support of top management in order to be accepted and survive.

(2) A written policy statement of overall philosophy concerning the health and well-being of employees or which addresses specific features, for example alcohol, should be available. This creates a positive climate in which employees can seek help.

(3) Managers and supervisors should be trained to identify employees with problems at an early stage and know how to confront them and make referral to the counsellor.

(4) Access to the counselling service should be available to all staff at all locations.

(5) The service should be credible in the eyes of the employer, managers, trade unions, and employees.

(6) Confidentiality should be explicitly stated, accepted, and understood by everyone.

(7) A continuation of care should be available, which includes referral and follow-up.

(8) The emphasis should be on self referral.

(9) The counselling service should be independent of any specific or single treatment-centre.

(10) A system should exist for evaluating the counselling service.

The counsellor needs to find a way of communicating the service to all employees on an ongoing basis; otherwise it will be forgotten. Although the number of self referrals received is the best way to assess whether the service is being accepted by employees, the counsellor needs to think of marketing the service in ways that will increase its accessibility for all employees.

Publicizing the service can be done in an number of ways, for example company newsletters, and although word-of-mouth recommendations are perhaps the favoured growth of counselling services in organizations where this type of service is new and unusual, this cannot be relied upon. Counselling still carries a stigma associated with people not being able to cope, and this needs to be reduced, particularly in organizations where the community is very close and the grapevine 'well oiled'. If the service is openly supported by the organization and access is freely available for all types of problems, then this will help. The counsellor also needs to be seen, since employees are more likely to contact someone they have met, even if only fleetingly.

Briefings of small groups of employees covering the scope and nature of the service are useful. Travelling to all company sites demonstrates that it is not just a head-office service. Visiting a night shift serves a similar purpose. It is not enough to have a title and office and wait for people to use the service. People need to be encouraged to do so and communication of the service and its personnel is vital to this.

The counsellor in the workplace

Many counsellors will not have worked in a private-employment context and should be aware that every counsellor–client contact is likely to have organizational implications. If this is lost sight of, the counsellor will find the service alienated by both management and unions.

The counsellor who is accustomed to seeing a client on a one-to-one basis needs to see the client in an organizational context and anticipate any problems others may have with the counsellor's assessment and recommendations for treatment. Recommending a course of counselling of once a week for 10 weeks in office hours to a production manager who has self-referred, during a peak production time when the concern was not interfering with his or her work and therefore not visible to the management, would not be understood. An alternative would be to refer to an external resource that could see him in the evenings.

The counsellor needs to keep up to date with available resources and assess their quality since it is impossible to attempt to see everyone and deal with everything. This is what is expected of the counsellor, however, and to meet this expectation the counsellor needs to draw on other resources. The counsellor also needs to be familiar with organizational structures and channels of communication if he or she is to be able to influence management to make changes.

Most counsellors in companies will work alone and will therefore need to look carefully at their own support, environmental as well as professional. Negotiations at the beginning of the introduction of a counselling service should include accommodation, its location, clerical support, answerphones, and so on. Employers often find these difficult to understand and accept. To provide a counsellor with an office – a basic tool of the trade – is often resisted by an employer who does not appreciate the need for privacy. Internal politics can easily get in the way of providing an effective service and reflect a lack of commitment to the service by the organization. Lastly, a careful balance needs to be kept between personal and professional life, perhaps taking some of the direction they provide to their clients.

Specific applications of counselling in the workplace

Redundancy counselling

The introduction of redundancy counselling is seen by some, for example, Novarra (1986), as the single most significant area of activity contributing to the acceptance of counselling in the workplace. As a term this is certainly true. As a way of increasing the acceptance of specialists this is true. As a way of helping some line and personnel managers recognize that the impact and repercussions of redundancy could not be alleviated by severance payments used in isolation this is true. Whether or not counselling takes place as opposed to the use of counselling skills and coaching is less clear. And it is this last aspect which has potentially given rise to most problems.

For many in the work context, counselling is synonymous with redundancy, an aspect which counsellors should work hard to dispel or else be tarnished with this until the demand for these services declines, at which time people working in this area are likely to find themselves redundant with few transferable skills relevant to counselling.

Redundancy counselling has shown how the use of specialist resources can assist organizations deal with discarded employees and encompasses advice, information, and guidance. This type of service is also supported and complemented by the organization's existing management and personnel. Counselling should however be extended to the remaining or stable employee population. Real progress in the workplace will only be made once counsellors are invited through the front door to meet people whilst they are experiencing the stresses and strains, challenges, and opportunities of their chosen work organization. Progress in this area is slow but there have been some notable advances, as discussed elsewhere in this chapter.

Redundancy counselling is described in more detail in Chapter 18 by Milne.

Alcohol counselling

The UK has seen agencies such as Alcohol Concern establish a government-funded workplace unit to promote the adoption of educative programmes and policies in the workplace. The Confederation of British Industry has produced a booklet in conjunction with Turning Point on the misuse of drugs, and the Industrial Society and IPM also have a booklet concerned with alcohol policies. There is an ever-increasing number of documents being produced by industrially recognized bodies, something which would have been unheard of 5 years ago.

Policy and education initiatives have been followed closely by the growth of private treatment centres. The value of these *vis-à-vis* NHS or voluntary units is debatable and an area that cannot be entered into here. Suffice it to say that generally private facilities are not available unless the employee has private medical insurance or the company is prepared to pay for treatment.

A number of companies do have their own in-house counselling services which can help employees cope with alcohol or drug abuse. However, where they rely on self referral only, they are less likely to be successful than if training is provided to first-line supervisors. Training should encompass identifying employees whose job performance has been noted as poor or irregular, approaching the employee on this basis only and using counselling skills within a disciplinary framework to motivate the employee to request or seek help.

An approach of this kind should be applied to all employees where poor job-performance has been recorded and not only where an alcohol or drug problem is suspected. Where this is applied consistently (supported by policy) it will be seen to be fair, consistent, and objective. As mentioned, actions of this kind are necessary to help the employee seek help and the supervisor is therefore actively involved in the intervention process and supporting the specialist counselling agency or counsellor.

The actual help the employee receives is itself an area of contention between different schools of thought. The majority of drug/alcohol counsellors subscribe to the disease model, while others regard controlled drinking to be a realistic objective. For the former counsellors, any other problems the person may present are seen as deflecting from the main and only problem of alcohol or drug abuse. These counsellors tend to regard the abuse as the cause of all other problems. The other school of thought, however, will tend to start with the 'other' problems – for example, marital problems, financial difficulties, job stress, and so on – advocating that once these are resolved the reason for the alcohol or drug abuse will be removed.

There is insufficient space to enter into this debate fully and the above is a very simple statement of the differences (see Chapter 23 for a fuller discussion of this debate). Counsellors and employers should be aware of the differences and consequent forms of treatment. This is particularly important if the existing trend develops further and alcohol and drug abuse is the key to unlock the organization's door to counselling as it has done in North America.

The area of alcohol and drug abuse is likely to be an important area for counselling in the workplace in the future. This is particularly true if the UK follows the pattern of growth seen in America, growth which has seen the development of employee assistance programmes, an area examined next.

Employee Assistance Programmes

Employee Assistance Programmes (EAP) were developed in North America in the early 1960s as a response to the adverse effects of alcohol in the workplace. A number of companies providing an EAP found that employees had other personal issues which needed help, counselling, and support and which also affected work performance. Consequently what has been termed 'broad-brush' EAPs were established in the early 1970s.

An EAP is essentially a short-term counselling and referral agency available to employees and their families. They are usually structured to provide an immediate 24-hour response to any personal concern or crisis, and are supported by a comprehensive referral network of community and private counselling resources.

EAPs were first introduced into Britain in 1981 through the influence of American parent companies and copying the structures already established. This structure includes, for some EAP services, autonomy from other in-company functions such as personnel, an advantage over functions like welfare. Outside provision of this service is also a cost-effective way for employers to extend counselling to employees.

The essential features of an EAP consist of the following:

(1) immediate access to trained professional counsellors;
(2) total confidentiality;
(3) training by EAP counsellors of line managers and supervisors in confronting and referring employees where job performance is affected due to personal problems;
(4) support to line managers and supervisors in dealing with troubled employees;
(5) efficient and professional referral capability;
(6) autonomy from the organization, i.e. not part of personnel department.

The EAP introduces counselling 'up-front' to employers and employees with a well-proven structure for providing the service. It is therefore one example of how counselling is being accepted in the workplace as a preventive and responsive service. Whether or not this area will continue to expand or be confined to US companies will be an area to watch in the next 10 years.

Future developments

Counselling in the workplace continues to struggle to gain a strong and consistent foothold. The 1980s have seen an increasing interest by employers in the use of counselling skills as a valuable managerial skill. Provided managers do not abuse these skills and acknowledge their limitations, then counsellors will be increasingly recognized for their contribution to employees' well-being.

Real progress will only be made when it is possible to demonstrate that an investment in an in-company counselling resource provides a return to the employer. Research aimed at giving valid evaluation of this area is beginning in a number of universities and management colleges in Britain. Once the results of these initiatives are available, employers will be in a position to assess for themselves the benefits – or otherwise – of counselling.

Employers who have decided to introduce counselling are often confused by the type of services available. There is a real need for a neutral professional body which can both advise organizations in this area and lay down agreed standards of good practice.

In addition counsellors need to be able to offer and demonstrate valid, professional, and recognized knowledge, experience, and qualifications. This also applies to all the different specialisms – for example, career counselling, redundancy counselling, and so on. If this is not achieved then industry is likely to be vulnerable to unqualified and unprofessional practice with little or no resort to action. There are already examples of companies extending their services into areas (where money can be made) like stress management and employee assistance programmes, without any previous experience or knowledge. The skill, knowledge, and training to be effective, for instance, redundancy counselling are not applicable to broad based counselling applications found in employee assistance programmes.

Criteria and guidelines for employers and a register of skilled and experienced counsellors encompassing all areas of workplace counselling need to be established, perhaps by the Counselling at Work Division of the BAC. If measures of this kind are not achieved people who want to work in this area and employers wanting these services will look to other professional groups, such as that provided by the British Psychological Society, which in 1988 offered psychologists the opportunity to become Chartered – an offer which has been accepted.

Counselling is very much in vogue in the 1980s and this consequently provides a real opportunity for counsellors to make in-roads into industry and prove their worth.

References

Aroba, T. and James, K. (1987) *Pressure of Work – A Survival Guide*, New York: McGraw-Hill.

Cooper, C. L. (ed.) (1983) *Stress Research: Issues for the Eighties*, Chichester: Wiley.

Goldsmith, W. (1982) 'Introduction to 1981 Stress Conference Proceedings', in L Booth (ed.) *Stress: Source of Positive Human Performance? or Human and Economic Disaster?*, Yelding, Kent: The Stress Syndrome Foundation.

Novarra, V. (1986) 'Can a manager be a counsellor?', *Personnel Management*, June: 48–50.

Orlans, V. (1986) 'Counselling services', *Organisation Personnel Review*, 15(5): 19–23.

——and Shipley, P. (1983) 'A survey of stress management and prevention facilities in a sample of UK organisations', unpublished report of Stress Research and Control Centre, Department of Occupational Psychology, Birkbeck College, University of London.

Prentice, G. (1976) 'Faith at work. The message is the mission', *Personnel Management* 8(3): 33–6.

Watts, A. G. (ed.) (1977) *Counselling at Work: Standing Conference for the Advancement of Counselling*, London: Bedford Square Press.

Chapter twelve

Counselling skills in the context of professional and organizational growth

Barbara Pearce

Introduction

This chapter presents a case for broadening counselling training through demystifying and disseminating the use of counselling skills to a much wider group of people than has previously been envisaged by those involved in the professional practice of counselling. The use of counselling skills is seen as both a generic helping-skill and as a means to assisting professional and organizational growth. It will be argued that this is an inevitable development and that major changes have already taken place within certain sectors, in particular, within the field of education. The chapter will compare counselling with other helping strategies and consider these in the context of the needs of other professions and their clients. It will also seek to demonstrate the fundamental changes which are taking place in vocational training in Britain and the growing demand for counselling in industry and commerce. Finally, the chapter will consider the next stages in the development of counselling skills.

Background to counselling-skills development

A growing number of people are undertaking counselling-skills training and it is of value to consider reasons for this growth. Perhaps the most significant is that of social change, which is producing an inevitable increase in recognition of, and demand for, counselling. This change can be demonstrated in a number of ways. A glance at popular contemporary literature written over the last hundred years shows us that, compared with the population a century ago, individuals today face a world in which relationships are more transient, mobility has increased, and change at all levels is a much more dominating influence on our lives.

Futurist writers such as Toffler (1970) and Stonier (1978) have described the likely consequences of the enormous revolution that is occurring in terms of personal, psychological, social, and technological change. Toffler talks of 'the roaring current of change, a current so powerful today that it overturns institutions, shifts our values and shrivels our roots' (Toffler 1970: 11). Hopson and Scally (1981a: 6) state 'we are living through a period of transition – and the demands on young people and adults will be similar. People will need to be adaptable, flexible and more personally competent than at any other time in our history.' Most poignant of all, Freire writes:

> The time of epochal transition constitutes an historical 'tidal wave'. Contradictions increase between the ways of being, understanding, behaving, and valuing which belong to yesterday and other ways of perceiving and valuing which announce the future. As the contradictions deepen, the 'tidal wave' becomes stronger and its climate increasingly emotional.
>
> (Freire 1976: preface)

It is probable, however, that we are best able to register the acceleration of change, and its impact on our lives, through our own experience. Professionally and socially we are meeting new people all the time. This is very different from the experience of our grandparents, whose lives as they describe them are like the still shots from a static camera rather than the fast-wind video lives which we all lead. Our parents have faced the transition to a faster and increasingly changing lifestyle and we are the product of that transition. Our own children are growing up and adjusting to a very different life. The world has shrunk, thanks to mass and immediate communication and easy accessible travel; education is rapidly changing to accommodate to new technology, unemployment, and changing circumstances, and the young now contemplate problems such as the emergence of AIDS, anorexia, drug-taking, and crime which would have been unimaginable to the young of earlier decades, as would also the bewildering array of opportunities and choices.

Is it surprising, therefore, that help of various kinds is necessary at many different points in people's lives? Perhaps not, and at one time, such help as was required would be supplied by the extended family. With the breakdown of this unit after the Second World War and more recently with the increasing incidence of marital breakdown, a helping vacuum has been created. Society has become responsible, under the welfare system, for providing material assistance for those in need, but has singularly failed to provide, within its limited resources, for the psychological needs of those at risk. Social workers, educational and clinical psychologists, and psychiatrists have done all that is possible, given their heavy caseloads, but have been forced to work at a crisis level rather than for providing at a development level for those who have become the victims of the increasing pace of change.

It is this vacuum in the helping arena which the counselling-skills movement is able to address. There will never be unlimited resources for the provision of the level of professional counselling which the changes in society are likely to require, and professional counsellors will therefore continue to be pre-occupied with crisis demands. Although there has been some resistance to, and suspicion of, the growth of the counselling-skills movement, it is in fact a natural response to growing demand and has frequently been triggered by those professionals who recognize that by imparting some of their skills to lay people, their own work can

185

more realistically be focused upon those most in need. In addition, as access to and understanding of counselling skills increase within the population, those skills can begin to have a supportive, preventive, and developmental influence within the wider community.

During the last few decades there has been a growth in the development of helping agencies, mostly working at a voluntary level. These have included, among many, the former National Marriage Guidance Council, now known as Relate: National Marriage Guidance, the Samaritans, Gingerbread, BACUP, and local Law Centres. They serve different purposes but share the common theme of providing assistance that is not part of state provision. They arise in response to a specific need emerging over a period of time and are themselves reflections of the transition through which we are all passing. Some, for example Law Centres or Citizens Advice Bureaux, will be concerned with providing advice or information, others, like Homestart, concerned with befriending and supporting, whilst yet others will help meet client or member needs through allowing individuals to explore the meaning of their situation and then to develop the skills and strategies for managing this.

We seem to be at the threshold of a greater acceptance of both the need for help and support in general, and for counselling in particular. This has been evident in several recent radio and television news broadcasts where discussions have taken place as to the value of counselling to help victims of kidnapping in the Middle East, major fire disasters such as the one in the Bradford football stadium and the King's Cross Tube Station, and massacres such as at Hungerford.

Definitions

Before embarking on a discussion of the principles involved in counselling skills it is important to the understanding of this chapter within the context of this book that differences between my different uses of the word counselling and counselling skills are made clear. There are basically five definitions which are relevant.

Counselling as a generic helping strategy

In this context counselling is one of a number of helping strategies which individuals use throughout their lives. Everyone has some of the skills required for each strategy but will become more skilful if they are aware of the different skills involved and are able consciously to use each strategy at appropriate times. These skills and strategies will be further explored later in this chapter.

Counselling as a professional practice

Those who are involved in the professional practice of counselling use the basic skills of counselling alongside a range of specific therapeutic approaches. Their work involves working with individuals, couples, or families at a deeper level and is often carried out over a longer period of time. The counsellors concerned may work in a voluntary or paid capacity and on a full- or part-time basis.

Counselling as advice

In historic terms the word counselling is associated with giving expert advice or recommendations, most often in relation to the legal profession. This creates confusion to many newly involved in the field of personal responsibility counselling, in which a major aim is to encourage individuals to take responsibility for their own actions and to help themselves. This confusion is further exacerbated by the media and by Government agencies such as the Manpower Services Commission who use the term in both senses. Thus, for example, they will recommend individual counselling and guidance in the sense used in this book for those on the Youth Training Scheme and yet also speak of counselling people *into* jobs.

Counselling skills

Wherever this term is used within this chapter it refers to the basic skills which are common to counselling as a *generic helping-skill* and to *professional counselling*. It is not concerned with the more specific therapeutic skills involved in the latter.

Counselling-skills movement

This phrase refers to those people who use counselling skills consciously and who have had some training but who are not professional counsellors. They would not regard themselves as part of a recognized movement but are distinguishable from those who have undertaken much more rigorous training and supervision in order to practise counselling in a more professional capacity. It is in this sense that those involved are referred to as a movement in this chapter.

Principles

Counselling-skills development

The counselling-skills movement owes most to the work of Carl Rogers (1951; 1957), who describes the qualities of empathy, genuineness, and warmth which are essential to the client-centred counselling relationship and which enhance all forms of helping. These qualities were later confirmed by Truax and Carkhuff (1967). Whilst it was stated above that the counselling-skills movement is neither recognizable nor homogeneous, thanks to the work of Rogers, who could rightly be called the father of the movement, there is sufficient common ground for those who use counselling skills to communicate effectively with each other. Sutton writes 'these principles are, up to a point, the very ones that common sense might have guided us to select as important' (Sutton 1979: 208). She then shows how the teachers, social workers, and health workers whom we most value demonstrate these qualities, and adds:

if we meet with kindness, compassion, respect and consideration, and continue to meet those attitudes, we lose our sense of vulnerability, our anxiety diminishes and we are able to perceive events and situations with a vision less clouded by self-protective emotion.

(Sutton 1979: 209)

Counselling and helping

It was suggested that counselling is one of a number of generic helping-strategies, and an exploration of counselling skills leads to an exploration of those helping strategies. Many writers, probably with a professional counselling-audience in mind, turn immediately to the different helping strategies, techniques, and theories within counselling. Okun (1982: 132) summarizes these in tabular form under the headings psychodynamic, phenomenological-client centred, gestalt, behavioural, cognitive–behavioural, and Transactional Analysis. Most people involved in using counselling skills at a basic level are unlikely to require such sophistication at the time of their initial interest, but may graduate to one or more such strategies at a later stage of development or as interest in the possibilities offered by counselling become clearer.

If individuals are asked to discuss the ways in which they have recently helped other people they will identify very different circumstances, but most of the strategies can be categorized as giving information, giving advice, teaching, counselling, or taking direct action on behalf of another person. Occasionally, someone will also identify working to 'change the system' as a helping strategy. These are among the strategies used by the Counselling and Career Development Unit (CCDU) in counselling- skills training since 1976 and discussed by Hopson and Scally (1981b) and Murgatroyd (1985).

More recently, a further helping strategy has been identified by CCDU, namely that of 'reviewing' (Pearce 1987). The use of this strategy is emphasized in Profiling and Record of Achievement schemes in schools and colleges of further education and in the various youth training schemes developed by the Manpower Services Commission (Pearce *et al.* 1981). In this context, 'reviewing' is defined as a process which enables people to say things about themselves relating to past experience, present situation and feelings, and future potential and need.

A first step in developing an understanding of counselling skills is therefore to help individuals recognize the ways in which they already help others and to explore the skills common and unique to each strategy. A further step in this development might then be to examine the advantages and disadvantages of each strategy for different helping circumstances. In this way it becomes possible to become a skilled helper, using specific strategies with awareness and appropriately instead of intuitively. During this process, for example, a given individual may for the first time become aware that what he or she had previously defined as counselling was, in fact, more related to giving advice.

Such a process of learning through understanding more clearly a wide range of everyday helping strategies can also lead naturally to an understanding of the importance of encouraging persons in need of help to take responsibility for making their own decisions, so that all helping strategies are employed in a more sensitive way.

Relationship-building skills

A first step in assisting the understanding of helping strategies is through the exploration of relationship-building skills, which are fundamental to effective helping and provide the route through which sensitive helping decisions can be made. Use of these skills, which are derived from the essential qualities of warmth, empathy, and genuineness as defined by Carl Rogers (Rogers 1951; 1957), respects the autonomy of the individual and is an enabling process. As a start to understanding the skills inherent within these essential qualities, they can be translated to respect, understanding, and being yourself.

Respect

Through exploring the skills of listening for non-verbal as well as verbal signals and recognizing that this is one way of showing respect for another human being, trainees quickly graduate to recognizing the many other concrete ways in which they can demonstrate this: for example, through giving time or displaying common courtesy to any individual. A teacher might identify ways of showing respect for pupils in the classroom and a manager can similarly recognize the means of conveying respect to colleagues and customers. The skills involved in demonstrating respect for another person are the foundation for the unconditional regard and warmth defined by Rogers.

Understanding

It is often easier for trainees to grasp the notion of understanding than it is to convey empathy, especially as empathy is frequently confused with sympathy. Empathy is concerned with recognizing and understanding the feelings of another *as if* they were being experienced by oneself, whereas sympathy involves being emotionally affected by the feelings of another. In a workshop it is possible to provide structured exercises which help trainees recognize and practise the skills of identifying the feelings of others and to understand the effect which it has when someone is similarly empathetic in relation to themselves. The feeling of being unconditionally valued at the same time as identifying the elements which give rise to this feeling is a very powerful learning process.

Being yourself

The most important aspect of being yourself is the recognition that there is no single model of helping or being that is the right one. It is liberating to know that, coupled with the other two essential qualities, comes permission to be genuine, and with that, to convey all the sincerity which this implies. The major skill involved in being yourself is that of self-disclosure. It often requires practice for an individual to learn to be able to be vulnerable enough to risk disclosing experiences or feelings, and to do this in a way which is appropriate to the helping relationship.

Helping and basic counselling-skills

Although relationship-building skills enhance the helping strategies of giving information, giving advice, teaching, reviewing, taking direct action, changing the system, and are essential to counselling, each strategy also has specific skills related to it. Some of these are common to basic counselling, others quite distinct. As a starting-point, consider Table 12.1, which lists some of the key skills specific to each helping strategy. The lists are neither prescriptive nor exhaustive and there will no doubt be other skills that readers will be able to identify. The skill of 'changing systems' has not been included as it requires a complex set of organizational and political skills not relevant to this book and the skills of 'taking direct action' on behalf of another person are also omitted as this chapter is concerned with strategies which leave the client rather than the helper in control. Those skills featured in bold type are those which are common to counselling and other helping strategies. It can be seen quite clearly that strengths in a range of helping strategies provide a basis for the development of basic counselling-skills.

Table 12.1 Helping skills

Informing	*Advising*	*Teaching*	*Counselling*	*Reviewing*
Interpreting	**Listening**	Designing	**Contracting**	Contracting
	Interpreting	**Listening**	**Listening**	Listening
	Analysing	Planning	Concreteness	**Questioning**
	Clarifying	**Questioning**	Immediacy	**Summarizing**
		Summarizing	**Questioning**	**Clarifying**
		Challenging	**Summarizing**	Giving feedback
			Clarifying	Asking for feedback
			Focusing	
			Confronting	

Focusing more specifically upon those skills which are specific to counselling the following brief definitions may be useful to those who are less familiar with the counselling process:

Contracting: This is the process which would normally take place at the beginning of a counselling session and which serves to clarify the purpose, duration, and structure of the session. It may be necessary to return to this process at later stages of the session if a new direction seems to be valuable for the client. Contracting is an important means by which the client is seen to be a partner rather than the subject of the counselling session.

Concreteness: Often a client will be vague about feelings and concerns and the skill of helping the individual concerned to be more concrete may be used to overcome this. The counsellor may ask the client to give examples of occasions on which a particular feeling has been experienced or to be more specific about a situation.

Immediacy: This is the skill of enabling the client to focus on the 'here-and-now'. It may involve asking for present feelings or, more often, discussing the relationship as it exists at that moment between the counsellor and client.

Questioning: It is normal to ask 'open' as opposed to 'closed' or 'leading' questions: that is, questions which require answers which are more than one word and which provide scope for the client to determine the direction of the answer.

Summarizing: The counsellor may at times find it useful to summarize all or part of what has passed during the session or to ask the client to do this. This is a clarifying procedure for both parties and is particularly valuable at the end of the session.

Clarifying: As different opinions are held about the exact meaning of different words and phrases it is important to clarify that the counsellor and client share the same understanding. It is even more vital to ensure that the client's feelings which have been identified by the counsellor are correct.

Focusing: In covering a wide range of concerns the counsellor may find it useful to ask the client to focus upon a specific aspect of concern and to explore this in more detail.

Confronting: Within the trust that has been established in the counselling relationship the counsellor will be able to confront contradictions which occur between words and behaviour in the client or sensitively to challenge uncomfortable aspects in the life of the client.

Action skills

The final phase of any helping strategy is that of taking action, although the emphasis on action to be taken will vary for different helping strategies and for different contexts. Ideally, in all situations the decision about the action to be taken will rest with the individual concerned, but the level of support required will vary; and in the case of both counselling and reviewing the action may be broken into a series of smaller actions taken after each session rather than one single action. In counselling, although it is not always necessary for action to take place, it is important to consider with the client whether any action is required at the end of a session.

To summarize, counselling is one of a range of helping strategies, all of which require an ability to build effective relationships. In addition, each strategy has its own unique set of skills as well as some which it shares with other strategies, and each strategy has an action phase – i.e.

Phase 1 — Relationship-building

Phase 2 — Skills specific to a given strategy

Phase 3 — Action

An individual who is able to use different strategies skilfully and with awareness is likely to be a more valued and skilled helper. There will be times when it is appropriate for a counsellor to turn to advising and there will be times when someone who is reviewing will need to counsel. The professional counsellor will need to develop a set of strategies and skills beyond those described above, which will not normally be part of the 'tool kit' of the person using basic counselling-skills, and will have taken part in a much more rigorous programme of training and supervision. The essential skill of the counsellor rests in the ability to use these skills at the appropriate times and with great sensitivity. Listening with every sense and with the whole of oneself is the key to achieving this. The basic skills of counselling are summed up in the Counselling Process as defined on courses run by the Counselling and Career Development Unit (CCDU) at Leeds University (Figure 12.1).

COUNSELLING		
The Counsellor		
uses		helps the client
RELATIONSHIP BUILDING SKILLS	Respect Empathy Genuineness	*to feel understood *to understand more about how s/he feels and why
EXPLORING & CLARIFYING SKILLS	Contracting Concreteness Immediacy Summarising Questioning Focussing Confronting	*to explore understanding *to explore feelings *to consider options *to examine alternatives *to choose an alternative
ACTION SKILLS	Objective Setting Action Planning Problem Solving	*to form action plans *to do, with support, what needs to be done

Fig. 12.1 The basic skills of counselling, as defined by the CCDU, Leeds University

Mapping the field

If, as suggested, the growth of the counselling-skills movement is both an inevitable and necessary response to social change, it may be useful to consider the circumstances in which individuals may wish to explore counselling as a means of helping others, particularly as in many cases their counselling work is voluntary, or at best peripheral to the main categories and tasks as defined in their job description. Many, it would seem, are people already involved in people-oriented, helping professions such as education and the health or social services. They are people who recognize their own helping limitations and who turn to counselling-skills training as an additional means of providing help.

Others, who perhaps have successfully faced a difficult situation in their own lives, turn later to help others facing similar situations; for example, women who have suffered the loss of a breast, might through the Mastectomy Association, begin to counsel other women and assist them in coming to terms with their loss. Given some guidance and training they can play a particularly important function since they act as a role model for their clients, as well as having the skills to help support them.

Lay helpers who may initially have been nominated by others to act in a befriending capacity must also be included. The Homestart Scheme, for example, uses housewives, who, after a short training period, provide a wide variety of support for families in temporary need. Their tasks could include looking after children, cooking the occasional meal, or just acting as a friend and providing a 'listening ear' for a lonely mother. The women in this group do not usually see the need for counselling or necessarily know about counselling skills, but recognize that they will need to respond to those they are helping in a sensitive and caring way. Their route through to counselling is via learning about active listening.

Finally, there are the many hundreds of people who have volunteered to train to join one of the voluntary services such as Relate or the Samaritans. These agencies are growing in number and cover an ever-increasing spectrum of need. Two recent additions are 'Childline', set up to provide a telephone link to children who are being abused physically, mentally, or sexually, and the Terrence Higgins Trust for those wanting help and advice about AIDS.

More recently, a new category of people recognizing and using counselling skills has become evident, namely industrial and other managers. Peters and Austin (1985) and de Board (1983) have written of counselling as a management skill and strategy. This will be returned to later in this chapter as it underlines the organizational thrust which the movement may need to take.

To summarize, I have defined a wide range of people concerned with helping others; some may formally recognize what they provide as counselling, while others may not recognize the label, but understand many of the skills. Some have received little or no training, while others have been rigorously trained and supervised. They are united only by the desire to be effective in the way they help. Those involved in the counselling-skills movement range across a very wide spectrum of helpers from those concerned with more effective listening through to those who will use counselling strategies at something approaching a professional level. It is essential for the community that a wide range of people are ready and willing to become helpers either in a professional capacity, as para-professionals, or as community helpers. It is only through this process that we will at least be able to withstand and at best creatively manage the trauma of 'Future Shock' (Toffler 1970).

Figure 12.2 illustrates two axes which may be helpful for mapping the field of the counselling-skills movement. It does not suggest that any given individual member of society is placed as shown on the diagram, for after all a solicitor may also be a Samaritan, a teacher, or a marriage-guidance counsellor. It is however likely that many social workers, whilst not formally trained as counsellors, will have an appreciation and some understanding of counselling, whilst teachers through their classroom training will have some training appropriate to counselling without necessarily recognizing its relation to the practice of counselling. The progression is likely to be around the diagonal line from the bottom left-hand corner of the figure to the top right-hand corner: that is, the higher the level of training, the greater the amount of counselling practice which is undertaken. This is not however always the case; for example, a teacher may have a recognized counselling diploma and yet have little opportunity to undertake counselling in its formal sense. There are many omissions from the figure but hopefully readers will be able to add those which have most relevance for them.

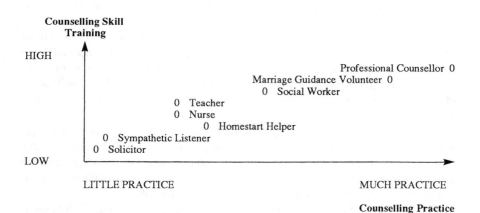

Fig. 12.2 Mapping the Field

Demystification of counselling

For more than a decade there has been a growth in the use of counselling skills as part of the process of organizational development. This has stemmed particularly from the field of education but is now spreading more widely through both the public and the private sector. In order to understand the reasons for this growth it is first necessary to explore the premiss upon which much of the educational growth has rested – the demystification of counselling.

The need for extending an understanding of the counselling process has been recognized by a number of writers. Indeed, Murgatroyd (1985: 5) writes:

> I cannot agree that only certain kinds of people (for example, professional counsellors with specified academic qualifications) should be allowed to provide particular forms of help ... helping is a process that can be and is widely used and available within a community and is not the sole prerogative of professionalized helpers and counsellors.

Hopson and Scally (1981b: 1) state that: 'It is vital that we 'de-mystify counselling', and that 'There is nothing inherently mysterious about counselling. It is merely a set of beliefs, values and behaviours to be found in the community at large.' (1981b: 8)

If this is indeed the case, the question arises as to how far it is useful or necessary to distinguish between professional counsellors and those who use counselling skills. Nelson-Jones (1984) makes the distinction between counselling interviews and helping contacts. He states that: 'Counselling interviews involve counsellors and clients in formal settings', whereas

> Helping contacts may be made by people who use counselling skills as part of different or more complex roles. For example, teachers, preachers, doctors, nurses, social workers and a host of others in the helping professions may each have opportunities to exhibit the skills of personal responsibility counselling.
>
> (Nelson-Jones 1984: 99)

Using this distinction some lay counsellors would be perceived as undertaking counselling interviews whilst many people in the helping professions who may have had considerable training but be forced to practice in anything but ideal formal conditions would be regarded as making helping contacts.

In Britain there are still comparatively few full-time counsellors and yet there is a growing recognition of counselling as an activity. Teachers who have a counselling diploma, for example, are unlikely to be employed in this capacity. They are more likely to use their counselling skills and knowledge within their teaching position as part of the pastoral care offered by the school. Even those Local Education Authorities which did employ school counsellors at one time have for the most part ceased to do so. This practice is reinforced by teachers themselves, who respect most those who continue to prove their ability to perform well in the classroom. It is these teachers who will have the credibility to add counselling to their other skills. In doing this they enhance their normal classroom practice as well as having additional skills when working with individual students. Indeed, Aspy and Roebuck (1977) have demonstrated that the best teachers already possess a high level of interpersonal skills. Similar views prevail throughout the people professions, ensuring that for a while at least counselling will most credibly be extended through encouraging a more universal understanding of the skills involved and their impact upon the present work of the professional person.

The work of CCDU

It was the belief in this process of demystifying counselling which in 1976 led the CCDU at Leeds University to launch a short but intensive counselling-skills course intended for teachers and other education-authority employees. The objectives of the course were to:

(1) identify the skills of counselling;
(2) compare counselling with other helping strategies;
(3) enable participants to identify their own skills and to build upon these; and
(4) explore the application of the course content to individual work situations.

The course was not intended to develop counsellors but to empower individuals to use counselling skills within their normal teaching practice, to help them deal more sensitively with pupil and staff problems, and to recognize when referral was necessary. The course used participative methods and gave all participants the opportunity to use closed-circuit television. Self-awareness exercises were also part of the course. Course members were explicitly discouraged from using role play because this was an opportunity not only to learn to use counselling skills but also to recognize the value of being counselled by another person and the vulnerability involved in being a client.

This course, with minor modifications, is still running and has been experienced by nearly 15,000 people since it was launched. It has only been possible to provide courses for such a large number of people because the underlying empowerment message contained within counselling became part of the organizational philosophy and practice of the CCDU.

A belief in demystifying counselling led to a process of demystifying training. Through the development of a training programme for potential volunteer trainers, large numbers of teachers and others (more than 400 at the time of writing) themselves became trainers. These trainers then undertook to run further counselling-skills courses with the support of the CCDU. In time, as the demand continued to grow, teams of teachers from individual or groups of local education authorities were trained, further increasing the number of counselling-skills courses which could be run. As a result networks of trainers began to develop. These trainers not only took part in running the CCDU course but also frequently became involved in training within their own institution, and, through their influence and enthusiasm, a demand for counselling training among their colleague teachers increased.

As for the teachers who have attended the courses, some, as described above, have become trainers, some have sought opportunities for further counselling training, some have become volunteers for helping agencies, and very many have reported that the course has been of benefit to their work as a teacher in the classroom, in working with individual staff and pupils and with parents. Some staff and trainers have left the field of education and are now working as trainers and managers in industry and the public sector and are influencing the system through their use of counselling skills.

The CCDU had started out with the intention of running short counselling-skills courses which would themselves reflect the central values of counselling. Through this process organizational decisions were taken by staff which were also congruent with those values, and the Unit became centrally concerned with helping individuals and organizations to help themselves. All other courses run by the CCDU were also influenced by this organizational perspective and the potential benefits of counselling skills and the counselling process to organizational growth began to be realized. Just as a counsellor may evaluate the effectiveness of a counselling session by considering how far the client has been able to take responsibility for themselves, so too does the CCDU evaluate its effectiveness by how far the organizations for which it has worked are able to continue that particular aspect of their work on their own.

There have been many counselling-skills courses designed with similar objectives to those of the CCDU, which makes no claim to being the first in this field. The aim in describing a small element of its work (Pearce 1986) has been to explore the opportunity afforded by taking an organizational, as opposed to an individual, view of counselling, for raising awareness of counselling to a much wider audience. Staff, voluntary trainers, and course members have continued to seek connections between different aspects of their work through counselling skills and it is this which has led to involvement in Record of Achievement courses, appraisal courses, and management courses.

The organizational approach

The task of disseminating counselling skills has, as described above, already begun and is particularly evident in the field of education and training. Guidance and counselling is part of the structure of the Youth Training Scheme (YTS), and although this is in its infancy, a start has been made which will bear fruit in the years to come, as staff expertise increases. In the education service, there has been a minor revolution in the last decade with the development of a large number of short counselling-skills courses. Probably of even greater importance is the recognition that counselling and reviewing have prospered within many of the newer initiatives within education. An increasing number of teachers accept the role of counselling within the pastoral-care system, and reviewing as part of the process involved in tutoring a group of students and within the emerging Record of Achievement. Most important of all is the provision of skill

197

development for students through personal and social development programmes. At their best, these courses are building a foundation for a generation of self-empowered individuals who may come closer to building a more caring society. This view of the growth of counselling is supported by the initial findings of a questionnaire on counselling provision in education conducted by the University of Warwick. This has shown that 'Whilst few Authorities now have a policy for employing full-time Counsellors in schools, most felt they were providing some sort of alternative counselling support if only through their tutorial system.' (Hooper and Laing 1987) The survey which was sent to all 113 Education Authorities in England, Scotland, and Wales had a 73 per cent response rate. The interim report goes on to illustrate the movement towards counselling skills through quoting some of the observations made by the advisers who replied to the questionnaire. The development of counselling skills is being further underlined by Government demands for appraisal for teachers. The teaching profession is anxious that this should be developmental and empowering rather than controlling and oppressive, and many recognize that training in counselling and reviewing skills could be helpful in ensuring this approach.

Similar movement, although not as yet so dramatic, is also becoming apparent in other public services and in industry and commerce. Peters and Waterman (1982) demonstrate that one of the factors which help companies to be successful in the commercial world is trust in employees and a constant attention to the needs of the individual in relation to the needs of the company. Peters and Austin (1985) go further and talk about the need for love and relate that to a range of practical helping strategies, including counselling, which are not dissimilar to those described earlier. They, like Rogers, have an optimistic view of the individual, a view which is beginning to be an increasing part of the value system of organizations which are aware of how this liberates the creative potential of the organization. Their approach and that of many other modern management consultants is that people are the most important resource within an organization whether as customers, clients, or employees, and that there must be constant attention to their needs. They reject the idea that this person-centred approach is a 'soft' option and suggest that true excellence can only be achieved by this means. It involves respect, trust, tolerance of mistakes, and encouragement to take risks. This is perhaps the most heartening aspect of sharing the principles of counselling. Inevitably the practice does not yet match the rhetoric but the 'window of opportunity' exists if we are prepared to recognize it.

Issues

There are number of issues relating to the use of counselling skills within the wider community, many of these are interrelated and are concerned particularly with the perception which counsellors have of themselves, their clients, and perhaps most importantly of each other.

198

Counselling as a profession

If we genuinely believe that counselling is about helping people to help themselves, then we must believe that they can take responsibility for the skills which some people in the professional field of counselling believe must remain exclusive to them. As Illich states: 'Professionals assert secret knowledge about human nature, knowledge which only they have the right to dispense.' (Illich *et al.* 1977: 19) In the same book McKnight (1977: 89) goes further and writes: 'We have reached the apogee of the modernized service society when the professionals can say to the citizen:

> We are the solution to your problem
> We know the problem you have.
> You can't understand the problem or the solution.
> Only we can decide whether the solution has dealt with your problem.'

I do not believe this to be true at the present time in the counselling profession, but there is a danger that such a view could be legitimized if counsellors claim 'legitimacy as the interpreter, protector and supplier of a special, this-worldly interest of the public at large' (Illich *et al.* 1977: 17). We must constantly question how far the systems and organizations which we have designed and supported are merely to protect the role of counsellors rather than to support the central ideas of counselling practice. As a member of the BAC, for example, it is important for me to question how far it is concerned with accrediting professionals and protecting their rights and how far it is an organization committed to helping individuals and organizations to help themselves.

The role of the counsellor

It is often difficult for those who are struggling to preserve a counselling service within schools and other institutions to come to terms with those similarly trained, who would prefer to work in a different way; in particular, to recognize that a counsellor who chooses to work within the system as a trainer or manager might be contributing to the eventual wider acceptance of counselling. This is perhaps an inevitable and potentially creative tension. It is important for all those involved in counselling to support the provision of counselling services and those who at present operate as counsellors can best serve this through being concerned with their provision in the present, whilst those working for system change have a long-term role to play. This will involve modelling the values central to counselling in the way they operate as trainers, teachers, nurses, social workers, managers, and so on. It will also involve setting up structures which encourage self-empowerment and which are concerned with people working and living together in a more sensitive and caring way.

It is this process which will cut through some of the apparent paradoxes which exist. Many counsellors, for example, may find the idea of Appraisal Counselling a contradiction in terms and yet at its best appraisal involves the right of an individual to know how he or she is perceived by co-workers and to plan how further to improve working effectiveness. Those who see appraisal as a developmental process are designing and running systems which are staff-centred, based on evidence, and are often peer-led.

Future developments

This chapter has been based largely upon the assumption that the counselling process and in particular the skills of counselling should be made available to a wide community of individuals – indeed that some aspects of counselling should be readily accessible to everyone. This notion of counselling-skills training for all might at first seem provocative. If broken down further, what is being suggested is the following.

(a) Counselling-skills training should be a normal and necessary part of the training of all professionals. The depth of training in those skills is likely to be greater for those engaged in the helping professions such as nursing, teaching, and social work than those who are lawyers, dentists, estate agents, and so on.
(b) At a lower level the foundation for counselling-skills training should be laid in schools with an increasing emphasis on providing training for students in active listening and on helping them to understand and practice the concepts of respect, empathy, and genuineness which contribute towards building effective relationships.
(c) Managers in industry and elsewhere need counselling-skills training in order to understand how counselling integrates with their other functions in working with people.

By adopting such a broad vision of demystification there is the opportunity to raise considerably the level of understanding and acceptance of the concept of counselling. It recognizes that the world is not divided into 'helpers' and those needing 'help' and that we can all assume some responsibility for responding to the needs of our fellow human beings. At the same time it would also ensure that each individual would understand more clearly the limitations of the help which they can personally provide and the necessity of turning to those with greater expertise at appropriate times.

By inviting an ever-increasing number of people to share an understanding of counselling we may begin to develop the notion of a truly caring society – not just through the provision of institutions such as the National Health Service or Social Services but also in the sensitivity of day-to-day contact between individuals.

Counselling-skills training

Not everyone agrees that the essential qualities described by Rogers can be acquired, or practised, by everyone who seeks to use counselling skills. Hamblin (1974: 11) writes:

> It is at this point that we begin to see that not all teachers can be counsellors. The personality of the counsellor will influence the transaction which occurs between him and the pupil, and not every teacher can create the conditions necessary for honest self-exploration and helpful communication.

The viewpoint adopted by Rogers for client-centred therapy is essentially optimistic about human nature and is based upon the belief that individuals can take responsibility for their own actions. This optimism can and should be extended to the potential of all individuals to take on a counselling role. It is based on the belief that, provided a given individual wants to understand and practice the essential qualities described by Rogers, and that they are willing to confront the personal growth this requires, then those qualities can be learned. Figure 12.3 shows the map of the field described earlier, alongside a further development of the model which shows the relationship between counselling-skill training and counselling practice necessary for professional counsellors, those who use counselling skills in a less formal capacity, and the community at large. There are of course many overlaps and there will be many people within the community who will wish to extend their understanding further, just as there will be some teachers, social workers, and so on who will operate at the same level as a professional counsellor. The model is meant to describe the minimum levels for which we should be aiming.

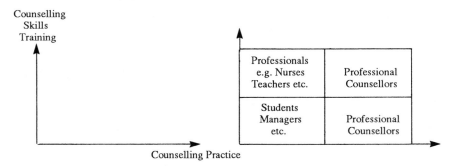

Fig. 12.3 A Model for Training

In figure 12.4 each sector of the model is considered separately. In the bottom left-hand corner it is argued that there should be a greater effort to disseminate the basic skills of relationship building throughout the community, in particular by providing young people with opportunities to learn and understand them and by ensuring that all those who work in the public arena are aware of the part these skills play in making them more effective.

		Basic Counselling Skills		Basic Counselling Skills	Advanced Counselling Skills
Relationship Building Skills		Relationship Building Skills		Relationship Building Skills	Advanced Counselling Practice

Students, managers, doctors etc.	Teachers, Nurses, Social workers etc.	Prodessional Counsellors

Fig. 12.4 Sectors of the model for counselling-skills training

Those in the counselling-skills movement will need to undertake basic counselling-skills training and through their understanding at this level may well graduate to gaining a greater understanding of counselling. It is only at this point that the more rigorous training and supervision necessary for professional counselling will be undertaken, as indicated in the final diagram in figure 12.4. It is beyond the scope of this chapter to discuss what is involved at this point.

In conclusion

Rogers (1978), who finally came to accept the political nature of the work in which he had been engaged throughout his life, summed up the challenge which faces counsellors in the following way:

> I believe it is the evidence of the effectiveness of the person-centred approach that may turn a very small and quiet revolution into a far more significant change in the way humankind perceives the possible. I am much too close to the situation to know whether this will be a minor or major event, but I believe it represents a radical change.
>
> (Rogers 1978: 286);

and 'A quiet revolution is underway in almost every field. It holds promise of moving us forward to a more human, more person-centred world.' (Rogers 1978: 290). It is this quiet revolution which this chapter has been addressing. I have demonstrated that it has already begun and our challenge now is to allow it to continue by recognizing, with Rogers, that our work is also essentially political in nature.

References

Aspy, D. N. and Roebuck, F. N (1977) *Kids Don't Learn From People They Don't Like*, Amherst, Massachusetts: Human Resources Development Press.

de Board, R. (1983) *Counselling Skills*, Aldershot: Gower.

Freire, P. (1976) *Education: The Practice of Freedom*, London, Writers and Readers Publishing Co-operative.

Hamblin, D. H. (1974) *The Teacher and Counselling*, Oxford: Basil Blackwell.

Hooper, R. and Laing, P. (1987) *Questionnaire on Counselling Provision in England, Wales and Scotland. Initial Findings,* Warwick: School of Education, Warwick University.

Hopson, B. and Scally, M. (1981a) *Lifeskills Teaching*, London: McGraw-Hill.

——(1981b) *A Model for Helping and Counselling: Implications for Training*, Leeds: CCDU, Leeds University.

Illich, I., Zola, I. K., McKnight, J., Kaplan, J., and Shaiken, H. (1977) *The Disabling Professions*, Boston: Marion Boyars.

McKnight, J. (1977) 'Professionalized, service and disabling help' in I. Illich *et al.* (eds) *The Disabling Professions*, Boston: Marion Boyars.

Murgatroyd, S. J. (1985) *Counselling and Helping*, London: Methuen.

Nelson-Jones, R. (1984) *Personal Responsibility Counselling and Therapy – An Integrative Approach*, London: Harper and Row.

Okun, B. (1982) *Effective Helping – Interviewing and Counselling Techniques*, Belmont, California: Wadsworth.

Pearce, B. (1986) *CCDU – A Living Philosophy*, Leeds: Counselling and Career Development Unit, University of Leeds.

——(1987) *Reviewing Skills*, Leeds: Counselling and Career Development Unit, University of Leeds.

——Flegg, D., Varney, E., and Waldman, P. (1981) *Trainee Centred Reviewing*, London: Manpower Services Commission, Research & Development Series No. 2.

Peters, T., and Austin, N. (1985) *A Passion for Excellence – The Leadership Difference*, New York: Random House.

Peters, T., and Waterman, R. (1982) *In Search of Excellence*, New York: Harper & Row.

Rogers, C. R. (1951) *Client-centred Therapy*, Boston: Houghton-Mifflin.

——(1957) 'The necessary and sufficient conditions of therapeutic personality change', *Journal of Consulting Psychology* 21: 95–103.

——(1978) *Carl Rogers on Personal Power – Inner Strength and its Revolutionary Impact*, London: Constable & Co.

Stonier, T. (1978) *Education in a Post-industrial Society. Exchange 3*, Leeds: CCDU, University of Leeds.

Sutton, C. (1979) *Psychology for Social Workers and Counsellors*, London: Routledge & Kegan Paul.

Toffler, A. (1970) *Future Shock*, London: Bodley-Head.

Truax, C. and Carkhuff, R. (1967) *Towards Effective Counselling and Psychotherapy*, Chicago: Aldine.

Part four

Themes

Chapter thirteen

Counselling and race

Colin Lago and Joyce Thompson

Issues

The subject of counselling and race is difficult to address in a clear manner, because as Jones (1985: 173) has put it, 'among other complexities, it is embedded in the fluctuating nature of race relations in our society and hence in a continually evolving sociocultural context.' At the heart of the subject there are several major debates that in part reflect contemporary views of 'race' in British society. The term 'race' used here is a broad one. We recognise that residing in Britain today are people from many races and racial origins. Many of these groups are likely to be disadvantaged, oppressed, or discriminated against by the dominant society (for example, the Irish, Jewish, Eastern Europeans, and so on). The specific focus, in this chapter, however, is concentrated upon the complex relationship between black and white people in Britain generally, and within counselling specifically. Nevertheless, in focusing on one specific set of relationships between black and white, it is hoped that more understandings might emerge implicitly for these other groups.

A major area of contention has centred around the extent to which counsellors require specialist knowledge of and sensitivity to race relations in Britain in order to counsel. One view holds that the knowledge and skills of counselling are all that is required with any client. The opposing view contains several major themes that may be summed up as follows:

(a) In order to understand relationships between black and white people today, a knowledge of the history between differing racial groups is required.
(b) Counsellors will also require an understanding of how contemporary society works in relation to race, the exercise of power, the effects of discrimination, stereotyping, how ideologies sabotage policies, and so on. In short, counsellors require a 'structural' awareness of society.
(c) Counsellors require a personal awareness of where they stand in relation to these issues.

From this debate a key question emerges that has sometimes keenly split different groups. Can or should white people counsel black people? In doing so, it is argued, they are substantiating, symbolically, the erroneous and pejorative view that black people are inferior, that black people require help, and worst of all that black people do not have, within their midst, their own capacity to resolve difficulties.

White people are already, self-evidently, rooted in white culture. Also, as counsellors they will have been trained in bodies of theory and practice that have either central European or US origins and emphases. Certainly, white US counsellors have often asserted that black people do not respond well to traditional methods of psychotherapy (Jones 1985). Some black people within Britain assert that such methods are also culturally encapsulated within a white western view of the world and are consequently insensitive and totally inappropriate in their unthinking application to all counselling situations.

So far, we have concentrated on the white-counsellor/black-client counselling relationship. We do not wish this early focus to blind us to the black-counsellor/white-client relationship. Increasingly, black people are training in counselling and indeed some have already formed an Association of Black Counsellors (ABC).

The issues of race and racism exist, potentially, if not explicitly, within the above pairings as well as in the same race counselling dyads, (black–black or white–white). Whether covert or overt, very real dilemmas confront counsellors in terms of how subjects related to racism are managed in the process of counselling.

Further questions also exist for counsellor trainers. What is the knowledge base required in preparing trainees to work with clients of different racial origins? In doing so, are there specific individual skills that need to be disseminated? Many other questions arise out of the initial complexities already presented here. At the core of this maelstrom of debate, some of which has been quite painful and bitter, there exists a deep underlying question that goes something like this. Given that relations between black and white groups over several centuries have been typified by oppression, exploitation, and discrimination, how might contemporary relationships within counselling be transformed into creative (rather than further damaging) experiences?

Racism – the major issue

It is our contention that the issue of racism has to be addressed and worked with by counsellors in training who plan to work in today's multiracial society. This view is not held by all counsellors and counsellor trainers in the field. Similar to earlier sentiments expressed by US psychiatrists (Thomas and Sillen 1972), many white counsellors see themselves as caring sensitive people who have chosen counselling precisely because they are concerned about other people. Therefore, they ask, how could they be racist in their practice? This genuinely held view does not take into account, however, a whole range of mechanisms, perceptions, and experiences to which white people have been exposed throughout their lives.

Such phenomena, if they remain unconscious, may affect the counsellor's behaviour and responses in ways that prove negative in cross-race counselling.

Notwithstanding the importance of this dimension, we are sensitive to the fact that any journey of exploration into the issues of racism will be, for many people, an intensely painful experience. White groups, after training, may experience vast realms of guilt and impotence. Black people, similarly exposed, may get in touch with powerful emotions such as depression and anger. Despite these apparently negative effects, our belief is that counsellors need to operate from a position of maximum awareness of self and of society.

Racism – the evidence

An abundance of research material clearly demonstrates that the black members of this society do not have equal access to the opportunities and provisions that exist within Britain (Hartmann *et al.* 1974; Smith 1977; Dummett 1980; Coard, 1971). As far back as 1971 the Census suggested that the unemployment rate among young people of Afro-Caribbean origin was twice as high as among white teenagers. In addition, Little *et al.* (1978) asserted that the incidence of young people going to an interview and not getting a job was four times as great for black teenagers compared with white teenagers. Smith (1977) also indicated that as total unemployment rose, the minority groups tended to make up a greater proportion of the total: in other words, unemployment rates for minority groups rose more steeply than rates of total unemployment.

In the educational arena, Coard (1971) produced some frightening figures concerning the disproportionate incidence of black children in educationally subnormal schools. One race-relations selected bibliography confirmed that a considerable amount of research had emerged indicating that the average teacher had differential perceptions and expectations of poor and minority-group children; that these differential perceptions were associated with differential treatment and teaching techniques; and that these in turn could lead to a depressed performance on the part of the children so treated.

The media also helps to perpetuate a view of black people that is pejorative. Research has revealed that a biased selection of issues concerning race is presented in the newspapers. Troyna (1981) reports that in a survey of major national and local newspapers, 47 per cent of all material on race issues were confined to the following themes; the National Front, crime, immigration, human interest, and 'normal'. Conversely, less than 10 per cent of items were devoted to housing, education, health, and employment. Some 25 per cent of all items in which West Indians were highlighted related to crime stories. Immigration was not dealt with as an issue of black people entering Britain but with seeking to keep them out. Perversely, 'white' hostility existed outside the framework of 'race' news; such discussions focused on issues such as democracy, the erosion of freedom, and so on. Conversely, black hostility was firmly placed within the framework of race-related material within Britain. Unfortunately, space does not allow other examples to be quoted, though there do exist substantial negative findings in other socio-economic areas (for example, housing, health, street arrests, and so on).

This consistent pattern of disadvantage and discrimination is so widespread and uniform across institutions in our society that the underlying issues of racism and racist attitudes are self-revealing and self-evident. Running parallel to this assertion and, indeed, extending it is the statement in the United States Mental Health Commission Report in 1965, which cited racism as the number one health problem in the USA. Within Britain in recent years violence has erupted in several cities and racism has been cited as one of the major reasons for these occurrences.

Consequently, in any counselling relationship between counsellor and client where there is racial difference, aspects of racism must be assumed to exist and might also require focused attention. One immediate area for concern, then, within counselling is that of the relationship between client and counsellor. This is explored in more detail in the next section.

The cross-racial counselling partnership – issues in practice

The following considerations have been devised by the authors in order to demonstrate the range of issues potentially present in various cross-race pairings of counsellor and client. Some generalized views and attitudes have been included in order to aid the visibility of such issues. However we acknowledge that they are somewhat simplified and are themselves in danger of serving to confirm stereotypes. We apologize if this occurs: it is not intended.

Let us imagine four scenarios featuring different racial pairings of counsellor and client, as illustrated in Figure 13.1.

SCENARIO 1: WHITE CLIENT BLACK COUNSELLOR	SCENARIO 2 WHITE COUNSELLOR BLACK CLIENT
SCENARIO 3 WHITE CLIENT WHITE COUNSELLOR	SCENARIO 4 BLACK COUNSELLOR BLACK CLIENT

Fig. 13.1: Possible scenarios of counsellor–client racial pairings

Scenario 1: Black counsellor / white client

The black counsellor It is most likely that the counselling training a black person would have received would have been, first, in a white, middle-class organization or institute, and second, theoretically and culturally Eurocentric and American (i.e. US) in origin. Additionally, they are also likely to have been taught by white, middle-class trainers. Consequently, and quite contrary to a simplistic view of the situation, black counsellors by virtue of their training and backgrounds, will have been predominantly geared to working with white people, not black people.

The aforementioned aspects of a black counsellor's rearing and training will hopefully constitute positive qualities towards working with white clients. However, in their lives as black people in white society, some will have experienced negative incidents and consequently feelings in relation to white people. For black counsellors, then, a serious element of their work with their white clients will be the nature of the countertransference that develops as the counselling unfolds (i.e. black counsellors' feelings and reactions to their white clients that occur during the counselling process). One might predict, therefore, that one element for discussion and exploration between black counsellors and their supervisors/consultants will be this very aspect, so that the negative elements of the countertransference can be dealt with professionally, rather than being expressed inappropriately within the counselling encounter.

The white client Obviously, it is difficult to predict accurately the nature of a white client's response to working with a black counsellor. However, the range of responses is likely to be stimulated by the following questions: what is the white client's perception of a black counsellor?; does this change over time?; would the white client be reluctant to expose his or her difficulty to a black person because of his or her own (erroneous) sense of superiority?; and to what extent would the white client presume that the black counsellor will not understand his or her predicament. In sum, what effects do the race, class, and culture of the counsellor have upon the client?

Questions in this section and the next have been deliberately employed to demonstrate the extent to which a multiplicity of responses might exist for each counsellor and each client. Unfortunately, space does not allow an expansion of these areas. Suffice to say that it is hoped that the questions themselves may stimulate counsellors' reflections upon their own position.

Scenario 2: White counsellor / black client

The white counsellor Again, a series of questions can assist us in addressing, briefly the issues for a white counsellor with a black client: how structurally aware of society is the counsellor?; do they have an understanding of the myriad disadvantaging mechanisms that exist in contemporary society in relation to black people?; what class background are they from?; what experiences of black people have they had?; and what effects, perceptions, and attitudes have these left upon the counsellor?

From experiences gained by the authors whilst involved in training groups, it seems reasonable to state that many white people are quite unable to cope with radical black-perspectives and black people's pain and anger, specifically in relation to racism. Rogers (1978) has noted this phenomenon and suggests that white people who are effective in responding to oppressed groups seem to learn two attitudes. One is the realization and ownership of the fact that 'I think white'. The other is the ability to respond empathically, to be able to enter into the black person's world of hate, bitterness, and resentment, and to know that world as an understandable, acceptable part of reality. To achieve this ability Rogers (1978) suggests that the white persons themselves need to listen to their own feelings of anger at unjust situations. This is clearly something that could most usefully be done in training and therapy, in order that the fullest opportunities for personal learning may be gained.

From the perspective of power, this combination of white counsellor with black client has a potential danger, namely a perpetuation of the notion of white superiority. The white person, as the counsellor in this situation, has the power. The sensitive handling of that power is absolutely crucial. White counsellors have to work out ways of enhancing their own sensitivity and knowledge beyond the counselling framework. To pursue their curiosity, however justified they might feel within the counselling process, would be an unethical abuse of their power. Black clients so used would have every right to experience further anger and a sense of injustice.

The black client One aspect of colonial conditioning that many black people have experienced is that of viewing white people as positive, powerful, know-ledgeable, intelligent, and so on. Consequently, such clients might have more confidence in a white counsellor. By contrast, black clients who are aware of the historical inequalities of the relationship between black and white people might be mistrustful of any meaningful interaction with a white counsellor. Indeed, it is unlikely that they would, knowingly, expose themselves to a white helper.

Some black clients might expect white counsellors not only to know their way around the British bureaucratic system but also to be able to influence that system on their behalf. The latter perspective raises further complexities as to the philosophical and theoretical nature of 'counselling' and how that equates with the reality of dealing with disadvantaged clients who are rendered less able, because of discrimination, to be effective in their world.

Suffice it to say, at least three different emphases have emerged in various counselling practices in relation to this quandary. One response has been for the counsellor to maintain the 'purist' perspective of engaging in therapeutic dialogue with the client, trusting that the client will learn sufficiently from this process to become able to deal with difficulties in their lives. An extension of this has been for some counsellors to offer educational teaching assistance to clients in areas such as assertion training. The third model has been the counsellor's adoption of an advocacy role on the client's behalf. Thus, based on the initial therapeutic work, the counsellor then moves towards negotiating with external agencies or persons on the client's behalf.

Scenario 3: White counsellor / white client

The white counsellor This is the commonly assumed combination of counsellor and client whenever counselling is discussed. Though race is not often an issue within such alliances, nevertheless it does from time to time figure within the dialogue. Indeed, when this occurs the counsellor may well be challenged in terms of his or her responses to the client. Thus, for example, what is the counsellor to do if the client uses racist language and conveys stereotyped views throughout the counselling? – confront these attitudes?; accept them?; ignore them?; continue to work with the client in order (hopefully) to gain an understanding of the significance of such utterances and views?; refer them to someone else?

Each of these questions contains significant quandaries for every white counsellor concerned with racial justice. Clearly, from the above questions dealing with a 'whites only' counselling situation, it seems self-evident to note the crucial importance of introducing issues of race into all counselling training courses. Race is still an issue even in non-racial situations. This question, which can have real consequences for the counsellor–client relationship, needs considerable thought by counsellors.

The white client From the client's perspective, of course, they have a right to their views and to express them within counselling, even though they may be experienced as negative or objectionable to the counsellor. Indeed, these sentiments will also exist for many subjects that clients may bring to counselling. Self-evidently, the activity of counselling exists precisely to facilitate the expression and exploration of problems perceived by the client.

The white client might also assume that the counsellor will agree with his or her sentiments. Further, some clients might attempt to coerce their counsellors into colluding with their views on issues of racism, in the knowledge that they are both white.

Scenario 4: Black counsellor / black client

The black counsellor The actual content and direction of the therapeutic interview between black counsellor and black client might well depend upon the counsellor's perception of the client's problems. The counsellor might for example be tempted to deal with the issue of racism and to explore this at the expense of other issues or problems with which the client is having to deal and cope with. Of course, the opposite tendency is also a possibility: that is, the counsellor may concentrate, perhaps inappropriately, on the other issues at the expense of acknowledging the issue of racism as raised by the client. From the perspective of professional development it would be most important for black counsellors to check themselves for either tendency in order to further explore their own perspective on the subject. Also, black counsellors, working with black clients, are likely to find themselves quite often, caught up in ethical dilemmas stimulated often by the client's own community. One such dilemma occurs when the counsellor supports the self-development of a client when that development is in conflict with the mores of the client's cultural group. Such dilemmas, if handled inappropriately or insensitively, could well create considerable difficulties, not only for the counsellor and client but also within the client's family, the local community, and the counsellor's agency.

In summary, the task of the black counsellor can be seen to have considerable consequences and is certainly beset with professional demands that would appear to exceed those of white practitioners. Blending British training with alternative traditional approaches and then having to cope with external consequences as well as with the client's internal world are formidable extra dimensions to the black counsellor's load.

The black client Some black people, because of their own upbringing, find it difficult to perceive other black people who themselves enjoy equal status to their white counterparts, as equally knowledgeable and skilful. Such people, as clients, might end up feeling that they have only received second best. Inevitably, this sense of disappointment could lead to a deterioration or withdrawal from the therapeutic process or a projection of inappropriate anger on to the counsellor. Conversely, there are often black people who would welcome the opportunity of being counselled by a black counsellor by virtue of a perceived positive identification of the same values and belief systems as themselves, for example, 'I find it easier to talk to you, you remind me of my grandmother.' Such initial positive feelings of transference are likely to be a foundation for a good working relationship.

Principles

Tentative guidelines for counsellor practice

Although the previous section on cross-race counselling relationships concentrated on complex issues, it also introduced some ideas in relation to what we consider to be good practice. The following guidelines constitute a development of such principles of practice.

(1) Attempt to gain an awareness and knowledge of your own culture and cultural style, race, and racial origins.

This apparently simple statement represents a considerably complex task for anyone to embark upon, certainly in relation to cultural 'style' (perceptions, behaviours, beliefs, and so on). As Hall (1976) has noted, 'Honest and sincere people in the field continue to fail to grasp the deep and pointing ways in which culture determines behaviour, many of which are outside consciousness and awareness.'

It is our contention that it is crucial that counsellors know where they are coming from, culturally, historically, and behaviourally. Only through having such knowledge and awareness will they be able to have a sense of their effect upon others as well as access to an understanding of the dynamic process that unfolds between them and their clients.

(2) Specifically, attempt to gain more understanding of the historical and contemporary relationship that has existed and presently exists between your own race and that of your clients.

Such knowledge may be of enormous value in understanding your clients' present perspective. Historically, most relationships between black and white races have been based upon traditions of conquest, colonialism, exploitation, oppression, and so on. Further, the evidence cited earlier stresses the contemporary existence of racism in Britain.

Both perspectives might yield insights for the counsellor into how they may be perceived by the racially different client. Such knowledge will hopefully contribute to the sensitivity and awareness that the counsellor brings to the encounter.

(3) Develop a 'structural awareness' of society.

This should include the effects of history, as well as an understanding of the myriad mechanisms of oppression and systems of discrimination that operate in society. Judy Katz's book *White Awareness* (1978) is an excellent reference work for training ideas and exercises. Indeed several trainees with whom we have worked have written essays and articles that have been stimulated by the impact of such exercises upon them. The importance of this guideline lies in its potential to demonstrate to each white counsellor how they, however unwittingly, can contribute to discriminatory procedures in society.

(4) Attempt to gain knowledge of the client's culture, culture style, race, and racial origins.

This is similar and complementary to our first guideline. One of the dangers of trying to learn about others is that of being tempted into simplistic beliefs and views of them based on inadequate, biased, or limited accounts. Such knowledge, therefore, has to be acknowledged as useful but limited. Indeed, willingness to change or modify one's views in the light of fresh experience is crucial.

In short, gain as much knowledge as is possible but also retain the ability to suspend that knowledge when working with a client. Extended awareness of how others live and view their lives will contribute to the extent to which counsellors may fully understand their clients.

(5) Hold in mind that any breakdown in communication may be attributable to the dynamic process between you.

Thus, you are not neutral in your communication form and the client is certainly not deficient, just different. Breakdowns in communication can be most disturbing to both participants in counselling. At worst, negative stereotypes may be reinforced on both sides. The following pointers might be helpful in this regard:

(i) attempt to be clear and concise;
(ii) avoid use of jargon and colloquialisms;
(iii) check out the accuracy of your understanding of what is being said;
(iv) be clear about what help it is that you are offering;
(v) possibly allow more time for the interview.

(6) Be aware of (and beware) your assumptions, stereotypes, and immediate judgements.

Some of these may be based on personal experience. Others may be gained from very old incidents, folk tales, parental influence, and so on. At worst, your assumptions and prejudices are likely to come between you and the client and operate as a barrier to real communication.

(7) Remember that many concepts like truth, honesty, intent, politeness, self-disclosure, and so on are culturally bound.

This may affect what the clients feel they can or cannot say and to what degree they can expose their feelings in relation to the issues they are bringing. Also, by holding this guideline in mind, counsellors may be further assisted in suspending initial judgemental attitudes.

(8) The dominant manner through which all counsellors operate is one that is underpinned by attention-giving and active listening to the client.

(9) Be alert to your usage of language.

Words and phrases can be loaded with connotative and ideological meanings. Gaining an awareness of the effect of the language we use is a very difficult process as we are so used to the words we utilize. Specific efforts have to be made to 'decode' and understand the implication of our utterances. Thus, for example, there are many such expressions that have racist undertones. To use them not only abuses the victim of them, and by association, your client, but also affects and reflects the speaker. At one level you become the abuser and as such, consequently, no longer the helper.

Another aspect of language usage is contained in the following anecdote. This concerns a West Indian woman who arrived in Britain during the 1960s. She kept going to the labour exchange looking for a job. On her second or third visit, the woman behind the desk said 'I'm afraid we still haven't found a job for you.' The West Indian woman replied, strongly, 'I don't want you to be afraid of me, I want you to help me find a job.'

It is virtually impossible to avoid such expressions as language is structured by them and is beset by them. However, what we can do, in addition to developing an awareness of them, is to broaden our ranges of vocabulary and expression in order that statements may be rephrased more appropriately or meaningfully. A sensitivity to client's responses to your usage of language will also enable you to monitor the effect of what you are saying upon them.

(10) Pay attention also to paralinguistic phenomena for they also can ensure that real communication does not occur.

Paralinguistic phenomena such as sighs, grunts, intonation, expression, silences, the structure of who says what and when, is determined by cultural and linguistic backgrounds. Research has revealed how powerful these phenomena can be upon the deterioration of the relationship between two people in communication.

This tenth guideline is intended specifically to complement the fifth, seventh, and ninth outlined above. Each, in their various ways, encourage counsellors to suspend initial negative judgements in response to their clients. Cultural and linguistic phenomena can have such profound negative effects on people who are culturally different. It is as if all the standard cues for understanding someone else have been removed. Yet the listener is not necessarily aware of this. They continue to hear the same language being used and fall into the trap of assessing the other person based upon their own regular criteria. Unfortunately, even these criteria are seldom conscious.

This general point is a most complex one and deserves considerable thought on behalf of counsellors.

(11) A more open and accepting approach to many models of counselling and helping is required within this sphere.

(Remember also that this statement implicitly incorporates non-Eurocentric models of helping.) At the moment in Britain there is available a whole variety of theoretically different courses of counselling training. Consequently, practitioners may become informed and skilled within a range of approaches to therapy. However, the vast majority of these have emerged from western societies.

What is more difficult to acquire are insights into non-western, traditional therapies that are based upon dialogue. Paradoxically, an insight into these therapeutic styles might greatly assist white western counsellors with black clients whose cultural origins are outside Europe. Thus, for example, one form of problem resolution in the Middle East is for the troubled person to consult various elders in the community. After gaining their views he or she then chooses a course of action based on the information gathered.

(12) Monitor your own attitudes during the interview, especially in relation to feelings of superiority or power over the client.

This point has been addressed briefly, earlier in the chapter. It relates specifically to the areas of oppression and racism. As elements of countertransference it seems crucial that the counsellor reflects on the case with his or her supervisor or consultant.

(13) There are circumstances in which it will be appropriate for white and black counsellors, in being sensitive to the issues of racism, to explicitly acknowledge and explore this topic within the counselling process.

The precise details of how, why, or when to do this can clearly not be predetermined by the guidelines here. It is however crucial that counsellors are knowledgeable and sufficiently comfortable with the subject that they can acknowledge its existence and facilitate the exploration.

(14) We would encourage counsellors to proceed cautiously and err in favour of minimum contact rather than long-term work.

The former will hopefully be helpful, and the latter may become intensely complex and have a poor prospective outcome. In these circumstances, appropriate referral arrangements might prove more satisfactory.

(15) Generate possible sources of referral to helpers or counsellors of the same race/culture as the client.

(16) Similarly, try to locate a suitable consultant who has experience of or is of the same race as the client, if the client becomes a medium to long-term one.

(17) Explore the experience of consulting racially different people with your own personal difficulties or for therapy in order to gain an insight into what it is you are attempting with your racially different clients.

Space does not allow any further exploration of the ideas contained in the above section. We offer these tentative guidelines as a basis for good counselling practice in the present. Hopefully, as interest develops in this aspect of counselling, the research might guide the development of future practice in more defined ways.

Future developments

Implications for counselling education and training

Counselling and race, as a topic, is still not dealt with on many existing counselling courses. Historically, also, such courses have not concentrated upon the society and the social milieux within which counselling takes place. Rather, there has been an emphasis on the development of self-awareness, the enhancement of existing skills and theoretical knowledge, and a concentration upon micro-skills. We are fully in accord with such emphases in training. However, the perplexities we can now appreciate through counselling in a multicultural and multiracial community make it crucial that future training courses also make efforts to adopt a wider 'sociological' approach. Here, the term 'sociological' is used within the definition of 'structural awareness' as described earlier. It serves to imply the following:

(a) an increased understanding of today's multiracial society and the historical pre-conditions that contributed to its formation;
(b) the provision of experiential training in the areas of racism and cultural awareness and the development of anti-racist strategies;
(c) simulated exposure of skills practice with racially and culturally different clients; and
(d) the opportunity for case discussion and analysis to highlight the complex range of data generated when counselling within this milieu.

Such a combination of approaches would hopefully help the individual trainees to develop a connectedness between their knowledge base, their attitudes and preconceptions, and their ability to practise.

Sue (1981) links five characteristics of culturally effective counsellors: (1) having self-knowledge; (2) possessing an awareness of generic counselling characteristics and their relation to culture and class; (3) having an understanding of socio-political forces affecting clients, especially racism and oppression; (4) having the ability to share world views of clients, without being culturally encapsulated; and (5) having mastery of an eclectic variety of skills and theories and ability to choose which are appropriate for a particular client. To this list we would add having (a) self-knowledge of our own cultural origins and one's present (culturally determined) style, and (b) an awareness of one's own perceptions of people who are racially different.

If a white person in counselling training pursues these general suggestions laid out above, then several implications are likely to emerge for their personal life as well as their professional one. These include:

(1) a development of an attitude of concern for the creation of a racially just society and the elimination of racist practices;
(2) a development of personal apprehension or fear that they will become 'marginalized' within their own groups (friends, work, family) and become the subject of conflict or ridicule for holding such views;
(3) a need to acknowledge that combating racism is a long and painful process and consequently they will require stamina of purpose and motivation;
(4) the exploration of personal attitudes and the development of a knowledge base of how society operates discriminatory practices and implicitly invites individuals to make political, professional, and personal choices in the present and the future;
(5) firmly held beliefs about the theory and practice of counselling might have to give way to a more open appreciation of other models;
(6) the possibility of adding a 'preventive' educative function to their work in addition to the existing one of counselling individuals through disseminating such awareness (via workshops, community activities, and so on).

At the present time, unfortnately, there seems to be a shortage of informed and skilled trainers within this specific area. Further, it would seem important and necessary for counsellors involved in mixed-race settings to avail themselves of supervisors who have the necessary width and breadth of knowledge required. Again, such consultants are few and far between.

The above elements somewhat reflect a 'chicken and egg' situation. Clearly this scenario constitutes a frustrating predicament in its entirety. Viewed from a slightly less pessimistic perspective, there exists a variety of short courses available (one-day, weekends) dealing with these phenomena. Indeed, increased demands have been made on members of RACE (Racism Awareness in

Counselling Education, a subcommittee of the BAC) and the BAC to provide such facilities over recent years.

We can appreciate in the near future that, as a result of an increasing incidence of mixed-race counselling partnerships occurring, appropriate training methods and consultative support mechanisms will develop. Beyond that, issues such as specialist accreditation of counsellors, supervisors, and trainers for this specific element of counselling might have to be considered by organizations such as the BAC and the British Psychological Society. However, the labelling of certain individuals in this way might carry the unfortunate implication that most of us do not need to address the problems.

The path towards the increased training opportunities for black counsellors will also not be an easy one. The authors are already aware of situations in some allied 'helping professions' where white trainers have been accused of racism for failing black students. The overriding concern of and challenge to training agencies is that of maintaining 'academic' standards whilst encouraging black students from a range of backgrounds, some of whom may lack prior qualifications. Unfortunately such predicaments may well cause many agencies to avoid offering training that is sensitive to the subject of this chapter.

We have begun to map out above a potential area of development for counselling courses and individual counsellors. Our own experience contributes to a view that these initiatives are long overdue and consequently require immediate attention. However, in reality, we fear that some of the challenges presented by this arena might prove too formidable to engage with directly. A shortage of existing trainers and supervisors has already been acknowledged, and so too has the difficulty of encouraging black students, lacking traditional prior qualifications. A further barrier to comprehensive development is the lack of systematic research in two crucial areas, training and counselling practice. Such research might guide the formulation of sensitive and effective training programmes. It is our experience that some programmes in anti-racism education have had contradictory effects: that is, some participants have been further consolidated in their prejudicial attitudes. Trainers and researchers must therefore develop approaches to training that enable participants to explore these very difficult issues, without producing the contrary effects alluded to above.

Given the above apprehensions we predict that developments in training in this field are likely to be slow and *ad hoc*. It seems reasonable to suspect that some counselling courses, whilst not fully incorporating major new modules on counselling and race, will offer short introductory seminars on the subject. A rather more modest expansion of general awareness might thus be created over time which might then act as a catalyst for the development of substantial initiatives at a later date. It is perhaps only in this way that enough experience might be generated for a coherent development of 'good' training to occur.

One example of a substantial initiative would be the development of a specific postgraduate counselling course focusing on this area. Certainly there is no shortage of theoretical or experiential training material to fill such a course.

Trainees could be drawn from the various professions which already use counselling methods. The course would offer a specific body of knowledge and skill to equip participants, first, more ably to counsel those who are culturally or racially different, and second, to counsel members of ethnic-minority groups.

Other considerations for organizations offering counselling

Counselling is often seen as a middle-class activity, and thus as élitist, or certainly distant from the experience of working-class people, white and black. We believe that more effort needs investing in education, health, and public-relations programmes to counter this view and to increase general counselling provision. Counselling needs to be seen as a legitimate process for problem resolution.

Recent developments in training, in education, Social Services, and the National Health Service have seen an increase in the spread of counselling skills generally. However, this has not yet been accompanied by a visible expansion of counselling facilities, especially in areas having a higher incidence of ethnic-minority peoples. With specific reference to counselling racially different clients there are very few specialist organizations offering help. Our view is that greater co-operation needs to take place between local authority and voluntary organizations and the different ethnic communities to stimulate the joint formation of projects that might be seen as directly relevant to the needs of those communities.

Much of this chapter has dealt with counselling as an activity that takes place between two people. There are other models of helping from around the world that are based on different assumptions, – for example, working with families, working with community groups, using a series of counsellors in turn, and so on. Co-operation and consultation between various elements of local communities might lead to the establishment of counselling agencies that are more sensitively and appropriately equipped to help specific local communities. If counselling providers work only on a one-to-one model they might not only be guilty of cultural domination but will fail to provide the most relevant forms of help.

Given the present nature of Britain's multiracial society, it seems incumbent upon those whose concern is for the quality of people's lives generally to imaginatively expand that concern to all groups resident within Britain. It is not enough to assume that there already exists an adequate network of informed agencies and counsellors. Developments in training, provision, research, and public information are all required so that any clients, be they black or white, may have access to helpful counselling.

References

Coard, B. (1971) *How the West Indian Child is made Educationally Subnormal in the British School System*, London: New Beacon Books.

Dummett, A. (1980) 'Nationality and citizenship', in *Conference Report of Further Education in Ethnic Minorities*, London: National Association for Teachers in Higher Education.

Hall, E. T. (1976) *Beyond Culture*, New York: Doubleday.

Hartmann, P., Husband, C., and Clark, J. (1974) *Race as News*, Paris: UNESCO Press.

Jones E. E. (1985) 'Psychotherapy and counseling with black clients' in P. Pedersen (ed.) *Handbook of Cross-cultural Counseling and Therapy*, London: Praeger.

Katz, J. H. (1978) *White Awareness: Handbook for Anti-racism Training*, Norman: University of Oklahoma Press.

Little, A., Day, M., and Marshland, D. (1978) *Black Kids, White Kids, What Hope?*, Leicester: National Youth Bureau.

Rogers, C. R. (1978) *Carl Rogers on Personal Power*, London: Constable.

Smith, D. J. (1977) *Racial Disadvantage in Britain*, Harmondsworth: Penguin.

Sue, D. W. (1981) *Counseling the Culturally Different*, New York: John Wiley.

Thomas, A. and Sillen, S. (1972) *Racism and Psychiatry*, New York: Brunner/Mazel.

Troyna, B. (1981) *Public Awareness and the Media*, London: Commission for Racial Equality.

Chapter fourteen

Counselling and gender

Jocelyn Chaplin

Why is gender important?

Gender is one of the main ways in which we differentiate between human beings. Yet it is not only about noticing those differences and trying to explain them. It is not only about having a womb or having a penis or about socially constructed expectations that women should be caring and passive and men active and aggressive. It is *also* about inequality. Gender differences whether physical or social are not equally valued differences. Gender is about power and inequality, hierarchy and oppression, because one gender, the male gender, and all the values and attributes associated with it, is deemed superior in most cultures of the world today.

In any unequal power relationship, those on the 'bottom' are far more limited by the differences than those on the 'top'. It is easier for men to argue that gender is not an issue, whereas for me as a woman, it is extremely important. The very way that I write this chapter, in a language and form that has developed in a male-dominated culture, makes me continually aware that I am a second-class citizen writing in terms laid down by my oppressor. I am living and working in a culture that was designed by the other gender, using values such as competition and linear thinking, that have been associated with that other gender. It often feels like an alien world for me in my female gender.

Yet I do not feel biologically determined by my gender. I feel fully capable of, for example, being assertive and thinking in a linear way. It is the other side of me, that which thinks in a more cyclical way and sees connections between everything, that is not equally respected in our culture. As a woman I am not treated as different but equal. I am reacted to as different and inferior, as marginal to mainstream society, as object rather than active subject.

At times I have felt that the world of counselling is one of the few areas of modern culture in which the values and ways of thinking associated with the female gender are genuinely respected. Even here, however, there seems to be an increasing male orientation.

However, there is a level on which gender is not important. In a spiritual sense we are all part of the same universal energy patterns. Energy has no gender, only electrical poles; but once this energy starts to take animal and human form, gender becomes important. Most known human societies have some form of gender division, yet this division has not always been hierarchical. There have been societies such as Minoan Crete in which women and female-orientated values were respected as much as men and male-orientated values.

Today, there is a great cultural variation in the expression of gender difference within Britain. I cannot possibly do justice to all these variations in one chapter. I am also myself the product of a particular middle-class, white, post-colonial background that I have rebelled against as a woman, but am still affected by. I am at present a heterosexual. All these factors limit my perspective, yet I hope that many of the issues raised in the following pages will have meaning for people involved in a wide range of counselling activities.

On the social level in which most of us live most of the time gender is intimately connected with our identity and being. The first question asked when a baby is born is, 'Is it a boy or a girl?' Questions about its health or its weight usually come afterwards. Gender is seen as of supreme importance and defines the child in its social context long before it has any say in the matter. From the moment of birth the baby is reacted to according to that gender: little girls are often held more protectively than boys, for example. If we see counselling as being concerned with a person's own self-definition and conscious development, then gender can be seen as an obstacle to self-fulfilment. The complex person trapped inside the box of limited social gender expectations is often screaming to get out. The woman who wants to drive a truck or the man who wants to care for children are only slowly being given social approval to 'be themselves'.

Many people who come for counselling have a wide gap in their perceptions of how they 'ought' to be and how they feel they actually are. Many of these 'oughts' are connected with gender. The man who feels deeply inadequate because he does not feel comfortable with the 'macho' expectations of his male friends is a familiar figure. So is the woman who feels that she ought to be the 'perfect mother'. As she cannot be, the result is often self-hatred and depression. In our male-orientated thinking we have to be successful or we are losers. Success is often defined according to gender: for the man it is success at work, yet even today for most women success means catching a good husband and being a good mother. Women's status is still determined largely through marriage. On our own we still often think we are just not good enough.

Many psychological problems, from depression to low self-esteem, can be traced back to gender issues (Nairne and Smith 1984). For women the reality of second-class status leads very directly to low self-esteem. For men it is more likely to be a mismatch between how they feel and how they think men should be and feel. Much of counselling is about getting underneath the 'shoulds' and discovering and then accepting what is *really* being felt. It is helping people to trust their guts. This includes getting to know and respect our bodies that in a male-orientated culture have been so devalued and split off from our minds, with which we are supposed to control everything.

Social gender expectations tend to be largely mental constructs that are deeply ingrained even before we learn to speak. Yet on another level we all inhabit gender-defined bodies. While in counselling we help people to question the social constructions of gender that they have learnt, we also need to help people feel comfortable in and accepting of their bodies, male or female. When we are grounded in our bodies then we tend to feel safer to question and make choices about social roles.

Indeed, there are today far more choices available to both women and men in terms of social roles. In some circles the 'new man' who shares fully in child care is the new hero. In fact, new and equally limiting role expectations can arise in subcultures which aim to reduce sexism. The need to belong is one of the deepest human needs; and as soon as we make a choice to belong to a particular group, certain role expectations connected with gender arise. Even in all-female groups, there may be expectations that all women should agree, for example. The idea of disagreements, conflict, and competition can be especially threatening for women's groups which may still have gender expectations concerning how women 'should' be.

At times the sheer range of possible roles can feel quite overwhelming. There is so much choice, in social terms. Yet because we have connected social role with personal identity we can feel split and torn apart by wondering whether we should be a career woman *or* a mother, a poet *or* a nurse. Yet all of us have many sides, some that are more associated with males at present and some that are more associated with females. In counselling we encourage people to explore these different sides, perhaps play-act them, try them out. After all they are just roles. The drag queen is often far better at playing the stereotyped 'femme fatale' than the female person who actually tries to be one. The drag queen knows that he is play acting. Seeing female and male roles as games, separate from our 'real selves', can help distance ourselves from them thereby reducing their power over us. We are not our roles. We are rather the process of change itself that can pass through the many roles. We are not the fantasies but we are the observers of our own fantasies. We are not the many costumes that we dress up in, but we are the bodies underneath.

The love of our own bodies in all their gender-specified glory seems paradoxically vital to our escaping the limitations of social gender expectations. Many people come into counselling hating their own bodies yet trying to live up to very rigid social gender expectations. The large woman who hates her figure because she wants more than anything to be slim is a familiar example. There is also the man who cannot even feel his own body yet desperately seeks to be the 'perfect' macho male.

To summarize, gender is important for counselling on four main levels. First, it is important because counsellors are working in a society in which male-related values dominate the culture and women are still basically treated as second-class citizens. Power structures in the society affect people psychologically in numerous subtle ways. Second, gender can be seen as limiting role expectations, that can be obstacles to full self-development and the expression of all sides of the self. Third, gender can be seen as a relatively superficial role, separate from individual personal identity, to be played like a game and not taken too seriously. We can *all* act many parts of ourselves, and some of these parts will be 'female' and some 'male'. Fourth, gender is simply the bodily form into which universal energies take human shape.

Principles

Process

Counselling is a face-to-face relationship between two or more human beings in which one or more of them are the centre of focus and the other one plays a helping role. Quite apart from the content of counselling, the *process* brings gender immediately into the foreground. The gender of the people in these face-to-face contacts is probably the first aspect of them that is noticed.

The client coming for the first time might already know that she or he will be seeing a man or a woman. She might have certain expectations as a result of this knowledge, for example she might expect a woman to be gentle and supportive and a man to be more judgemental and confrontational. She might even be taken aback if they do not fit her role expectations.

On the other hand she may not know which gender they will be. A client going to see a psychiatrist, for example, might expect 'him' to be a man, and be surprised and even suspicious if 'he' turns out to be a woman. A female client may react with immediate submissiveness, perhaps combined with flirtatiousness, to a male counsellor, just because he is male, regardless of any more complex psychological considerations.

Strategies for 'gender aware' counselling

Awareness of gender-related reactions to the counsellor

It is very important that the counsellor be aware of gender-specific reactions which may be superimposed over the client's 'deeper' problems. It is vital to keep a look-out for the kinds of learnt reactions, especially to the opposite sex, that do not necessarily reveal the client's 'normal' behaviour patterns. A male counsellor, for example, might assume that a woman's submissive behaviour towards him, is the way she behaves with everyone and is not mainly simply a learnt response to male authority figures. At home she might be a little tyrant! If he did not recognize the importance of the particular male–female context of the counselling he could limit himself to working with only one side of her. He might fail to recognize her strengths or her temper, for example. He might even continue to treat her as the victim that she presents to him in her 'feminine' role of wanting the big strong man to help.

Awareness of power relationships in counselling

The power relationship is often the hidden agenda. In our male- orientated culture anybody in a 'helping' role tends to be seen as having power over the person being helped. Co-counselling, self-help groups, and notions of self-healing are all more connected with female-orientated ways of 'helping' and try to minimize unequal power relationships. Yet because the whole society is so permeated by concepts of competition and control, these issues still emerge in most helping relationships.

Female client/male counsellor For most women growing up in patriarchal society, men are still seen as the experts, the all-knowing ones. And men seem to collude very effectively in this myth. Thus, for women going to see male counsellors there can be particular difficulties concerning her wanting to give him great authority but resenting it and him rejecting but still enjoying that authority. Most clients feel the contradictions of wanting an authority to tell them what to do and yet resenting that authority and basically wanting equality.

Both female and male counsellors need to be aware of the power that is being projected on to them, but male counsellors need to be especially careful. They need to examine honestly their own feelings about being in such a powerful role. They need to find ways of minimizing the inequality in the counselling situation. Thus, for example, the arrangement of chairs or couches needs to be taken seriously and placed in a way that does not make the counsellor seem 'higher' or more important as when he sits behind a desk. For men, power is perceived as sexually attractive, so he needs to underplay his sexual charms and be careful not to sit in a way that might be experienced as sexually threatening to the woman, nor should he touch her unless totally convinced that it feels appropriate for both parties.

However, there are also many subtle messages that a male counsellor might give out unintentionally to retain control of the session, for example by interrupting her or asking too many questions. Clearly, this depends on the style of counselling, but generally in the more directive counselling approaches there is a danger that the counsellor may exert too much control over the client. If the counsellor is a man and the client a woman, such control may serve to reinforce the pattern of dependency and low self-esteem that she has experienced every day of her life in patriarchal society. Men have a greater tendency to interrupt women than vice versa; so a male counsellor needs to pay particular attention to his listening skills and his ability to respect and take seriously whatever the female client brings. Women's reality has long been invalidated by men and counsellors should not therefore collude with society by disbelieving clients or invading them with their own views of the world (for example, through their interpretations).

Underlying many of the problems mentioned above is the prevailing social stereotype of the strong male doctor curing the weak female patient. Although most counsellors do not see themselves in this way, many clients still have this model deeply embedded in their unconscious. Indeed, it is possible that some male counsellors are themselves still unconsciously affected by this image. Such images need to be examined with great honesty by the counsellors. At times it might be appropriate to bring attention to such stereotypes if they are referred to by the client: for example, 'You seem to think that all men are strong.' A male counsellor could even disclose something about his vulnerable side at this point.

Male client/female counsellor A male client with a female counsellor might be particularly prone to power struggles as he may be used to the idea that men should always be in the controlling position in relation to women. He might try to invade her boundaries, for example by staying late. It is especially important for female counsellors to be firm about their boundaries, stopping at the time given and not talking about themselves unless it is absolutely necessary. She may need to protect herself, for example, by having other people on hand if she is working alone at home. She might have to avoid encouraging him to talk a great deal about his sexual fantasies as many of these may include degrading women and no woman, in whatever role, should be forced to submit herself to male violence, even at a mental or fantasy level.

Male client/male counsellor Male clients with male counsellors may get into the stereotypical male competition for supremacy that still lurks underneath so many supposedly helping male relationships. The male counsellor needs to monitor his own feelings about competition and control even as the sessions are taking place. The client may just say something that triggers off the counsellor's old feelings of needing to be in control, on top, or even just right about something. In fact the counsellor is not always right and needs to be aware that there are many paths to truth, many realities and ways of seeing. Counselling is not about winning arguments or proving to clients that you are right.

Female client/female counsellor Woman-to-woman counselling can sometimes seem almost too cosy and similar to talking things over with friends, as women do 'counsel' each other in their everyday lives more than men. Yet counselling as described in this book is of a more formal kind in which there are two very different roles. The counsellor does not generally talk about herself, nor does she rescue the client as she would want to do with a friend.

There might also be a danger of overempathizing with the female client and losing a clear sense of being separate people. Women are more used to connecting with each other and sharing what they have in common than sitting back and being different. Female counsellors need to keep reminding themselves that they are in the role of counsellor.

Content

In terms of the content of counselling, there is a need for the counsellor constantly to look out for the influence of gender-specific expectations. Many clients reveal beliefs such as women should not be angry or men should not cry. As counselling is partly about helping people to own and express all the feelings that they actually have, such gender-specific beliefs play a major role in preventing people from developing their full selves.

The counsellor's self-awareness

Counsellors need to question all their own assumptions about gender through reading, consciousness-raising, and thorough self-examination. This can require a ruthless honesty that can be painful as well as exhilarating. Only when counsellors have gone through this process themselves can they genuinely help their clients to question their own gender expectations and discover what they really feel and want. These expectations can be seen as obstacles to self-fulfilment rather than as goals to be achieved through counselling. Many counsellors may still think that a 'mentally healthy' woman ought to be more giving than her 'mentally healthy' husband, for example (Broverman *et al.* 1970). Some may still think that marriage, or at least a close heterosexual relationship, is a mark of mental health in women, while many women say that they feel 'healthier' outside such relationships with men. There can also be an assumption that women must be neurotic if they do not want children.

Exploring different gender roles

The counsellor can help the client to explore images and roles relating to gender without judgement. Clients can be encouraged to see their lives like plays in which they play many parts including those of the opposite gender. Some of these roles might feel comfortable while others can feel strange at first. A gestalt-orientated counsellor might get the client to put two different sides of themselves on two different chairs. One might be male and the other female. One woman client had a female queen side and a naughty little boy side. She was encouraged to act out these two parts.

Painting or cutting out images from magazines can also help a client to explore the roles and images that they relate to, including images that fascinate but seem unacceptable. Thus, for example, a shy person might have a strong warrior image in the unconscious that represents the other side. A man might have a strong mother-earth image or a prostitute image that represents hidden sides of the self, often of the opposite gender. Astrology or Tarot cards can help supply us with gender-specific images that make up the complex and varied beings that we all are.

Beyond gender

Yet ultimately it is important that counsellors work with and acknowledge the aspects of their clients and of themselves that is not gender-specific, that is beneath (or above) the form visible to our eyes. Counsellors need to be able to tune into the level on which they can 'see' the human soul in front of them. The soul is neither male nor female. It is simply their being, their essence, their point of connection with all the other energies that dance around the universe. To be able to connect with and love this aspect of the person, whatever is brought to the counselling session in terms of problems, is a vital part of the healing process.

Being here in our bodies

On another level it is also important to keep the focus actually on the person in front of us. Women in particular often talk more about partners, children, or friends than about themselves. This is a result of the gender expectation that women *should* care more for others than themselves. To be able to bring them back repeatedly to themselves and how *they* are feeling is an invaluable technique in counselling. It also brings them back to their bodies and grounds them in the here-and-now. Their bodies, unlike their souls, *are* gender-specific and need to be fully accepted in whatever shape or form. Dissatisfaction with our bodies can keep us operating solely on a mental level, while we believe that everything can be controlled through our heads and ignoring feelings. The counsellor needs to help provide a safe setting in which there is a sense of two human bodies of particular genders here in this room together at this moment.

Sexuality in counselling

Sexual energy may be present in counselling between people of the same or different gender, as it is so intimate. This energy *can* however, be transformed into healing, loving energy without threatening the client (or the counsellor). We are so used to associating intimacy with genital sex in our male-dominated culture that it may be hard at first to accept and use the sexual energy that may be present. This is especially true for men in either the client or counsellor role as they generally have less experience of intimate friendships and talking out feelings outside their sexual relationships.

Clearly, however, there do have to be rules about not having sexual intercourse while in a counselling relationship. In the past some well-known male therapists have had sexual relations with female clients which would be unacceptable today. We would see the male counsellor as exploiting his power. It is well-known that for many women in our male-orientated culture, power itself is the 'greatest aphrodisiac'. Female clients with male counsellors are especially vulnerable, although clients often 'fall in love' with their counsellors regardless of gender. However, the counselling sessions need to be seen as quite outside the everyday world in which sexual attraction may actually lead to affairs.

It may also be important, however, for the client to feel that he or she can express sexual and other fantasies without fear of being judged. This may include fantasies about the counsellor. It may also include ones of which the counsellor does not approve, such as sado-masochistic fantasies. These will be much less dangerous if expressed, without fear that the person him- or herself will be rejected. The fantasy is not the person. However a female counsellor needs to feel able to stop a male client whose fantasies make her feel uncomfortable, as might be the case if they involve degrading women. She could share with him her feelings and stress that she is not rejecting him as a person. She might even talk about the influence of society on male sexual fantasies. He could be advised to talk to a man about them or join a men's group; but the female counsellor has a right to refuse to listen. No woman, in whatever role, should be forced to be in a position of submitting herself to male violence, even at a mental or fantasy level. We already live in a culture in which such male violence has caused women untold psychological as well as physical misery. For men, such violence is often a symptom of their own insecurity, inferiority, or humiliation. However, as women have been used as scapegoats for so much male pain, it may sometimes be more appropriate for male clients to see male counsellors when they are uncovering some of these very deep pains and resulting rage.

Not all counsellors, however, go deeply into the client's childhood experiences; but even when working in a short-term way with immediate problems, gender issues are likely to be very important. Below are two examples of counselling situations in which gender plays a major role.

Examples of the role of gender in counselling

Sue came to counselling for depression. She had not asked to see a woman counsellor but was in fact allocated a woman to work with. At first she had seemed disappointed, but after counselling admitted that she could never have opened up so well with a man. By the end of counselling she had also stopped looking up to men so much.

Sue was married with two teenage sons, and before marriage had been a science teacher. At first she told her counsellor she had everything one could want – a nice house, plenty of money, a good husband – and yet she could not understand why she was depressed. When questioned more deeply about her life, it was clear that she played a fairly stereotyped housewife role, with which she claimed to be happy. She talked a lot about her sons and husband. The counsellor had to keep asking her about herself, for example 'But how did you feel when your son called you a silly cow?' Gradually her anger was expressed.

It eventually emerged that she was depressed because she was so put down and taken for granted at home. She believed she was not so important as the others. The counsellor pointed this out to her and spent many of the early sessions helping her to feel more important and to find out what *she* really felt and wanted. Sue's denial of her feelings and desires was directly linked to her beliefs about a wife's and mother's role. She would say things like, 'But I have to be home to cook dinner.' The counsellor would say, 'Who tells you that you must?' and 'What would happen if you weren't there?'

Later in the sessions it turned out that a whole side of her was being ignored too. Her mind had stagnated, she said. Her confidence to go out and work was very limited. The counsellor helped her to list her skills and abilities, including the devalued one of managing a home.

She was also encouraged to write down her feelings in a diary to get to know herself better, Eventually her image of herself began to change. She drew on paper and acted out a variety of images of herself. These included the 'clever scientist', the 'career woman', the 'earth mother' and the 'shy little girl'. They *all* turned out to be parts of her. She did not have to stay stuck in the 'earth mother' and now obsolete 'perfect wife' image with which she had so totally identified. Her counsellor also did some assertion training with her to help her stand up for *her* rights at home.

Tom was a very shy, tall man who came to counselling because of anxiety attacks. He worked with a male counsellor. Tom had great difficulties making relationships with women. He could only approach them when drunk, yet he had lots of fantasies about women that at times became obsessive. The counsellor used relaxation techniques with him a lot at first to help him get to know his body and to allow him to express his fantasies without too much fear. He then encouraged him to imagine that he was some of the female characters in his fantasies. He had one image of a female warrior. By putting himself in that role he began to feel more confident about himself. His mother had been a rather dominating woman, but now he was able to incorporate that aspect into himself. The counsellor also encouraged him to walk around the room feeling his fully male body, to move his pelvis, swing his shoulders and to feel OK about being male. He role-played encounters with 'real life' women, and then acted out the women themselves. So while on the one hand he became more comfortable about his own male body, on the other hand he could recognize and use the 'female' aspects of himself.

Issues

The gender of the counsellor

One of the most important issues is the gender of the counsellor *vis-à-vis* the client. Many female counsellors will not take on male clients for the reasons mentioned above such as the fear of male mental (or even physical) violence, but also because they feel that women have been doing men's emotional 'work' for them for centuries and they would rather concentrate their energies on women who have usually been giving rather than getting emotional support.

Many female clients choose to have a female counsellor who will also have grown up as a female in a male-orientated society with whom they would feel more comfortable in opening up. The wish of a client to see a counsellor of a particular gender should, I believe, always be respected. I have often heard counsellors say that clients may not know what is good for them and perhaps if they ask for a woman, what they need is a man! There are many situations, such as counselling after a rape (of a woman by a man), where it would be totally inappropriate for a woman to see a male counsellor. Yet many women feel metaphorically raped by men every day of their lives.

Clients do project on to counsellors feelings that they had towards parents or siblings of both sexes. A male counsellor can sometimes have feelings about mother projected on to him. However, it is more likely that issues connected with the client's father arise when working with a male counsellor. Even women who need to work with women counsellors at first may later choose to work with a male in order to look at specific 'father' issues; but it must be the client's choice.

A male client may choose to work with a woman because he might feel safer and less threatened. However, a time might come when he feels that he wants to 'face up' to his fear of confrontation with men and work with a man, It depends very much on the stage of her or his personal journey as well as on the individual's background, as to the appropriate choice of a female or male counsellor. Availability may sometimes limit choices too.

Differing values

Another issue for counsellors is how to remain true to themselves and their values while working with clients with very different beliefs. Clients may come into counselling full of stereotyped notions of gender roles. Men may come describing ways in which they put down their wives. Women may come in hoping that counselling will simply make them into better wives. The counsellor needs to respect the client and his or her values without having to agree with those values. The counsellor does not judge the client as a person but may judge the ideas she or he has. This can be a difficult contradiction.

The counsellor is there to help clients question their assumptions about all aspects of their lives, all their 'shoulds'; and gender expectations create a lot of 'shoulds'. Any sexist assumptions such as '*All* men are strong', 'But I'm *only* a woman (housewife)' can be questioned, gently. The counsellor could ask 'Who says all men are strong'? or 'I noticed that you said "only" a woman; that implies to me that you don't think much of being a woman.' Often just pointing out the revealing word like 'only' will be enough. Sometimes, as a woman counsellor working with women, I say, 'A lot of women feel that way' or 'We women often fall into that trap, don't we?', or even 'There is a lot of pressure from the society to make women feel that they should be slim (want children) and so on'. The counsellor is not going to deliver long lectures about sexism in society, but there are many subtle ways of exploring gender issues. In the early stages of counselling it is vital for counsellors to have some sense of how clients view the world, and then to start exploring these from where the clients are. Many clients will have already questioned many gender-defined role expectations; others will be starting from a less conscious position. Indeed, there are so many different ideas and attitudes towards gender that the counsellor cannot make any assumptions about her or his client's beliefs before getting to know her or him.

Nature versus nurture

Another important issue is the question about how much people can actually change through counselling and how much of the way we are is biologically determined? Does the mere possession of a womb, for example, lead to a natural maternal instinct? For academics these questions are still unresolved. For counsellors the issue relates to the range of choices actually available to our clients (and ourselves). A woman in counselling who clearly does not want to have children needs to be encouraged to explore all her feelings about her choice, including any losses or pain that may be involved, but it cannot be assumed by the counsellor that she is going against any 'natural' instinct. She is not mentally 'unhealthy' because she does not want children.

On the other hand, we are all born with certain potentials and biological characteristics such as colour and gender. Normally these cannot be changed, so a counsellor needs to help people accept their limitations as well as their choices. Indeed, what may be perceived as a limitation may also be a strength. People often come into counselling wanting to get rid of what they see as a vulnerable, unacceptable side of themselves. In modern society vulnerability and sensitivity, dependence and gentleness are generally associated with the female gender. Such characteristics are often especially unacceptable to men. Yet there is great strength in them too. Creativity often comes from this side of the self. Counselling helps people to accept and then perhaps transform and express these devalued sides. It may even help to talk to clients about the way that any characteristics associated with women are looked down on in our society. The counsellor needs to show that she respects these sides as much as the more acceptable ones by giving them her full attention, getting clients to draw or act them out, and by sharing feelings she might have about those vulnerable sides, such as relief or increased affection for the client. Or she may simply say 'It's OK to cry.'

It is equally important to stress the enormous range of choices that clients actually do have once they have begun to question gender-role expectations. Gender is often far less limiting than people believe. There seems to be far more variations of abilities, personality characteristics, and so on within each gender than between them. The limits are more likely to come from the way we think about gender than from our actual bodies.

Counsellors can use images of famous or ordinary, modern or ancient people to help clients recognize the range of characteristics available to their gender. Many Jungian-influenced counsellors today use myths and stories of ancient goddesses such as Artemis and Innana (Perera 1981) to help women empower themselves both by re-enacting the myths, visualizing or painting them, or simply learning about times when the female gender had more respect and value than it does today. And for men there are increasing numbers of films and television programmes showing men who express the so-called 'feminine' side of themselves. Counsellors can refer to these images and they can also be models themselves of people who can express both 'masculine' and 'feminine' characteristics. Most male counsellors do seem to have accepted their own 'feminine' side to some extent or they would not be engaged in such a caring, so-called, 'female' type of profession. Most female counsellors are fairly firm and assertive, which could be seen as an expression of their 'masculine' side. I use inverted commas with the words 'feminine' and 'masculine' because the socially constructed meanings around them are so limiting when we try to talk about groups of characteristics that do not need to be gender-defined at all.

Future developments

Where is this field going in the future?

The whole field of counselling seems to be increasingly taking gender issues more seriously. There is more and more encouragement of the client's expression of the side of themselves previously associated with the opposite gender. The mushrooming number of assertiveness training courses reveals one way in which women are exploring their 'masculine' side. It is often harder for men to develop the 'feminine' because it is still relatively devalued in our society. However, there are now men's groups, books, and courses to explore feelings about 'being a man'. In the past 20 years there has been an increase in the number of opportunities for men and women to do counselling in groups or with individuals separately and away from the opposite gender. Many women still feel intimidated in mixed groups and men still have a tendency to take over in these groups.

Places like the Women's Therapy Centre in London were set up to provide a safe place for women to explore their feelings honestly with other women. Women connected with the centre like Orbach and Eichenbaum (1983) have written about ways in which gender affects women at deep psychological levels. Factors such as lack of funding and the present 'conservative' climate, however, make the increase of such facilities seem unlikely in the near future. However, the range of women coming to the few women-only facilities that do exist seems to be increasing, for example to include more black and working-class women.

Another trend is the increase of problems associated with questioning stereotyped gender-roles and the need for counselling to help people come to terms with these changes. Thus, for example, many men are having sexual problems such as erectile dysfunction partly because the old gender roles are changing. Their sense of being a 'man' may be undermined through unemployment or even the increased assertiveness of their wives or girl-friends. Women, on the other hand, are often suffering from feeling that they have to be superwomen and always play every role available to them, from mother to career woman, and so on. The stress involved can be enormous. Many counsellors are beginning to use stress management and relaxation techniques more and more in their work. They are having to look at the whole person, body and mind, within society. Counselling cannot be seen as separate from the society of which it is a part, and changes in social attitudes and behaviour affect both the process and content of counselling. Further, gender roles are changing quickly in society as a whole.

Gender issues are also related to sexual orientation and one direction for the future is an increase in counselling and self-help groups for gay and lesbian people, in which their orientation is *not* seen as a 'problem'.

Where should this field be going?

Both women and men need to love and express the power, joy, and sexuality of their own bodies, of whichever gender and of whatever shape, age, or colour. This can be through just fully being and living, or through relationships with people of the same or opposite gender. Counselling can play a vital role in this process. Feminism does not imply that men should start hating their own bodies and genuine undistorted sexuality, in the same way that women in the past were taught to hate theirs (Rowan 1987). We all need to explore ways of expressing our sexuality in non-oppressive, creative ways.

At the same time as loving and accepting our gender-defined bodies we need to open up the choices in terms of roles and gender-associated characteristics. In other words we need to move towards psychological but not necessarily physical androgyny (Singer 1976). People who have available to them abilities and characteristics associated with both sexes do seem better able to cope with the modern changing world (Bem 1977): they are more flexible, adaptable, and are psychologically 'healthier'. Counselling needs to help people to become more psychologically androgynous. We all still have to survive in existing society, however, and until much deeper changes are made within that society, many people are likely to remain in 'unhealthy' gender-split ways of being, even after counselling.

References

Broverman, I. K., Broverman D. M., Clarkson, F. E., Rosenkrantz, P. S., and Vogel, S. (1970) 'Sex role stereotypes and clinical judgments of mental health', *Journal of Consulting and Clinical Psychology* 34: 1–7.
Bem, S. (1974) 'The measurement of psychological androgyny, *Journal of Consulting and Clinical Psychology* 44: 155–62.
Nairne, K. and Smith, G. (1984) *Dealing with Depression*, London: The Women's Press.
Orbach, S. and Eichenbaum, L. (1983) *Understanding Women*, Harmondsworth: Penguin.
Perera, S. (1981) *Descent to the Goddess*, Toronto: Inner City Books.
Rowan, J. (1987) *The Horned God*, London: Routledge & Kegan Paul.
Singer, J. (1976) *Androgyny*, New York: Doubleday.

Chapter fifteen

Counselling and sexual orientation

John Sketchley

Introduction

This chapter deals with the counselling of homosexual men, lesbian women, and bisexuals, but not transvestites, transsexuals and paedophiles, who have different needs.

What are the problems experienced by the group under consideration? The presenting problems may be inability to meet others, loneliness, wishing to meet a person of the opposite sex, a divorce and its sequel, custody of children, arrest by the police or a court case, or a prospective engagement and marriage. There are precipitating factors that may bring the problem to a head, such as falling in love unexpectedly, a significant birthday (30 or 40), the growing independence of children, discovery by a relative of a private life. However, underlying these events may be fundamental problems, upon which the counsellor will need to work with the client. They are such matters as: self-hate, guilt, shame, a lack of self-worth, self-doubt, internalized oppression, religious doubts, fear for the future, and isolation.

Principles

Is there a problem?

It should not be assumed, from what has been said so far, that all gay men and lesbian women have deep problems to be resolved through long sessions of counselling. Quite a number will need nothing more than the opportunity to talk, to be accepted by the counsellor, to be given permission to be the person they are, and to be given information about local gay and lesbian groups. The counsellor will at the first meeting therefore need to display a particularly accepting attitude, so that clients will feel able to disclose their true nature. A particular strategy of great use is not to take statements at their face value. Thus, for example, the client may state: 'I think I may be homosexual', or 'I think I may be bisexual.' Another version is: 'I'm not sure whether I'm homosexual/gay/lesbian or not.' These seemingly simple statements are in fact quite complex. People use them to test the ground, to find out the attitude of the counsellor. A cautious statement can easily be withdrawn if the counsellor displays surprise, disapproval, or a cold lack of interest. As Kinsey *et al.* wrote, sympathetic counsellors show their reactions

> in ways that may not involve spoken words but which are, nonetheless, readily comprehended by most people. A minute change of a facial expression, a slight tensing of a muscle, the flick of an eye, a trace of change in one's voice, a slight inflection or change in emphasis, slight changes in one's rate of speaking, slight hesitancies in putting a question or in following up with the next question, one's choice of words, one's spontaneity in enquiring about items that are off the usual routine, or any of a dozen and one other involuntary reactions betray the interviewer's emotions, and most subjects quickly understand them. Unlettered persons and persons of mentally lower levels are often particularly keen in sensing the true nature of another person's reactions.
>
> (Kinsey *et al.* 1948: 42)

Much later, Masters and Johnson commented that if the homosexual population expected the worst from health professionals they would rarely be disappointed (Masters and Johnson 1979, Douglas *et al.* 1985).

The initial statement may conceal other complexities. A sudden conversion to a new sexual orientation is most unlikely and, though unacknowledged, the persons's sexual orientation will have been there for some time, probably years. People will have thought about it before, perhaps put it to one side, only to be confronted by it again in fantasy, dreams, or even experience. They will probably have detected some underlying truth about themselves, and weighed this up against anticipated family and societal reactions. Though as yet inchoate and inarticulated, these experiences and thoughts are very real and influential. A part of them may be a strategy for dealing with the counsellor – namely not revealing too much at once, stating things rather vaguely so that different interpretations can be placed upon them. Thus, the counsellor will need to explore something of the history that has brought the client there at that time, so as to understand what is happening.

The first statements by the client may indicate only superficial doubt. There are people, especially bisexuals, who are confused. However, the great majority of men and women will be concerned, not so much about their fundamental orientation as about the way they are to live their lives. They may hesitate to conceptualize themselves as 'gay' or 'lesbian', because they think there are implications for the way they walk, talk, dress, and the company they keep; and further implications about their ability to accept or reject a sexual proposition, and about where they live. Will they have to be promiscuous, or treat relationships as impersonal, or regard all friendships as asexual, or become a sexual predator? Such is the power of social conditioning.

A further point the counsellor needs to explore is whether the hesitancy of opening statements is simply nervousness in using unaccustomed words, talking about the intimate self with another, and anxiety about the nature of counselling. More importantly, however, the clients may be misreading their feelings in saying: 'I'm not sure whether I am gay or not.' Thus, a gay man may reason: 'If I were gay, then I would be able to say it. But I am not able to say it, therefore I am not sure.' The fear of social rejection is thus read as uncertainty. Lastly, young people may purport to be enquiring either on behalf of another person, or about their own relationship with a third person. 'There's this gay boy I know' is a typical beginning (Woodman and Lenna 1980).

As with other clients, the counsellor needs to treat the beginning of the first session with the care demanded by these complexities. Exploring past history, events, thoughts, and feelings about them, can help, but most of all, making encouraging statements such as: 'It is OK to be gay; many good people are homosexual; many lesbians lead their lives without a great deal of worry; for many, homosexuality is just an ordinary part of their lives.' In this way, the counsellor will quite quickly detect whether there is an underlying problem to be the subject of further counselling intervention. Where there is no underlying problem, straightforward information about where to meet others (perhaps through a local Lesbian and Gay Switchboard) and where to buy the gay press is all that is needed, with the offer of further support if needed.

Disposing of myths

Many of the problems experienced by the client are caused by accepting unexamined myths. The counsellor will therefore need to invite the client to confront them. As in other areas of counselling, one way to dispose of the myths is to enable the client to analyse their factual element, their emotional content, and the way they are perceived and expressed by others.

The myths are numerous, and each client will have favourite one(s) to which he or she clings. Amongst them are the following: you can tell a homosexual man or a lesbian woman by the way he or she walks, talks, dresses; homosexuals are liars and not to be trusted; a homosexual is stuck in a stage of adolescent development; everyone is against homosexuals; homosexuals are a special danger to children; no homosexual can be happy; they are incapable of long-term relationships, interested only in sex, and emotionally unstable.

The counsellor, by listening carefully, can usually pick up what myths are operative in a particular client. Direct questions, such as 'What evidence do you have for that?', is one way of enabling the client to confront a particular myth. Another is to give information from the counsellor's own experience, for example 'But I know teachers, clergy, doctors, shopkeepers, who are openly homosexual.'

The myths are the outward manifestation of society's hostility to gays and lesbians, and may be the inward cause of internalized self-oppression in the client. This will need skilful counselling, so that the client can overcome the negative image of self that is held and build up a feeling of self-worth after years

239

of secrecy. Apart from a rational disposal of the myths, which may need combating every time they reappear, the counsellor gives permission to the person to be him- or herself. This is best done by encouraging the client to talk freely, with no condemnation or expressions of surprise; to accept the self as a legitimate sexual person with emotional and physical needs; to accept that being gay is not a strange deviation ('Am I the only one?' is a feeling that nearly all gays and lesbians experience at some time) but a quite normal situation that many ordinary people take in their stride. While working through this agenda, the client may bring to the surface painful episodes, disappointments, broken relationships and trusts, shame, religious and moral fears, all of which serve to distort the perception of the self and to induce self-hatred.

The counsellor can best help through unconditional acceptance of all that is said, and reflecting back what is happening: 'I see how painful it is for you to say this; you seem to condemn yourself very hard – would you condemn another person in the same position? I think it is very courageous of you to tell me these things, and I feel flattered to be entrusted with them.' As the feelings begin to flow more easily, the counsellor can present a useful analogy: 'It seems you feel like a person who has lived all life so far in the dark and is suddenly brought out into the painful light.' This feeling persists for some time in several people, and the counsellor may need to repeat the analogy and provide encouragement to live with the 'painful light' until a feeling of normality returns. Furthermore, the counsellor should praise the effort to reach out for a sense of integrity, where public and private selves are reconciled, and personal growth is achieved.

Choices and decisions

Having elicited the feelings, the counsellor can now invite the client to examine the choices available for movement and progress. Some clients will have a feeling of having no choices at all. Skilful counselling can enable the client to formulate some alternatives. A useful technique here is to ask the client what choices are theoretically possible for another person in the same position: this removal from the directly personal can be sometimes very illuminating. The choices will range from doing nothing to telling everyone the truth. Each choice will have consequences which the counsellor should ask the client to outline. A further line to pursue is whether making a choice is a once-and-for-all thing, unalterable. The counsellor could well point out here that personal growth is what matters, and that choices can be seen in a developmental way, each being a stage in a process towards a greater goal. Choices relate not only to telling other people, but to style of living, meeting other lesbian or gay people, frequenting social events or gay places, reading the gay press, moving home, being political, and so on. The counsellor can help each client construct a programme of change incorporating a number of these choices, leading to the re-perception of self as valuable, in control of one's life, and lovable. Each programme should be scrutinized by the client, with the counsellor's help: is each particular choice relevant, practicable, and realistic? How can a particular choice be implemented? If the programme happens by design rather than by chance, then the client will increase in confidence.

Validity of different sexual orientations

The client will almost certainly view homosexuality, and more particularly his or her own homosexuality, as invalid. The counsellor may therefore need to help the client to explore what sexuality can mean. It can be pointed out that human sexuality has a personal significance over and above society's need for propagation; and this significance can be found in homosexual and heterosexual relationships. Ample evidence for this is found in psychology, sociology, and anthropology (Ford and Beach, 1951; Nilsson Schönnesson 1988). However, in our society homosexuality has been condemned variously by the Church as sinful, by doctors as sick, by the law as criminal, and by education as unmentionable. The counsellor will therefore need to enable clients to see how this very negative image of homosexuality has induced them to have a negative image of themselves.

To initiate the change from self-condemnation to self-acceptance, the counsellor can ask the client to list all the things that have been said by Church, doctors, the newspapers, and any other source, about homosexuals. Some of these will be good, but most will be unflattering. The next step will be to ask what feelings these statements generate in homosexual men and women, and in the client. Next, how are these feelings enacted? – for example, if a person feels angry he might hit someone or sulk, or break something. Gay men and lesbians, upon hearing what is said, may feel sad, angry, depressed, and act out these feelings by retreating into themselves, or throwing themselves into their work, or going on political marches. In extreme cases, they may resort to suicide. Lastly, the client can be asked: 'When society sees gay men and lesbians acting out their feelings in this manner, how does it describe them?' Probably, the same words of condemnation as in step one will reappear. So the counsellor can move on to ask how the client can break the vicious circle just revealed.

Another way is to elicit the things that are commonly said about gay men and lesbian women, and then to examine them one by one. Of each, the following questions should be asked, so that the client can provide answers: Is it factually true (like saying 25 December is Christmas Day)? Does it express an opinion (for example, I think it will rain tomorrow), or does it express a feeling? Whose feeling? Do the statements therefore tell us about the homosexuals or about the people saying and writing the statements?

Some of this can be done by way of homework, whereby the client collects statements from newspapers, books, television, and radio before the next session.

Telling others

Gays and lesbians have a unique experience. Unlike blacks, for example, they are invisible in an environment that is apparently totally heterosexual (Beane 1981). They therefore have a sense of being strangers in the world. The counsellor will need to enable clients to see themselves as one of a class. Counsellors are familiar with people who are unable to accept some important truth, and are blocked off from personal growth and functioning. The person needs to see the facts in a different way, and to perceive the self differently. The counsellor can praise the client for work already done in this direction before coming for counselling: the client will have been thinking, rehearsing statements about the self, establishing new boundaries for things that can be talked about, tentatively applying words like homosexual, gay, bisexual, or lesbian to this newly perceived self – and all that without the help of a counsellor! How much more can they do with a little help. The client is now in the position of Humpty Dumpty: 'How do I know what I think until I hear myself say it?' There is a deep psychological need to put the thoughts into words and the counsellor is very often the first person to whom the client can say 'I am gay'.

In due course, clients need to address the feelings of being unlovable and unloved. The counsellor must enable them to construct a realistic programme whereby they can test out the validity of these feelings. The best way is to start telling others. By telling others, especially people who have known them for some time, they can find out that a gay or lesbian person can be loved, and is therefore lovable. A progressively more difficult programme can be constructed with the client, perhaps starting by looking at a mirror and saying: 'I am gay: I like myself; I expect others to like me.' From there, the client can move on to writing such thoughts on paper, showing the paper to the counsellor. Once clients are more at ease in calling themselves gay, they can consider which person to tell first. The new definition of self can produce a dramatic release of energy used hitherto for suppression. The counsellor should reflect to the client that this is progress and praise what is happening. Some clients decide to go no further, and the counsellor may have to accept this, pointing out that the client is entitled to make such a decision, but also is entitled to change his or her mind in the future.

The programme, if pursued, will be different from client to client. Some prefer to tell a friend first, others a member of their family. The counsellor may need to review strategies for dealing with the wide range of reactions of others, drawing a distinction between first and second reactions. The client can usually tell how friends and relatives are likely to react, and these intuitions should be explored, and challenged if unrealistic. A young man, for instance, might be worried that his parents will throw him out of the home, but previous reactions and the existing relationships can be good pointers to a more realistic appraisal. It may be helpful to rehearse through role-play what can be said and how it can be said, through a graduated series of situations with the counsellor taking the role of a brother or sister, and then a parent. In this way clients will feel that things are happening by design, and at any stage they can stop, pause, and resume the process. It would be useful to point out that though in one sense the process never stops, it is not necessary to make it a lifetime's career (Hart 1982), lived openly on the public stage.

In particular, the counsellor should be prepared to help teenage clients who are still under the legal control of their parents. If possible, the counsellor should either refer to an agency that deals specifically with gay and lesbian teenagers, or be prepared to meet the parents, who may feel alienated and guilty of failure, blaming the situation on their own sexual problems. Threats of going to the police and sending to a psychiatrist may be issued but, fortunately, physical violence is rare. In the case of teenagers, counselling should ideally include the family so that normal family life can be restored, and the educational and psychosocial issues covered with the young person and the family.

Married gays and lesbians

Many gay men, lesbian women, and bisexuals marry and may be parents by the time they confront their sexual identity. The relationships between the spouses need examining by the client in the counselling sessions as the history often reveals pretences, denials, and collusion in both spouses, though the counsellor should not assume or propound that divorce is necessarily the answer. Couples constantly surprise with their imaginative problem-solving once the reality is acknowledged, and this potential should be explored by the counsellor. A very straightforward approach is to say to the heterosexual spouse: 'You know the truth, and you need to decide whether and how you can live with it.' It should not be forgotten that this statement should also be made to the gay, lesbian, or bisexual partner, who also needs to decide whether the new situation is tolerable, and how to fulfil deep needs.

The counsellor may need to examine the feelings of both spouses towards any form of open marriage. In particular, if the gay, lesbian, or bisexual needs some freedom for fulfilment of personal needs, the heterosexual spouse may begin to claim some of the same freedom. Where this happens, it can lead to a new independence for both spouses (Wolf 1985). The first feelings may be, in a wife, grief and isolation, loss of self esteem, feeling unattractive and unlovable, and in a husband, disbelief (perhaps feigned), anger, and insult. These feelings should be explored with the help of the counsellor. A particular aspect for the counsellor to examine, especially if the spouse never comes for counselling, is an illusion that some gay men have, connected with their own self-condemnation and fears. The gay or bisexual man may imagine that he has told his wife and that 'she understands'. This can deceive both client and counsellor. Disclosure probably needs repeating in gradually more and more explicit ways, and new crises will need resolving (Gochros 1985).

If a gay or lesbian presents for counselling before a planned marriage, the counsellor needs to help the client discover what he or she is trying to achieve:

children, escape from family pressure, or inability to accept the truth about themselves, or, in some cases, the wish for marriage as a cover. The potential problems that ignorance and pretence can provoke should be carefully explored, while remembering that some couples who have been open with each other from the start have had successful marriages with children.

Lesbians

A special word has to be said about lesbian women. Raised to view themselves as a half-person without a man, they may see marriage as the door to personal growth, adulthood, freedom, and motherhood, with sex construed as the price to be paid for the benefits. An unsatisfactory sex life may thus be no more and no less than expected. When the benefits are also not forthcoming, lesbian women may become aware of their orientation later than gay men. With this increased awareness, they can experience profound unease about their social role as women. The counsellor may therefore need to enable the lesbian to redevelop a complete sense of self, as her very concept of being a woman (defined as mother and wife) may now be empty of all meaning. The issues raised by the women's movement are fruitful areas to go into: the ability to be oneself, independence of men, self-assertion, personal growth and development. Perhaps more than with gay men, the counsellor will need to help the lesbian build up a sense of self-worth and self-acceptance.

Bisexuals

Behind bisexuality is the troubling actuality of homosexuality, and much of what has been said so far applies to bisexuals. However, there are some unique aspects. It is not unknown for some counsellors to hold and suggest the opinion that 'we're all bisexual really'. This oversimplification may be taken by the client to mean that it is alright to have homosexual feelings as long as you have heterosexual ones, and in any case dismisses the problems as simple and unimportant. To state 'you have the best of both worlds' fails to understand two separate worlds: bisexuals cannot easily reveal their heterosexual interests in the gay world, even less can they reveal their homosexual interests in the heterosexual world. Thus, they may feel trapped in two separate closets.

Kinsey *et al.*'s (1948) seven-point scale, showing relative components of heterosexual and homosexual experience and interest in individuals, is a useful educative and therapeutic tool that the counsellor can use. Most people can estimate where they are on the scale, some even rating themselves as exclusively interested in the same sex, while still labelling themselves bisexual. It is of great solace to know that they are not alone, and that many people are bisexual. Once the counsellor has helped the client to quantify the degree of homosexual and heterosexual interest, the client can be asked to estimate how urgent are the needs to fulfil the desires. If the client considers homosexual interest to be small, he or she may wish to tolerate it but do nothing further.

Since many bisexuals state that they are confused, the counsellor needs to probe this feeling to bring out its full dimensions. As a therapeutic intervention, the counsellor can reflect to the client that confusion is a sign of mental health, not neurosis. The counsellor can also educate by pointing out that sexual attraction is not a matter of choice, and by giving permission to the client to have fantasies and feelings without guilt, since he or she does not need to act on them unless they choose.

There may be deep feelings of guilt to assuage if the bisexual is in a heterosexual-couple relationship. The guilt arises from self-oppression, as in gays and lesbians, but has an extra dimension because of the relationship to a heterosexual person, and possibly because of the presence of children. The counsellor may need to invite the bisexual to bring the partner to counselling sessions so that their mutual relationship can be enhanced. It is interesting to note that the heterosexual partner sometimes finds his or her own homosexual impulses triggered off by the revelation that the partner is bisexual (Lourea 1985). However, with a heterosexual spouse, the counsellor may need to enable the person to work through shock and anger to gradual acceptance.

After dealing with the feelings of guilt and shame, the counsellor will need to help the client to work on his or her own needs, and to balance out what they owe themselves and what they owe others, while forever faced with the paradox of a conventional public image and a secret private life. For those who come to terms with this paradox, bisexuality can be fulfilling (Brownfain 1985), and the counsellor should lead the client to explore the positive aspects and to resolve the negative ones.

Couples

Gay and lesbian couples may have problems and experience the need for counselling if one person is 'out' and the other not. A good strategy is to bring them to realise that all couples have problems, and that solving them is part of the relationship. The couple can be invited to ventilate their feelings, describe possible solutions, do homework on a realistic solution, and evaluate their progress with the help of the counsellor.

Other problems can arise out of the absence of traditional sets of rules for their relationship, social hostility, lack of external supports, and the absence of gender roles. The counsellor can best help by enabling the couple to air their feelings honestly to each other, and to lead them to consider the unique power they have to act in their adult selves and produce a way of living that works for them, and that is not in need of legal protection, religious validation, or public approval.

A couple may sometimes have given up so much and suffered a great deal to achieve their relationship, and may expect it to be perfect. The counsellor can explore the different expectations that each has of the other and of the relationship, help them assess what is realistic, and lead them to select realistic solutions, which they can try out as homework and evaluate with the counsellor at a subsequent session.

Issues

Prejudice in the counsellor

Counsellors are children of their own culture, and may therefore unwittingly and unintentionally display prejudice when dealing with gays, lesbians, and bisexuals. There may, for example, be prejudice in assumptions about the origins of homosexuality, possible explanations being either genetic or environmental, but with no compelling evidence one way or the other (Feldman 1973). The view in this chapter inclines to the genetic explanation, if only because the environmental ones, often psychoanalytical, appear as attempts to explain homosexuality away, based on the assumption that heterosexuality has no need of explanation. It is like saying 'Where does the moon come from?', without realizing that the question also means 'Where does the earth come from?' Other authors examine the question of origins in some detail (Hart and Richardson 1981; Plummer 1981; Hart 1982). For the counsellor, however, it is an issue that can prejudice the counselling relationship, blinding the counsellor to the evidence that homosexuals and bisexuals can lead fulfilled lives.

Another area of prejudice finds expression in language. The word 'homosexual', coined in 1869 by an almost unknown Swiss physician, Karoly Maria Benkert, was part of the medicalization of sexuality and of the growing prejudice towards people who were different from the expected norm (Hetrick and Stein 1984). Just as women eventually began to revolt against the medicalization of childbirth, so homosexual men and lesbian women revolted against being defined as a medical problem. For this reason, the words 'gay' and 'lesbian' are now used to assert the right to define oneself, put aside the notion that sex is the only aspect to consider, portray a positive self-acceptance, and emphasize the validity of the orientation. A deliberate or embarrassed avoidance of the two words by the counsellor will reveal some prejudice to the client. At the present time of writing, this has even more force, as the Government, Church, and media line up to express condemnation of homosexuality.

The evidence from gay men and lesbian women leading ordinary lives in the community is that their homosexual interests were well-established by the age of 12, and often before, and that even at that age they were not confusing friendship with sexual orientation. For the counsellor to allude to possible confusion at an early age, or to adolescent crushes, misses the target, and is a further example of unexamined prejudice.

Further prejudice is found in the imagination and fantasy employed by the media, and even professional counsellors, to describe the sex life of gays and lesbians. Thus, for example, gays and lesbians are assumed to play out masculine and feminine roles in their relationships. Counsellors asking questions based on this assumption sound as if they are talking a foreign language to the client. The assumption is based on a deeper one – namely, that all gays and lesbians are confused about their maleness or femaleness. They are, of course, complete persons, emotionally, socially, and sexually, but their deepest feelings and needs are fulfilled by a person of the same sex. As one young gay man said, 'There comes a time when you realise that what you feel for and want from a man is the same that a heterosexual man feels for and wants from a woman.'

It has to be said that even gay counsellors can fall prey to the prejudice described here, since they, too, may have to contend with their own self-oppression. This takes the argument further forward into the question of whether a gay or lesbian should be counselled by a gay counsellor.

A gay counsellor or not?

The client often asks the counsellor 'Are you gay?' A positive reply can reassure, encourage more open disclosure, and speed up the process of readjustment: the counsellor may be the first known gay person to whom the client has spoken. For these reasons, some gay agencies and counsellors have espoused the view that only gay and lesbian counsellors should counsel gays and lesbians.

There are also political arguments, important for the development of gay culture, behind the proposal. One is that of self-help: no-one else has been interested, the establishment structures have been destructive, and therefore the best way is to help oneself. The other strand is that described above when talking of prejudice, namely that even liberal-minded helpers unconsciously carry within them a tradition of hostility to homosexuality, which can be expressed non-verbally and verbally in the counselling sessions.

The situation has been modified by three factors. First, gay organizations have influenced the counselling and therapeutic work done in Britain. By inviting others to attend training days, by contributing to the training of establishment personnel, by joining counselling organizations such as the British Association for Counselling, the gay organizations have themselves come out. The second factor is that the establishment structures are appointing known gay people into helping professions, where they will be counselling heterosexuals (Rochlin 1985). Third, heterosexual counsellors and non-gay agencies are committing themselves to combating oppression by working on their own homophobia.

There are further thoughts to consider. To suggest that only gay and lesbian people can counsel gays and lesbians carries the implication that only heterosexuals can counsel heterosexuals. Gay and lesbian counsellors generally would contest the suggestion that they are not suitable for counselling heterosexuals. Another consideration is that to say to any counsellor that he or she is incapable of counselling a given group, simply on the grounds of sexual orientation, is a very deskilling and undermining suggestion. Finally, this suggestion also removes responsibility from non-gay counsellors for dealing with their own homophobia through further training.

Coming out

Coming out is the name given to the process of accepting one's inner sexual orientation and gradually revealing it to others. The process is not a once-and-for-all event, for each new acquaintance requires a further decision. It is probable that the process begins with close family, then friends, total strangers, people at work, and finally becomes as natural as telling someone your name. Coming out does not have a unified meaning. For some it means confrontation with anyone raising issues of sexual politics: a definition so narrow that only a few people fit into it. For others it is a question of degree: some people may know, others not.

Is coming out an optional extra, or is it a fundamental part of personal development, and therefore to be encouraged by the counsellor? On the one side, it can be said that your life is your own, and privacy over sexual and emotional matters is a right, and that coming out, therefore, is unnecessary. Such a view is naïve. While there is no compulsion to tell others, there is often a deep psychological need to do so. Coming out can bestow greater inner unity, release energy for more constructive endeavours, reduce fear, induce a feeling of being lovable, and help to integrate feelings with intellect. Most of all, the person regains a sense of control over events and an ability to make important life decisions. It produces a feeling that one's life has validity, unity, and emotional fulfilment without the burden of secrecy. Bit by bit the person may find that the 'problem' of sexual identity diminishes, and the self is accepted for what it is, without shame. This description could of course fit many issues brought to psychosexual counsellors. where acceptance of reality produces a renewed feeling of being in control.

It is the contention here, therefore, that coming out is a central therapeutic strategy for helping gays and lesbians. It has to be underlined, however, that it is the process, not the final goal, which is important. The process begins with the self, being able to apply, first inwardly, and then in the presence of the counsellor, the words gay and lesbian, or homosexual, to oneself. Thereafter the counsellor should discourage the client from drawing up a list of people to tell, as such an approach is performance- and-goal-orientated. It is probably better to examine situations where it is important for the truth, or partial truth, to be openly acknowledged: for example, in relationships, with one's own children, where ambiguity can mislead another person emotionally, where lying may produce unacceptable constraints, and where movement and growth are important.

Changing one's sexual orientation

With the technology developed in the sixties, there was a belief that deconditioning and aversion therapy could change a person's sexual orientation.

Some clients still ask if change is possible, and thus it is still an issue to be addressed. The issue is not well-illuminated in the research literature, and the political criticism of it by the gay community has given way to something like incredulity that it was ever thought possible. The approaches have been abandoned (Hart and Richardson 1981; Pinkava 1987). Even before they were abandoned, however, they were heavily criticized for failure in scientific method, with outcomes based on self-report a few months after treatment and seldom after two years (Weinberg 1975).

Psychoanalysis has not produced any convincing evidence of its ability to change a person's sexual orientation. As Weinberg (1975: 38), referring to gays and lesbians, writes: 'In most such cases, if the psychoanalytic patients instead of spending years on the couch, had been looking for their own self-defeating activities, they would be much better off.' Counselling towards self-acceptance, greater inward and external openness, living with uncertainty but still developing and growing, are more fruitful avenues down which to go.

Future developments

The debate about whether counsellors of gay persons should themselves be gay or not will continue. There will, however, be a change of direction, in the view of this writer. In the last few years properly trained non-gay counsellors have begun to inspire confidence in gays and lesbians, but a renewed climate of oppression will almost certainly make the gay and lesbian community return to the older position of antipathy to non-gay counsellors. In this climate US sources will be cited which suggest that even those counsellors who have developed a broadmindedness through working with different lifestyles are not sufficiently prepared to deal with homosexual couples (di Bella 1979). A sympathetic counsellor, it may be argued, is an asset if a client, fearful of being homosexual, refuses to see a gay or lesbian counsellor (Beane 1981), but it is likely that even this will be challenged by the gay community.

Prejudice is the frequently cited reason for discounting the efforts of non-gay counsellors. The prejudice may be 'scientific', [for example, psychoanalytic theory finds its structure threatened by the view that homosexuality can be considered a normal variety of human sexual response – Hart 1982] or it may reside in the 'traditional' condemnatory position taken towards homosexuality in Britain. It is regrettable that, in the opinion of the present writer, some counsellors, perhaps unwittingly, will go along with the new tide of opinion against homosexuality.

Another change in the near future will be in the counselling made available to young gays and lesbians. Over the last few years some counsellors have tentatively and sensitively helped them to come to terms with themselves, and to experience an adolescence characterized by psychological growth and under-standing. With the law forbidding local authorities to fund anything in schools or elsewhere which 'promotes' homosexuality now effective, counsellors (and teachers) may find themselves expected to condone self- oppression, to sow doubt in the minds of those young people who already define themselves as homosexual, to permit and even encourage mistrust in children whose parents are gay or lesbian, and to prevent young gays and lesbians meeting others in warm relaxed surroundings.

In the adult gay and lesbian world, counsellors, however, will be able to discover insights into human nature, relationships, and sexuality. Gays and lesbians have developed the courage to break out of stereotypical male and female roles by exploring alternative lifestyles and surviving without social validation. Homosexual people have much to teach their heterosexual counterparts about personal commitment, rather than external pressures or sexual activity, serving as the basis for committed relationships. In this regard they show both a parity of roles similar to what feminists have been arguing for (Peplau 1982), and open relationships without recrimination (Winkelpleck and Westfeld, 1982). These insights are valuable to all people who feel constrained by stereotypes and traditional family models. It is to be hoped, therefore, that trained gay and lesbian counsellors will be invited to contribute to training courses for the education of other counsellors. This indeed has already started to happen in some courses, for the benefit not only of the trainee counsellors but also of their future clients, whether heterosexual or homosexual.

References

Beane, J. (1981) 'I'd rather be dead than gay: counselling gay men who are coming out', *Personnel and Guidance Journal* 60(4): 222–6

Brownfain, J. J. (1985) 'A study of the married bisexual male: paradox and resolution', *Journal of Homosexuality* 11(1–2): 173–88.

di Bella, G. A. W. (1979) 'Family psychotherapy with the homosexual family: a community psychiatry approach to homosexuality', *Community Mental Health Journal* 15(1): 41–6.

Douglas, C. J., Kalman, C. M., and Kalman, T. P. (1985) 'Homophobia among physicians and nurses: an empirical study', *Hospital and Community Psychiatry* 36(12): 1309–11.

Feldman, P. (1973) 'Male homosexuality', in H. J. Eysenck (ed.) *Handbook of Abnormal Psychology*, 2nd edn, London: Pitman Medical.

Ford, C. S. and Beach, F. A. (1951) *Patterns of Sexual Behavior*, New York: Harper.

Gochros, J. S. (1985) 'Wives' reactions to learning that their husbands are bisexual', *Journal of Homosexuality* 11(1–2): 101–13.

Hart, J. (1982) 'Counselling problems arising from the social categorization of homosexuals', *Bulletin of the British Psychological Society* 35: 198–200.

——and Richardson, D. (eds) (1981) *The Theory and Practice of Homosexuality*, London: Routledge & Kegan Paul.

Hetrick, E. S. and Stein, T. S. (eds) (1984) *Psychotherapy with Homosexuals*, Washington: American Psychiatric Press Inc.

Kinsey, A., Wardell, B., Pomeroy, M., and Clyde, E. (1948) *Sexual Behavior in the Human Male*, Philadelphia: W. B. Saunders.

Lourea, D. N. (1985) 'Psychosocial issues related to counselling bisexuals', *Journal of Homosexuality* 11(1–2): 52–62.

Masters, W. and Johnson, V. (1979) *Homosexuality in Perspective*, Boston: Little Brown.

Nilsson Schönnesson, L. (1988) *Guidelines on Certain Aspects of Homosexuality*, revised edn, Copenhagen: WHO.

Peplau, L. T. (1982) 'Research on homosexual couples: an overview', *Journal of Homosexuality* 8(2): 3–8.

Pinkava, V. (1987) 'Logical models of variant sexuality', in G. D. Wilson, (ed.) *Variant Sexuality: Research and Theory*, London: Croom Helm.

Plummer, K. (ed.) (1981) *The Making of the Modern Homosexual*, London: Hutchinson.

Rochlin, M. (1985) 'Sexual orientation of the therapist and therapeutic effectiveness with gay clients', in J. C. Gonsoriek (ed.) *A Guide to Psychotherapy with Gay and Lesbian Clients*, New York: Harrington Park Press.

Weinberg, G. (1975) *Society and the Healthy Homosexual*, Gerrards Cross: Colin Smythe.

Winkelpleck, J. M. and Westfeld, J. S. (1982) 'Counseling considerations with gay couples', *Personnel and Guidance Journal* 60: 294–6.

Wolf, T. J. (1985) 'Marriage of bisexual men', *Journal of Homosexuality* 11(1–2): 135–48.

Woodman, N. J. and Lenna, H. R. (1980)) *Counseling with Gay Men and Women: A Guide for Facilitating Positive Life-style*, San Francisco: Jossey-Bass.

Chapter sixteen

Pastoral counselling

John Foskett and Michael Jacobs

Principles

Defining pastoral counselling

'Pastoral' can be used in different senses. It applies equally to the caring function of teachers, particularly in primary and secondary schools, as well as to the major part of the ministry of parish clergy. In this chapter our concern is to describe counselling which takes place within and around the religious context, although too precise definition of the nature and aims of pastoral counselling would limit the variety of its expression.

We use the term 'religious' because the interest in pastoral counselling not only brings together those of different Christian traditions, but also provides common ground with members of the Jewish faith, as well as with those who belong to no church, but who consider matters of faith and ultimate concern as of relevance to them and their clients. In part pastoral counselling and its corollary, which is psychologically informed generic pastoral care, continues the ministerial tradition of 'the cure of souls', healing, spiritual direction, and the confessional. However, a distinctive feature of pastoral counselling is that it is practised by as many (if not more) 'lay' people as it is by ordained ministers, in the context of church-affiliated counselling centres, as well as in private work. Pastoral counselling is not to be defined as that which is practised by those who are ordained, or who are paid by the churches.

Nor can pastoral counselling be limited either to an ecclesiastical setting or affiliation. It also refers to counselling which takes religious problems seriously, and which is informed by the counsellor's concern for ultimate values and meanings – religion in its widest sense. This does not mean that the pastoral counsellor is only interested in religious problems, nor that matters of faith will automatically find their way on to the agenda. As we illustrate below, apparently 'religious' problems often disguise common issues such as personality and relationship problems, which are typical of many clients in other counselling settings. On the other hand, long- term counselling and psychotherapy can give rise to deeper questions of meaning, which may also form part of the content of pastoral counselling.

The ambience of pastoral counselling

Given the similarity between the types of problem, and indeed the variety of therapeutic approaches used both in counselling generally and in pastoral counselling, it is only perhaps the general backcloth against which the counsellor works which gives the term 'pastoral' its distinctive emphasis. Following in a long tradition of spiritual guidance and pastoral care, pastoral counsellors see themselves as working in a framework which includes other dimensions than the psychological, and more than concern for the individual client(s).

A well-tried definition of pastoral care is that it consists of 'helping acts, done by representative religious persons, directed towards the healing, sustaining, guiding and reconciling of troubled persons, whose troubles arise in the context of ultimate meanings and concerns' (Clebsch and Jaekle 1964: 4). Developed to apply to pastoral counselling, the *healing* function is seen in long-term counselling and pastoral psychotherapy, although the latter term is not widely used in Britain. It has much in common with what other counsellors offer for people with major personal and relationship difficulties. The *sustaining* function is more typically seen in supportive counselling, as in the long-term care of those with chronic problems and disabilities, or in crisis intervention with the bereaved. The *guiding* function is expressed in the counselling offered to those seeking direction in their lives, vocation or work, such as preparation for marriage, for career moves, or for retirement. Such guidance does not imply advice-giving, but involves helping the client to make her or his own decisions. The *reconciling* function is most often expressed in work with couples, families, or groups, although we could also emphasize the importance of reconciliation within individuals. Here, the traditional religious language of atonement between persons and God helpfully reflects the need for inner reconciliation or at-one-ment of persons to themselves, which is cherished by modern psychodynamic practice. This is especially true for those who understand God as being within the depths of themselves. Finally, in addition to the four functions in the definition, some writers add a fifth, *nurturing*, as seen in work with individuals and groups which encourages personal growth and development (Clinebell 1987).

An alternative definition of pastoral counselling, which expresses the philosophy and in religious terms the theology behind a counsellor's work, is that it is for the whole person, as an individual as well as part of a family and social unit, and as a whole person, body, mind, and spirit, but with particular reference to the person's psychological, ethical, and theological frames of reference (Schlauch 1985). In this description, the inclusion of the term 'spirit' raises complicated issues with which religion has had to grapple since the advent of a separate psychological understanding of persons. Yet there is more to people than body and mind. Whether spirit is a separate entity, or is a description of the whole body–mind unity is a difficult question, on a par with definitions of the 'self' in psychodynamic psychology. What is more obvious is that the term 'psyche',

253

which lies at the root of different terms such as psychology and psychoanalysis, is the same as the more traditional religious concept of 'soul'. Pastoral counselling, therefore, is especially concerned with the whole person, and, when appropriate, with helping people find their own meanings for, and relationship to, the transcendent. In this respect the pastoral approach has something in common with the fourth of the major divisions of therapy and counselling, transpersonal psychology. (The other major divisions are behavioural, psychodynamic, and humanistic psychology.)

Pastoral counselling itself does not espouse one particular counselling orientation; pastoral counsellors differ to the degree to which they draw upon the techniques and theories of person-centred counselling, psychodynamic psychotherapy, Transactional Analysis, gestalt, and so on. Nevertheless Freud and Jung and their modern counterparts have had a major influence upon many pastoral counsellors. Freud's criticism of religion has proved invaluable in helping pastors understand the neurotic aspects of religious belief, while Jung's frequent use of the symbols and imagery of world religions, and his apparent endorsement of a religious outlook on life as being central to the recovery of people in the second half of life, makes his thinking especially attractive to some pastoral counsellors. 'God' in Jungian terms is an 'archetype', and there is as much debate about the existence of archetypes as there is about the existence of a deity.

Nevertheless, the psychodynamic schools are concerned to understand the nature of persons, and tend to be less optimistic about people's capacity to change through their own efforts alone. Many of the issues which are tackled by psychodynamic theory therefore find parallels in the debates that have taken place in traditional theology: whether, for instance, the deterministic, and often unconscious, influences of infancy and childhood allow any place for the exercise of free will; whether persons are by nature good or bad, angelic or devilish, how the past influences the present, and the present influences the future. Similarly, pastoral counsellors find parallels between existential issues in therapy and theology. Anxieties about death, about meaninglessness, and about guilt constitute religious as well as therapeutic problems.

Pastoral counselling is not easily separated from pastoral care, so that while there has been the development of a specialized ministry of pastoral counsellors, this is a small, albeit influential, group in Britain. The majority of pastors have many duties in the course of their oversight and care of congregations. They are often sought out at crucial times in people's lives, such as the birth of a child, the blessing of a marriage, the advent of illness or tragedy, coping with death, and coming through bereavement. Faced with these expectations upon them, pastors have turned increasingly to the insights of pastoral counsellors, who themselves have tried to integrate the social and behavioural sciences with their religious and theological studies. Clergy and laity are increasingly benefiting from training in counselling skills, personal awareness, and from a grasp of sociological and psychological perspectives. This is leading to them offering a less directive, less

254

authoritarian, and less moralistic ministry. In its place has emerged a greater capacity to help individuals and groups explore their own needs and aspirations, to resolve their own problems, and to seek their own direction. Indeed, pastors seek to be alongside people as, in biblical terms, they 'work out their own salvation with fear and trembling' (Philippians 2: 12), helping them to acknowledge that their God is as much within them as within the church or those who have traditionally been seen as speaking on God's behalf.

From 1960 onwards a number of major pastoral counselling organizations have developed, some of which have had as much impact outside the churches as within them. These include the Clinical Theology Association, the Richmond Fellowship, the Westminster Pastoral Foundation, the Raphael Counselling Centre (one of the specifically Jewish organizations), the Dympna Centre (primarily for the counselling of clergy, priests, and those in religious orders), and the Salvation Army Counselling Service. These and others came together to form the Association for Pastoral Care and Counselling, which is now also the pastoral division of the British Association for Counselling (Foskett 1985). Furthermore, locally based church groups have formed their own training and counselling services, sometimes linked to one of the major national organizations.

There is also a rather different type of religious counselling, mainly stemming from the evangelical churches. This is more explicitly Christian, and may involve the use of prayer and other more traditional pastoral practices such as the laying on of hands and the use of scriptural texts to guide and support the client. As yet this latter type of religious counselling has not fully entered into dialogue with the pastoral counselling described in this chapter. In the authors' opinion, a pastoral counsellor needs to use her or his religious base sparingly and implicitly, and only to address religious issues explicitly if and when these are introduced by the client.

Two examples of pastoral counselling

Most of the pastoral work which pastors undertake, whether using counselling skills in pastoral care or working as counsellors, has much in common with the problems presented to counsellors and carers working in other settings. Pastors, like other helpers, are confronted with problems of all kinds, only some of which have any clear religious component. However, the initial presentation of a person to a pastor may take a specifically religious form, such as a question about belief or moral attitudes, just as the presentation to doctors usually takes the form of a physical illness. Clients expect pastors to be interested in religion, and therefore perhaps only to be interested in them if they present in religious terms. Yet the training and practice of pastors and pastoral counsellors has made them more aware of the deeper issues which underly the initial presentation. In the following example, we show how the client presented a religious problem, but that in the course of counselling there turned out to be significant personal and relationship aspects.

Jean had become increasingly depressed, and was treated first by her general practitioner and then by a psychiatrist, before being admitted to a hospital. She did not, however, respond to treatment, and became more and more obsessed with her badness. At one point she decided that she was possessed by the devil, and that only an exorcism could help her. She insisted on seeing the chaplain of the hospital, and then a priest who was responsible for handling such requests. Both chaplain and priest agreed that in their opinion there were no grounds for thinking that Jean was 'possessed'. The chaplain therefore offered her the opportunity of counselling, to explore what it was that made her so sure that she was in the grip of the devil.

Jean was reluctant to accept this offer, and did so only on the understanding that she could tell the pastoral counsellor all about the devil inside her. She found this very difficult to describe at first, but gradually she painted a picture of herself as someone who was utterly revolting, and to whom something unspeakable had been done. She was now contaminated and a threat, especially to her husband and children. For a long time she could not bring herself to describe what it was that had happened to her, but eventually she related that she had visited a faith healer, because she had been suffering from recurrent back trouble. Only afterwards did she think this was wrong, because the healer was not a Christian.

The counsellor encouraged Jean to describe what precisely had happened when she had visited the healer. She explained that the man had put his hands on her back, and she had felt a strange sensation run all through her body. Jean then refused to discuss the matter further, and returned to the belief that it was only an exorcism that would save her. Re-telling the initial experience had clearly strengthened her anxiety.

Firmly but patiently the chaplain refused to act on her request for exorcism. Counselling continued, and Jean came back to the original incident, and to recognition of the strong sexual feelings aroused in her by the healer. That the chaplain could accept such feelings amazed and relieved her, and Jean slowly began to countenance the idea that her feelings, even if they had been disturbing, were not evil; and that because she had not acted upon them, there was no need to continue to feel such strong guilt. She was not wholly able to give up the idea of a devil within her, but the idea featured less and less in her counselling with the chaplain; and, bit by bit, Jean was able to discuss with her husband some of the things that had happened.

The second example demonstrates the close connection between a person's religious feelings and behaviour, and other dimensions of their past and present relationships. It confirms the view of some theologians, philosophers, and psychologists that many of the images that people have of God are projections; and that by working through the negative projections in particular, religious belief can contribute to more positive views of self and others.

George and his wife approached a counsellor for help with problems in their marriage. After they had seen the counsellor for a short time together, George elected to go on seeing her on his own, because counselling had already uncovered his deprived and traumatic childhood. With the help of the counsellor, George was able to face his sense of rejection, and get in touch with the enormous anger he felt towards his parents, and in particular towards his father. As counselling progressed he began to drift away from his church, realizing that when he worshipped he felt similar explosive feelings towards the church and especially towards the minister. The counsellor suggested that George could approach the minister to discuss his feelings, but he was afraid of offending the minister, whom he by now felt was too much like his father.

As an alternative he agreed to go and see a pastoral counsellor, and with her help he was able to explore the way in which his religious belief-system had been retarded in the same way as his emotional development. The pastoral counsellor was able to show him the selective way he drew upon religious resources to reinforce his retardation and sense of oppression, and she gradually helped him to accept the idea of being angry with his God. In time this helped George to return to his church with much greater satisfaction and enjoyment.

This example demonstrates one of the particular advantages of working with a pastoral counsellor when it comes to matters of faith and 'religious' practice. While counsellors with no particular faith are often able to respect a client's own religious views, many of them are too respectful, and unsure of challenging false assumptions and distorted beliefs. Perhaps they are hesitant about entering the potential minefield of theological speculation; or see faith as primarily an intellectual position which has little to do with feeling. Some counsellors also fear that questioning a client's faith could lead to the collapse of an important belief system, leaving the client devoid of its comfort. They fail to appreciate that confrontation and analysis of unhelpful beliefs and practices often lead to more healthy religious attitudes, which in turn free the person to grow emotionally as well as spiritually.

Issues

Faith and psychology

In a pluralistic and largely secular society religious belief often seems an outmoded way of viewing life. Those who retain faith in the transcendent can easily be confused with those who use religious belief as a defence against taking more responsibility for themselves. Jean, in the example above, thus believed that she was possessed by the devil, rather than accept her own sexual excitement, and the anxiety that accompanied it. Yet the chaplain, and other people who were consulted, could see no evidence of possession. As her counsellor, the chaplain was faced with the question of how literally to respond to her conviction. He did not challenge her devil, but began to explore around it.

Carried to its logical conclusion, such an approach leads to dilemmas for many pastors, since the psychological tools which a pastor brings to her or his work tend to question the meaning and validity of many expressions of religious belief.

Psychological explanations have a way of casting doubt upon more transcendent understanding of religious experience. There are tensions here for pastors. Some of them go overboard on psychological insights, although we have to ask whether in doing so they are responding to the latest fashions in knowledge in order to conform to the age. Other pastors try to see psychological and religious insights as running in parallel, and use both in a blended form. An example of this can be found in the work of Frank Lake and his development of clinical theology, where each discipline is used to interpret the other (Yeomans 1986). Finally there are those who recognize the trends towards counselling, and the value of using many of the techniques, but who actually make less use than they might of psychological insight. 'Christian counselling', for instance, often favours a more mixed approach combining counselling methods with practices like prayer therapy and healing of memories. There is, however, a danger is using such methods lest they encourage a magical idea of religion, which fails to recognize the significance of the unconscious. It is sometimes difficult for counsellors and healers to realize the importance, for good and for ill, that they have for their clients. As good objects they represent much which can help their clients attain the health and understanding they seek. However, the same attachment can foster an unhealthy dependence upon the counsellor and the counsellor's abilities, and this can have a disabling effect upon the client. Much of the training of pastoral counsellors in self-understanding, together with their subsequent supervision, is to help them to manage the transference relationship with their client, whether or not they explicitly draw attention to it.

Another development which has been of indirect importance to pastoral counsellors has been the attempt to understand the nature and development of religious belief, in the same way that intellectual, moral, and emotional development has been studied by psychologists and psychoanalysts. The research by James Fowler (1981, 1984, 1987; Jacobs 1988) led to his proposal of six stages of religious development, from mythical and literal views of faith to its highest expression in the lives of people like Ghandi or Mother Teresa. Fowler uses the term 'faith' to denote belief and value systems which are not necessarily theist. Faith is common to all humanity. The first part of his somewhat wordy definition of faith describes it as: 'People's evolved and evolving ways of experiencing self, others and world as (they construct them) as related to and affected by the ultimate conditions of existence (as they construct them)' (Fowler 1981: 92–3).

Paul Tillich is an example of an important modern theologian whose work combines theology and psychology, and which usefully informs a pastoral counsellor's thinking about faith and meaning. He suggested three different religious world-views, starting with unconscious literalism in the person of simple and unquestioning faith; proceeding to conscious literalism in the person whose intellectual integrity has been challenged by other disciplines and has to find some way of reconciling literal faith with modern thought; and reaching the stage of broken myth, where a person treats religious ideas as essentially symbolic and metaphorical, to be believed in only so far as they have the power to express the ultimate when the symbols are broken, and used as pointers to ultimate concerns (Jacobs 1987: 114–18; Baldridge and Gleason 1978).

Such views of religious faith and development underline the subjectivity of the beliefs and practices seen in clients and congregations alike. Pastoral counsellors often find hope in the more radical theological positions espoused by people like Tillich or Don Cupitt. This kind of thinking has sometimes led traditional religious institutions and the more conservative-minded clergy and laity to dismiss the insights of pastoral counselling as doctrinally unsound. Pastoral counsellors' willingness to work with those aspects of persons which some religious people define as 'sinful', 'bad', and 'immoral' has in some cases prompted outright rejection of their ministry.

The understanding which pastoral counselling has brought to some of the major ethical debates within the churches also contributes to a certain amount of tension. Issues like the role of women in the Church, attitudes to gays, lesbians, second marriages, and AIDS have been liberalized in the churches, partly through the work of pastoral counsellors. At the same time, those churches that espouse more dogmatic and moralistic attitudes, and offer their adherents a greater sense of certainty about faith and morals, are flourishing. Although pastoral counselling, with its more questioning outlook, helps balance this drift to the right, and heads off the return to religious certainty as a type of security blanket, inevitably these quite different approaches to religion and faith lead to tensions between radicals and conservatives.

The relationship of pastoral counselling to pastoral care

The fact that counselling can often carry greater status and value than general pastoral care has also created some tensions within the movement itself, particularly with pastoral and practical theologians. These latter point to the danger of pastoral counselling becoming an egocentric preoccupation of the somewhat neurotic and narcissistic middle classes (Jacobs 1987: 130–6, 144–9). The criticism goes further, suggesting that counselling, like institutionalized religion, is in danger of making 'misfits' conform to society's expectations. Pastoral counselling may neglect the more prophetic aspects of pastoral care, where criticism of society and concern for the corporate and the social is as important as concentration upon the individual and the personal. Although it is not in practice easy to integrate the pastoral and the prophetic aspects of a pastor's work, we believe that to separate them is to make a false dichotomy, and that the conflicts between pastoral counsellors and pastoral theologians are potentially very creative. These issues are being addressed more squarely, as those who teach pastoral studies and those who train pastoral counsellors bring their respective insights to bear on common issues. Some pastoral counsellors are also beginning to address issues like the effect of the threat of nuclear conflict upon individuals and society, and forming their own subgroupings, linking in this case with the peace movement.

The international community

The wider awareness of pastoral counsellors has been helped through membership of international conferences and congresses on various themes related to pastoral care and counselling. These have brought British pastoral counsellors face to face with the application of counselling in other political regimes, such as the Eastern bloc, and in cultures and amongst peoples of other faiths, such as the countries of Africa, Asia, and South America. Pastoral counselling can easily become another means of trying to westernize and colonize, and pastoral counsellors can lead the way in accepting the essential need to listen, observe, and learn from others, rather than impose one's own views upon them. In Africa and Asia counselling is having to learn to take its place alongside equally effective folk myth and medicine (Dumlagan *et al.* 1983; Chanona and Sharif 1987).

The development of training

The training of pastors in counselling skills has developed rapidly from 1975 onwards, and increasingly, Anglican dioceses have been appointing Advisers in Pastoral Care and Counselling, with responsibilities for training and supporting clergy and laity. Theological colleges and seminaries offer more practical training in pastoral care than once they did, with placements in health, community, and social-service agencies. Lay training is much more common in all the major denominations. Such exciting developments nevertheless raise a number of issues and tensions, such as those between clergy of different generations; and between clergy, the traditional custodians of pastoral care, and the laity, who are often more open to training, and who become more skilled practitioners than many of the ordained.

There are also questions about the accreditation and monitoring of pastoral counsellors, and, what is more difficult, of those involved in general pastoral care. The British Association for Counselling accreditation procedures, to which the Association for Pastoral Care and Counselling subscribes, often fail to attract those clergy and laity whose principal loyalty is to their work within the Church, rather than to the wider but more specialized field of counselling. The Association for Pastoral Care and Counselling still offers a national accreditation scheme for pastoral supervisors and trainers. While monitoring and supervision is vitally important as pastoral care and counselling mushroom, there are problems with accreditation, lest by implication it deskills the effectiveness that the majority of pastors bring to their ministry, by creating a minority élite who simply practise as professional pastoral counsellors. There are also signs that the latter can grow to work more and more independently of any ecclesiastical organization or group, and that this in turn can heighten the sense of alienation between the theological and therapeutic aspects of pastoral care.

Future developments

Living in a multifaith society

Although pastoral counselling has been one of those arenas of joint action and concern that has helped co-operation across the divisions between churches, and has gone further by drawing Christians and Jews together, pastoral counselling has not yet addressed the multicultural and multifaith realities of the society in which it is practised. This is probably due to a number of different factors.

First, pastoral counselling, like most other kinds of counselling in Britain, is an activity predominantly involving the white middle classes, both as counsellors and as clients. It is therefore inclined to be racially and culturally exclusive (see Chapter 13 by Lago and Thompson). Second, pastoral counselling is a relatively small movement, which has been preoccupied with establishing its own position and credibility within Jewish and Christian traditions. As we have already shown, it appeals to those who seek in their faith an integration of the secular and the sacred; conversely it tends to be avoided by those who wish to preserve the unchanging traditions of their church or synagogue, or those who are attracted by the new spirit of their born-again beliefs. Adherents of other major faiths, like the many practising Jews and Christians, tend to fall into either of these two latter categories, and are therefore unlikely to be attracted to the pastoral care and counselling movement. The answers to their questions are found in their scriptures and tradition, or through their belief in divine inspiration, and they have little understanding of or sympathy for a non-directive approach.

Third, there are no obviously comparable developments within Buddhism, Hinduism, Islam, Sikhism, or other religious groups. The priests, imams, or other spiritual leaders, do not have an explicitly pastoral function, and pastoral care is practised informally within the extended family and kinship groupings. So while there are natural pastors and wise and understanding people within these traditions, no one would think of them specifically as being pastoral carers and counsellors; nor at first glance see what they have in common with Jewish or Christian pastors. In fact, we sense that they have much in common and much to share with one another if an appropriate medium can be found; but as yet that does not exist in Britain. There is evidence, however, from Africa and Asia that indigenous and western forms of ministry can complement one another, provided there is a context of mutual respect and understanding (Dumalagan *et al.* 1983; Lartey 1987; ma Mpolo and Sweemer 1987). To some extent the conditions which may provide this context are beginning to appear in this country, in the following ways.

There are similarities in the different faiths and traditions in patterns and methods of spirituality. Meditation is an obvious example. There are also communities and groups of different religions such as Interfaith Network UK (see Reference Addresses) who meet to share some of their practices with each other. There are also a small but significant number of counselling and caring agencies provided by and for ethnic minorities. Some have explicit religious connections, and all aim to help their clients with cultural and religious issues as well as other problems. The differing attitudes towards religion espoused by different generations are often a focus for their work for example at NAFSIYAT, (see Reference Addresses, and Chapter 13 by Lago and Thompson).

Christian and Jewish pastors working in areas with many minority groups are being encouraged to develop patterns of care to which members of those groups can contribute. Churches have appointed race relations advisers from amongst the members of minority and ethnic groups, and guidance is now available to all pastors working in multicultural areas (Hooker and Lamb 1986).

In some institutions too, particularly in the health service, chaplaincy teams have been extended to include pastors of other faiths. In one instance known to us there is also a multifaith worker. As pastoral counselling is a major part of a chaplain's work, this means that there are beginning to be opportunities for pastoral counsellors of different faiths to share and compare their work with one another.

The significance of story

The therapeutic model which dominated pastoral care and counselling from the sixties to the eighties has been complemented by a new model, which aims to integrate the theological and the therapeutic, through the common element of story and narrative. In different generations and amongst those of various religious traditions, one story tends to dominate: for instance, amongst counsellors it can be the client's story, whilst amongst pastors it can be the religious story. In fact three stories can be identified – the client's, the counsellor's, and the religious story – and in pastoral counselling all three have to find their place and interaction with each other for the ultimate benefit of client, counsellor, and the religious vision (Foskett and Lyall 1988: Chapter 5; Bohler 1987).

Counselling which is practised as an integral part of the life and activities of members of a church, congregation, or other religious group, is most likely to provide the context in which all the stories can be given equal weight, and their integration actively sought. This is much more difficult if pastoral counselling is practised in isolation from the rest of pastoral care. The same is true of two other possible developments: the contemporary interest in holistic approaches to health, and the rediscovering of the prophetic aspects of pastoral care. These too require an environment which encourages the containment of different approaches and perspectives, rather than an atmosphere which divides them into specialties.

The holistic approach

The contemporary interest in holistic and non-medical approaches to health has met with a ready response in some religious groups; pastoral counselling is often included amongst the resources offered within church health and healing centres and services, as a means of initial interview and assessment, and then as one amongst a number of other therapies and treatments, such as the Churches Council for Health and Healing (see Reference Addresses). Similar connections are beginning to be made with those involved in spiritual direction. Until recently, questions about spirituality have remained largely unexamined by pastoral counsellors. Given the essential body–mind–spirit unity which underlies theological ideas about the nature of persons, current thinking about spirituality, and the concerns of holistic healing, there are grounds for a greater *rapprochement* between these different activities. There is evidence that those who guide the spiritual development of others are finding parallels between their own discipline and Jungian thought in particular. As pastoral counsellors begin to realise this interest, it is to be hoped that they will in turn explore the benefits of closer links with spirituality.

Rediscovering the prophetic role

Pastoral counselling is part of more general pastoral care, but pastoral care has other areas of specialized interest, such as the sociological and the political. Pastoral counsellors, like the counsellors in other settings, are faced with issues about the use of knowledge gained in private and in confidence (suitably disguised to preserve anonymity) to inform public decisions and policies. The growing divide between those who have and those who go without, and issues about caring for one another, are essential areas of interest to many pastoral counsellors who realize that major social problems and international concerns cannot be tackled simply by counselling individuals and families. As churches attempt to address the major problems of both inner urban areas (Selby 1983; *Faith in the City* 1985) and poor rural areas, and focus their attention upon issues of social responsibility and cultural and racial justice, pastoral counselling will need to play its part in underlining the significance of external deprivation upon emotional, relationship, and spiritual problems. Since political pressure often gains from the weight of numbers as well as the force of argument, this is one field in which pastoral counsellors need to organize, on the one hand with other counsellors generally, and on the other, with the churches' social responsibility officers and boards.

Returning to roots

As pastoral counselling finds its identity, and shows the significance of its contribution to the counselling milieu generally, the time will come when many of those who found new insights in psychology and counselling methods will feel more confident about revisiting their original disciplines and training. They will want to look afresh at theology, in order to see in what ways theological reflection might enhance pastoral counselling. Furthermore, since religion has in the past provided one of the principal ways of trying to understand, explain, and come to terms with the mysteries of life and death, the needs and problems of persons, and the interrelationship between people and the world in which they live, the religious tradition has the potentiality for providing an even richer perspective on the issues with which pastoral counsellors are daily involved.

Reference addresses

Churches' Council for Health and Healing, St Marylebone Parish Church, Marylebone Road, London NW1 5LT.
Interfaith Network UK, c/o 124 Court Lane, London SE21 7EA; also the British Council of Churches Committee for Relations with People of Other Faiths.
NAFSIYAT, Inter-Cultural Therapy Centre, 278 Seven Sisters Road, London N4 2HY.

References

Baldridge, W. E. and Gleason, J. J. (1978) 'A theological framework for pastoral care', *Journal of Pastoral Care* 32 (4): 232–8.
Bohler, J. (1987) 'The use of storytelling in the practice of pastoral counselling', *Journal of Pastoral Care* 41(1): 63–71.
Chanona, C. and Sharif, S. K. (1987) 'Pastoral response to the oppressed and the oppressor', in *Pastoral Ministry in a Fractured World*, Third International Congress of Pastoral Care and Counselling, Melbourne, Australia, pp. 92–106.
Clebsch, W. and Jaekle, C. (1964) *Pastoral Care in Historical Perspective*, New Jersey: Prentice-Hall.
Clinebell, H. (1987) 'Pastoral counselling' in A. Campbell (ed.) *A Dictionary of Pastoral Care*, London: SPCK.
Dumalagan, N. C., Becher, W., and Taniguchi, T. (1983) *Pastoral Care and Counselling in Asia*, Makati Medical Centre, Metro Manila, Philippines: Clinical Pastoral Care Association of the Philippines.
Faith in the City (1985) Report of the Archbishop of Canterbury's Commission on Urban Priority Areas, London: Church House Publishing.
Foskett, J. (1985) 'Pastoral counselling', *British Journal of Guidance and Counselling* 13(1): 98–111.
——and Lyall, D. (1988) *Helping the Helpers*, London: SPCK.
Fowler, J. W. (1981) *Stages of Faith: The Psychology of Human Development and the Quest for Meaning*, San Francisco: Harper & Row.
——(1984) *Becoming Adult, Becoming Christian*, San Francisco: Harper & Row.
——(1987) *Faith Development and Pastoral Care*, Philadelphia: Fortress Press.
Hooker, R. and Lamb, C. (1986) *Love the Stranger*, London: SPCK.
Jacobs, M. (ed.) (1987) *Faith or Fear: A Reader in Pastoral Care and Counselling*, London: Darton, Longman and Todd.
——(1988) *Towards the Fullness of Christ*, London: Darton, Longman and Todd.
Lartey, E. Y. (1987) 'Intercultural pastoral care and counselling in Africa', in *Pastoral Ministry in a Fractured World*, Third International Congress of Pastoral Care and Counselling, Melbourne, Australia, p. 124.
ma Mpolo, M. and Sweemer, C. D. (1987) *Families in Transition, The Case for*

Counselling in Context, Geneva: World Council of Churches Publications.

Schlauch, C. R. (1985), 'Defining pastoral psychotherapy', *Journal of Pastoral Care* 39(3): 219–28.

Selby, P. (1983) *Liberating God*, London: SPCK.

Yeomans, M. (ed.) (1986) *Frank Lake: Clinical Theology*, London: Darton, Longman and Todd.

Chapter seventeen

Careers counselling and guidance

Diane Bailey

Introduction

Work is a major source of identity and status in our society. Changes in work patterns and practices have strong repercussions in individual lives and experiences. Over the last decade such changes have included relatively high levels of unemployment, often concentrated amongst young school-leavers and in certain parts of the country; shifts in the patterns of employment away from manufacturing industry and towards the service economy; and a significant increase in part-time, often low-paid, work, especially amongst women. At the same time there is evidence of skills shortages and of the inadequate training of the workforce. Political responses to these conditions have included more emphasis on vocational elements in the curriculum, such as the Technical and Vocational Education Initiative (TVEI) and the Certificate of Pre-vocational Education (CPVE), and the creation of the Training Agency (formerly Manpower Services Commission) in 1973 to improve the fit between training and employment through schemes like the two-year Youth Training Scheme (YTS) and the Adult Training Strategy.

These changes have had implications for all those involved in careers counselling and guidance. Practically, there are problems in maintaining a current information-base of labour-market and of training-scheme information. Operationally, there are difficulties in liaising with the numerous education, training, and employment agencies relevant to helping clients make decisions about work. Furthermore, counsellors and helpers are being challenged by wider conceptions of work, paid and unpaid, and by increasing awareness of how social factors, such as class, gender, age and ethnic group, affect work opportunities.

'Guidance', is used in this chapter as an umbrella term encompassing the helping activities of informing, advising, counselling, coaching in appropriate skills (for example, decision-making), assessment, and providing advocacy and feedback to agencies (see Watts 1980). 'Careers counselling' here means, more specifically, offering the client a non-directive relationship in which to explore issues and carry through decisions about work. Guidance and counselling may both involve face-to-face help or may be mediated by telephone, letter, text, or computer program.

Principles

The relationship of theory and practice

Far-reaching changes in patterns of employment and in our conceptions of work have led to shifts in the models and forms of careers guidance which individuals need in order to cope with change. Theory and practice exist in a two-way relationship here. All practitioners work from sets of assumptions that inform their working styles and relationships. Careers workers express their theoretical perspective every time they conduct an interview or run a group session. It is the role of theory to challenge and develop these assumptions and to give practitioners tools to improve their grip on working issues. Likewise, models and principles need constant testing in the field to ensure their relevance and utility. Theory and practice are interlinked and both are embedded in social, economic, and political structures. In response to the changes in employment and work, there has been a broad shift from models of career development, which explain how people come to do the jobs they do, towards theories of guidance which provides a basis for action (Watts 1981).

A developmental model of careers guidance

One broad model of careers guidance with a wide currency is a three-stage process model adaptable to many contexts. The interactions are essentially developmental, based on a dynamic view of the person, and drawing on a range of helping processes. The three stages are:

(1) *Reviewing*: in which the helper explores with the client her or his needs in relation to work and ways in which available options might meet these.
(2) *Goal-setting*: in which the client is helped to clarify and set achievable goals.
(3) *Action planning*: in which an action plan is agreed, undertaken, and evaluated.

The key helping-process here is probably counselling which may be provided in an interview or may be facilitated through self-exploration or through group discussions. However, other processes may be of considerable importance. Giving clients accurate, current, and relevant information is crucial to careers guidance, in order to help them realistically to assess options and make choices. This might include occupational information, up-to-date labour market information, and information about relevant training and education. To give the information in a form and with the reinforcement which the client can use is a skilled business: a simple information sheet may be more helpful than a complete Courses Guide or direct access to a training database. Assessment, broadly defined to include structured self-assessment as well as external assessment and to cover values, interests, work experience, skills and aptitudes as well as achievements and qualifications, is also important. Information and assessment both feed into the reviewing and goal-setting stages of careers guidance.

In moving forwards and in translating goals into action plans, clients may need forms of help which are less obviously person-centred and are more concerned with active interventions in the worlds of work and training: advising, coaching, and advocacy. However, it is important to conceive of these processes within a model of careers guidance aimed at promoting the individual's control and independence. Advising, the making of knowledge-based suggestions, can give the client access to other people's experience, expertise, or 'inside' information. Thus, for example, careers officers may advise on which occupations are resistant to women's advancement; a YTS co-ordinator may advise on which employers are sensitive to issues of race. Coaching involves providing structured learning experiences for clients to gain the necessary competence in, for example, self-presentation at interviews, writing job-applications, or job-searching skills. Advocacy involves taking action on behalf of and with the agreement of the client. One underlying assumption in advocacy is that the clients see the appropriate action or behaviour modelled by the helper and are thus able to act for themselves next time. Thus, for example, (in the early stages of job-seeking) a jobcentre adviser may phone on behalf of a client to make an appointment with an employer, but may suggest that the client subsequently does this for her- or himself.

The existing provision of services

This comprehensive developmental model of careers guidance, drawing on plural interrelated forms of helping, is useful for practitioners who deal with clients from various age-groups and categories. However, the reality is that constraints often prevent agencies from providing this level of comprehensive, client-centred, and developmental guidance. Young people in school preparing for and seeking entry to work and adults planning mid-career changes, re-entry to work, or retirement may find it difficult to get the kind of careers guidance which they need.

There is a very wide array of agencies, services, and individuals with a remit for some aspect of careers guidance or counselling. This provision for the pre-18 age-group, involving careers teachers, college counselling, and Careers Services, with community and employer links, is relatively coherent, However, provision for the post-18 group, especially the majority of adults not in higher education or training, is uncoordinated, underresourced, and involves agencies with widely differing purposes. A gap often exists between the models of effective guidance to which practitioners subscribe and what is possible in day-to-day practise. Any evaluation of which helping activities particular agencies undertake reveals gaps.

Jobcentres and placement agencies offer mainly information on vacancies, job-types, and training opportunities, with possibly some advice and advocacy.

Private vocational-guidance services charge their clients fees for assessment, usually by psychometric tests and for advice on occupational suitability, with relatively little counselling or advocacy. Employer-based services might include programmes for career development, pre-retirement, or redundancy, with built-in counselling assessment and coaching in the appropriate skills (for example, decision-making, assertiveness, or working in teams). At the other end of the scale, they may be confined entirely to information on training. The Careers Service offers counselling as the core of its guidance provision and aims at a comprehensive model of helping. Nevertheless, most services can provide this level of help only for younger clients, and offer adults only the use of their information base. This overview shows that relatively few agencies offer objective client-centred careers counselling as a primary service.

In addition to this comprehensive model of careers guidance, a variety of more specific concepts and principles has been developed in relation to particular client groups (for example, pupils, students, and adults; employed, non-employed, and unemployed groups; mid-career changers and women returners) and also in relation to particular helping agencies (for example, placement services which match job-seekers to employment opportunities and not workplace counselling services which help employees develop their careers). A review of some of these concepts and contexts, with examples of good practice, shows the range – and perhaps the limits – of careers guidance at present.

Careers education

The concept of careers education has been very influential. It refers to a structured approach towards teaching individuals the skills and knowledge needed to manage their future work-roles. Its aim is educational, to foster learning relevant to transitions from one life stage to another. Usually, the transitions are from education into employment or unemployment and it is most developed in the context of school–work transitions. Its principles would however be transferable from, say, employment to retirement or from unpaid work in the home to paid employment. The four main objectives of careers education have been identified (Law and Watts 1977) as the promotion of: opportunity awareness; self-awareness; decision learning; and transition learning. The first two objectives are relevant to the reviewing stage of careers guidance; decision learning relates to goal-setting; and transition learning relates to action planning.

Developing an awareness of opportunities is probably still the core of much careers Education undertaken in schools. Increasingly, this includes opportunities in further education, leisure, the community, and the family, as well as in paid employment. Not only the formal economy, but also informal, alternative economies figure in the experience of many individuals, young and adult. Careers education needs to recognize this wide spectrum of opportunities if it is to be effective. A survey, *Careers Education in the Secondary School* (DES 1973),

269

identified two possible approaches: the infusion approach in which the syllabuses of many subjects included learning about work; and the separate approach in which careers education was timetabled as a distinctive element. The survey noted that neither approach was then widespread, though more recently both have been extended throughout secondary education. Table 17.1 sets out what could be included in specific tasks and activities to enhance opportunity awareness.

Table 17.1 Tasks and activities for enhancing opportunity awareness

Opportunity Awareness: Tasks	*Activities*
• Reviewing curriculum options at school or college	Group discussions individual interviews
• Gaining information on further education and training	Talks, visits, careers conventions
• Increasing job knowledge (entry requirements, occupational styles, rewards)	Job-knowledge indices
• Widening knowledge of occupational fields and families	Games, visits, occupational interest checklists
• Building a base of sources of occupational information	Careers-library work
• Gaining knowledge of local employment	Work experience
• Increasing perceptions of all kinds of work, paid and unpaid	Work shadowing, community and voluntary work

Developing self-awareness involves helping individuals to evaluate their strengths and weaknesses, including abilities, aptitudes, practical and interpersonal skills, personal qualities, and physical attributes. For adults this could mean a reappraisal of work experience to include domestic and parenting roles, voluntary work, and skills not accredited by exams. Of equal importance is the exploration of how individuals feel about work and themselves as workers. Young people and women may have underdeveloped or fragmented self-images because their work experience has been limited, interrupted, or in low-status and undervalued areas. Many clients have blocks or anxieties about their own potential in the job-market and about their saleable skills and competencies.

Counselling is the appropriate response to unblocking development and to strengthening self-images. Careers Service staff are trained and supported to offer such counselling. Many careers teachers may, however, feel uncomfortable in such a role. Indeed, although developing vocational self-awareness may be seen as a general objective of the curriculum in most educational settings, this is difficult to translate into successful programmes. The emphasis remains on subject-related assessments rather than on helping students towards an integrated self-assessment. For young pupils, the General Certificate of Secondary Education and the proposed national curriculum will bring changes as yet unquantifiable. For adults, broader formats of assessment are being tried, with greater client involvement and ownership: profiles, portfolios, self-assessment programmes, and the accreditation of experiential learning are all moves in this direction. However, these remain essentially experimental and small-scale developments.

Table 17.2 sets out some specific tasks and activities in developing self-awareness.

Table 17.2 Tasks and activities for developing self-awareness

Self-awareness: Tasks	*Activities*
• Reviewing qualifications and attainments	Profiles
• Reviewing interests and hobbies	Interest inventories
• Self-assessment of aptitudes, competencies, and attributes (intellectual, social, practical, physical)	Self-diagnostic tests
• Eliciting likes, dislikes, and values	Checklists of likes/dislikes, self-portrayals
• Examining perceptions of sex roles	Role-plays, paired interviews
• Exploring ideal life-styles and occupational preferences	Guided fantasies, questionnaires

Decision learning and transition learning are akin. The first concerns both raising the individual's awareness of how decisions are made and helping her or him to make decisions wisely. This might include reviewing particular decision styles (for example, quick and intuitive, slow and deliberate) and practising strategies for actually making decisions (collecting and collating information, ranking needs, and evaluating outcomes). Transition learning is active preparation for coping with changes. This could involve searching out information about work organization, tax rates, or retirement benefits, and practising the skills appropriate to managing change (for example, writing a curriculum vitae). Providing opportunities for an individual's decision and transition learning, structuring the practice, and giving feedback on progress could be undertaken for clients of all ages by a range of helpers: careers counsellors and teachers, personnel or training managers, and educational-guidance service workers.

The concrete tasks and activities involved are set out in Table 17.3

Table 17.3 Tasks and activities for developing decision and activity learning

Decision Learning: Tasks	*Activities*
• Raising awareness of personal descision-making styles and evaluating those of others	Video, simulations, games role-plays
• Seeking and using feedback	Small group or paired work
• Outlining strategies for logical review of options	Career-decision programmes
• Identifying priorities	Critical-incident reflection
• Crystalizing work choices	Career-decision programmes
Transition Learning: Tasks	*Activities*
• Acquiring study skills	Learning management programmes
• Acquiring coping skills (stress management)	Peer counselling, groupwork
• Knowledge of un/employment rights and benefits	Talks, visits, information sheets
• Practising applications and interviews	Role-plays, groupwork
• Gaining job search and job-retention skills	Role-plays, work-shadowing
• Induction to the workplace (structures, time-keeping, relationships, finance)	Mentoring

Further and higher education

In further and higher education the emphasis is still largely on placement into employment and on general guidance. Increasingly, however, careers counsellors are rethinking their services, despite financial constraints, to prepare clients more adequately for frequent job changes, 'serial' careers, possible unemployment and plural work-roles. Group explorations and decision learning programmes are being provided, in addition to standard interviews. Even more radically there is at least one experiment in infusing the curriculum itself with careers education in an integrated BA course with an 'enabling studies' component (Ball 1984).

Adults

Adults now make on average five significant occupational changes during their working lives. This suggests a large-scale need for both careers and educational guidance. Furthermore, since work affects other major aspects of people's lives – their economic and social status, their self-image and confidence, their intellectual and emotional states – this has implications for other kinds of counselling. However, since the closure of the Occupational Guidance Units in 1980, the provision of work-related guidance has been inadequate and uneven. A pilot study undertaken in one town found a substantial demand for vocational guidance amongst particular groups: the unemployed, women returners, recent job-changers (two-thirds of whom see themselves as future clients for guidance), and the uncommitted (half the economically active sample were 'open to occupational change') (Killeen 1986). The specific forms of guidance they asked for (unprompted) were:

(a) testing and advice to enable them to identify jobs which match their existing abilities, skills, and training;
(b) information on vacancies, training, salary scales, and companies;
(c) counselling for goal-setting and decision-making;
(d) direct assistance in job-getting, or in getting particular types of work.

Existing services certainly do not provide this range or scale of help, but areas of good practice exist.

For a small proportion of clients the Training Agency offers courses with emphasis on confidence-building, self-evaluation, and decision-making. The Wider Opportunities for Women (WOW) courses offer re-appraisal and bridges to further training or employment, with the additional benefits of peer-group support. Career-development courses help redundant professional and managerial staff to rethink their vocational profile and future work-roles and to practise career planning. Counselling supports participants in coping with the stress of change and in rethinking their options.

Educational Guidance Services for Adults (EGSAS), though concerned primarily with further education, also recognize the vital links between adults' roles as learners and workers. A recent report, based on the practice of over eighty services, emphasized that they should be: client-centred, confidential, open and accessible to all, free, independent, widely publicized and able to contribute to the development of education and training (UDACE 1986). As well as being client-centred, with all that implies for staff training, services are also extremely local in character and responsive to specific target-groups.

Workplace services

It is obviously beneficial to have careers guidance available in the workplace, since it is here that employees clarify their aspirations about their current and future jobs. One difficulty in employer-led services is their lack of independence. Ultimately, they may serve organizational goals rather than those of the individual. Nevertheless, if the aim is to develop a closer correspondence between the goals of the organization and those of the employee, then in-house careers guidance can be productive for all participants. Services can range from comprehensive career-development programmes to occasional discussions about training needs. Three kinds can be identified.

First, some companies provide guidance linked to particular stages: mid-career appraisal, resettlement services for employees who leave early, and redundancy and pre-retirement courses. Employers and unions are increasingly able to help employees cope practically and psychologically with these watersheds in employment. Transition programmes might include self-appraisal, counselling, retraining, and advocacy to external agencies.

Second, career-development programmes are now widely undertaken by major employers and professional associations. Ideally, the employer develops a more flexible and motivated work-force and employees gain in skills, job satisfaction, and a more open discussion of their career paths. Some large companies employ careers counsellors. Others, such as ICI, adopt a plural approach including peer counselling by volunteers, career and life-planning workshops, and training for senior managers in careers-counselling approaches (Hopson 1985). Many organizations now develop the basic counselling skills of managers and supervisors, adopting a generalist rather than a specialist approach, and some encourage mentoring or co-counselling arrangements (de Board 1983).

Finally, some workplace training includes careers-education elements and transferable skills such as stress and conflict management, assertiveness, and group working. Training needs analysis itself can prompt individuals to review their existing roles and skills. This kind of work-related learning, although not systematic or accompanied by counselling, can increase participants' self-awareness and adaptability. It may, in fact, be the only careers guidance which some employees get.

Issues

Distinctively, careers counselling spans both the internal psychology of the person and the external contexts of education and employment. Indeed, part of any practitioner's training is to develop a rationale for the interrelation of the two, so as to help clients as effectively as possible. Most of the current issues in careers guidance and counselling revolve around divergent or even conflicting accounts of this relationship between the individual's requirements in relation to work and the social and economic structuring of work opportunities. All guidance agencies have to formulate their objectives in terms of this relationship – and moreover, as employers themselves, to ensure that their own employment practices match their principles for dealing with clients (for example, in equal opportunities for training and promotion).

Three areas currently reflect the divergence of views on how individuals and occupations relate and, as a result, what are the proper roles for careers guidance and counselling: initiatives to create wider definitions of work; the long-running debate on whether people choose or are selected for particular occupations; and the rise of 'vocationalism'.

Wider definitions of work

There are widely differing views of what constitutes a 'career'. Narrowly, a career can be seen as a succession of jobs, often of increasing status, which people move through in a more or less planned sequence. This view is deeply entrenched in the perceptions of employers, as well as of the general public, despite its divergence from the work experience of large numbers of people, including women and the unemployed. In fact, in lay terms it is almost true to say that the middle classes have careers and the rest have jobs. More comprehensive theoretical definitions emphasize that career development, like other human development, covers the life-span and includes *all* a person's learning, decision-making, and adjustments in relation to paid and unpaid work, 'beginning early in life and proceeding along a curve until late in life'(Super 1957).

One result of these wider definitions is that practitioners who have 'careers' in their job or agency title often wish to clarify with clients what this means. Clients with narrow conceptions of careers can have unrealistic expectations of what careers services can deliver. Their role is not that of helping clients match themselves to an occupation which they then climb like a ladder until their particular ceiling is reached. The emphasis may be rather on helping unemployed or non-employed clients to assess their work-related skills on the basis of voluntary or domestic work; or on exploring with clients what kinds of rewards they need from paid employment (for example, status, money, generous free-time, no travel, job satisfactions) and what compromises will best meet their particular priorities. Counsellors may see their role as helping clients recognize the pressures created by narrow conceptions of work and of occupational status, pressures which are only too evident in statements like 'I'm only a housewife.'

The psychology of occupational choice versus the sociology of opportunities

One of the most significant debates in careers guidance over the past decade is that between the psychologists of occupational choice (Daws 1981) and the sociologists of 'opportunity structure' (Roberts 1981). Basically, the debate is about how people come to do their jobs: do they 'choose' them, in any meaningful sense; or are they selected for them by combinations of labour-market forces and class stratifications? Psychological explanations stress personality differences, individual aspirations and striving, and the personal meanings which people give to their work-related behaviour. Sociological accounts, by contrast, stress the social and economic structures which shape people's life-chances in education and in employment and the social and family groups which shape their work attitudes and values.

In general, counselling theory, especially person-centred, Rogerian models, draws more heavily on psychological than on sociological perspectives. Psychological accounts have more immediate appeal to practitioners, and theories of occupational choice are useful training for career workers. Two theories have been particularly influential in careers guidance: matching and developmental accounts.

The first involves evaluating individual differences in abilities, aptitudes, values, or personality types and matching these to existing occupations. Private vocational-guidance services and labour-market policies often assume 'matching' models with a resulting emphasis on assessment. In fact, a range of assessment tools and resources has proved useful to practitioners who would not necessarily subscribe to matching theories of how people choose their occupations.

Developmental theories have had a much more powerful effect on careers-counselling practice. They stress occupational choice as an evolutionary process, encompassing the person's life-span, rather than as a few, isolated decisions. The most comprehensive model is that of Donald Super, based on five life stages: Growth (birth–14), Exploration (15–24), Establishment (25–44), Maintenance (45–64) and Decline (65 onwards). Through these stages, the individual develops her or his self-concept, including core constructs about work and oneself as a worker, by making occupational choices. More recently, Super has outlined a model of a life-career rainbow of nine major roles (child, student, 'leisurite', citizen, worker, spouse, homemaker, parent, and pensioner), played out in four 'theatres' (home, community, education, and work) (Super 1981). Developmental models provide a useful framework for practitioners to support clients in implementing their self-concept. The notion of multiple life-roles is also a useful one for helping clients to map their lives and work on potential role conflicts.

Sociological explanations of occupational choice and of related areas such as social mobility, work entry, gender, and class have proved far less usable and comfortable for careers practitioners, although of evident relevance to their work.

The 'opportunity structure thesis' explains occupational entry in terms of selection and employers' recruitment practices, rather than of individual choice (Robert 1981). People do not choose their jobs; they take what is available. Furthermore, access to different levels of employment depends on educational attainments and, to some extent, on family and social group. Even people's expectations are formed by 'anticipatory socialization' in family and community.

These sociological perspectives represent a major challenge for careers workers. Roberts identifies two possible positions for guidance agencies: an acceptance of placement as their primary function, as part of the social-control apparatus; or an emphasis on clients' self-development, possibly leading them to unrealistic aims that are discordant with the opportunities available. Careers work is either aligned with 'realistic influences' or it is counter-cultural. It cannot be neutral and it is, in any event, marginal.

Rather than confronting these challenges head on and seeing psychological and sociological accounts as mutually exclusive, careers practitioners may prefer to see them as complementary. Many careers workers are fully alive to the contradictions in their work, especially with regard to unemployment, the YTS, and the real options available to people of all ages. Ball (1984: 15) argues that many 'would be happy to admit that one of their major roles was helping young workers to adjust to work as much as it was to help them choose between work alternatives'. Individuals are still rational and purposive in their work-related behaviour. However problematic, practitioners may develop a framework that draws on both the psychology of choice and the sociology of opportunity.

New vocationalism

Related to this issue is that of the 'new vocationalism' and its relationship to careers education. The 14–19 curriculum increasingly contains vocational elements, which has implications for careers, education, and training agencies. Many Careers Services employ specialists in TVE and YTS guidance and course tutors occupy defined roles in vocational preparation. Programmes for all age-groups have been developed with social and life-skills components and strategies for coping with unemployment. The arguments for such elements are based on 'realism' about the probable life chances of participants. Critics argue, however, that such vocationalism, by being directed at supposedly non-academic groups, functions divisively and actually restricts opportunities and self-awareness. Vocational elements are not available equally across the ability range, but introduce a segregated curriculum at an early stage. As a result, some participants adjust their occupational goals downwards and psychological deskilling is subtly reinforced.

These issues affect not only the way all careers guidance activities are constituted and funded, at the level of policy, but also the daily relationship of helpers and clients. Overarching questions of how society structures and rewards different kinds of work and how work opportunities are allocated or chosen are constantly translated into daily decisions about resources, priorities, and counselling styles. For this reason practitioners need to engage with them as actively as possible.

Future developments

It seems unlikely that further resources for careers guidance and counselling will be available on a scale that would match existing demand and the increased need likely to be created by current trends. These trends include women's increasing re-entry to work after breaks for child-rearing (two in five of the work-force are women); greater job mobility and more career changes amongst all adults; emphasis on adult retraining and continuing education, often in part-time, flexible, or open and distance learning forms which require learners to be clearly motivated and independent; and far-reaching, as yet unmeasured, changes in the school curriculum. Many practitioners in the field are wryly aware of the gaps between policy and experience, between, say, the rhetoric of lifelong learning and actual participation rates in adult learning or between fluctuations in unemployment figures and the hopes and frustrations experienced by many of their clients in relation to work.

Future developments are likely to consist of small steps in the direction already apparent, rather than in any radical reformation of services or new commitment of resources. The most likely areas for development are in the technologies for delivering services, in the more plural and flexible models of careers guidance and counselling, and in the training which underpins both these changes.

Self-help resources

One route for achieving more accessible and – possibly – more economical guidance is in the extended use of self-help resources and technology-assisted systems. There is now a wide range of aids and programmes which, either mediated by careers workers or acting as 'stand alone' facilities, meet some needs for information, assessment, and counselling (many are listed, with addresses, in Ball 1984). As far as text-based resources are concerned, careers counsellors have a large repertoire of tools for assessing clients' aptitudes, interests, and work values, or for exploring their knowledge of different occupations. More recently, however, workshops and packs have been developed which people can buy or borrow in order to clarify careers issues, working either alone or in groups. Popular examples are *Build Your Own Rainbow: A Workbook for Careers and Life Management* (Hopson and Scally 1984), designed to help users' career decision-making, and *Work Choices* (Open University 1985), designed to help users review their work options and locate sources of help. Such packs are helpful in several ways. If used alone, they can prompt structured self-exploration, for example in eliciting what priorities the user has for employment. If used by a group, they can stimulate support and peer counselling. If used before a counselling interview, they can clarify issues and prompt more focused and purposeful questions by the client.

Computer-assisted services

Computerized guidance resources are of two kinds. There are database systems for information retrieval and processing which are becoming increasingly comprehensive and efficient. Second, there are programs for self-exploration, assessment, and decision learning which are being developed for specific user-groups (school pupils, higher-education students, job changers, and so on).

In the first group are databases of national and – increasingly – local information which underpin much careers and educational guidance. ECCTIS (Educational Counselling and Credit Transfer Information Service) provides records of all further- and higher-education in the UK of more than 6 weeks and leading to a qualification. On-line access is via Prestel–Gateway and records are also available on microfiche and compact disc. MARIS-NET (Materials and Resources Information Service) has records of over 9,000 work-related open-learning packages and can be searched by subject, qualification, or package supplier. The PICKUP (Professional, Industrial and Commercial Updating) database covers work-related short courses, with information for employers on customized training programmes. These three major systems can also be accessed via TAPs (Training Access Points), which are experimental regional networks of information, guidance, and employer agencies with on-line computer points in places such as libraries, workplaces, Careers Services, and Shops.

Computerised systems have obvious advantages over paper-based systems. There are, however, important questions about who should bear their considerable updating costs: providers of information, such as employers and colleges; guidance agencies and intermediaries; end users, either individuals or organizations; or government? Moreover, should such systems be developed as tools for guidance workers or as direct, hands-on information sources for clients?

Computerised systems for helping users to clarify options or to develop vocational learning are also being designed. Some require users to feed in information, either directly or in questionnaires, about their work preferences, aptitudes, and interests so that the job suggestions, with relevant entry information, can be generated. JIIG/CAL (Job Ideas and Information Generator – Computer-Assisted Learning) and CASCAID (Careers Advisory Service Computer Aid) have been widely used with school pupils and versions are available for adults and higher-education students respectively. Besides these matching systems, there are more interactive programs. Here the emphasis is on reviewing preferences rather than on generating job suggestions. Prospect HE, developed as part of the DES's Computer-Assisted Guidance Project, is currently being piloted. The project aims ambitiously to develop systems that help users to understand career planning and decision-making; to assess their own current career-development; to evaluate information about careers; and to formulate goals and action plans.

The potential of such systems is hardly glimpsed as yet. Evaluation shows some success in both raising self-awareness and developing vocational learning. Furthermore, people enjoy using them. As one element in a guidance process they can open up issues for counselling very creatively. As 'stand alone' systems their potential remains to be tested. They can offer complete privacy and limited structures for exploration; but they are costly to develop and need expensive refinement for various client groups and purposes. With the inevitable growth of information technology, the availability of all these systems will increase. How far development will be towards more truly accessible and client-owned guidance systems depends rather on political and economic factors than on technological innovation.

More integrated services?

In the wider context the most significant improvement in guidance provision might be in the better integration of agencies. This would mean a rationalisation of services for all ages and client groups. It is, for example, inequitable that higher-education students, already privileged, have provided for them a level and quality of careers counselling not available to other groups with equally distinct needs. The integration of educational and vocational guidance, if not well developed in conceptual models and theories, is slowly happening on the ground through regional networks, referral procedures, and Local Education Authority co-ordination. Education and work links are improving through work experience schemes and community-interaction projects. Field research is important to evaluate the outcomes of specific schemes and to contribute to developmental models of guidance and counselling.

In a different dimension, more integrated services would also provide stronger links between careers counselling and personal or psychotherapeutic support. Choices about work frequently involve people's core identities, arousing powerful feelings about self-worth and self-image, which guidance workers may feel ill-equipped to acknowledge and cope with. In extreme cases, such as long-term unemployment, mid-career frustration, and direct conflict between roles as mother/wife and employee, the client's affective state may prevent any constructive careers guidance as such. To discuss work preferences with clients who are suffering from chronic indecisiveness or acute anxiety caused by repeated rejections in the job market or who are experiencing paralysing guilt over leaving their children, albeit temporarily, is unlikely to be productive. Guidance workers need to know when and where to refer their clients for personal counselling that responds to their pressing needs. Only after coping with these blocks can clients benefit from specific careers counselling.

In more general terms, it is arguable that existing models of careers counselling pay insufficient attention to the affective dimensions of decision-making and to the profound repercussions that work roles have on clients' personal lives, including their marriages, parenting, and psychological well-being.

Since any significant increase in resources is unlikely, the better integration of services depends not only on improved networking but also on improved training. Career specialists would benefit from knowledge of personal or psychotherapeutic strategies. Those who include careers guidance amongst other roles would gain from specific training in careers work. Managers, trainers, union and association representatives, tutors and teachers, broadcasters, and advisory-service staff all deal on a daily basis with clients experiencing work-related problems or considering career opportunities. Counsellors in medical or personal contexts often encounter career conflicts which have a sharp relevance to their client's well-being, although not the presenting issue. Providing training in careers guidance and counselling for a wide range of people in managerial or advisory roles is likely to prove both satisfying for them and cost-effective for organizations. Modularized programmes, open learning, and self-contained courses on, say, careers-counselling interviewing would allow participants to select the level of training that matched their needs. Modules on both the practical and theoretical approaches to careers guidance, as well as awareness training on gender, culture, and class in relation to careers structures and opportunities, might be appropriate.

All these developments are towards the wider, if gradual, dissemination and co-ordination of careers guidance as a range of helping processes. It is not simply that more means better. More information, on occupations, relevant training, prospects, vacancies, and so on is not enough, unless ordinary people can locate it, relate to it, and use it. Information is a commodity which is unequally available, resulting in the 'information rich' and the 'information poor'. It is important to develop systems which are not only comprehensive, but fully accessible. This means that alongside information systems should be other forms of help – advice, counselling, assessment, and advocacy – if careers guidance is to be more effective and more equally available.

References

Ball, B. (1984) *Careers Counselling in Practice*, London and Philadelphia: Falmer Press.

Daws, P. P. (1981) 'The socialisation/opportunity-structure theory of the occupational location of school leavers: a critical appraisal', in A. G. Watts, D. Super, and J. Kidd (eds) *Career Development in Britain*, Cambridge: CRAC/Hobsons.

de Board, R. (1983) *Counselling People at Work*, Aldershot, Hants: Gower.

Department of Education and Science (1973) *Careers Education in the Secondary School*, London: DES.

Hopson, B. (1985) 'Adult life and career counselling', *British Journal of Guidance and Counselling* 13(1): 49–59.

——and Scally, M. (1984) *Build Your Own Rainbow: A Workbook for Career and Life Management*, Leeds: Lifeskills Associates.

Killeen, J. (1986) *Vocational Guidance: A Study of the Demand in One Town*, Hertford: National Institute for Careers Education and Counselling.

Law, B. and Watts, A. G. (1977) *Schools, Careers and Community*, London: Church Information Office.

Open University (1985) *Work Choices*, Milton Keynes: Open University.

Roberts, K. (1981) 'The sociology of work entry and occupational choice', in A. G. Watts, D. Super, and J. Kidd (eds) *Career Development in Britain*, Cambridge: CRAC/Hobsons.

Super, D. E. (1957) *The Psychology of Careers*, New York: Harper & Row.

——(1981) 'Approaches to occupational choice and career development' in A. G. Watts, D. Super, and J. Kidd. (eds) *Career Development in Britain*, Cambridge: CRAC/Hobsons.

Watts, A. G. (1980) 'Educational and careers guidance services for adults: I. A rationale and conceptual framework', *British Journal of Guidance and Counselling* 8(1): 11–22.

——(1981) 'Career patterns', in A. G. Watts, D. Super, and J. Kidd (eds) *Career Development in Britain*, Cambridge: CRAC/Hobsons.

Unit for the Development of Adult Continuing Education (1986) *The Challenge of Change: Developing Educational Guidance for Adults*, Leicester: UDACE.

Chapter eighteen

Counselling in the context of redundancy and unemployment

Tony Milne

Introduction

The redundancy of a job can lead to the unemployment of the job-holder, who may then wrongly describe himself[1] as redundant. Redundancy, in the proper use of the term, occurs when the need for a particular kind of work in an organization decreases or ceases. It may be compulsory or voluntary and the term has legal implications. Unemployment may be taken here simply to refer to the state of not having a job, when one is desired – without entering the argument about whether that is paid or unpaid.

Of course, reasons other than redundancy may lead to unemployment – resignation, dismissal for misconduct, ill-health, or early retirement, which is sometimes a euphemism. Counselling people in several of these categories was usually covered by the term 'redundancy counselling.' Today, however, 'redeployment counselling' is often a better term. This is mainly so because today the individual employee is frequently told that the organization cannot offer her the sort of future which she would want for herself: there is no question of compulsory redundancy, but the organization would expect her to be gone within, say, a year. Redeployment, sometimes internal, often external, is the appropriate word, since there is no compulsory individual redundancy; nevertheless, there is a move to another job. Certainly, redeployment, like redundancy itself, may generate a great deal of painful feeling, which blocks rational decision-making. Counselling is the appropriate way of helping. Many individuals and agencies are today engaged in this. A common, if rather inappropriate, term used by some agencies is 'outplacement', meaning that redundant individuals are assisted to find a place outside their previous employing organization.

As our own experience has been mainly in counselling the recently redundant, redeployed, early retired, or longer-term (up to, say, 2 years) unemployed managers, executives, professional people, and other white-collar employees, the focus of this chapter is on them.

Principles

Redundancy counselling in this country started in the early 1970s, when it was pioneered by CEPEC (the centre for professional employment counselling), whose founder – himself made redundant – soon discovered that people in a similar situation needed a phase of counselling, in the professional sense, before they could concentrate on coaching issues. After coaching comes communicating. The world refers to the whole process (counselling, coaching, and communicating) as 'counselling' but it is helpful to distinguish when appropriate between the three phases. We are here concerned with the first – counselling – but it may be helpful to explain what we mean by the other two terms. Coaching is a more problem-centred activity than counselling, and involves the counsellor being more directive than in counselling. An example of a coaching task would be helping a client to write a better curriculum vitae (CV). Communicating covers the drawing up by the client, with the counsellor's help, of a marketing plan, learning how to identify potential employers and approach them in ways likely to result in selection interviews: this phase, too, demands more managerial skills than the earlier ones. One phase merges gradually into the next, with loop-backs, the helper turning in a sense from a true counsellor into someone managing the client's management of his own job-search.

There are two ways of writing about the phase of counselling: by taking a counsellor's framework for approaching it, and by examining some of the commonest themes which clients bring to the counselling. Both approaches will be adopted in this chapter.

The counsellor's framework

Clients bring to redundancy counselling the widest range of problems and it becomes clear that you cannot tease apart, so to speak, a person's job and career from other aspects of his life. The Manpower Services Commission (MSC), now the Training Commission, when we did some extensive work for them a few years ago, wanted us to do this. It was initially felt that the unemployed people, whom they were sponsoring for help in finding new jobs, should pay privately to get their own, separate, personal counselling elsewhere. We explained that this separation is impossible and it was subsequently accepted that a whole-person counselling approach is essential.

Being redundant at least gives the individual an opportunity, rare in normal working life, to stand back, look at where he has come from, where he is currently, where he wants to get to, and the strengths and areas for development which he has for this journey. This is best done with the help of someone who is not emotionally involved, as a member of the family will be; has no power relationship, as a boss will; and is trained. Such a person is of course a counsellor, and counsellors have indeed helped a great many redundant people to find a new direction in life. One of the best tributes I had was from a client who said, 'I came into counselling to find a job, but I have found myself.'

The range of issues which may come up is well covered by a useful mnemonic for redundancy counsellors, the Flouch Factors, named after John Flouch, a pioneer in redundancy counselling:

F Financial

L Leisure interests

O Occupational history

U Understanding of self and others

C Care of time

H Health

The redundancy counsellor needs to see that each of these is covered, though not necessarily in that order.

Financial

When your job is made redundant and you have to leave the organization for which you may have worked for many years, there is an initial phase of shock. When this feeling has subsided, there remains a worrying uncertainty about the future: how long will the money received as compensation have to last? This leads to two difficulties. First, the redundant person may tend to cut himself off socially: 'We can't afford to entertain.' He is in danger of becoming socially rusty, which will show at an interview for a job. Second, if his employer has not provided counselling for him, he may be reluctant to spend his own money on counselling help. Redundancy counsellors do not need to go in detail into a client's finances. A simple first question will suffice to establish the facts: 'What is your financial situation, in general terms?'

Investment of large lump sums is best left to an appropriate financial adviser, who may need in some cases to be a tax expert as well.

Leisure interests

A client's hobbies and other ways of spending non-work time, past as well as present, will often tell a counsellor a good deal about the client. In addition, they may lead to a new career. An example would be the ex-RAF officer who had been interested in clocks and watches in earlier years. A course in horology enabled him to set himself up in the country as a restorer and repairer of antique clocks.

Occupational history

A matter for early determination is whether the client has considered, if only to reject, the possibility of self-employment. Some outplacement agencies seem to assume that all their clients want to go back into similar employment. Not all do, if given the opportunity to consider matters. Of course, they must have a clear idea of what product or service they want to offer. Above all, they must have the right personality; too many people fail in self-employment when this could have been predicted on the basis of a simple personality inventory. A valuable device is Dr Max Kostick's Perception and Preference Inventory (PAPI), which demands a dialogue between counsellor and client. Its focus is personality at work and it covers such items, relevant to self-employment, as degree of need for the support which a structured organization offers; need for rules and supervision; ability to seize a chance, plan, market self or services; and so on.

The counsellor may in practice first take the client's most recent job situation, perhaps the period leading up to the job loss, and the circumstances surrounding it. There is often a great need to discharge feelings. These feelings have been well described elsewhere (Harrison 1976). There is commonly a phase of shock and anger, often followed by one of somewhat unreal optimism and then a stage of depression. The counsellor's approach in each phase needs to be different. In the first case, she needs to help the client to express the anger; in the second, to see that there are things to be learned about today's job search, and the counsellor can teach them; in the last case, the task is to restore the client's optimism and self-assurance.

Next, an occupational history should be taken, with particular emphasis on interpersonal relationships. The counsellor is always asking herself, 'What are the job-stoppers here?' In other words, what most stands in the way of this client finding and keeping a satisfying job as quickly as possible? The words 'keeping' and 'satisfying' are important. Is the counsellor really helping if the client finds another job but loses it again within three months? Again, a job as a petrol forecourt-attendant may not be very satisfying to a manager. The emphasis on interpersonal relationships will sometimes throw up that these have been bad. The personal qualities in the client leading or contributing to these problems may become apparent in a selection interview, leading to rejection. The counsellor may need to help the client to tackle the difficulties. If they concern maladaptive behaviour, for example, the counsellor needs to help the client to effect a deep change in behaviour, using whatever approach the particular counsellor favours.

Transferable skills must also be analysed by the client, with the counsellor's help; or they may need expression in terms attractive to employers. Former members of the armed services and police officers, are sometimes poor at this. A Police Constable, for example, may think that keeping a notebook, which he has done for years, is of no interest to a future employer. He can be helped to express this activity in terms like, 'the ability to write concise but accurate reports'. This is often a sought-after strength. Unemployed people are very unsure of their strengths; their self-image has been battered and it is a counsellor's task to help restore this. 'Tell me about your strengths' and 'Tell me three things you like about yourself' are helpful questions in this area.

Understanding of self and others

The counsellor needs to know about the client's family: both the original one from which the client came and any present relationships. Whether the client is an elder, middle, younger, or only child may well have its significance, as will, quite certainly, the general pattern of childhood. 'How do you remember your childhood?' is a question whose answer in itself will be revealing. The parents' methods of controlling the child are also significant: was it predominantly squash, ignore, or rescue (Lake 1987)? There seem to be no alternatives, and each method of control will produce characteristics in the adult. Home is where we start from, and we all carry forward unfinished childhood business into adult life. As to present family, the attitude of the spouse to the unemployed person may be important.

How far does the client understand herself? What values does the client have? Clients in transition – and redundancy is commonly a transition – are people whose values are changing. What is the client's motivation? Can he make decisions without difficulty? Does she have an action plan for the future? What use does the counsellor make of all the information gained? Some of it is to understand the client better, and so empathize more accurately. Elder or eldest children, for example, are commonly more affected than others by rejection; acceptance is particularly important to them. They may react more strongly than others to redundancy, a form of rejection. Other information guides the counsellor on how to react best to the client: those ignored in earlier years, for example, need a different approach from those squashed. Lastly, such matters as poor presentation in interviews must be discussed with the client, and help offered in improving this. A counsellor can only do this on the basis of a good understanding of the client.

Care of time

When the client has been assisted to explore every part of his life, the counsellor may think that each part separately (for example, family and job) is without any serious problems. Nevertheless, when put together, the balance between them may need further exploration. Thus, for example, a client at this time may realize that previously 95 per cent of his time has gone to work and 5 per cent to family, and this is not what the client wants for the future. Again, getting the client to take you as counsellor through a typical day can be helpful and revealing. The counsellor is here acting like a mirror, holding up to the client what she is, perhaps without realizing it, doing with her life.

Health

This may cover both mental and physical aspects. At redundancy, there may appear to be an excess of mental or severe emotional problems, or of marital difficulties. Have they been produced by the redundancy? In our experience, they commonly have not. It may in fact be the other way around: they have led to redundancy; or they have been there all along but have been covered up, the individual holding himself together with the help of the structure to life which employment provides. The health problems have been ignored for a long time; this is no longer possible when the structure to life goes, with the job loss, and the difficulties come to the surface.

Physical health may also be a problem, often for older people, although of course individual cases vary enormously. When appropriate, a medical opinion should be sought. Certainly, most counsellors are not medically qualified, and their task is often, under the heading of health, to refer the client to others, being careful not to give the client the feeling of being rejected.

The clients' themes

Probably the main counselling theme in redundancy is that of uncertainty. There is uncertainty about so many issues: 'Shall I get another job? Am I too old to do so? How long will it take? What sort of job will it be? Should I go self-employed? How shall we manage financially? Can we afford a holiday? Can we entertain like we used to? What will our friends and neighbours think? Shall we have to relocate? Should I take the company to an industrial tribunal? How will my spouse and the children take it?' – and so on. All this uncertainty can be stressful.

'Shall I get another job?'

The counsellor must be able to answer this convincingly. The answer is almost certainly 'Yes'. There are plenty of ways in the economy of earning money; not all of them are satisfying. The client may also impose limitations: 'It must be the same as I was doing before, within 2 miles of my present home, and at a higher salary...' In CEPEC, we can point to our experiment for the MSC in counselling 100 unemployed men and women; job-placement rates were used by the MSC as the measure of the success of counselling. Those counselled were shown to find jobs significantly faster than members of a matched control group, who just had other 'mechanical' help, like CV writing, but with no counselling, available to them. Thus, our work has been validated – a unique piece of research in the field of employment counselling (Coolbear and Fairbairns 1981).

Unemployed clients tend to talk in terms of, 'If I get another job...' It is important for the counsellor to encourage them to say, 'When I get another job...' Altering the words affects the client's inner world of thoughts and feelings. This in turn affects his body language and behaviour, which become more positive.

'Am I too old?'

We have no laws in this country against age discrimination. An Institute of Personnel Management code urges companies against it, but it still seems entrenched. It is only necessary to study job advertisements to see that organizations rarely say that they can consider anyone over 45. They usually seem to want someone aged 27–35. I often wonder about the fate of the personnel staff who place these advertisements, if they themselves have to change jobs after 45. However, the counsellor can do a lot to help the client in this field. A great

288

deal depends on the feelings of the client about his or her age. If these are negative, that will come across in an interview, with consequent rejection – reinforcing the age stereotype which the client has. There are some twenty ways in which more mature and experienced people have more to offer than younger ones. These include greater experience of the world and of people; therefore greater common sense; better judgement; less casual absenteeism; and much more. The counsellor's task is to get the client to think of as many of these as possible.

'How long will it take to find a job?'

This varies greatly and while one person will be lucky enough to be out of work for only a matter of days, another will take months to find a position. Statistics will not help an individual. The counsellor should prepare the client for the possibility that it may take months rather than days.

'What sort of job will it be?'

In some redundancy helping ('outplacement') agencies, there seems to be an assumption that clients will want to go back into exactly the same sort of job as they had previously. This is by no means always the case. When, in counselling, clients reflect on the past, they may realize how unsatisfying it really was, or how unfulfilled they were. The counsellor needs to help the client to identify the most satisfying career direction in which it is practical to go.

Satisfying careers and jobs for people depend on four factors as far as the individual is concerned: ability, aptitude, personality, and occupational interest. A counsellor must take all four into account and has the possibility of using an inventory to get some measure of the last two. 'Test' is an inappropriate word, as they cannot be measured, and therefore cannot be tested. However, good inventories are available: PAPI, mentioned above, for personality, and Rothwell-Miller for occupational interest. The new unisex version of the latter produces much useful dialogue between counsellor and client.

'Should I go self-employed?'

As has been noted above, too many people fail in self-employment for reasons connected with their personality. Inventories are available which enable these failures to be predicted and they should be used. In self-employment, for example, there are few rules laid down by others. The self-employed person writes the rules, so that very structured personalities, with a high need for external rules and supervision, may find that self-employment is not for them.

'How shall we manage financially?'

Unemployed people often need some simple financial coaching, on how to draw up a budget, how to deal with the mortgage, and how to find sources of income – perhaps some part-time activity, consultancy, or selling the junk in the garage. However, where large sums are involved – as from redundancy payments – it is essential to involve a financial expert, probably also knowledgeable in tax matters.

'Can we afford a holiday, or to entertain?'

Whether a holiday is affordable must be determined by the budget forecasts, but entertainment is in a special category. There are three great perils in unemployment: mental stagnation, social isolation, and getting physically run down (leading to mental laziness). These may show at an interview for a job ('He seems rather out of touch...') Mental stagnation can be avoided in many ways: a correspondence course, a structured reading programme, membership of some local committee. Social isolation must be avoided; there is no need to entertain on the same scale as before, but at least ask friends in for a cup of tea. Lastly, the unemployed client should be encouraged to take an amount of exercise appropriate to her build and weight, to avoid the difficulties mentioned above.

'What will friends and family think? Will we have to relocate?'

There are many stories of husbands, when unemployed, continuing to leave the house at the same time every day, because they have not told their families. These cases do, in our experience, exist, but they are rare. A lack of openness with the children, on the other hand, seems more common. People cannot be supportive if they do not know the facts, and it is important to an unemployed person to have support. People are often reluctant, when a company closes one site, to relocate to another site owned by the same company. The fear is that the second site may then close, with no alternative, leaving the person to live among strangers. It is hard for a counsellor to help with this question; it is more a matter for a national housing policy. Certainly, children's education may be important in considering relocation. Every counsellor has heard from clients about the problems in family life which may follow from a company's need for complete managerial mobility. In that regard, counsellors concerned with family issues – and few are not – are probably glad that more and more managers are against national mobility – i.e. the possibility of being posted anywhere in the country.

'Should I bring an action against the company?'

Often, the unemployed client is angry against the organization which has made his job redundant. He wants to get back at 'them' in the organization. If there has been real injustice, this may be appropriate. However, the counsellor should consider helping the client to see that the future is more important than the past; that awards at tribunals, even after devoting much time to them, are commonly quite small; and that the employer, if challenged, will probably bring out publicly in the tribunal matters which the client would prefer left unsaid. We have known too many clients who, before coming to us, had become obsessed with revenge: they cherished huge files of papers on their cases, but rarely thought about the job-search. Some of these clients are clinically obsessed and require specialist help.

Issues

One of the first issues in redundancy counselling is: 'Who offers it?' CEPEC has always advocated three levels of counselling skills for employing organizations: line managers should have elementary skills – probably best referred to simply as listening and observational skills – while personnel and related staff need more developed counselling skills. Then there is the need from time to time for independent external counsellors. Line managers can probably not offer redundancy counselling, as individuals may see them as having been responsible for their redundancy. These managers will, however, benefit from some instruction in how to break the news of redundancy. Even personnel staff will, with one exception, often be seen as too close to the organization responsible for an individual's situation. The exception is where an organization has had some of its own staff professionally trained in counselling skills, and has set up an independent Resettlement Unit, or something similar. That can be effective, particularly where there is redeployment rather than true redundancy.

In most cases, this leaves the independent external redundancy counsellor as the only possible helper. Even where an internal Resettlement Unit has been established, some cases will be beyond them, in terms of time or competence, so that referral to an external agency will alone make sense.

How can an organization best choose an external redundancy counsellor? There are a number of outplacement agencies which offer help, and at different levels of staff. While a few of them employ accredited counsellors, many do not – whatever title they may use. The employer seeking the best help is advised to ask a number of questions:

— does the agency employ staff trained in counselling in the professional sense, with at least a proportion of them accredited?;
— does it adhere to the codes of ethics of the British Association for Counselling? (see Chapter 25 by Charles-Edwards *et al.*);
— does it put professional considerations before commercial ones, or the reverse?;
— has its placement record been validated with a proper statistical study?; and
— does it take on virtually any client, or refuse to register some whom it considers poor placement risks, liable to spoil its placement record?

Some employers adopt the practice of giving redundant staff a list of several outplacement agencies, and asking the staff to choose whichever they prefer. This is not good practice. Redundant people are not necessarily in the best frame of mind to make a rational choice. In addition, as CEPEC knows well from many cases, the staff sometimes have a tendency to choose the most expensive agency, to get back at their employers, who will pay the fees.

Who should pay?

Some employers, on the grounds that they have made a large financial settlement with the individual, will not pay for outplacement services, leaving the employee to do so from the settlement. In fact, many employees, uncertain how long the money will have to last, are reluctant to pay out for resettlement help. It would in fact be better for the employee if the employer would, instead of giving the employee, say, £10,000, give him £8,000 cash and pay the balance for outplacement help. But should the employer pay everything? This is a general issue in work counselling, applying also to developmental counselling (when the job is not lost, but there are issues affecting performance at work). There is much to be said for the client making a contribution, but the mechanics of this are not easy to arrange, and it will be some time before employers and employees accept this.

At what stage should a redundancy counsellor be called in?

Some employers like to have an outplacement-agency representative in the next room at the announcement of redundancy, so that the employee, probably in a state of shock, can be taken straight in to see his counsellor. This may result in the counsellor spending most of his time persuading the employee to use his agency, and come and see him in his office. This does not seem very ethical. A counsellor should certainly be involved within a day or two, away from the employer's premises, but not quite so quickly as in the preceding case!

The stages of life

We have found it valuable to think about redundant clients against a background of understanding of the stages of life, in developmental terms. We have repeatedly found the work of Jung (1960) and Levinson (1978) valuable. Is the client at mid-life transition? Does he feel on a developmental plateau? Has he had, does he have, could he become, a mentor? It assists the counsellor to understand the client if he realizes that the client is, say, at mid-life transition; there is so commonly much inner turbulence at this time, a questioning, a revaluing, an urge to change careers. It helps the client, too, if the counsellor can explain that the client is not unique in these feelings, but that they are common.

Future developments

One important spur to counselling at work in this country was the situation in the 1970s of mergers and take-overs, often leading to redundancy. Having established Resettlement Units offering counselling, the companies concerned realized that they had a resource which could be used for career development counselling. This is likely to become more established in the future, so that people will become increasingly aware of their career plans and how to achieve them. This may well relieve redundancy counsellors of time otherwise spent on career counselling, enabling them to give more time to personal issues affecting performance. Counsellors will probably also be able to give more attention to the clients' self-presentation, exploring with them how they are likely to come across to potential employers.

Computers are beginning to be used in redundancy counselling. Some outplacement agencies are beginning to provide computer links between their offices and their clients' homes; one wonders about the feelings of isolation which may result from this. Outplacement agencies can also tap into extensive computer networks giving information for their clients' benefit on, for example, potential future employers. There are also an increasing number of computer programs on careers guidance, the best taking values and motivating factors into account, as well as qualifications and crude career categories. Work on such computer guidance services will grow. Can counselling itself be computerized? The Training Commission (TC) seems to thinks so, having recently solicited project submissions for this. A counselling program was in fact written years before the TC interest, and was tested out by CEPEC counsellors. It was indeed intriguing, but maddening. The computer got you to type in your name, and then the program proceeded:

Computer: Hello, Clarence! What do you want to talk about?

Client: Sex.

Computer: What aspect of sex do you want to talk about?

Client: Performance.

Computer: How do you feel about your performance?

and so on. *Talking* to a *visual* computer produces some neuro-linguistic programming (NLP) horrors. The NLP thesis (Lewis and Pucelik 1982), which we believe to be correct, is that different people access and process information within themselves in different ways; three of the main ones are visual, audio, and kinesthetic (touching and feeling). Thus, visual processors tend to use phrases like, 'As I see it, the picture is rather dark...', while audio processors prefer words like 'From what I hear, it doesn't ring a bell at all...' It can thus be seen how communicating with a computer can benefit most those who process information visually and benefit least those who are kinesthetic processors.

Could we use the computer in a different way? I think we could. BUPA reports that people will often be more truthful – for example about sex – to a machine than to another person. Could we usefully use a computer before person-to-person counselling? It could gather a large volume of data about a person's life, prompting the counsellor on areas to help the client to explore.

Next, there is likely to be a significant change in this country in attitudes to counselling itself. The future of counselling at work, including redundancy counselling, will be affected by these changes. It is the author's speculation that most people will have dialogues with a counsellor from time to time, starting from some point in childhood; thus, counselling will not be seen as weak, or indicative of problems or difficulties, but as entirely normal. This will make redundancy counselling more readily accepted, and hence easier for the counsellor, freeing time to help with more difficult issues in the client: personal matters, behavioural problems, and so on. This implies that redundancy counsellors will have to become even more professional and highly trained, in order to be able to assist the client with these issues. Accreditation by the British Association for Counselling, with its insistence on supervision, will assume greater importance. Work counselling, including redundancy counselling, will become a more widely accepted branch of counselling, with its own special training.

Lastly, there is the matter of the emergence of some kind of Association for redeployment counsellors or their organizations, to ensure ethical standards and practices, together with appropriate training. Some form of Association, perhaps a European one, must emerge. Too many agencies use the word 'counsellor' when they mean 'consultant'. All trained counsellors know of so many ethical issues that can arise; hence the Code of Ethics of the British Association for Counselling (see Chapter 25 by Charles-Edwards *et al.*). People who have suffered redundancy are vulnerable. There have been cases, for example, of such clients being asked to invest money in the outplacement agency that is helping them. An example of another difficult issue would be that in which an outplacement agency rejects applicants because they might be poor job-placement risks – difficult to help to resettle in another job. To accept them might, in the eyes of the agency, damage the agency's placement statistics, but is this refusal ethically acceptable?

Just as redundancy counsellors have to know something of many branches of counselling, so other counsellors in the future should know more about the world of work in general and redundancy counselling in particular. Just as general counselling issues are taught on work counselling courses – for example, matters concerning bereavement counselling, marital matters, or psycho-sexual issues – so work counselling should be more widely taught on general counselling courses.

Redundancy, or enforced job-change of some kind, will continue, and perhaps accelerate in our society, so that the need for redundancy counselling will not diminish. Hopefully, as the process develops, the stigma so often associated with redundancy will begin to diminish, and the event be seen as an opportunity, rather than a crisis, for the individual.

Note

1   I have written 'himself' partly because there are many more men than women in the groups which are the focus of this chapter, but from now on I shall use the masculine and the feminine interchangeably and more or less alternately.

References

Coolbear, J. and Fairbairns, J. (1981) *Evaluation Study of an Experimental Career Counselling Programme for PER Registrants*, London: Psychological Services, Training Services Division, Manpower Services Commission, Report DTP 23, June.

Harrison, R. (1976) 'The demoralising experience of prolonged unemployment', *Department of Employment Gazette* (April): 330–49.

Jung, C. G. (1960) See especially 'The stages of life' in *Collected Works* (volume 8), London: Routledge.

Lake, T. (1987) *Defeating Depression*, London: Penguin.

Levinson, D. J. (1978) *The Seasons of a Man's Life*, New York: Alfred A. Knopf.

Lewis, B. A. and Pucelik, R. F. (1982) *Magic Demystified: An Introduction to NLP*, Oregon: Metamorphous Press.

Chapter nineteen

Counselling, death, and bereavement

Averil Stedeford

Principles

Many of the chapters in this section of the handbook are about minority groups within the population, who are suffering because of their situation or the attitude of others to them, and it is generally accepted that counselling will be beneficial to them. Dying and bereavement are not like this. They happen to everyone and cannot be avoided; nor is it always appropriate to attempt to relieve the distress they cause, temporarily disabling though it may be. The dying person who has rich inner resources to draw on, and who has adequate support from family or friends, has no need of professional intervention. This may be equally true of the bereaved individual or family. However, many people are not so fortunate and for them counselling is likely to be necessary and effective. Unless they are asked for help, counsellors first have to decide whether to offer it or not. If they do, one of their main tasks will be to act as monitors, watching their clients go through a process which, though normal, may be very painful. They aim to offer their clients support, to help them to understand what is happening and find meaning in it, and to cope with it in a way that causes least suffering to all concerned. People can grow emotionally and spiritually while they are facing their own death and during the suffering of bereavement, and counsellors may be able to recognize and reinforce responses that lead to such growth (Pincus 1976). They also need to be aware that the normal process can be altered: responses may become maladaptive and destructive, leading to an escalation of suffering which might be prevented or relieved by appropriate interventions. Counsellors must therefore be familiar with the range of experiences that happen to the dying and the bereaved so that they know when to support and reassure and when to intervene more actively. They must also recognize those psychological complications of terminal illness and bereavement which would be more effectively treated by another professional, and be able to co-operate with that person or hand the case over if necessary.

The dying person is facing the loss of his or her own life, and those around that person are facing bereavement: the loss of a significant relationship. There is a cluster of responses which is common to any loss, and each kind of loss imposes its own variation on this basic theme. Familiarity with this core group of reactions enables counsellors to understand more easily what is happening to the dying and the bereaved and to choose and time their interventions appropriately.

Responding to loss

At the moment of recognition that something valuable has been or is about to be lost, there is a sense of *shock* and a disruption of the activity that was going on at the time. What has occurred may seem unbelievable, and if the trauma is severe, a protective emotional *numbness* may occur, temporarily preventing the person from being overwhelmed by the full impact of the event that has hit him or her. Also protective but in a different way is the response of *denial*. The person who vigorously declares that something is not true is putting up a fight against his or her growing suspicion that it might be, and is searching for a way of avoiding the distress which will accompany acceptance of the abhorrent idea. Once it begins to be accepted, questioning starts. It seems to be part of human nature to try to make sense of events, so people ask 'Why has it happened to me?' If they conclude that someone else is to blame, they will be *angry* and may take action accordingly. If they think it is their own fault they feel *guilty* and may regard the loss as a punishment for some misdemeanour in the past. Sooner or later *grief* will become the predominant emotion. They will reminisce about what has been lost, recognizing its value, sometimes idealizing it, and longing to retrieve it. Self-blame may occur again as they wonder whether there is anything they could have done which might have prevented the loss from happening. But it *has* happened, and gradually there is acceptance that nothing will bring the lost object back. A sense of emptiness and despair takes over. This is the 'rock bottom' of grief, when it seems as if life will never be worth living again and even activities unconnected with the loss may lose their value or meaning. Fortunately, there is in almost everyone a capacity to recover and people gradually realize that to remain in the depths of such grief is intolerable for them and for others. They realize that it is essential to learn to live without that which has been lost, and they begin to find satisfaction again in other aspects of their lives. *Recovery* does not involve forgetting, but learning to live as well as possible in the new situation.

The dying patient

All people who recognize that they have an illness which will end in death in the foreseeable future go through some of the experiences just described. They do not necessarily occur in an orderly sequence, nor do they happen only once, but may recur with each exacerbation of the disease as it entails a new loss – for example, of role, or of independence. A counselling intervention is only required if patients remain disabled by their emotional distress in a way that prevents them from doing things they are still physically able to do or disrupts their relationships with others. Even then, attentive listening from counsellors may be sufficient to relieve their feelings of isolation and help them to make sense of what is happening to them.

Shock and denial

People who are feeling shocked or numb need space and relief from responsibilities while they begin to come to terms with what they have just learned. More active intervention is sometimes needed if denial persists. People who say that they are sure nothing is seriously wrong, but show by their behaviour that they are indeed very anxious, often benefit from being given the opportunity to acknowledge their suppressed fears. Letting them know that there is nothing shameful in being worried about themselves and that most people in their situation would feel the same, facilitates this. The content of their dreams or nightmares may also provide counsellors with an opening, as may the expression of (displaced) anxiety about other patients in the ward. Occasionally, gentle confrontation is appropriate, but patients should always be left able to hold on to their denial if they really need it. Some of the fears that are revealed turn out to be unrealistic and dissipate with informed reassurance. Others are appropriate and then patients need to know what can be done to alleviate the threatening situation if necessary. Thus, for instance, patients often wonder how they will die; whether they will have severe pain, or choke to death, or be left alone when *in extremis*. Talking about such fears and knowing that others will be able to respond and help is often very effective in relieving anxiety.

Anger

Anger in the dying causes problems if it is displaced. Some people, perhaps because they have not fully accepted the reality of their situation, blame others for their plight and are very critical of their treatment and of efforts made to help them. Their irritability can alienate them from professional carers and from family whose best efforts are rejected. Counsellors who first listen patiently to the long list of complaints may then be able to correct the displacement by saying something like 'Even if everything you have told me about had gone well, I suspect that you would still be angry. Perhaps the real problem is that you are so ill and can do so little about it.' Once patients can redirect their anger against the disease itself, and talk to the counsellor about their feelings, their belligerent attitude towards others changes and relationships may be improved.

In some people anger takes the form of childish rage. They are so incensed that the illness is stopping them from doing many things that they used to take for granted that they refuse to do even that which is possible. Thus, a patient who had become paralysed from his waist downwards refused to learn to use a wheelchair. 'If I can't walk out of here, I don't want to go at all' was his attitude. If counselling had not helped him to recognize that he was depriving himself of much that he could enjoy, he would have remained bed-bound and miserable for many months instead of going home again to his family.

Grief

People who are dying are often sad as they realize that they are losing so much that they value, both in their personal lives and in their relationships with others. Most people assume that they have a right to live to be old and feel deprived when they realize they will not be able to share, for example, the growing up of their children, the achievement of work goals, the reward of retirement, or the pleasure of grandchildren. The grief work which they do as they come to terms with all this is like a doorway through which they must pass before they reach acceptance. Attempts to cheer them up or distract them from their sorrow show a lack of understanding of their need to grieve. Those caring for them must recognize this and learn to offer them quiet support and space.

Resignation and acceptance

Not all people come to accept that they are dying; some young people in particular remain angry and want to fight to the very end, and who is to say that this is inappropriate? Witnessing their distress is painful for those who love them. They may request that the patient be sedated because it would be so much easier to stay with them if they were apparently peaceful. Such relatives need much support to go on bearing their pain if the wishes of the patient to remain alert are to be respected. The counsellor's primary task is to help the patient to go as far as is appropriate for him or her on the route to acceptance. Some only reach a stage of resignation; they seem hopeless and give up, withdrawing from others and waiting for death. The struggle is over but there is no sense of triumph. A few travel further, into a more positive attitude. Knowing that they will die soon, they are determined to get as much as possible out of the time that is left. Priorities change and a new interest or skill may be discovered to replace an active pursuit which has become impossible. While it is appropriate to fight, they do so, but as the illness progresses they do not exhaust themselves by attempting the impossible. As weakness and helplessness supervene they recognize that others want to care for them and they accept their dependency without shame. Some people seem to achieve these transitions by themselves or with the help of their families; others need the help of a sensitive counsellor who notices the beginning of change and reinforces it. Reassurance is needed that the acceptance of care and giving in is not failure but is a yielding to the love of others who want to make the last days or hours as easy as possible.

Dying patients who are depressed or anxious are not usually suffering from a depressive illness or an anxiety state in the psychiatric sense. Their emotional distress is more often an indicator that they are grappling with problems related to their illnesses and short prognosis and the counsellor's first task is to establish good rapport with them and to find out what these problems are. For convenience sake these can be divided into four groups:

(1) coming to terms with their own mortality;
(2) problems related to communication with the professionals and with the family;
(3) problems directly related to effects of the disease or treatment; and
(4) problems related to adjustment in role as the illness progresses.

The first has already been dealt with in some detail.

Communication

Communication problems cause more suffering to dying patients than anything else except unrelieved pain, and they are sometimes quite easily solved. Many patients do not know as much as they would like about their diagnosis or prognosis, either because they have not asked, or because information has been withheld from them. It is still the practice of some doctors to be evasive, even when patients ask directly, and some doctors tell the relatives more than they tell the patient. Families may be insistent that patients not be told, and doctors sometimes accept their judgement in this matter without sufficient consideration of the wishes of the patients themselves. Counsellors should take a history of the development of the illness from the point of view of communication, asking questions like 'When you first went to the doctor with this, what did you think it was? What did your doctor say? Did you tell your family?', and so on. This approach will indicate interest in how patients feel about their illnesses, reveal how much they know, and how much information has been shared with others. If patients want more information than counsellors can provide, they can be encouraged to ask, or their physicians can be approached and the situation discussed. Occasionally it will transpire that patients have been told but have not understood or are using denial. Some doctors are more willing to talk frankly with patients if they are convinced that they really want to know, and will be supported if they react with much distress. Good liaison is important here.

The dying and their families

Counsellors will often discover that people guess or know how ill they are, and their families know too, but neither are able to be open for fear of upsetting the other. This makes for tension whenever they come together. Visits may be kept brief and conversation brisk and cheerful, with everyone avoiding that which is uppermost in their minds; the question of how the patient is and how long he or she has left to live. Patients often experience conflict between the wish to confide and be comforted, and the wish to protect their relatives from distress (and themselves from witnessing it). Their choice of confidant is determined partly by how strong they perceive the other to be. There is a tendency to ignore the fact that even elderly parents and little children, vulnerable though they are, need to be prepared for a death. They will cope better if they have some time to adjust and to say those special things that are not often put into words in everyday life. Given the opportunity, many people will use counsellors to help them think through what to say to their spouses or other relatives. Counsellors will sometimes arrange to see a couple or family together, to facilitate such conversations. Other people, having gained confidence from the individual interview, would rather be alone with their families when such news is shared, and perhaps report back about it after. The provision of this kind of enabling support leaves people with a sense of accomplishment and control and is to be encouraged. Once the true situation is acknowledged within a family, practical help can be requested and given more freely, important questions can be asked and answered, and anxiety levels often fall dramatically.

Problems related to disease and treatment

Patients often fear that, as their disease progresses and they lose weight or become jaundiced or change in other ways, they will become unacceptable to their family. A few people hold mistaken beliefs, for instance that cancer is contagious, and unnecessarily deny themselves the intimacy of sex or the kiss and cuddle of a grandchild. Some do not come to terms with disfiguring operations like mastectomy and colostomy and they and their family need help with this. Others, particularly women, find the loss of hair which may follow chemotherapy, or the moon face that accompanies steroid treatment, makes them too self conscious to go out and mix with their friends any more. Understanding support from counsellors, who may also involve other family members in boosting the confidence of such patients may make a big difference in situations like these.

There are some diseases, notably the cancers, where treatment aimed at cure or at prolonging life may have severe side effects. The time may come when a decision has to be made about whether such treatment should continue. A stage can be reached when it is no longer effective or the distress it causes outweighs the possible benefits. Some patients find it difficult to tell their physician that they feel it is time for active treatment to end. A few want to give up prematurely because they have become depressed and see stopping treatment as an easy way out of their struggle to live. Others, perhaps because they are so afraid of death or of the shame of what they see as accepting defeat, want to persist when it is clear that they would be better off with symptomatic treatment only, gaining a few weeks of comfort and tranquility with their family before death. Because a counsellor can be a neutral figure, not in direct charge of treatment, he or she is in a good position to explore these issues with such people and help them make the best decisions for themselves.

Problems in role adjustment

Terminal illness brings with it a series of changes in role, from, for instance, active, care-giving, wage-earning parent to weak, helpless, dependent patient. Counsellors can help such individuals and their families to adjust appropriately to these changes. Some individuals give up too soon or are pushed into the sick role by over-anxious relatives when there is much they can still do. They then

301

become bored and depressed because they feel useless and a burden. Others cause their families undue distress because they are unable to accept care that they really need. They wear themselves out trying to prove to everyone that the illness is not getting the better of them. Most people find it hard to watch someone else take over jobs that they regard as theirs. Resentment and jealousy about this may turn relationships sour at the time when the family most needs to be able to pull together.

Occasionally dying individuals and their families get out of step in the adjustments they all are required to make. Sometimes, patients feel ready to stop fighting and rest but their families cannot bear to let them go. They encourage them to try to get up when they are too weak or to eat when they are no longer hungry, and do not realize that in their longing to keep their loved ones with them a few days more, they are making those days even harder for them. Counsellors can act as an intermediary here, showing the families that they understand that it is love that is prompting their behaviour, but then pointing out that the person's greatest need now is to be left in peace.

Bereavement

The responses to bereavement can be seen as another set of variations on the 'reaction to loss' theme. Even when death had been expected and relatives have kept a vigil by the bedside, they are often shocked when it really happens and cannot 'take it in' at first. Temporary emotional numbness can be an advantage in that it allows the person to get on with the many practical tasks which immediately follow a death, without being overwhelmed and disorganized by unmanageable feelings. Sometimes, one member of the family will take on this coping role, relieving others of responsibility so that their grieving can begin. Such behaviour is useful but can also be defensive, and such people may need the help of an outsider to point out to them that they too have lost someone and need space and time of their own in which to grieve.

Many bereaved people feel that the dead person has only gone away and will return in due course. This is a form of denial and allows time for the full implication of the death to be realized and accepted gradually. In the mean time the bereaved often behaves as if the deceased can still be found. They search for them and restlessly visit the grave or places where they used to be during their lifetimes. Habits change only slowly and the widow or partner continues to set the table for two, she hears her husband's footsteps or his key in the door; she dreams he is still alive and wakes distraught at the empty space beside her. Hallucinations of the dead person are normal in the first few months of bereavement and counsellors should offer reassurance about this, since some people fear they are an indication of impending breakdown. Even more common is a sense of the presence of the deceased, which may be comforting.

The need to go over the events of the last illness and death is strong and there is questioning; 'Why did it happen? Was anyone to blame? Could I have done something to delay or prevent it?' Some guilt is usual and anger is common. As with the dying patient, anger can be displaced, leading to disturbances in relationships; or suppressed, making later depressive illness more likely. Bereavement counselling is hard work, for the newly bereaved person only really has one desire; the return of the deceased. Nothing anyone says or does can accomplish this so helpers may be perceived as useless, even if well meaning. Unless counsellors can accept this as part of the anger of grief, they will feel rejected and may withdraw, unaware that unappreciative people still need someone who is able to stand by them and wait, offering continuity and support while they come to terms with their losses.

The grief that follows a major bereavement can be very disturbing and some people are frightened by the intensity of feeling and wonder if they are about to break down. They may be surprised at how physically ill they feel. The pangs of grief, which usually begin a few days after the death, are prompted by reminders of the deceased and expressions of sympathy, or just come 'out of the blue'. They are like pain but no one can put a finger on the place that hurts. In addition, sleeplessness is likely, especially if the deceased died at home and the grieving person had been in the habit of listening for him or her during the night. Poor appetite, indigestion, and bowel upsets occur, as do other physical manifestations of anxiety such as palpitations, sweating, urinary frequency, and a dry mouth. Physical symptoms can also occur as a result of the psychological mechanism of identification. Taking on some of the mannerisms, interests, and attitudes of the deceased is a normal part of identification; a way of holding on to the memory of the dead person. However, experiencing their symptoms is not normal and often leads to fear that they have the same condition that caused their relative's death. The clinical picture can be confusing as the palpitations of anxiety may be interpreted as indicators of impending heart disease; diarrhoea or constipation may be seen as evidence that the bereaved person has bowel cancer. When symptoms of this kind persist the bereaved individuals should be encouraged to discuss them with their general practitioners, who have to decide whether investigation is necessary.

Emotionally, grief is characterized by despair and a loss of any sense of purpose in life. At its height the bereaved individuals cannot imagine that they will ever feel normal again. Attempts to cheer them up at this stage usually antagonize them and make them feel that no one understands. However, they may need reassurance that people do recover from grief, and support from someone who is able to wait. When the first signs of recovery appear, perhaps renewed interest in the house or garden, or a willingness to go out again, these should be gently encouraged by counsellors. Occasionally people feel that their grief demonstrates how much they loved the deceased, and that to be cheerful again is a kind of betrayal. A timely reminder by counsellors that the person they loved would not want them to go on grieving for ever may help them to accept that the relationship really is over and that it is time to begin to make a new life.

During bereavement the first task of counsellors is to assess the adequacy of support that is being offered and to help to mobilize more if that is possible and necessary. The second is to monitor the progress of grief so that they can reinforce and encourage those aspects that are healthy, and intervene more actively or refer the person on for more expert care if the process becomes pathological. In order to make this assessment, counsellors have to have a concept of what can be regarded as normal grief. This can be formulated in terms of the reactions to loss already described, and complemented by a more dynamic view which recognizes that grieving is a process. 'The tasks of mourning' as set out by Worden (1983) can be used by counsellors to help in assessing whether someone is making progress or has got stuck and is in need of help to move forward again. These tasks are:

(1) to accept the reality of the loss;
(2) to experience and bear the pain of grief;
(3) to adjust to a world in which the dead person is missing; and
(4) to withdraw and reinvest the emotional energy bound up in the relationship which has been lost.

Varieties of grief

There is no sharp dividing line between normal and abnormal grief and counsellors have rather to ask themselves 'What reactions would I expect for *this person* with *this loss*?' Grieving varies according to the age of the person concerned. Little children do not have the same concept of death that adults do and they express their anxiety and distress in different ways. Their need to grieve may go unrecognized by those around them; they may seem little affected at the time but have difficulty in making close relationships later in life, and may then become depressed. Adolescents often keep their grief to themselves, but it may show in poor school work, delinquency, or promiscuity. How people grieve is influenced by their upbringing and whether it is acceptable to them to show feelings. Many relatives expect grief to be over quickly and counsellors may need to make it clear that prolonged grieving may not be a sign of weakness, but is a measure of the seriousness of the loss that has been sustained and the adjustment that has to be made. Some elderly widows or widowers do not go through the full grieving process, partly because they regard the separation as temporary and think that all they have to do is wait until their own time comes.

A person's previous experience of death also influences his or her coping. Those who have been helped to accept it as part of life, perhaps through the death of pets in childhood and later of grandparents, neighbours, and so on, are less vulnerable than those who have been shielded from it and whose first close encounter with death comes in middle age. Several losses occurring close together, so that there is no time to recover from one before the next happens, also increases vulnerability.

Some losses are more traumatic than others. Death which comes suddenly and unexpectedly is shocking and the grieving process may be delayed by numbness and disbelief. The bereaved person's confidence in the security and on-going quality of life has been shattered and he or she is anxious and vigilant. Often they cling to surviving members of their families and for a while are unable to be left alone or take ordinary risks. Anger is prominent in this kind of grief, often because the person who has died is young or has been 'cut off in his or her prime' and the bereaved person has a need to find someone or something to blame.

Parents who lose a child in late adolescence or early adulthood are often very slow to recover from their grief, and may never do so fully. Deaths where the extent of the loss is not openly acknowledged and little or no support is provided can also be associated with prolonged or delayed grief. Among these are miscarriages and still births, or the loss of a very close friend or lover who has not been recognized by others as having a key place in the life of the bereaved.

The pattern of grieving may be altered if the relationship which has been lost was ambivalent. There may be relief at first that the tension and strife is over, and the anxiety level is often low. When grieving does begin, the person realizes how much he or she misses someone who was familiar even though there was often hostility or resentment, and guilt and regrets may become intense. The grief may be prolonged and self punitive as if it might in some way make reparation for the past. Such individuals may need help from counsellors to get the memories in perspective, to forgive themselves for their share of the problems, and to recognize that they were not the only contributors to the unhappiness they both experienced.

Bereavement may be especially disabling if the relationship that has been lost was one with a high level of dependency. The survivor who was the more dependent partner is left helpless because he or she literally does not know how to live without the other and needs to acquire new roles and practical skills just at the time when the capacity for innovation and learning is at its lowest ebb. Those who are initially drawn into care for such a person may resent the tendency to chronic dependency which can emerge if the bereaved individual discovers that manipulation of others is easier than learning to care for him- or herself. Sympathy must be balanced with firmness when counselling such people and their families. The survivor who was the more dominant partner may be equally lost in bereavement because that person derived too much of the meaning of his or her life from caring for, or exercising power over, the other.

The end of counselling

Knowing when counselling should end is important. With the dying, the counsellors' tasks may be complete when patients and their families are comfortable together, giving and receiving all the help that is needed. Only when the dying continue to want their counsellors, either because a precious new relationship has been added to the ones they had before, or because their counsellors have become the most important person for them, should those counsellors remain in a close relationship to the end. Often it is right to slip into the background, relinquishing the clients into the care and love of their families. This is the counsellors' own bereavement and it carries with it the satisfaction that the work has been completed in the best possible way. It may or may not be appropriate for them to continue the work with the families, or take it up again, and this will depend on circumstances to be discussed later.

Bereavement counselling ends when clients are able to manage without their counsellors. The process of grieving may not be complete (the end-point is almost always indefinable) but it has become clear that it is moving towards resolution. Old interests and relationships are being revived or new ones entered into and the person concerned has his or her own momentum to move forward into a new life.

Issues

Who most needs counselling?

It is impractical, and probably also undesirable, to offer counselling to all who are facing death or are bereaved. To be most effective, it should be offered to those who are most likely to suffer severe and distressing reactions, and for bereavement, ways of predicting risk are being researched (Raphael 1977; Osterweis et al. 1984; Parkes 1986). Factors which probably increase risk include poverty and deprivation; being a single parent with young children at home; the presence of unusual levels of anger, guilt, clinging, or other distress before the death; other recent or concurrent losses; a history of drug or alcohol abuse; and previous history of psychiatric illness. Outcome research shows that counselling these people reduces their morbidity to that of low-risk groups who have not been counselled. The need for counselling for people facing death has not become generally accepted, except for special groups such as those suffering from cancer or AIDS, where it is particularly obvious. The author's own work (Stedeford 1984) suggests that adults who have young children and elderly parents both depending on them suffer most intense feelings of guilt. People who have little to be satisfied with in their lives find it very hard to die, as do those who have been very independent and have never been ill before. At present, whether counselling is offered to the dying is determined more by the sensitivity, knowledge, and resources of those near to them, than it is by the intensity of their need.

Who should do the counselling?

There is no clear division between the support offered by a caring community and friends to an individual or family in crisis and the more clearly defined interventions of professionals who may become involved. Nor is support required only by those who are judged psychologically inadequate; almost everyone needs someone else when they are facing death or are newly bereaved. Whether professional help is required depends partly on the degree of isolation of the individual concerned. Problems of the dying and their families are most likely to be identified by a member of the general practice or hospital team, or by clergy if the patient is associated with a church. Among the medical and nursing professions, some see psychological care as part of their work and equip themselves to give it; and others see their role as limited to the treatment of the physical illness. They may ignore other needs or they may recognize them and refer on, for example to a social worker. However, many patients are still left to assume that emotional anguish is an inevitable part of terminal illness and that nothing can be done to relieve it.

Help is increasingly being offered by voluntary organizations (such as BACUP and Cancerlink for cancer patients) and a great deal of effective counselling is done by them. Their support is particularly appropriate for those who have become very anxious, or who feel helpless and isolated in the face of their disease. Patients who become severely depressed, confused, or paranoid, or whose physical symptoms do not respond to measures that would be expected to bring relief, should be referred to a psychiatrist if possible. In dying patients, good liaison is particularly important between counsellor or psychotherapist and the medical team because many psychological symptoms can be caused either by stress, physical or biochemical changes related to the illness, side-effects of medication, or any combination of these. Optimum treatment can only be decided upon when an assessment has been made which takes the various possibilities into account.

When in bereavement the general practitioner and his or her team have been the principal carers, follow-up will usually be offered by them. When the death occurs in hospital or in a hospice, opinion is divided as to whether those involved in the counselling of patients and their families should continue working with the latter during bereavement. The decision may be made on practical grounds because distance or shortage of staff often means that it is impossible for follow-up contact to be made on more than one or two occasions. These visits provide an opportunity for the carers to complete their own grief work and to make sure that the bereaved family is put in touch with sources of further support if it is thought likely that they will need these. The psychological care of the bereaved requires less knowledge of the interaction of physical and emotional factors than is usually necessary for the dying. It is therefore appropriate to use trained volunteers more often in this area as organizations like Cruse and many hospices do. There is a clear end-point to the care of the dying patient but recovery from bereavement is a slow process, more like growth, and involves readjustment and re-integration into the life of the local community. For this reason community-based care is often the better choice, and for some the Church can offer long-term support, especially where clergy and lay people have received training in bereavement counselling.

The local social worker, health visitor, or volunteer who visits the bereaved family for the first time may feel at a disadvantage because he or she did not know the deceased, but this lack of continuity need not be a drawback. The bereaved person often welcomes someone new to whom the story of the illness and death can be told, to whom photographs and mementos can be shown, and who makes it clear that he or she is interested in getting to know what the dead person was like and what the loss means. This facilitates the beginning of grief work in an effective way.

What counselling techniques should be used?

From the description of the wide variety of problems that are encountered in the dying and bereaved, it should be clear that counselling must be equally varied if it is to fit closely with the clients needs. Work may be with individuals, couples, families, groups, or any combination of these. Sometimes it will be mainly supportive or aimed at reducing isolation and improving communication. It may include the giving of information or helping someone in his or her search for meaning in suffering. Interpretive work is needed when defences block progress and sympathetic confrontation is occasionally appropriate in maladaptive denial or angry regression. Facilitating the expression of feelings is often very important and counsellors must be able to tolerate the negative aspects of grief, neither withdrawing or retaliating if they get hurt in the process. Because physical changes are paramount in the dying person and physical illness is also increased during grief, good liaison with the medical team is essential and familiarity with the common bodily changes in dying and bereavement is a useful adjunct to the counsellors' general knowledge.

Grief or depression?

A particularly difficult area is the transition between anticipatory grief in the dying or normal mourning in bereavement, and depression. This has been of concern at least since Freud (1917) wrote 'Mourning and Mélancholia'. Biological indicators of depression are obscured in the dying by illness or the side-effects of treatment, and the diagnosis rests on recognition of the presence of low self-esteem and inappropriate guilt, both of which may have a delusional quality. The dying and the bereaved often have regrets about the past; when these are excessive, depressive illness should be suspected. Individuals who think they are a burden when others do not regard them as such, or who withdraw and cannot enjoy activities that are still physically possible for them, are also likely to respond well to antidepressants. In both groups, suicidal ideas should be explored before it is assumed that they are depressive. In the dying they may occur if life becomes intolerable because of unrelieved pain, or they may be an expression of the wish to retain control and to die while faculties remain intact. Good care and symptom control usually relieves such an individual's distress sufficiently for them to feel able to wait until nature takes its course, or even to enjoy the last part of their lives more than they thought they would.

In the bereaved, suicidal ideas may be an expression of the longing to be with the person who has died, or a way of communicating about the intensity of distress, rather than a wish to be dead. If counsellor and client can talk about them and agree that this is their meaning, they are less likely to be acted out. The risk of suicide is increased in bereavement and here again good liaison with the medical team is essential. Depressive illness in both groups does respond to medication and one of the first changes often seen may not be a relief of suffering, but a movement towards more active and specific grieving in which the counsellor again has a role to play.

Future developments

Counselling for the dying and those close to them is a relatively new development and is growing rapidly in certain areas of obvious need, for example AIDS and cancer. Lay groups are often ahead of the medical profession in recognizing deficiencies in the service and responding to them. This may have a balancing and beneficial effect as they tend to emphasize the individual's wish to retain control of their lives including their treatment, wherever possible. Co-ordination of the activities of these groups is important if resources are to be pooled and inappropriate gaps and overlaps avoided. Among the professionals, clinical psychologists, social workers, clergy, and psychotherapists and counsellors of various kinds all have a role to play, both in working with clients and in training volunteers to share the task effectively. On-going professional education and the careful selection and teaching of volunteer counsellors is essential if high standards are to be achieved and service is to keep pace with need.

Bereavement counselling has been going on much longer, but here too standards are variable and methods of selection and training need to be developed and refined. More accurate identification of those who are at risk and progress in adapting counselling techniques to fit the many different expressions of grief is needed. This will enable interventions to be more effective and thus more satisfying to client and counsellor alike.

Work with the dying and the bereaved in an intensive way and for a long time is very stressful. It is becoming clear that this fact must be taken into account in selection and training and the provision of on-going support. Professional isolation must be avoided and the exposure to suffering and loss diluted by breaks for teaching and learning, research, or work with clients with different kinds of problems. Unless counsellors themselves are cared for in this way, some very capable people may withdraw from this work because they find the strain intolerable.

References

Freud, S. (1917) 'Mourning and mélancholia', in *Sigmund Freud: Collected Papers, Volume 4*, New York: Basic Books.
Osterweis, M., Solomon, F., and Green, M. (1984) *Bereavement: Reactions,*

Consequences, and Care, Washington, DC: National Academy Press.

Parkes, C. M. (1986) *Bereavement*, London: Tavistock.

Pincus, L, (1976) *Life and Death*, London: Sphere.

Raphael, B. (1977) 'Preventive intervention with the recently bereaved', *Archives of General Psychiatry* 34: 1450–4.

Stedeford, A. (1984) *Facing Death: Patients, Families and Professionals*, London: Heinemann Medical Books.

Worden, W. (1983) *Grief Counselling and Grief Therapy*, London: Tavistock.

Chapter twenty

Counselling and sexual dysfunctions

Grahame F. Cooper

Sexuality is ever-present in human life, and sexual dysfunctions have plagued humankind for a long time. Although the treatment of sexual dysfunctions is often considered to be a recent phenomenon, Bancroft (1983) has reminded us that some 180 years before Masters and Johnson started the 'new sex therapies', John Hunter, of surgical fame, used similar psychological methods to cure a man with erectile dysfunction. Most people do not seek or obtain help from a specialist in sexual dysfunctions, but many could be helped by those other professionals who, in addition to basic counselling-skills, have an awareness of sexual functioning and dysfunctioning and a willingness to help by using well-established principles of sex counselling. In this way nurses, general practitioners, health visitors, occupational therapists, social workers, clergy, and others may (within their existing work contacts) be able to offer help which would otherwise be unobtainable, unacceptable.

The sexual dysfunctions

Sexual dysfunctions of psychological origin are a clear example of psycho-somatic conversion, i.e. an alteration or disruption of a bodily function occurring as a result of emotional trauma such as anxiety, guilt, anger, or grief. In describing the sexual dysfunctions and their treatment through counselling, a four-phase model of human sexual response will be used here. Table 20.1 demonstrates the relationship between this model (Cooper 1988), the four-phase model of Masters and Johnson (1966), and the three-phase model of Kaplan (1979).

In planning treatment, some of the important factors are discussed below.

Occurrence

Any of the sexual dysfunctions may be of *general* or *specific* occurrence. The sexual dysfunction is of general occurrence if it occurs with any partner and (in so far as it is applicable) when attempting to masturbate alone. If the dysfunction only occurs when with a particular partner and not in other situations, then it is said to be specific.

Table 20.1 The phases of human sexual functioning

Cooper (1988)	Masters and Johnson (1966)	Kaplan (1979)
		Desire
Arousal	Arousal	Arousal
	Plateau	
Orgasm	Orgasm	Orgasm
Resolution	Resolution	

Origin

A sexual dysfunction is of *primary* origin if the person has always had it. When a previously satisfactory sexual function is lost or impaired, the dysfunction is of *secondary* origin.

A dysfunction can be both secondary and specific – for example, a client who is sexually functional with one partner may be dysfunctional when with another partner.

Physical and psychological causes

The particular tasks of counselling people who have disabilities are discussed in Chapter 21 by Segal. Four relevant factors here are:

(1) Physical disabilities can cause sexual dysfunctioning either by directly affecting genital responses or by indirectly affecting the capacity for sexual acts and interactions.
(2) In some conditions there is no clear distinction between physical and psychological causes for sexual dysfunction: for example, in multiple sclerosis or diabetes intermittent dysfunctions caused by the disorder can set up anxieties which then disrupt sexual functions.
(3) Some people with physical disabilities have sexual dysfunctions of purely psychological origin, as able-bodied people do, for example due to the grief response to loss.
(4) Some malfunctions in the hormonal systems cause sexual dysfunctions.

The principles and practice of sex counselling will be described here in relation to heterosexual dysfunctions. Homosexual people suffer similar dysfunctions and the principles of treatment described here are equally valid for them.

Table 20.2 presents the psychogenic sexual dysfunctions, and shows that there are no distinctions between female and male dysfunctions within the desire and resolution phases.

Dysfunctions of the arousal phase

These are due, in both male and female, to a failure of the normal mechanisms which lead to increased blood flow and vaso-congestion in the genitals.

Dysfunctions of the orgasm phase

These show interesting and important differences between men and women. A comparison of the so-called orgasmic 'dysfunctions' of women with the orgasmic dysfunctions of men shows a gradation of degree of dysfunction in both sexes. However, orgasmic dysfunctions are much more common in women than in men. Both the nature and function of the orgasm differ between the sexes, despite the similar rhythmic contractions at 0.8 cps of comparable groups of muscles.

For the male, orgasm and ejaculation are often used synonymously and are assumed to be the same event, but under some circumstances these two functions can be separated – pre-pubescent boys, for example, often experience orgasm during masturbation before they are sufficiently developed for ejaculation to occur. Dysfunctions of this phase in the male are commonly described in terms of ejaculation – the outward and visible sign of the male orgasm. In the male, orgasm is the sensation experienced during ejaculation, a vital process in procreation. There is no such connection in women between orgasm and procreation and the biological function of the female orgasm is unclear.

Although some women are able to experience multiple orgasms, a significant proportion of women have difficulty in achieving orgasm during heterosexual intercourse and furthermore some women fail to achieve orgasm at all. Recent evidence has indicated that in some of these women, certain pelvic reflexes are absent or weak, thus raising the possibility that their orgasmic dysfunctions may be neurogenic rather than psychogenic. For some women the multiple orgasm has become the norm which they 'ought' to attain and failure to do so may lead to anxieties and to dissatisfaction with self or partner. It is generally held that the male orgasm differs in that it is followed by a refractory period, during which further stimulation is ineffective, rendering multiple orgasm impossible. Lowndes Sevely (1987), however, contends that the difference is only an ageing factor in men.

Treatment – counselling or therapy?

The terms counselling and therapy are, unfortunately, often used synonymously. Although the boundaries are not absolute, this author finds that a useful distinction can be drawn between counselling and therapy, both theoretically and practically.

Table 20.2 Heterosexual dysfunctions of psychological origin

Female dysfunctions	Male dysfunctions
DESIRE PHASE	
Inhibition of sexual desire: Lack of interest in seeking or attaining sexual interaction. Not available to sexual arousal.	
AROUSAL PHASE	
Dyspareunia: insufficient vascular engorgement leads to lack of vaginal lubrication and relaxation, hence acceptance by the vagina of fingers or penis is painful. Masturbation may also be difficult.	(a) *Partial erectile dysfunctions:* insufficient vaso-congestion occurs to initiate and/or sustain full erection of the penis, hence masturbation or penetration may be difficult.
Vaginismus: pain and tightness make acceptance of penis or fingers impossible. In severe vaginismus, powerful reflex adduction of the thighs may occur.	(b) *Total erectile dysfunction:* no significant enlargement or erection of the penis occurs.
ORGASM PHASE	
Orgasmic 'dysfunction': this occurs to varying degrees: (a)Orgasm not achieved by vaginal intercourse unless simultaneous direct stimulation of clitoris. (b)Orgasm not achieved by simultaneous intercourse and direct clitoral stimulation. It is achievable by masturbation when with a partner or when alone.	*Orgasmic/ejaculatory dysfunctions:* (a)*Premature ejaculation:* ejaculation occurs 'too quickly' for the man and/or his partner. (b)*Retarded Ejaculation:* difficulty in achieving ejaculation 'within a reasonable time' (maybe associated with partial erectile dysfunction).

Female dysfunctions	Male dysfunctions

ORGASM PHASE

(c)Orgasm not achieved by simultaneous intercourse and direct clitoral stimulation nor by masturbation when with a partner. Achievable by masturbation, but only when alone.
(d)*An-orgasmic*: orgasm not now achievable with any stimulus or
Pre-Orgasmic: orgasm has never been achieved.

(c)*Ejaculatory Failure*: ejaculation retarded indefinitely. It cannot be achieved by intercourse, direct penile stimulation, or masturbation.

RESOLUTION PHASE

Dysphoria due to guilt, anxiety, or revulsive reactions.

Counselling

Counselling is a working process appropriate for helping people with difficulties of recent or immediate origin – that is, due to a recent traumatic event or conflicting feelings or beliefs associated with a recent event. In general, it is a process which helps people through those transitions of life that many people overcome simply with the help and support of relatives and friends. An example in sex counselling might be a person who fails to become sexually aroused whilst suffering stress or fatigue. This failure produces anxiety and on the next occasion that anxiety alone is sufficient to prevent sexual arousal from occurring and so a self-sustaining condition is set up arising from recent causes.

Therapy

Therapy is a working process appropriate for helping a person with a problem which is of remote origins (Kaplan 1974), i.e. which has its roots in distant events of childhood and infancy that are deeply buried or in the unconscious. In general, psychotherapy may be appropriate where there is distress or behavioral disturbance which can be traced back to early experiences by utilizing the transference within the helping relationship. In sex therapy, resistances to the treatment programme may indicate such early traumatizing experiences.

The author's usage of a clear distinction between counselling and therapy encompasses Kaplan's (1974) concepts of sexual dysfunctions of 'remote' or 'immediate' origins and is influenced by, amongst others, the concepts of Worden (1983).

Principles

The principles of the new sex therapies provide a means of understanding sexual dysfunctions. This understanding can be used by those helpers who are not specialist sex therapists to offer counselling and 'sexual first-aid' to people in need. These principles have already been presented in a form suitable for use by the public (Brown and Faulder 1979).

New sex therapies

Masters and Johnson (1966, 1970) provided easily explicable models of human sexual functioning, dysfunctioning, and therapeutic principles. Their approach, which emphasizes the active involvement of the client in the therapeutic process, has wide application and it brought together existing concepts and developed new ones. Their methods have since been modified and developed by various practitioners (for example Kaplan 1974, 1979, Bancroft 1983, Fairburn *et al.* 1983, Hawton 1985) as part of the natural progression towards positive eclectic practice.

Kaplan's contributions (1974, 1979) clarified the distinction between disorders of desire and disorders of arousal, and provided appropriate therapeutic

316

strategies. She emphasized the psychodynamic aspects of this approach which Masters and Johnson did not *explicitly* address in their writings.

The following principles can be clearly seen and are commonly, though not invariably, adhered to by current practitioners in Britain.

Working with the couple

Even though only one of the couple may present symptoms of sexual dysfunction, it is usually appropriate to work with them as a couple in sex counselling, since both will be affected and a positive outcome is more likely if both are actively involved in the counselling. If the partner is unable or unwilling to attend, then Bennun's (1985) unilateral marital therapy model might be applicable, but the limitations must be recognized.

Stress reduction

Anxiety is a major factor in causing or sustaining psychogenic sexual dysfunctions. Fear of failure and other performance anxieties are eliminated or reduced by asking the couple to agree to a total ban on sexual intercourse or other 'performance achievements' in the early stages of treatment.

Communication

Communication difficulties are important in precipitating and sustaining sexual problems, and work will focus on *verbal* communication, including sexual vocabulary and communication of feelings, both positive and negative; and *physical* communication, the giving and receiving of sensual and sexual pleasure. Mutually pleasurable sexual intercourse may be seen as the ultimate communication between the couple.

Motivation

The couple must be sufficiently committed to the treatment contract and programme to endure discomfort which may arise from exposing, and perhaps challenging, the nature and strength of the relationship. Many sexual problems are symptomatic of the state of the relationship and the level of communication, and high motivation is essential for a successful outcome.

Education

Sexual ignorance, misinformation, and myths (see Zilbergeld 1980 and Dickson 1985) contribute significantly to dysfunctioning, and hence education in sexual functioning and dysfunctions is important in the treatment. Useful resources for clients' use include Docherty (1986) and Ward (1976). A common example of an anxiety-creating myth is the belief that the vagina has to be *penetrated* (a forceful act requiring a stiff penis), part of the dominant male view of sexuality. This anxiety can be reduced by education about the positive female action of *accepting* (taking the penis into the fully aroused vagina) an act which does not require an erect penis.

Practical aspects of sex counselling – general

The general application of these principles in treatment programmes is given in brief outline here and illustrated by some specific case materials relating to erectile dysfunction.

Counselling

Couples often arrive with a double load of anxiety: they are anxious about their problem and anxious about coming into counselling. Helpers must therefore be able to offer the core conditions of acceptance, empathy, genuineness, and clear communication in order to establish a relationship (a therapeutic alliance) within which help can be given and received.

Anxiety reduction

General anxiety is reduced by forming a good relationship, and problem-specific anxiety is reduced by (a) exploration of stress and negative feelings, thus improving communication between the couple; (b) educative work to increase understanding of sexual functioning and their specific dysfunction; (c) reducing sexual performance demands by banning sexual intercourse and encouraging sensual love-making which is not performance-orientated, through a sensate-focus programme.

Sensate focus

Using the sensate-focus programme modified from Masters and Johnson (1970) removes the anxiety of sexual intercourse and provides opportunities for non-demand sensual love-making. In the first stage the couple are asked to take turns in giving and receiving sensual pleasure in a warm and safe environment of their choice, by touching, stroking, kissing, caressing and so on, but avoiding stimulating the genitals, breasts, or other erogenous areas. Talking about it afterwards increases communication skills and in these ways they learn to give and receive sensual pleasuring and to share their emotional responses.

The second stage includes the specific sexual areas in the pleasuring, but continues the principle of non-demand. If arousal occurs, it may be enjoyed and allowed to come and go, but it is not an objective of the exercise and the absolute ban on intercourse remains.

Illustrative case note 1: Alan and Brenda

Alan's erection failed when attempting intercourse with Brenda. He was fatigued after a stressful week and had drunk some alcohol. Despite Brenda's understanding response, he became worried when on two further occasions he again failed. In the first counselling session, the mechanisms of sexual arousal and the causes of his dysfunction were explained. They accepted a total ban on sexual intercourse and a sensate-focus programme to provide non-sexual pleasuring, and increased mutual understanding and communication.

They were seen weekly; progress in the sensate-focus home assignments was monitored and any difficulties explored. In this non-demand experience Alan's confidence (and his erectile function) recovered. Intercourse was resumed in similar non-demand conditions, with Brenda on top lowering herself on to Alan so that her fully-aroused vagina *accepted* and contained his penis, without performance demands upon him.

By the time counselling ended after five sessions, they were able to have intercourse as before, and with a much greater sense of mutual understanding and security than ever before.

Applications of sensate focus

The change factors necessary in counselling to bring about transformation and the building of sound foundations for positive sexual functioning from the specific blocks which precipitate or sustain negative sexual functioning have been described elsewhere by this author (Cooper 1988). Sensate focus is an important component of these processes which offers a valuable double-effect. First, by listening carefully to the clients' accounts of their usage, or avoidance, of sensate-focus exercises, the counsellor gleans valuable diagnostic information as to the causes and the effects of their sexual dysfunctions. Second, sensate-focus offers people immediate, active involvement in their own treatment by physical, verbal, and non-verbal communication exercises, thus overcoming one of the specific blocks.

Participation in the sensual, non-demand exercises of sensate focus may highlight beliefs about non-sexual love-making and about the participants' own bodies. Negative beliefs will need to be discussed in counselling to overcome blocks, whilst further individual physical assignments are appropriate where there is a negative body-image.

There are full accounts of sensate-focus work in Fairburn *et al.* (1983), Hawton (1985), and Cooper (1988), and a well illustrated massage sequence in Kitzinger (1985).

Sexual vocabulary

What are the right words to use? For many people there are no comfortable sexual words, only the awkward, clinical vocabulary of the professionals (vagina, penis, coitus) or the unacceptable, derogatory vocabulary of the football ground (cunt, prick, fucking). This difficulty, arising from family and cultural influences, exacerbates sexual dysfunctions for the couple by making it impossible to discuss the problem either between themselves or with the therapist.

Every helper must ensure that he or she is familiar with the wide colloquial sexual vocabulary to ensure that inappropriate reactions are not shown. McConville and Shearlaw (1985) is recommended for this purpose.

319

The word game

This author uses the following exercise to enable clients lacking a sexual vocabulary to discover usable words for themselves. (A modified version is used for training sex counsellors and therapists.) Each partner writes down all the words he or she knows under headings such as female genitals, male genitals, sexual intercourse, masturbation, orgasm, and so on. The lists are then shared, one at a time with the partner and they then discuss their reactions. With which words do they feel uncomfortable? With which words do they feel comfortable? Which words would they like to use in their own discussions and with their sex counsellor? If they do not like any of the words listed they can invent their own. Through this exercise the couple establish a vocabulary so that the therapeutic work can proceed.

'Making friends with your body'

Many women suffering from sexual dysfunctions appear to be alienated from their own bodies. They lack a vocabulary with which to talk about their bodies, and are often ignorant of its basic structure and functioning. Their negative self-image includes adverse comparison with other women. Although this difficulty is more commonly presented by women, it also affects some men who have sexual dysfunctions. In sex counselling, individuals have the opportunity to effect important positive changes in their self-image and beliefs.

It is often difficult to love another unless one can love oneself. Specific individual work, as described below, will often help people to 'become friends' with their own bodies. Sensual bathing (purely for pleasure) is encouraged before visual and tactile exploration and appreciation of his or her own body. This is followed by self-massage with appropriate oils, lotions, or talcum powder, which leads to erotic appreciation and stimulation. Complete privacy in a warm, comfortable, and conducive environment is essential. Brown and Faulder (1979) and Zilbergeld (1980) give fuller descriptions.

Illustrative case note 2: Eric and Freda

Family attitudes and shyness had left both Eric and Freda ignorant about their own bodies and sexual functioning. They had not been able to consumate their marriage. Their shyness slowed the building of the counselling relationship, but they were well motivated and welcomed the learning opportunities, including the sensate-focus programme. They enjoyed the 'freeing up' which came from the word game; prior to that Freda's only words had been 'You know – round the tops of the stockings'. Her strong negative feelings about her body initially made the 'making friends with my body' programme difficult for her. In the bath, she would only touch her vulva with a flannel 'because it's dirty down there', but eventually, she felt comfortable about touching herself and partially inserting her own finger into her vagina.

Practical aspects of sex counselling – specific dysfunctions

Having described treatment concepts of general application above, additional techniques for other specific dysfunctions follow with illustrative case material.

Disorders of arousal

Dyspareunia

Dyspareunia means painful intercourse. It can be of physical or psychological origin, and is more common in women. In men it is mostly of physical origin – for example, inflammation (balanitis) or tight foreskin (phimosis). Some physical causes in women are infection (for example, thrush, genital warts, genital herpes), incomplete healing after childbirth, and oestrogen deficiency atrophy.

Psychological inhibition of arousal leaves the vagina dry and relatively tight instead of well lubricated, soft, and relaxed. When the vagina is dry and unready to accept penis or fingers, penetration will inevitably be painful. Arousal can be inhibited by anxiety, guilt, embarrassment, grief, or anger. Previous pain of physical origin can cause anxiety which prevents arousal and so causes pain of psychological origin.

The origins of dyspareunia may be immediate, easily recognizable, and treatable in counselling, or they may be due to remote, traumatizing past events which require therapy. Treatment of dyspareunia in women by counselling is based upon anxiety reduction and education through sensate-focus programmes and individual work on 'making friends with your body'. When full arousal is being achieved, genital intercourse may then be included in the pleasuring, but initially the woman controls the rate and depth of acceptance of the penis into her vagina by being on top of the man.

Vaginismus

In dyspareunia penetration is possible but painful, whilst in vaginismus the reflex reactions are so powerful that it is only possible to penetrate by force. In severe cases, even touching the genital area or thighs will cause a powerful reflex adduction of the thighs. Treatment is similar to that for dyspareunia but the counsellor must be aware of resistances to psychological penetration which indicate underlying conflicts. Sometimes behavoural interventions are needed to overcome the conditioned reflex, in addition to counselling. This is illustrated by referring again to the case of Eric and Freda (see earlier).

After learning to accept her own finger in her vagina, Freda began using Stanley Vaginal Trainers (Stanley 1982). She inserted these size-graded smooth plastic rods for increasing periods of time, using a lubricant (K-Y jelly). In this way her vagina was *trained* to accept increasingly large objects without triggering the reflex and with greatly reduced discomfort. The principle here is of *training* the vagina to accept the object, *not* dilating the vagina. When accustomed to the largest trainer, she felt ready to accept her husband's penis.

With Eric on his back, Freda lowered herself down on to his penis, thus controlling the depth and speed of entry herself and so minimizing anxiety. After ten counselling sessions they were confidently enjoying sexual intercourse in various positions.

Disorders of female orgasm

Table 20.2 shows the range of these disorders. Treatment is usually based on the general techniques described above and sensate-focus programmes. The following describes the treatment of a women with primary anorgasmia who was fully capable of sexual arousal, but had low sexual desire:

Illustrative case note 3: Gill and Harry

Gill loved her fiancé Harry, but her sex drive was low and although she became aroused when he initiated love-making, she was anorgasmic. Progress with sensate-focus was good although in Harry's keenness 'to get on' the intercourse ban was sometimes broken. Gill was delighted to discover, through pleasurable bathing, self-exploration, and eventually masturbation, that her vagina was not 'yukky' and that she was a fully sexual women capable of orgasm. The use of literature (particularly Friday's *My Secret Garden* 1975) enabled her to accept sexual fantasies and to develop her own. After six counselling sessions Gill was regularly orgasmic and had a greater sexual appetite than Harry, somewhat to his surprise!

Disorders of male orgasm

Premature or retarded ejaculation are defined by the clients' own words: 'He comes too quickly for me to be satisfied' or 'It takes me so long to ejaculate I feel like giving up.' In clinical practice, measurements of time to ejaculation from entry will not define these conditions adequately.

Premature ejaculation

Sensate focus forms the initial basis of counselling treatment but later, direct behavioural interventions, based on the concepts of Semans are indicated (see Bancroft 1983; Fairburn *et al.* 1983; Cooper, 1988).

Semans's treatment actively involves the partner in 'retraining' the man's response to intense sexual arousal. The man learns to recognize when ejaculation is about to become inevitable, so that stimulation can be reduced and hence ejaculation controlled. Once good recognition, and thus control, has been achieved, intercourse can be resumed but with the man underneath so that he can concentrate on recognizing the sensations and controlling his partner's movements on to his penis. In this way gradually increasing the periods of containment and then movement can be achieved by the man before choosing to ejaculate in the vagina. Zilbergeld (1980) gives useful modifications of this technique for the man to use alone.

Retarded ejaculation

In counselling, sensate focus is used and individual homework assignments may be devised for the male, similar in principle to those for female clients. This increases sensory awareness and implicitly 'gives permission' for masturbation and orgasm (see Brown and Faulder 1979; and Zilbergeld 1980).

Illustrative case note 4: Ian and Janet

Ian's ejaculatory difficulties started after Janet had spontaneously aborted, and he had been totally unable to ejaculate in intercourse or by masturbation for the past four months.

During a lengthy treatment which included individual therapy for Ian, masturbation became enjoyable but ejaculation did not occur until, watching an erotic video alone, he masturbated and ejaculated. He then used this graded series of steps with Janet's willing approval and help:

(1) ejaculation when alone in the house,
(2) ejaculation with Janet in another room,
(3) ejaculation with Janet in the same room,
(4) ejaculation when in bed with Janet,
(5) ejaculation whilst cuddling with Janet,
(6) ejaculation onto her pubic area,
(7) ejaculation into her vulva,
(8) intercourse with ejaculation in her vagina.

This behavioral programme was successful after his individual therapy had dealt with his introjected beliefs and his hidden anxiety that he would be responsible for further painful suffering if he made her pregnant again.

Janet's individual counselling and homework assignments had included the Kegel exercises which trained her to contract her pubococcygeal muscles. These muscles can constrict the vaginal cavity, thus gripping the inserted penis, enhancing the woman's sexual pleasure, and providing greater stimulus for her partner.

Gillan (1987) gives details of the Kegel exercises. The principles are: *identifying* the sensation of pubococcygeal muscle contraction by voluntarily stopping urine flow during micturition; *enhancing* awareness and contractions by practising contractions when not micturating; *strengthening* the muscles by contracting them frequently – as the muscle strength increases with regular training, a woman will be able to feel the contractions in the vagina with her finger.

Issues

Use of co-worker or single-worker models

Masters and Johnson (1970) considered it vital to use a man–woman co-therapy team in the treatment of couples, but treatment outcomes with single therapists are not significantly different (Kaplan 1974). The author's survey of sex therapists in the UK (Cooper 1988) found that only 14 per cent normally used a co-worker model, and some were all-female teams. Non-specialist workers, wishing to use the single-worker model may do so without fear of it being significantly detrimental.

Clients as individuals or couples

Clients without a partner may request help for sexual problems such as disorder of arousal, anorgasmia, or premature ejaculation. The non-specialist worker should not be deterred from helping single clients with sex problems, provided that the worker can create a good counselling relationship, can discuss all aspects of sex and sexuality comfortably and knowledgeably, and has the skill to adapt techniques for use by single clients. Within a good counselling relationship, much relief can be provided by giving accurate information to counteract taboo and ignorance, by the implicit permission-giving which comes with 'the word game', and with 'making friends with your own body' for both men and women. The Kegel exercises can be taught and there is a description of the Semans technique suitable for the single male in Zilbergeld (1980). Much help and relief can be given to the individual with a sexual problem simply through acceptance, and real understanding, both at the factual and the feeling levels, by an interested counsellor.

Groupwork

Group treatment for sexual dysfunctions has developed slowly, apparently due to participants' anxiety about confidentiality, and therapists' anxieties that people might change partners in a group for couples. The participants receive support from others with similar dysfunctions whilst for the administrator there is improved cost-effectiveness. Gillan (1987) has written about single-sex, mixed-sex, and couple groups. This interesting technique should only be used by counsellors experienced both in groupwork and in sexual-dysfunction work.

Therapeutic approaches

The principles and practices of the 'new sex therapies' have been deliberately emphasized here because they are readily accessible to, and usable by, helpers who are not specialist sex counsellors. Other 'schools' of sex counselling and therapy, with differing beliefs about the nature and origin of sexual problems, are

324

described elsewhere (Cooper 1988). These schools include psychodynamic therapy, behavioral sex counselling, cognitive therapy, and rational-emotive therapy.

Sexual dysfunctions are seen as arising at different levels in the psyche by these different schools, with comparable differences in the level of the treatment intervention (Cooper 1988). The levels should not be considered as 'watertight compartments'; there is dynamic interaction between the levels, and intervention at one level will also affect other levels. This author firmly believes that sex counsellors and sex therapists should always be aware of, and ready to take appropriate account of, the psychodynamic level of the clients' functioning.

Towards a positive eclecticism

Although some of the 'schools' mentioned above are seen as purist, there are historical connections between them. None developed in isolation and this opens consideration of the concept of a developing positive eclecticism.

To develop the clarity and confidence necessary for effective functioning whilst relatively inexperienced, it may be necessary to train in a specific school. However, with experience, the practitioner will (unless completely rigid and closed) begin to explore the potential of other approaches, recognizing that certain clients may require variations of what has been learned in the primary training. Almost inevitably, then, there is a move towards a positive eclecticism in that within the coherent philosophy which is reflected in the formation of the therapeutic alliance, the experienced practitioner will select appropriate techniques and interventions which match client needs. Thus, micro-level events reiterate the macro-level development and interweaving of ideas throughout the history of sex counselling and sex therapy. The individual practitioner's philosophy and practice of working will necessarily be dependent upon his or her beliefs about the nature of human life and the meaning of sex and sexuality.

It is therefore unlikely that a single method or therapeutic approach can be found which will give the best results with *all* clients. The very nature of the sex-counselling relationship inevitably means that the practitioner's personality (influenced by his or her own sexual history) will always determine what can be available for the client. The individuality of self and other must be accepted and not denied. This individuality is determined by the imagery of the inner world within which the person lives, and effective therapy can only be offered or received, if the *meanings* are congruent with that inner world.

Future developments

Physical diagnosis

The increasing range of investigative techniques (Bancroft 1983; Kaplan 1983) may now detect physical causes for cases which previously would have been labelled as 'psychogenic' – an unfortunate mis-labelling, since 'not proven' would have been more accurate and helpful.

Hormonal disturbances cause sexual dysfunctions comparatively rarely, but continuing advances in theory and in assay methods should improve diagnosis and treatment.

Selective arteriography provides useful evidence for the state of the penile blood-supply. There appears to be a considerable lag in developing comparable techniques for investigating genital blood-flow in women with disorders of arousal.

The direct injection into the penis of vaso-active substances which produce erections (for example, papaverine) has been quickly accepted. This has diagnostic as well as therapeutic uses, but the technique is still in a comparatively crude stage of development and refinements of technique can be expected, including the method of injection.

Future treatments

Male erectile dysfunctions continue to attract more effort and attention than other aspects – perhaps an unfortunate reflection on the undue emphasis which our society places on the importance of a stiff penis. No doubt expensive penile implants of increasing sophistication will continue to be developed and used owing to the persistent misconception that erection is essential for genital intercourse.

Outcomes

Outcome research shows that in addition to couples who are cured, there is a significant percentage whose dysfunction persists but who are no longer troubled by it because of their increased understanding and communication.

In the urgent quest for a cure, it may be overlooked that counselling is often concerned with the 'inner world' rather than the 'outer world' i.e. with the client's ability to integrate that which cannot be cured or changed, whatever its origins.

Whilst the purist schools, particularly perhaps the behavioural, will continue to produce new treatment procedures such as the 'negotiated timetable for sexual intercourse', these should be assimilated and used within the framework of positive eclecticism. Treatment can then be based more on the accurately perceived needs of the clients, than on the practitioner's need to adhere rigidly to a particular school.

In addition, as research continues to clarify the essence of effective therapeutic relationships, sex counselling and sex therapy may become more effective in *brief* interventions.

Preventive measures

The wide adoption of the following educative measures could lead to a significant reduction in the prevalence and severity of sexual dysfunctions, thus reducing treatment needs.

The cases presented show how ignorance and poor communication exacerbate and sustain psychogenic sexual dysfunctions. A plea is therefore made for a threefold change:

(1) a programme of *sensual* education from an early age to familiarize individuals with their bodies, thus leading to a higher level of self-acceptance and positive body-image;
(2) a *sexual* education programme which ensures that individuals have a comfortable sexual vocabulary and adequate information about psychological factors in sexual functioning and dysfunctioning, as well as basic anatomy and physiology; and
(3) positive efforts to prevent the perpetuation of damaging cultural myths about both male and female sexuality through the media, particularly by the advertising industry.

The AIDS epidemic

The shadow of the AIDS epidemic looms over all of us, over sex and sexual relationships, and over sex counselling and therapy. The epidemic and its accompanying publicity have affected some people's sexual habits. The campaign for 'safer sex', whether heterosexual or homosexual, underlines the need for urgent programmes of *sensual* education for present and future generations. AIDS is already a factor causing anxiety amongst clients in general counselling, as well as sexual counselling, but there may also be some positive effects.

The publicity has led to sex becoming an acceptable topic of conversation to an extent previously unknown in our society. If this increased openness can be sustained, it will lead to more available sexual information and increased ease of discussion for couples with sexual difficulties, thus reducing the likelihood of exacerbation and the need for sex counselling.

Endpiece

Whither sex counselling?

The last three decades have seen powerful changes in public attitudes to sex and sexuality. After emerging from an earlier restrictive period, there was a liberal movement through the 'swinging sixties' and the 'permissive seventies', but now, in the late eighties, there is a resurgence of a restrictive sexual morality.

From facets of the work discussed in this chapter, it can be seen that these changes are both reflected in, and affected by, sex counselling and therapy. It will be interesting to observe the movement during the next decade and to see if the interactions between current attitudes and sex counselling result in a changing balance between counselling and other treatment approaches to sexual dysfunctions.

References

Bancroft, J. (1983) *Human Sexuality and its Problems*, Edinburgh: Churchill Livingstone.
Bennun, I. (1985) 'Unilateral marital therapy', in W. Dryden, (ed.) *Marital Therapy in Britain, Vol 2: Special Areas*, London: Harper & Row.
Brown, P. and Faulder, C. (1979) *Treat Yourself to Sex – A Guide to Good Loving*, Harmondsworth: Penguin.
Cooper, G. F. (1988) 'The psychological methods of sex therapy', in M. Cole and W. Dryden. (eds) *Sex Therapy in Britain*, Milton Keynes: Open University Press.
Dickson, A. (1985) *The Mirror Within: A New Look at Sexuality*, London: Quartet Books.
Docherty, J. (1986) *Growing Up*, London: Modus Books.
Fairburn, C. G., Dickerson, M. G., and Greenwood, J. (1983) *Sexual Problems and their Management*, Edinburgh: Churchill Livingstone.
Friday, N. (1975) *My Secret Garden – Women's Sexual Fantasies*, London: Virago.
Gillan, P. (1987) *Sex Therapy Manual*, Oxford: Blackwell Scientific Publications.
Hawton, K. (1985) *Sex Therapy – A Practical Guide*, Oxford: Oxford University Press.
Kaplan, H. S. (1974) *The New Sex Therapy*, New York: Brunner/Mazel.
——(1979) *Disorders of Sexual Desire*, London: Baillière Tindall.
——(1983) *The Evaluation of Sexual Disorders*, New York: Brunner/Mazel.
Kitzinger, S. (1985) *Woman's Experience of Sex*, Harmondsworth: Penguin.
Lowndes Sevely, J. (1987) *Eve's Secrets*, London: Bloomsbury Publishing.
McConville, B. and Shearlaw, J. (1985) *The Slanguage of Sex*, London: Futura Publications.
Masters, W. H. and Johnson, V. E. (1966) *Human Sexual Response*, Boston: Little, Brown and Co.
——(1970) *Human Sexual Inadequacy*, London: Churchill.
Stanley, E. (1982) 'Vaginismus', in S. Lock, (ed.) *Sex Problems in Practice*, London: British Medical Association.
Ward, B. (1976) *Sex and Life*, London: Macdonald Educational.
Worden, J. W. (1983) *Grief Counselling and Grief Therapy*, London: Tavistock Publications.
Zilbergeld, B. (1980) *Men and Sex* ,Glasgow: Collins.

Chapter twenty-one

Counselling people with disabilities/chronic illnesses

Julia Segal

Introduction

There are more than one million people registered as disabled in Great Britain today. Some have physical disabilities, some intellectual, and some emotional. Some were born with disabling conditions; some developed them later in life. Some know approximately how their condition will affect them throughout life; others suffer great uncertainty.

Many people with disabilities or disabling chronic illnesses are not registered disabled, either because they do not want the label or because they do not qualify.

Principles

I have spent 3 years counselling people with disabilities, using an approach influenced mainly by Kleinian psychoanalysts but also by people with disabilities themselves and by others working in the field before me (Segal 1985). There are some principles I find useful.

General Principle: People will make efforts to distance themselves from the disability or illness in many different ways.

These can be usefully challenged.

Principle 1: Use of language should reflect the fact that people with disabilities or illnesses are first and foremost people.

Attempts are being made to alter usage in such a way that people with disabilities are not labelled simply by their disability.

Current opinion maintains that if I lose my hand I have an *impairment*. If as a result I cannot write, I have a *disability*. If, as a result I cannot get a job, I have a *handicap*. The concept of 'the handicapped' is being challenged on the grounds that a handicap depends on society as much as the individual; being unable to read is no handicap in a non-literate society. This change of language is not yet

329

current in the population. Feelings and assumptions reflected in the terms 'the handicapped', 'spastics', 'epileptics', for example, are still powerful determinants of social and emotional reactions in counsellors and clients and their families.

It is helpful to consider how everyone has some kind of disability or impairment. It is normal to be short-sighted, physically weak, or lack artistic, mathematical, or musical abilities.

It is when we unconsciously perceive our own 'monstrous', weak, ugly, disturbing, or bad self reflected in a person with a disability that we are most likely to behave badly. We may behave as if they were not people but cartoon characters, with only the one characteristic, knowledge of which is derived from a part of ourselves rather than from the reality of the other person. Thinking about the way we would feel if we were in their shoes can help to mitigate this.

Talking this through with someone else is probably an essential preparation for counselling someone with a disability. The discussion can allow similarities and differences between the counsellor and the client to be explored realistically.

Principle 2: A disability, chronic illness or handicap affects whole families and social networks, not just the individual.

In this chapter I do not systematically distinguish between feelings and behaviour which affect those with disabilities and their families or the professionals around them. There are often important differences, but it can be very useful to point out to clients, whether disabled themselves or not, how feelings are shared.

Principle 3: The meaning of the disability is as important as the disability itself.

It is useful to consider two aspects of the meaning of a disability or chronic illness; the practical and the emotional. Getting up and going to bed may take two or three hours because of a disability. Going to the shops may have to be organized weeks in advance and may break down because someone fails to arrive. Getting an alteration to the house paid for by some Authority can take many months. All of this can give rise to perfectly understandable feelings which need to be acknowledged when counselling someone with a disability or their partner. Of equal importance are questions such as 'Can anyone love me when I'm like this?'; 'What have I done to deserve this?'; 'Would the family be better off if I/they were dead?'

In counselling, people with disabilities and their families can examine and change the emotional meaning of a condition. Changing this can often affect lives significantly even where the condition itself is unaltered. Many disabilities are in fact caused by the *reaction* to an impairment or illness.

A physically and mentally impaired teenager used to sit silently, curled up, his face hidden by a distorted posture. A counsellor sat and spoke with him for an hour every week for several months before it became clear that his position was a result of his hiding a very slightly distorted face. His distorted speech was a way of avoiding social contact where his face would be seen. The counsellor's understanding of this led to him beginning to speak differently and to interact with others. His mental and physical disabilities were far less severe than had appeared at first.

This example shows, first, how this very impaired boy had perfectly understandable and 'normal' reactions – he wanted to hide his 'odd' face from view. It also shows how important social interaction is in determining meaning; the boy's exaggerated fears about his face had never been tested in social conversation since they had led him to withdraw totally from company. Once someone took the trouble to try to understand how he felt, the quite ordinary fear could be changed, with social and physical consequences.

Principle 4: People with disabilities and handicaps should be offered counselling which is as near to 'normal' as possible.

Attempts to maintain normal rules of counselling (and of social behaviour) are important. One of the frustrations faced by people with disabilities is the difficulty in persuading others to treat them like anyone else. If the counsellor 'kindly' behaves in a different way with a disabled client, the client may feel the loss of the normal situation keenly. Most rules for counselling in any setting have developed for good reason; these reasons are likely to have just as much force for the client with a disability. Any deviation from the normal can usefully be discussed by a counsellor, preferably with their supervisor, but possibly with the client too. It may be necessary, but it may raise important issues within the relationship which should not be avoided.

Home visits are a particular case of this. A client who has the freedom to break appointments by not turning up is in a different situation from a client who can only refuse to open the door or arrange an interruption. Some people feel invaded when their condition seems to give others the right to intrude into their home and their body. The social-status implications of being visited rather than visiting are also significant.

Principle 5: Confronting reality in a skilled way is an essential ingredient of counselling, whatever the problem involved.

People often seem to have difficulty sorting out what they have lost, what they have to give up, and what they may choose to keep if they pay a price.

For 20 years a man refused to use a leg-bag for his urine in spite of his family's whole life being disrupted by the urgent need to get him to the toilet every hour. He was sure that his wife would stop being sexually attracted to him if he had one. In counselling he faced this and discovered it could not be true. The life of his whole family was changed.

People are sometimes afraid that their relationship would be damaged by acknowledging really upsetting fears or facts. They can also be afraid that their statements or questions would be self-fulfilling prophecies. This can apply to people with disabling conditions, to their families, and to counsellors. Realities are often avoided because people are afraid of them; they feel that illusions are safer: 'I know he's being unrealistic but isn't it better to let him keep his illusions? What good would it do to face him with reality?'

Unfortunately, maintaining illusions takes a lot of energy. In fact, experience shows that denial and illusions are used as defences against fears which are *far worse than reality*. With the right person and in the right setting, facing up to fears and unpleasant beliefs, however painful, can be experienced as a relief. Sometimes it shows up frightening beliefs as unrealistic. At worst, it leads to sharing and acknowledgement of real cause for grief or mental pain.

> A young man with serious difficulty in social relationships and some physical disabilities kept insisting that his father was far less competent than he was. He changed considerably after work following on from the counsellor (against her own resistance) pointing out that his father had been able to have a wife and son, whereas he could not.

Counsellors as well as others can be caught by the assumption that illness, a distorted body, a difficulty speaking, or a slowness of intellectual grasp must all be accompanied by a lack of emotional strength. Work presented at an informal workshop at the Tavistock Clinic, Hampstead, London, run by Valerie Sinasson and Jon Stokes, has repeatedly demonstrated that insight and understanding as well as the ability to experience grief, depression, or any other emotion in a realistic way – and to hide them – can be evident in people who are extremely impaired, both mentally and physically.

It is the able-bodied who consistently have difficulty in coping with their perceptions of others' disabilities. They frequently 'cover up' rather than take opportunities to discuss them. This means that they do not discover or challenge either the illusions or the realistic perceptions of the person with the disability.

The difficulty for the counsellor or caring professional can be simply not to block the direct expression and sharing of painful beliefs; for example, by some spoken or unspoken encouragement to 'be positive' or to maintain some other one-sided illusion or pretence.

Issues

Professional health workers and counsellors can benefit from discussion of the issues which affect their clients, some of which I describe below. Preparation for facing such issues (particularly the 'tricky' ones, such as death, suicide, sex, and family violence) can make the difference between a counsellor who can 'contain' fears and anxieties, and a counsellor who by his or her behaviour confirms to the client that certain fears or anxieties are quite unthinkable.

These issues affect not only clients but also their families. Any issue which is of importance to a person with a handicap or illness or disability must affect his or her family, and vice versa. Other people's reactions, cares, and fears affect all those around them and may need to be understood in counselling.

Grief

Whole families have to cope with grief in connection with impairments or illnesses in one member. Grief arises with the giving up of some past reality, which may include ordinary hopes and expectations for the future. The development of new ways of thinking, behaving, and living cannot take place without grief for the old. The pain involved should not be underestimated. It often gives rise to anger. Sometimes this anger is not expressed directly but is evoked in someone else who responds either angrily or with rejection.

Growing older with a disability (particularly your own, your child's, or your parent's) gives rise continually to a new set of losses appropriate to the age and life stage. Each of these must be somehow acknowledged and incorporated into the automatic assumptions made by the individual and those around. The pain that accompanies each new awareness of a loss caused by the disability may be avoided at times; long-term avoidance causes social and emotional difficulties.

The ability of a counsellor to bear grief with a client without minimising, exaggerating, or denying it may be of enormous value. It seems that grief which is expressed can be better tested against reality and may be more easily worked through. Other opportunities for this may not be available to the client.

Grieving for real losses (such as the loss of a leg) may enable people to discover what they can salvage (such as the ability to socialize without playing tennis). Grieving in company may reduce the feeling of being alone and abandoned which often arises with any loss.

Earlier losses are evoked by new ones and may give rise to grief which seems unrealistic in the new context. (A common example of this is when the death of a cat or dog releases grief for a father who died two years earlier.) Grief for the losses caused by a disability may be disentangled from grief for losses which have nothing to do with disability, yet which are themselves in some way crippling.

A woman came for counselling about her multiple sclerosis (MS) and spent her sessions grieving for the loss of three babies by miscarriage and abortion (unrelated in fact, though not in fantasy, to the MS), and talking about an incident when as a teenager she was sexually assaulted. Her relationships with her daughters and her husband improved, in particular in connection with the family's handling of her disabilities.

How each member of the family deals with personal grief affects the others. The grief of losing one's own faculties and the grief of the watching partner are closely connected. The grief of being born deformed or imperfect is connected powerfully with the grief this brings to the mother. A mother's difficulty grieving about her child's physical impairment may cause the child as many problems as the condition itself.

'Accepting the illness/disability'

This is a phrase often used, particularly by family members and professionals. Sometimes it seems to be used as an unrealistic accusation: 'I want you to help him to accept that he is really useless, that he can't do anything.' Sometimes it seems to be used more realistically, though impatiently: 'She hasn't accepted it; she won't use the wheelchair.'

Acceptance is clearly bound up with recognizing reality and grieving for what has to be given up. It seems to take in general about two years to accept any significant loss in the sense that nearly all the automatic assumptions made about the world will include the loss rather than deny it. This means that people with progressive illnesses or disabilities are often mentally about two years out of date in terms of their physical situation. Awareness of this can help people who would otherwise think that grieving behaviour was going to last for ever.

Exploring what 'accepting it' or 'fighting it' means to the people concerned is often valuable.

A young man felt that if he accepted that he had MS it would mean he would lose his only chance of getting rid of it, which was to bargain: 'if I don't ask too much, and don't accept it, I will be given back the use of my legs'. Once he realized this was how he thought, he could not maintain it.

Making sense of the situation

People often feel the unfairness of their fate. It is as if we all have certain expectations: a reasonable lifetime of good health; work to be followed by retirement; that our children will outlast us. When these expectations are not fulfilled, we feel something has gone wrong.

The need to make sense of the situation can throw people back on to very primitive beliefs, often superstitions (for example, God is punishing us so we must suffer). These beliefs can sometimes be more disabling than the condition itself.

A young woman who was physically scarcely affected at all, felt that because she had MS, she ought not to look for a husband; she should dress badly and stop going to parties in case someone was attracted to her.

'Being bad'

Any illness or loss may give rise to a sense of guilt, blame, or envy of others, and a feeling of being 'bad'; a bad person, bad inside, to be avoided like the plague.

A woman in her twenties, diagnosed MS 12 months previously, said she had suddenly 'seen' horrible fungus growing out of a filing cabinet at work. 'That's me', she said; 'that's how I think of myself, full of fungus, vile, really yukky inside.'

These feelings can have disastrous effects on relationships.

Parents with handicapped children often unconsciously believe that the child is the result of 'bad' sex, or a consequence of their own inner badness. This can affect their treatment of the child.

People sometimes talk of 'wishing' their condition on to someone else. This can make them feel wicked and bad. Mothers can also feel they are bad if they do *not* wish their children's disabilities or illnesses on to themselves.

The desire to make people better

This is terribly important for family and friends, and it can also help to discuss their frustration with the person who has an incurable illness or disability themselves. Sometimes the people who are closest are the least able to show their concern, if they feel too guilty for not being able to make the person better. This can cause a husband to withdraw or attack whenever his wife tries to tell him she feels ill or in pain, but it can happen in any close relationship. Understanding when this is happening can uncover buried love between the people concerned.

Sometimes those around try to take control of the condition (illness/disability) by controlling the person who has it, partly out of misguided attempts to *make* them get better.

Children with a severe disability or chronic illness can have strong desires to make their parents better, including making them happy when they are sad. Where their own condition brings grief to their parents, this can cause the child enormous distress which they may cover up in order to try to keep the parents happy.

Dying

Disabilities and chronic illnesses often face people with anxieties about dying. Parents worry about what will happen to their children who have a disability; people with a present or potential disability worry about being a burden or being abandoned. People have very mixed feelings about wanting to be dead themselves or wanting a member of the family to die, especially if severe pain is involved.

Since it is seldom a topic of social conversation, ideas about death and dying are often quite unrealistic. They may include the fear that if you talk about death, it will happen, or you will be wishing the person dead. Often these ideas seem to have been formed in childhood and not to have changed much since.

Sharing thoughts about dying and death often seems to help, particularly where they have not been clearly articulated. Realistic ideas about how, when, and where death is likely to happen may then replace more terrifying ones.

A bright, busy woman in her thirties 'never thought about dying', though she smoked thirty cigarettes a day and had a progressively disabling disease. On being pressed to think about it, she imagined herself in a large public ward. Asked where her husband would be, she was surprised to realise he was not there in the picture. She then described a quite different place she knew, where she felt she would be able to die with dignity and with her husband close by. At the end of five sessions of counselling she no longer had to keep doing things all the time and said she was much more relaxed. She also gave up smoking.

Counsellors and other health professionals who have never discussed their own feelings about death and dying may be unable to hear or to respond when clients or patients raise these issues or hint that they worry about them.

Suicide

People who hint or mention that they have considered suicide often find it a relief to speak of it openly. The desire to be rid of pain and the problems of life may need to be acknowledged, and the frustration and anger which may accompany the decision not to hurt the family and friends in this way.

It can be useful to look at hidden aggressiveness behind suicidal wishes; the question of who would suffer is often important. People who initially say simply that they want to relieve their family of a burden may on further discussion express their anger with these carers and their failings, and a desire to punish them and make them suffer: 'I'll kill myself and then they'll be sorry.' Uncovering the mixed feelings involved can be helpful. Again, counsellors need to have discussed these issues *before* they arise in counselling.

Loss of role

There is a common idea that one should be relieved of other troubles and duties when ill, and by extension, when disabled. This however lays the basis for excluding people with disabilities from ordinary social roles, and can be examined and challenged.

A particular case of this involves the assumption that the person with a chronic illness or disability should not be worried or made angry. This can have the effect of seriously weakening that person's ability to take on normal roles such as that of parent or spouse or adult son or daughter.

336

An 8-year-old girl said she had not told her mother she had been homesick when she stayed at her friends' house for the night, because her grandmother had said she should not worry mummy. Before her mother was ill (with MS) she had always told her things like that.

Not only the family but also the person with the disability or chronic illness themselves may encourage this behaviour.

A disabled mother spoke of herself as one of the children and persuaded several social workers to do so too.

The behaviour of the medical profession

This is an issue which often arises. Disappointment, resentment, and unrealistic expectations mingle with experience of unthinking behaviour or mistakes on the part of doctors. Both the reality and the exaggeration, and the guilt and upset they can arouse in the patient may need to be understood and acknowledged. People often feel guilty if they catch someone else in the wrong, and they often desperately want to keep the doctor as a good, helpful figure who can do no wrong.

Counsellors may need to 'practise' their own neutrality in such situations, where they have to acknowledge the reality and the feelings involved, without being drawn into taking sides.

Social stigma

For many people their or their children's disabilities mean some kind of social stigma. People can and do make life difficult for those with disabilities. They can be positively unpleasant; patronising; over-protective; unhelpful and thoughtless. The feelings aroused by such behaviour may need to be acknowledged. There is often a furious indignation and resentment: 'I have to cope with the illness/disabilities; why should I have to cope with other people's inability to handle it too?'

An assumption that somehow you have paid your debt to society if you or your child have a disability, and that everything else should be made easy, often gives rise to wry laughter when discovered and clarified.

There is a serious problem where the disability or illness arouses great anxieties in those around. The film 'The Elephant Man' graphically illustrates the horrified and horrifying reactions of people viewing a severely disfigured face for the first time. Revulsion and disgust – and fascination too – may flicker across the most well-disciplined face in such circumstances. It is painful to empathize with someone who has to endure it with every new person they meet.

As with any kind of counselling, if a client is complaining about the attitude of 'society' or someone close to them, it can be useful to ask '... and is there a part of you that agrees with them?'. The power to do something about it may be regained, or the grief for a real loss may be owned, without denying that the attitude of others may be a real problem. This can help to combat the temptation to see 'the disabled' as poor, helpless victims who bear no responsibility for the way they are treated.

One woman felt that she could not talk to friends about her MS because everyone pitied the disabled. When asked about her own attitudes she said that she had had a boss who was in a wheelchair. It appeared that what she had actually felt towards this woman was a mixture of envy and resentment: why should a woman with a disability have a husband, children, and a prestigious, well-paid job when she herself had none of them? After one session of counselling she was able to tell friends about her MS and it then took up less of her attention.

Control, dependence, and independence

Control of your own life often becomes more restricted if you have a disability or if you care for someone with one. This can be for reasons of reality: it may be really difficult to get up at a time you choose if you live in a residential institution or depend on someone else's help, or if someone else depends on you. Unrealistic assumptions can also be involved.

A woman said she was afraid that if she went into a wheelchair it would be awful for her husband. Asked in what way precisely, she said, 'well, you know, the *responsibility*'. The counsellor said it sounded as if she felt that loss of her legs would mean she abdicated all responsibility for herself; she looked astonished, and then laughed.

Reactions to constraints on independence vary with individuals. Some people cannot imagine being happy without a caring and cared-for partner; others cannot imagine being happy without the option of living alone.

Reactions are also affected by the sensitivity of those in control. People pushing wheelchairs can do so making it clear that they are in the service of the person in the chair, or they can simply treat the occupant as if he or she is part of the chair itself, with no mind or opinion to be consulted. People being pushed too can treat the pusher with consideration or rudeness.

Fears of losing control of one's life often depend on unrealistic beliefs about how much life can ever be under control, and about how much independence of others is ever possible or desirable. Experiences of being unable to control nurses or other helpers – when needing bedpans or being fed, for example – also colour attitudes to dependence.

For some people being dependent means reverting to childhood; their experiences as children will affect how they feel about this.

A farmer with a disability refused to go out on his scooter since he had fallen off and been unable to get up. He was not found for several hours, but it was not this that worried him, he said. He could not bear to have to tell his wife where he went in the future; this to him meant being a child again, and he preferred to stay at home.

Counselling can sometimes help people discover a new concept of 'dependent mature adult', where previously they only had 'dependent child' and 'independent adult'. The dependence of others on the person with a disability for love and comfort, for example, may also be newly recognized and valued through counselling.

Some people fear that others will not love them if they do not keep control: loss of control then means loss of being loved and may be very frightening indeed.

Unfortunately, people who are put in a position of power by someone else's disability may use it in ways which are not to the benefit of the person on the receiving end, either from ignorance or malice.

It is hard to make decisions on someone else's behalf. Often people seem to feel they must 'play safe' by keeping control, in spite of the fact that this control may disable. A child who is never given any responsibility does not grow up normally; but giving responsibility to a child with a severe disability may be extremely difficult.

A woman on a ward for the terminally ill was told by the nurses she should not smoke. She asked a passer-by to get her a cigarette. The nurses felt this was manipulative behaviour. It had not occurred to them that she could be allowed to decide whether to end her life smoking or not.

Sometimes unreasonable attempts to control others can be ways of trying to get rid of feelings of powerlessness. These feelings can be brought about by a body which will not obey or by a social situation. Where someone feels they have no rights and respect themselves, they may treat others as if they have no rights and respect due. This can clearly apply both to people with disabilities and to those who care for them professionally or voluntarily.

Sex

The attitude that sex is inappropriate for 'the disabled' may still be detected in the general public, including people with disabilities themselves. There are many situations connected with disability where sex needs to be considered. Here I mention only a few.

(a) Teenage anxieties about sex (and aggression) may not be modified by normal private interactions with other teenagers if impairment brings too much adult supervision.

(b) Incest is not uncommon with children with physical and mental impairments: private discussion of anything that has happened to them may be helpful, though difficult. Adults who were sexually assaulted as children may blame the assault for later illnesses or disabilities in themselves or their children.

(c)Not everyone finds disabled or impaired or weak bodies unattractive: sexual attraction may be unaffected or increased by disabilities. People sometimes find this surprising or even shameful. People with severe disabilities do fall in love and do marry.

(d)People often find that they cannot combine the roles of sexual partner and nurse/carer. They may have to take this into account when deciding whether or not to allow someone else to take care of their partner's bodily needs.

Relationship difficulties connected with disabilities

I have grouped these into a separate section because there are particular issues which affect relationships between people with disabilities and others. The counselling relationship as well as other professional and non-professional relationships may be confused by them.

Those who have little experience of others' disabilities are often afraid: 'I won't know how to behave; I'll say the wrong thing; I'll make a fool of myself.' It can be difficult to know how to behave when first meeting someone with a gross deformity or odd social behaviour.

'Normal' social rules may also not apply easily, and it can be difficult to know what new rules to use in their place. It can seem rude to sit and watch someone struggling to put on their coat rather than helping them: deciding when and how to offer help and when to assume that the person can do what they are doing in their own time can be difficult. The individual concerned may have strong personal beliefs about when help should and should not be offered, and these may not be easily guessed.

Experience helps; so too can discussing the difficulty straightforwardly with the person concerned. They have probably been in the situation before, and if they have not, they may well value insight into someone else's reactions to their condition. Local disability groups sometimes offer 'consciousness-raising' workshops.

Relationships can often be distorted in particular ways as a result of assumptions made about 'the disabled'.

Assumption 1: You have to be kind to the disabled and think nicely about them; they've got enough to put up with as it is.

A psychologist rang to discuss counselling a woman who had MS. She said she felt so sorry for her. I asked if there was something in the client which gave rise to this feeling, or did it come from the psychologist herself? There was an embarrassed silence and the psychologist then said that actually the woman made her feel extremely irritated, but she felt she shouldn't feel like that about someone with an illness like MS.

The feeling that one should not experience irritation with 'the poor dears' can be a serious barrier both to real work (for professionals) and to close relationships (in the family and socially) and can maintain unnecessarily asocial behaviour.

A deaf boy was being very nasty to a small girl. His mother told him off. The girl's mother said, 'oh, you can understand how he feels' – meaning, don't be so hard on him, he's deaf. The mother said no, he had to learn he could not treat other children like that or he'd never have any friends.

Assumption 2: No-one can understand what it is like to have a disability unless they are disabled too.

People with similar disabilities can often help each other considerably in many ways, but they may not understand each other any more than any two people taken at random would understand each other. The problem is that no two disabilities are the same since the people who have them are different.

The effort and skills people need to try to understand someone with a disability may be no different from those needed to understand anyone else whose outlook and situation differs from their own.

Assumption 3: It is not fair to be happy and satisfied yourself when others are disabled and suffering.

A counsellor working with disabled people said that at first she felt guilty about enjoying her work; it did not seem fair that she had the work satisfaction and they had the disabilities.

A mother said she felt guilty every time she enjoyed the sun; how could she be happy when her son had multiple sclerosis?

This assumes that people have no more to their lives than their disabilities, and that these totally ruin all happiness and satisfaction in life. This is not necessarily true. Even if people's satisfactions are limited by their disabilities, they may still have satisfactions the counsellor or their mother do not have. Not everyone reacts with envy and jealousy at seeing others happy; people can enjoy others' happiness and can obtain pleasure from participating in a different way.

A blind woman enjoyed going to the cinema.

A man who used to go fell walking with his wife enjoyed hearing her describe walks she took without him.

A woman thought her husband would be unhappy seeing his children playing on the beach as he would get upset that he could not join in now due to a severe disability. He said he did want to watch them, and he liked seeing them enjoying themselves.

Future developments

There have been many changes in attitudes to disability in recent years, often brought about by the efforts of people with disabilities themselves. The Open University and Age Concern (for example, Mace *et al.* 1985) are particularly important disseminators of new attitudes and approaches in this field. Pioneers such as Miller and Gwynne (1972), Alison Norman (1980), and Wendy Greengross (1976) have written influential books for professionals. The work of psychotherapists such as Shirley Hoxter (1986) are contributing to new understanding of the effects of disabilities on people. One future development I feel fairly hopeful about is a possible increase in writing of this kind, as psychotherapists as well as counsellors become interested in discussing the issues around disabilities and chronic illnesses.

Both the demand for counselling and the attitudes of counsellors have also been changing as a result of general changes within society. People with disabilities are less likely to be seen as objects of pity or charity and more likely to be seen as active participants in society.

Availability of counselling

There is more work to be done. Counselling is still not fully recognized in this country as a practical and useful way of helping people to live better with their own or others' disabilities. Counsellors themselves are seldom employed in this capacity: there is an assumption that anyone can offer counselling, and that it can be fitted in by social workers, teachers, doctors, or anyone else, whether or not they have the time, training, supervisory support, personality, or inclination. Some of course do have all these things, but by no means all.

SPOD (in London) is an organization which attempts to offer sexual counselling to people with disabilities as well as training for professionals working in the field. It would be good to be able to say that in future I see such organizations increasing in number and effectiveness; but unfortunately they are instead under financial threat and may not survive.

With the increase in self-confidence of those with disabilities, many self-help groups have developed. These offer practical help to those who are prepared to accept the necessary label, and also to those who wish to learn about and perhaps change their own attitudes. Some of these offer counselling. A few fall into the trap of suggesting that only those with disabilities can help others with disabilities; others are more concerned with the quality of their counselling.

ARMS (a self-help charity for people with multiple sclerosis) has a policy which says that everyone with MS should be offered at least one counselling session with a professional counsellor. Organizations for people with other illnesses may be slowly following suit. When rung up to ask if they offer counselling the response can be an apologetic 'no' rather than a total rejection of the idea.

There are also organizations run by people who say 'our people do not need it'. The difficulty is that the people with power and resources have to be convinced that counselling is worthwhile. Deciding to find or spend the money needed is of course difficult, but sometimes it seems that the idea of counselling is either threatening or seems insulting, implying a lack of something which one ought to have. Some charities are run by people who seem continually to rush around in order to avoid knowing what they think or feel. Some people are terrified of 'cans of worms' being opened. Where they control policy, counselling is less likely to be on offer.

Change in attitudes to disability

As disabled people become more visible (via 'Equal Opportunity' employers, for example) and integrated into schools, disabilities become less unfamiliar and frightening. This is already influencing opinions and behaviour. So too are books written by people with disabilities, particularly those with an autobiographical component. Counsellors will be affected by these changes just as others are.

Counsellors' own attitudes and assumptions

Most counsellors will have to make some efforts to modify both their own expectations and their lack of expectations towards people who are overtly disabled or chronically sick. They may have to learn how to avoid patronizing or 'taking-over' approaches. They may have to work to uncover hidden prejudices in themselves, just as has been necessary with racism and sexism. This applies whether they have an obvious disability themselves or not.

Within the general population, assumptions about the kinds of allowances which have to be made, and which should or need not be made, are at present in a state of flux. Counsellors are in a position to influence the development and direction of such attitude changes by their willingness to look carefully at attitudes and beliefs with clients and to challenge assumptions. To do this best they need considerable awareness of their own attitudes and assumptions.

Discussion with colleagues and personal therapy for counsellors are both in my opinion essential for future developments in counselling in general. They are particularly important when counselling this particular client group. The ability to grieve with clients depends upon the counsellor's own experience of sharing grief and of being understood by somebody else. The experiences of being dependent on somebody else, of being offered something you do not have yourself, and of coping with the very mixed feelings this arouses, are all experiences common to people with disabilities and people in therapy themselves. Counsellors who avoid this dependency relationship with a therapist cannot fully understand the difficulties their clients face. The counsellor's own mental and emotional disabilities need to be uncovered and worked with in a therapeutic context if clients are not to be used to cover up the counsellor's own difficulties.

One of the problems of having a disability is that you may become the butt of other people's projections: you may come to stand for parts of themselves which are disabled and perhaps pitied, despised, or rejected. Counsellors need to work on their own mental state in order to do their best to avoid adding to the problems of their clients. I would like to see increasing recognition of this amongst all counsellors; and I think it is particularly vital when working with people whose circumstances make them especially likely targets for emotional exploitation. People who have been ill-treated as children are also in my experience particularly vulnerable to arousing the counsellor's worst side, and where people with chronic illnesses or physical disabilities have also suffered violence as a child, the counsellor is likely to need considerable help.

Demand for counselling

New assumptions about the abilities of people with disabilities can create new pressures. For some, these pressures will be unwelcome and they will want to be left alone to do things their own way. For others there may be a new thought that if they are not living to the full then they could ask for help or they could be offered it. Like anyone else, people with disabilities and those who live with them can sometimes feel extremely insulted at the idea that they might 'need' counselling, particularly if they see it as yet another way of distinguishing them from the rest of the population, imagined somehow not to 'need' counselling. Others have more of an idea that people can help each other to handle difficult situations rather than simply mock their inabilities. For these, counselling may be seen as a possible aid to real self-determination.

It is likely that people whose experiences have shown them that talking to others can help will be more likely to come for counselling than those whose experiences have been less encouraging. Offering counselling to people with disabilities produces just the same reactions as offering it to anyone else.

However, it may be that where people have chronic illnesses which lead to some kind of deterioration, there is an increased sense that people *should* be offered some kind of help with dealing with the emotions aroused. Beginning with AIDS and cancer, it is perhaps slowly becoming accepted that people with certain conditions should be offered counselling, not only for themselves but also for their families.

Demand for staff or group counselling

Changes are taking place in terms of the behaviour expected from and tolerated in people with chronic illnesses and/or disabilities. Once people are not patronized they may be treated with more dignity, but the same allowances may not be made for them. Asocial behaviour in people with physical or mental disabilities may be tolerated and even condoned in some circumstances at present, when it is assumed that normal standards of politeness and respect are not valid. These allowances may permit and encourage segregation, but losing them means real losses as well as gains.

In other circumstances, such as residential institutions, standards of behaviour demanded from people with disabilities at present may be higher than those demanded from the general population, if only because of the pressures of living communally. The movement seems to be towards recognizing the right and potential of people with disabilities to live alone or in company of their own choosing, or in smaller groups. Such small units might well benefit from relationship counselling.

Tolerance towards both sexual and aggressive feelings amongst people with disabilities also seems to be increasing slowly amongst professionals. This demands new behaviour from 'carers' anywhere where people rely upon the assistance of others. What kinds of behaviour are to be tolerated and what can be rejected? Balancing the rights of the individual and the group, the 'cared for', and the carer, in a day centre, a nursing home, or any kind of group living situation (including a family) is far from easy. Do staff or parents have the right to say 'I do not like to see this happening'? Do they have the right to enforce their likes and dislikes? Who has the power in fact: the helper or the helped, or is it somewhere divided between the two?

Staff in some institutions are discovering the value of staff support-groups or work discussion-groups led by outsiders. Counsellors are being brought in to help such groups to look at their own feelings and behaviour in the new climate of opinion, and to find new ways of working which incorporate an increased respect for the client.

Need for counselling

Some pressures on people with chronic illnesses and disabilities are increasing. The shortage of staff in the NHS and the run-down of institutions means that good nursing is seldom available even on a 'respite care' basis. This is actually life-threatening (for example, increasing the incidence of pressure sores, which can kill.) It also raises the anxiety level of both nurses and patients. The increase in numbers of divorces and remarriages means that people who behave badly or are 'difficult', either as a result of their condition or in reaction to it, may be less easily tolerated at home if they threaten a new relationship in which they have no secure place. They are also more likely to lose their own marriage relationship. The run-down of Social Services financing is bound to affect people with disabilities or chronic illnesses seriously, particularly those who do not fit easily into neat categories, such as those who can *sometimes* work.

All of these add to the difficulties faced by those who depend on the aid of others, and add to the likelihood of social or emotional 'breakdown' of some kind. Counsellors may well be called in by hard-pressed social workers to help pick up the pieces – but will they be available to be called in? Someone has to pay them. Counselling and psychotherapy are sometimes funded by private health insurance; this source of funding may unfortunately become of increasing importance in the future in Britain. Will this be yet another way in which social divisions are exacerbated?

Conclusion

Counselling people with disabilities, their families, and professionals involved with them is work I personally find extremely rewarding. There is often so much which can be achieved in such a short time, simply because no one before has ever sat down with the people concerned and discussed openly and honestly the 'unspeakable' things they have believed and feared. Even one or two counselling sessions can sometimes uncover and remove difficulties which have prevented normal social interactions from taking place. The changes brought about in people's feelings about themselves and their consequent behaviour can be dramatic. In the process, with good supervision, the counsellor too learns and changes – and perhaps prepares for his or her own future.

References

Greengross, W. (1976) *Entitled to Love*, London: Malaby Press.
Hoxter, S. (1986) 'The significance of trauma in the difficulties encountered by physically disabled children', *Journal of Child Psychotherapy* 12(1): 87–102.
Mace, N. L., Rabins, P. V., Castleton, B. A., Cloke, C., and McEwan, E. (1985) *The 36 hour day*, London: Hodder & Stoughton with Age Concern.
Miller, E. J. and Gwynne, G. V. (1972) *A Life Apart*, London: Tavistock Publications.
Norman, A. J. (1980) *Rights and Risk. A Discussion Document on Civil Liberty in Old Age*, London: The Centre for Policy on Ageing.
Segal, J. C. (1985) *Phantasy in Everyday Life*, London: Pelican Books.

Chapter twenty-two

Counselling people affected by HIV and AIDS

John Sketchley

Introduction

The title of this chapter embraces AIDS patients, the HIV- infected, people near to them, and the worried well, all of whom may become clients of the counsellor. Given the incurability of HIV infection, health education and counselling have assumed an importance hitherto denied them. The Scottish Health Education Group with the British Association for Counselling is in the process of producing a training manual for training counsellors to deal with clients affected by HIV. The House of Commons Select Committee has given a positive endorsement of counselling in this field, and the World Health Organization has appointed an international group of consultants to advise it about counselling people with AIDS and all people affected by HIV.

To understand the following principles and issues, a review of the medical background appears necessary. The human immunodeficiency virus (HIV) is transmitted through blood, semen, and cervical secretions, and from an infected pregnant mother to her unborn child. This means that precautions need to be taken during sexual activity and injections, the main protections being the use of condoms and not sharing needles. Everyday social activities, such as shaking hands, kissing, and using lavatories, do not constitute a risk. The World Health Organization's guidelines on HIV and breast-feeding continue to advocate it, as breast milk is not regarded as a high risk.

Once HIV enters a person, a range of possibilities lies ahead. Within 3 months the immune system produces an antibody, which is almost powerless against the virus, but which can be detected by a blood test. It is important to note that a negative result of the antibody test does not mean the person is uninfected, because of the delay between infection and the production of the antibody. The antibody-positive person may remain in that state for years, perhaps without knowing, apparently healthy but able to infect others. There is thus a difference between HIV infection and HIV-related diseases.

At any stage, the HIV-infected person may move along the spectrum into manifestations of HIV-related diseases. The first and least serious possibility is generalized lymphadenopathy, when the glands in the neck and armpits are

347

persistently swollen. The second is AIDS-related complex (ARC), a collection of symptoms such as tiredness, constant fevers, loss of weight, diarrhoea, night sweats, and sometimes shingles, herpes, and thrush in the mouth. These are profound changes, and not just an occasional sleepless night or attack of diarrhoea. These two conditions may be episodic, with periods of remission. The third possibility is dementia, similar to that in the elderly, and results from the virus attacking the central nervous system.

Lastly, there is AIDS itself, which can appear at any time after infection by HIV, or after episodes of other manifestations. The HIV virus causes a severe defect in certain cells which are critical in the body's defence system. The virus incapacitates the immune system so drastically that illnesses normally repelled by the body seize their opportunity and take hold. The main ones are Kaposi's sarcoma (a skin cancer) and pneumocystis carinii (a type of pneumonia). Virtually unchecked by the immune system, they can kill, though the patient may be able to lead a reasonably normal life at home for some of the time.

There is no way of telling when a person with HIV will progress to ARC, AIDS, or any other manifestation; but it is thought that in time all HIV-infected people will die of HIV-related diseases. Infection by HIV is for life, and the infected person may unwittingly transmit the virus to others, while appearing to be healthy. HIV and AIDS, furthermore, are no chooser of persons, and can infect men, women, or children who are exposed to them. It is therefore more helpful to think of risk activities rather than risk groups, though numerically homosexual men and drug-addicts have suffered most in Britain.

Principles

Before HIV antibody test

Counsellors and most health professionals in the field agree that all people seeking or advised to be tested for HIV antibodies should be properly counselled before the test. The counselling should provide information about what the test can and cannot do, with a clear explanation of the difference between HIV infection and AIDS, and the main means of transmission of HIV. During this process it may become obvious that the client has been involved in risk activities, such as sex with an infected person, sharing a needle, or a transfusion of infected blood. Alternatively, the client may reveal that he or she has not engaged in high-risk activities, in which case it would be relevant to help them examine more closely why they wish to be tested, as it may be unnecessary.

The information in effect consists of explaining modes of transmission of HIV and how to prevent it, and looking at the advantages and disadvantages of the test. The advantages are that some people want to be certain one way or the other, available treatment can be applied, decisions can be taken about behaviours and relationships, and decisions made about healthy living and about pregnancy. The disadvantages include possible depression if the result is positive, rejection by family, friends, and employers, and problems about insurance if others learn of the positive result or even about the request for the test. A negative result leaves a person still uncertain, either because it may be a false negative or because the antibody is not yet detectable. In this case, a person engaging in high-risk activities may need to consider having a further test after 3 months.

The main focus of pre-test counselling will be on the psychosocial issues, arising from known and unknown factors. A positive result cannot be received neutrally, and will have serious implications for the person's life, loved ones, family, and work. The counsellor should explore the feelings that a positive result will arouse in the client, and the effects in other quarters. At this stage it is worth trying to understand more fully the motives behind the request to have the test. If the motive is to discover whether the client needs to change his or her behaviour, it is necessary to underline that whether a person has the test or not, whether the test is positive or not, the client should develop safer behaviour. The reason is that the ways to avoid being infected and the way to avoid transmitting HIV to others are the same, i.e. using a condom and not sharing needles.

The illumination of motives may reveal fears, guilt, and apprehensions: fears of possible or probable infection, guilt about behaviour and the likelihood of having infected others, apprehension about the results of the test and its implications for living and relationships. As in all counselling, the counsellor has to elicit these feelings in a non-judgemental way and probe them further to enable the client to resolve them and to give permission to the clients to be the persons they are. Feelings, it may be pointed out, naturally arise in us. In the author's view, we are not responsible for their presence, but we are responsible for what we do with them.

The aspects of responsibility can cover: whom to protect, organizing one's life to ensure protective measures are available at the right time, leading a healthy life, reviewing one's system of values and beliefs, and taking a realistic decision about having the test or not. It is easy to take on an air of moralizing when addressing these points, and the counsellor must guard carefully against such an eventuality.

Some clients who have engaged in known high-risk activities resist the idea of possible infection. This denial needs confronting by the counsellor, as it is an unrealistic response. Behind it may lie a deep fear of dying, being 'found out', guilt over a casual sexual experience or a one-off homosexual encounter, belief that he or she is being punished, worry that certain freedoms or behaviours will have to be given up, concern for actual or desired children, and anger with the person who transmitted the virus to them. The inability to accept these feelings may lead to denial, and thus the counsellor must enable the client to bring them to the surface. Once the feelings are acknowledged and owned, the range of decisions that may help to resolve them must be examined and a realistic choice made by the client. The counsellor may need to provide support during the implementation of any decisions.

At the end of the counselling session a decision has to be considered. The client, whether referred by others or by self, must be the one to decide whether to go ahead with the test. This decision will embrace also the responsibility for dealing with the consequences of the result, such as making changes in behaviour and relationships, and living with an uncertain future.

After the HIV antibody test

Negative result

The relief afforded by a negative result has to be tempered by other considerations. A sexually active person or drug-addict must consider changes in life-style and sexual behaviour to avoid infection, and to avoid possible transmission since a negative result is never conclusive, for the reasons given in the introduction to this chapter. The uncertainty and fear outlined when describing counselling before the test may therefore still remain, and the counsellor may need to help the client review many of the issues again, as a negative result may be perceived as 'no progress'. A further consideration here is that the partners of the client may also experience a sense of relief, but uncertainty and mistrust may return as they wonder why the test was requested in the first place. The counsellor may need to be available for future sessions to enable the client to cope with the uncertain situation. The background of risk may help the client to decide whether to ask for a repeat test after three months.

Positive result (Miller 1987a)

The test is conducted by health professionals, but the counsellor may be asked to give the result. There are bad ways of doing this: over the phone, by letter, in a hurry, just before the weekend (Richards 1986), without the possibility of immediate counselling and further information. There is no easy way of giving a positive result, but it should be direct, face to face, simple, and brief, so as to avoid confusion and misunderstanding. Whether the news is imparted by the health personnel or by a counsellor, there must be time immediately available for the counsellor to deal with the client's reactions.

The first reaction in the client is deep shock (Grimshaw 1987), described by one health adviser like this:

> It is as if the patient is suddenly reduced to an impotent point. The will or ability to talk may vanish. Thought processes and feelings seem suddenly to shut down. The person feels a completely powerless victim who can do nothing to avoid the inevitable, having lost all control, being a victim and not an agent. This is the reversal of the usual state of mind, producing despondency and anger, while thoughts of illness and death fill the mind.
>
> (Palmer, personal communication 1987).

How can the counsellor proceed? The first aim will be to enable the client to talk and discharge the feelings verbally; the second will be to help restore the feeling of being in control; the third will be to take stock of the implications; and lastly, to make realistic decisions for the future based on meaningful motives.

The first aim is to enable the client to talk and discharge the feelings. As a first step the counsellor must respond to feelings with feelings. The only possibility may be non-verbal, perhaps holding the client's hand, or embracing the person, and sitting together in silence, allowing the client to weep and show despair, or simply being there and available, and sharing the distress. Gradually it may be possible to encourage the client to put into words what information has been received. He or she may believe they have been told they have AIDS, or that they are going to die, or that they must be hospitalized immediately. The counsellor should not condemn any misunderstandings, but will need to repeat many times the difference between HIV infection and AIDS. Questions such as: 'Try and tell me in your own words what you have understood', 'What did the doctor (or other informant) tell you?', 'What did the doctor say you had to do?' may be ignored by some clients. An alternative is to ask closed questions, where the client can signal assent or disagreement by movements: 'Did they give you the result?', 'Was it positive?'; 'Did you understand it?', 'Is anyone (friend, spouse) waiting for you?'; 'Do you remember what we discussed before the test?' From general questions the counsellor can move into specific ones: 'Can you remember the difference between HIV and the illnesses it can cause?', 'Do you remember that condoms are a good form of protection?' The counsellor will need also to provide a great deal of feedback to the client: 'I see you are very distressed', 'You are obviously worried about yourself'; 'I understand how concerned you are about partners/children'; 'I see how confused you are.' The effect of this feedback is to give a sense of reality to the client.

As speech returns, the understanding of the information needs to be checked, since misunderstandings can provoke extra anxieties and are not a basis for decision-making. Many of the educational issues reviewed before the test will need revisiting. At the same time the feelings will be verbalized, probably in a random, poorly articulated fashion. Guilt, fear, anger, isolation, rejection, and, most importantly, lack of control, are commonly experienced. Suicidal thoughts can be serious and should be addressed if present (Miller 1987b).

The second aim of counselling the antibody-positive client is to help the client regain a sense of control, the key to dealing with the other feelings. The lack of control should be explored: 'What is uncontrollable?'; 'Who is uncontrollable?'; 'There's nothing I can do' is a statement that must be analysed so as to undermine its universality. Can the client continue to work? Go to the cinema, a football match? Take exercise, eat well, avoid stress? The stark truth that HIV infection is for life must be acknowledged, but in its turn it can be a motive for doing other things such as deciding whom to inform of the news, how to protect others, how to avoid illness, and how to lead a satisfactory life amid the uncertainty. Clients who are blood donors should inform the transfusion service, so that appropriate action can be taken to protect others.

351

A further decision to consider is whether to join a support group, such as Body Positive (an offshoot of the Terrence Higgins Trust), where hope is maintained, solutions to practical problems may emerge, new social skills can be practised, friends can be found, and knowledge about HIV infection is updated.

There are other areas where control can be taken. It is known that prolonged anxiety reduces the effectiveness of the immune system (Coates *et al.* 1984), and thus stressful situations should be avoided where possible. This can be enhanced by eating properly, taking regular exercise, proper rest and recreation, treating any infections promptly, and having regular health checks every 3 months. Yet again, it may help clients to put their affairs in order and perhaps write a will, do things that have been put off, such as patching up a family relationship, and generally dealing with what is called unfinished business.

During the few weeks following the imparting of the positive result, the client may want access to further counselling. The counsellor, therefore, will need to agree with the client how this can be done: by appointment, by phone, at what times. This is yet another matter where the client must have the feeling of control, initiating the contacts when necessary. Alternatively, the client may wish to find another counsellor, or another sympathetic person with whom he or she can share feelings. In any case, this person is likely to be outside the immediate circle of friends and family. Time made available in this way can take on a symbolic value, indicating the person's worth and acceptability to others.

Third, the client needs to take stock of the implications. While everyday social life and work may continue, the antibody-positive person has to consider how to protect others, and the implications for life insurance, medical and dental care, family planning, and pregnancy (perhaps even abortion).

Finally, after the review of all the feelings, issues, and implications, the client has to make realistic decisions for the future. The counsellor has to keep two issues to the forefront: first, that the client may need support in implementing the decisions, and, indeed, some homework to practise the implementation (for example, buying condoms, exchanging needles, rehearsing how to tell someone of the antibody status); and second, that the decisions have to be based on the values and beliefs of the client, so that they can be incorporated into an operational system of personal motives. Religious, social, moral, and family considerations may be important in providing the motives to underpin the decisions. How have important decisions (such as leaving home, settling down with a partner, changing jobs) been taken before? On what principles? How have uncertainty, bad news, and events been dealt with in the past? Can the same principles help now?

It is interesting to note from this description that counselling has a contribution to make to encouraging individual growth and personal development in a positive way: it is not just for helping to resolve problems and crises.

Some counsellors working with HIV-infected people have noticed paradoxical behaviour in some clients, with an increase of risk behaviour once the positive status is confirmed. Often this arises out of the unconscious use of denial as a coping mechanism (see Chapter 19 by Stedeford on death and bereavement). It is however usually found to be temporary, and the counsellor needs to be particularly accepting during this time, while encouraging the client to face up to the reality and implications of the infection.

Counselling people with AIDS

Learning that one has AIDS is traumatic. The counsellor will probably need to deal with it as already described for the counselling of a person with HIV. In other words, the initial counselling will concentrate on opening up communication with the client. All the feelings of guilt, anger, and denial may be resurrected. It is vital that they be expressed and acknowledged rather than challenged by the counsellor at the outset.

It will probably be necessary to review the information about HIV and its various effects, relating what is known to this particular client's state of health, and giving some idea of what may be expected. Issues of control, leading a normal life, and work have to be addressed and decisions made.

The psychosocial issues are considerable, and the need for counselling may increase as medical care looms larger and normal life diminishes. Different emotions emerge as new developments appear, and the client may need repeated counselling to adjust.

The first stage is crisis, manifested in shock, fear, and denial. The counsellor's role will be to establish effective communication without challenging the denial.

The second stage is one of adjustment to the news, although denial will probably continue intermittently, associated with anger, anxiety, depression (Burton 1987), and guilt. Thoughts of suicide are less common in people with AIDS than those who are antibody positive, who seem to be in greater uncertainty (Miller 1987b). During this stage, social disruption and withdrawal is common. Clients may abandon their jobs, refuse to see family and friends, hide away, and even leave their present accommodation, as an expression of guilt, shame, and fear. They may ask the health carers and the counsellor to collude with them in telling lies to family and employers. The counsellor's response will need to help them ventilate the feelings that prompt these actions, to own them, and decide how to deal with them. The counsellor can help clients restructure relationships with family, friends, and employers by examining with them their system of values and beliefs, so as to uncover deep personal reasons for realistic action. The counsellor may need to rehearse with the client coping strategies for dealing with the reactions of others. The client may want the counsellor to be present when family and friends come visiting and this can be helpful if the client and others know what is happening.

During this time of social adjustment, the counsellor can encourage the client to participate in a peer group where more support becomes available. This may be particularly necessary if the client is receiving psychiatric and medical treatment, which can arouse feelings of anxiety and isolation. The counsellor, of course, will probably deal with these feelings during counselling sessions, but a peer group can also help. The counsellor may need to have the client's permission to liaise with the health professionals about the progress of the illness, so as to adjust the counselling more closely to the client's needs.

The third stage is one of acceptance. The client takes on a new sense of self within the limitations imposed by the illness. This is a positive achievement, and the counsellor's response is to encourage and reinforce it by reflecting back to the person this new perception of self. Some clients will take on an altruistic outlook at this stage, and may wish to become involved in helping others with HIV-related conditions, in the belief and hope that some good can come out of the situation. They will also begin to return to activities and relationships that existed before, rebuilding bridges and connections. The support of the counsellor can be expressed in helping to review options, within the constraints of the illness, and to make realistic decisions for implementation.

The fourth and last stage is preparation for death. Predominant issues are fear of dependence, pain, being abandoned, isolation, and death itself. The chapter on dying (see Chapter 19) contains a fuller account of these issues than is necessary here. However the counsellor's response will be to encourage the client to complete any unfinished business, to employ a constructive approach to any legal or family matters (Miller 1987c), and to talk about the feelings.

This sequential account of four stages sounds more logical than is the case in reality. The client may regress from one stage to another. The uncertain progress of the disease can engender new fears. There may be apprehension about the disease's future effects. The gradual loss of physical strength and appearance, sexual activity, social life, status, and privacy can increase the feeling of being dependent. The counsellor may need to encourage family, friends, and health-care staff to allow clients to make their own decisions. They must be further encouraged to touch and embrace the clients, for whom physical closeness and contact are as great a need as ever. Without such contact the person's feeling of loss of self-esteem, personal identity, and isolation are increased, leading clients to stigmatize themselves yet further as immoral people, deserving of punishment (Boyd 1987). The client remains a sexual being, with sexual needs, but fear of infecting others or of being infected may undermine sexual identity and worth, leading perhaps to sexual dysfunctions (see Chapter 20 by Cooper).

Other concerns may be brought to the counsellor because of health-related issues and treatment. A morbid fear of everyday infections like influenza may develop, and the client may be bewildered by the claims for experimental drugs or alternative therapies, unsure of what to do. Dementia, anticipated or actual, can be one of the greatest concerns of a client. How can the counsellor respond to these issues? By enabling clients to distinguish the real from the imaginary, by encouraging them to focus on being alive and on what is possible, and by helping them to plan future activities, especially enjoyable ones. A meal out with friends, a visit to the cinema, choosing some new clothes, going to a football match, reading a book – each client will have a different list. By capitalizing on the moment when they wish to help others, clients may see themselves anew as a positive resource, and this can be reflected back to them.

Throughout, the counsellor may find the client's family and friends themselves seeking counselling, as they struggle to accept the person with the illness and with possibly a newly revealed nature as a drug-user, homosexual, or a person with many sexual partners. Some will exhibit considerably more worry, and perhaps depression, than the client: they feel helpless as they see the decline, while the client may be reconciled to the truth. Counselling will address the same issues as hitherto described.

Women

An antibody-positive woman wishing to become pregnant will need special counselling. Pregnancy may precipitate AIDS; the baby may be affected; her male partner will have a view to be considered; she may need to re-establish her perception of self as a woman if she decides to avoid pregnancy altogether. The counsellor must help the woman ventilate her feelings, so that she can take realistic decisions with her own value system. If she does become pregnant, then abortion may have to be considered (see Chapter 8). In all cases, marital and sexual problems may arise (see Chapters 4 and 20).

Issues

Language and attitudes

The language used by the counsellor can profoundly affect the counselling process. By language the counsellor reveals his or her own nature and ability to enter the world of another. The temptation is to talk about 'victims of' and 'sufferers from' HIV infection and AIDS. This has been criticized by the gay community in particular, and by many people dealing with the issues. It is suggested that it is better to talk of people or persons with AIDS/HIV, so as to avoid the possible moral overtones associated with other words.

Further, there is the wider issue of moralizing. Counsellors are less likely than others to tell people to change their attitudes. The exasperation of such a message is heard as moralizing and is angrily resisted. Correct information, honestly given, in a context of unconditional regard, can help the client change behaviour, especially if it is coupled with interaction with others in self-help groups. However, counsellors can, nevertheless, fall into the moralizing trap if they are unaware of their own attitudes; for example, how to impart the information that reduction of the number of sexual partners can lessen the danger of infection. The tone of voice, a slight movement, a look – all these can betray a hidden morality that will be detected by the client, who might reject the message along with the morality. Another example is this statement made by a health professional: 'If you stop homosexual activities you will not catch the virus', which barely conceals the person's distaste for homosexuality. Finally, advice to footballers not to embrace, kiss, or bathe together is about macho behaviour, not about HIV or AIDS.

The last consideration of language is that it must always be in terms the client can understand. As HIV and AIDS counselling has to consider intimate sexual behaviour, there is room for misunderstanding from euphemism or scientific terminology. Frank, explicit language is required.

Counselling, education and advice, and changing behaviour

In considering the need for behaviour change, the issue of non-directive counselling arises and its relationship to education and advice. The educational aspect is perhaps the easiest to accept: it covers the modes of transmission and infection of HIV, the consequences of HIV infection, safer-sex techniques.

In turning to advice, the situation is less clear. It could conceivably cover matters like: dealing with vomit, blood, menstrual flow, whether to work, whether to send a child with HIV to school. But what about: whether to have sex, whether to use safer-sex techniques, whether to tell one's sex partners? There emerges a higher order of consideration: the balance between the social responsibility of both client and counsellor, and the freedom of the individual, and the rights of other parties. Counsellors already have experience of dealing with clients who wish to find a way of fulfilling their own needs while respecting the needs of others, but the presence of a potentially fatal virus brings the dilemma into the counsellor's own conscience, to affect not only his or her relationship with the client but also the commitment to confidentiality. Does counselling of HIV clients therefore involve advice? The counsellor will try to help clients to consider their social responsibilities at a moment when their personal needs are most demanding, and to help clients think through the implications of behavioural change, not simply as an option for personal growth, but as a responsibility (a duty?, a moral obligation?) towards other people, whose safety has to be taken into account.

I would like to propose a different counselling response, to be called prevention counselling,[1] which could legitimately include education and advice. Figure 22.1 illustrates this. The education circle covers information about HIV, modes of transmission, methods of prevention, and techniques of safer sex. The advice circle deals with, for example, how to deal with vomit and blood, whether to send an HIV-positive child to school, whether a reasonably independent person with AIDS should continue to work, and how to use a condom. The psychosocial circle deals with the feelings and motivation of a person with HIV or AIDs, but also with his or her relationships to others who may be potentially and mortally threatened by that person's HIV-positive status. The counselling process is the place where the three overlap. In the process, one way forward is to invite clients to elicit their own reasons for change and to put them into their own words, thus feeling they are in control of their own life. Using existing values and beliefs, the counsellor can help them gradually build up a sense of social responsibility to others. Since change will need to be incorporated into an existing life-style, the counsellor will need to assist the client to construct a programme of implementation, differentiating perhaps between decisions with immediate effect, such as using a condom, and long-term decisions like informing other people, or joining a self-help group.

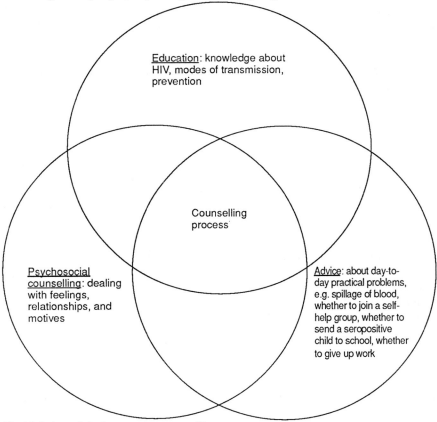

Fig 22.1 A model of prevention counselling

The implementation will take time to incorporate into the client's own belief and value system, which covers such basic questions as: Where do I come from?, Why am I here?, What will become of me? In other words they refer not just to reasons for doing things, but one's very existence, self-worth, and the symbolism between action and being. If, for example, a man thinks (or more likely, feels) that condoms render him less manly, he will find them difficult to use. If a person feels marginalized living in an industrial, uncaring society, sexual intercourse may be one of the few moments when he or she feels fully human: any attempt to interfere with the number of sexual partners or to introduce condoms may be resisted.

The programme of change will therefore need careful consideration of feelings, relationships, and motives, as well as information and advice. The gradual implementation of change can be helped by homework. At first it would include fairly undemanding actions like finding out some information, reading, writing a letter, talking to someone; but it can move on to more difficult things like informing someone of the positive status, buying condoms, learning to use condoms, trying out new (but safer) forms of sexual pleasure. The programme of change and related homework needs working out according to the unique needs, opportunities, and personal strengths of the client. As in other areas of counselling, progress needs evaluating by clients themselves with the help of the counsellor, who can reinforce success with praise and avoid blame for failures or shortcomings. In this way, supportive counselling leaves clients feeling they are in charge.

The unwilling client

A few people with HIV infection or even AIDS show no wish to change behaviour or life-style. People working with them think the explanation is a deep feeling of guilt: the person believes he or she is not worth protecting, and should be punished, perhaps for being homosexual, unfaithful, sinful, or immoral. Open acknowledgement of what is happening is advocated: the person does not care for self, and apparently has no concern for others. Once low self-esteem is admitted it can become the focus of counselling work. The work can look at relationships with parents in particular, and at issues of the locus of control, i.e. does the client generally experience the self as an agent, in control of life from the inside, or as helplessly passive, with control from outside?

The worried well (Miller 1986)

The distinction between a person who has engaged in risk behaviour and one who is well but worried is not always easy to make, especially in people at marginal risk. One way to resolve this is to review the possible sources of infection to see where they impinge on the client's life. The problem will not always be resolved, however, because some people are convinced that they are mortally ill. Some doctors have said that some people who were always asking if they had cancer are now asking if they have HIV and AIDS. Counsellors are used to dealing with irrational feelings by confronting people with realistic evidence (or lack of it – no or little risk behaviour, in the case of HIV) that contradicts the feelings. A small number of the worried well may need psychiatric intervention, and the counsellor may therefore have to refer a client to the medical services (Miller and Green 1985).

Drug-users

Perhaps even more than homosexuals, drug-users may be perceived by carers as 'having brought HIV/AIDS upon themselves'. It is as if they have no right to be ill and no right to sympathy or access to resources. Counsellors therefore will have to be aware of their own attitudes to drug-use, provision of free needles, and the current laws on drugs. Counsellors find that at an intellectual level, drug-users often seem to understand all the associated risks, showing great concern for others; but emotionally conditioned by the need for drugs, they find it almost impossible to embrace a programme of change. They may also be fearful of police interest at places where free clean needles are available. In order to establish motivation for change, three issues seem worthy of exploration: first, the concern for others, especially sexual partners and children in the womb; second, to set sights on changing ways of ingesting drugs rather than on giving up the drug: for example, not injecting, using sterilized equipment, not sharing equipment, and changing to the oral use of drugs where possible; and third, the clients should be asked to draw up their own programme for change within the constraints as perceived by them.

Confidentiality

This is an area of controversy, illustrated by the following discussions:

(1) should general practitioners have the automatic right to be told of the positive status of one of their patients? And if a counsellor attached to the practice is informed by the client of positive status, what are the rights of the GP?
(2) if the counsellor knows that an antibody positive drug-user goes abroad to sell blood, plasma, sperm, or even organs, does the counsellor have an obligation to inform others?
(3) if an antibody positive person continues unprotected sexual activity with an unsuspecting partner, does the counsellor have to maintain confidentiality?
(4) if a newborn child is found to have HIV or AIDS, and the mother insists the father should not be told, what then?

While the guiding principle must always be that the confidentiality of records is paramount, the above cases illustrate some of the issues that are exercising the people working in the field. The situation may become worse if laws are made compelling counsellors and others to reveal such information. It is therefore urgent that counselling organizations deliberate on the issues and provide some clear guidelines, perhaps establishing some distinctions between the various types of case. Thus, for example, it might be possible to inform an agency that an unnamed person has donated blood or sold sperm to it on a given date, whereas a person in no danger (for example, a general practitioner) may have no right to the information.

Secret testing

The British Medical Association (BMA) passed a resolution at its conference in 1987, to the effect that a doctor could test a patient for HIV antibodies without his or her knowing. The executive officers of the BMA subsequently took legal advice and did not implement the resolution as BMA policy. However, the resolution illustrates the issue, and counsellors need to be clear where they stand on it. Perhaps the position to take is that of the Royal College of Nursing, which instructed its members not to co-operate with any doctor proposing to take blood for an antibody test from an unsuspecting patient. This implies that permission to be tested must be given explicitly. Certainly counsellors, who promote the individuality and independence of their clients, should not co-operate in deceiving any client into giving blood for an antibody test without knowing what is happening.

The needs and rights of counsellors

At the beginning of the HIV crisis, there was much talk of 'burn-out' produced by the stress of dealing with infected clients. Some protested that working with dying children, in an abortion clinic, and with people with mental handicap was equally stressful. While this may be so, there are special features of HIV/AIDS counselling that can produce stress. First, it is mainly young people in their prime who are affected. Second, the virus is new, and much is unknown about it; an ignorance bound to produce anxiety. Third, rumours have circulated about the infection risks to people caring for clients with HIV or AIDS, and have aggravated the stress. At the beginning also, and fourth, many counsellors working in the field were dealing for the first time with people whose lives were threatened, or who were actually dying.

The consequences of this situation are that counsellors have an obligation to obtain whatever training they need to deal with HIV clients. The BAC/SHEG training pack provides a good basis for such training, as it covers all the aspects, such as dying, death, bereavement, sexuality, homosexuality, haemophilia, and drugs. The pack lays emphasis on the necessity of counsellors dealing with their own feelings and attitudes towards such emotive matters. Another consequence is the advisability of setting up mutual support groups, where peers can develop each other's professional and personal strengths.

Counsellors have to be clear, as in all other areas of counselling, that they have rights: rights to rest, recreation, a private life, not to be available all the time, not to give their private telephone number, without feeling guilty. A less obvious right is the right to respect from other professionals for one's professional position. The first people with HIV or AIDS were diagnosed in the sexually transmitted disease clinics, where health advisers quickly responded by organizing counselling before and after the blood test. Now other departments, such as gynaecology and obstetrics, are conducting their own tests. In at least one case, a young husband of a mother-to-be was diagnosed positive, and he was referred to the health adviser in the clinic for sexually transmitted diseases who was asked to inform him of the news, and take the matter from there. The health adviser felt used and indignant that the health professional who had initiated the test then failed to carry the consequences of his own action.

Future developments

The issue of confidentiality, and the disputed 'right to know' if someone is infected with HIV, continues to be debated and will no doubt become an area in which the counsellor will come increasingly under criticism. Professional and other counselling organizations might have to produce a more detailed rationale than hitherto, and perhaps now is the time to do it before the pressures increase further (Elliott 1987).

Confidentiality affects the relationship between counsellors and their clients, the willingness of clients to come forward for help if confidentiality is not guaranteed; but the opposition to absolute confidentiality is coming from insurance, employers, and the temptation to blame sexual and ethnic minorities.

Counsellors will inevitably be drawn further into the debate about compulsory testing (Miller et al. 1986), as its multiple facets develop (Gillon 1987). Some governments are already imposing testing on certain groups. Since counselling is advocated before and after testing, what is the ethical stance to be taken by the counsellor?

The distribution of free needles to drug-users is under trial by the British Government. This is surrounded with controversy and the arguments continue about its possible encouragement of drug use. Counsellors have to take stock of their own ethical position on this, as it can affect the counselling process. The same can be said of the provision of free condoms to prostitutes (Parry and Seymour 1987). It has been said that offending people's feelings does not kill anyone, while AIDS is fatal.

There are a number of infants born with HIV and even AIDS. If they survive they will start school in the 1990s. Parents have already expressed strong feelings towards existing school children – for example, boys with haemophilia – who have HIV infection. There is no reason why such children should not attend school: the others are in no significant position of risk, and indeed the infected children may be more at risk from them if they catch colds and influenza, which they may then find hard to overcome. Thus, the matter is already a cause for concern. But with greater numbers the concern will grow, and will affect school and family counsellors, with the consequent problems of confidentiality.

The counsellor of a person with HIV or AIDS may be approached by family or friends of the client, who seek counselling for themselves. Should the same counsellor deal with them? Could a conflict of interest arise? Could confidentiality be breached in either direction? Where can the counsellor find the principles to resolve these questions? The situation is somewhat similar to that found in counselling couples (for example, husband and wife), but there are differences. The HIV-positive person may not hitherto have had a relationship problem with family and friends but the infection may produce one, whereas in a couple with a relationship problem but where neither has HIV there is no danger to physical health. If more than one counsellor is involved, what principles can guide the professional relationship of the counsellors? Clearly clients need to give permission if their separate counsellors are to confer with each other. The issue of whether to have separate counsellors will depend on the people concerned: clients expressly worried about the possibility of factual information being given to a third party may insist on family and friends having a separate counsellor; but on the other hand there are people who are close to their family and friends and do not wish to keep secrets from them. Where the same counsellor deals with the various people concerned, it is essential that he or she is not in a position of go-between, carrying messages from one person to another, and therefore may need, when establishing the counselling contract, to foresee the possibility of referring any of the parties to another counsellor.

What is certain is that, in the absence of cure, counselling will have a new importance. It will help people not only to deal with their feelings, but also to make important decisions about their behaviour and relationships. Counselling thus will assume a social as well as an individual significance.

Note

1. This term was invented by Dr G Lloyd of Tulane University, New Orleans, who, with the present author, is writing The World Health Organization training materials on HIV/AIDS and counselling.

References

Boyd, K. M. (1987) 'The moral challenge of AIDS', *Journal of the Royal Society of Medicine* 80: 281–4.

Burton, S. W. (1987) 'The psychiatry of HIV infection', *British Medical Journal* 295: 228–9.

Coates, T. J., Temoshok, L., and Mandel, J. (1984) 'Psychosocial research is essential to understanding and treating AIDS', *American Psychologist* 39(11): 1309.

Elliott, J. (1987) 'ABC of AIDS: nursing care', *British Medical Journal* 295: 104–6.

Gillon, R. (1987) 'Testing for HIV without permission', *British Medical Journal* 294: 821–3.

Grimshaw, J. (1987) 'Being HIV antibody positive', *British Medical Journal* 295: 256–7.

Miller, D. (1986) 'How to counsel patients about HIV disease – those who have it and those who fear it', *Maternal and Child Health* 11(10): 322–30

——(1987a) 'ABC of AIDS: Counselling', *British Medical Journal* 294: 1671–4.

——(1987b) 'HIV counselling: some practical problems and issues', *Journal of the Royal Society of Medicine* 80: 278–81.

——(1987c) *Living with AIDS and HIV*, London: Macmillan.

——and Green, J. (1985) 'Psychological support and counselling for patients with acquired immune deficiency syndrome (AIDS)', *Genito-urinary Medicine* 61: 273–8.

Miller, D., Jeffries, D. J., Green, J., Willie Harris, J. R., and Pinching, A. J. (1986) 'HTLV-III: should testing ever be routine?', *British Medical Journal* 292: 941–3.
Parry, A. and Seymour, H. (1987) 'AIDS and female prostitution', *Health Education Journal* 46(2): 71–3.
Richards, T. (1986) 'Don't tell me on a Friday', *British Medical Journal* 292: 943.

Chapter twenty-three

Counselling people with alcohol and drug problems

Richard Velleman

This chapter will start by making some general points about the nature of work with people who experience drug- or alcohol- related problems. It will then examine some of the major issues which are current in this growing area of help before outlining some areas in which changes and growth may be predicted.

This chapter is about 'counselling'. Although there certainly are distinctions which can be drawn between counselling and other forms of help, none will be drawn here. Instead, the term 'counselling' will be used in a very broad way, and for the purposes of this chapter such terms as counselling, intervention, help, and so on, will be used interchangeably. Similarly, it is recognized that alcohol is a psychotropic drug, with effects comparable to a range of other drugs.

Principles

Alcohol- and drug-related problems are areas in which stereotypes abound. If members of the general public are asked about people with these problems, common views are of male alcoholics on park benches drinking cider, or of drug addicts injecting heroin in dingy squats in run-down urban areas. Yet, whereas there are individuals who conform to these stereotypes, the reality is that the range of people with drug- and alcohol-related problems is vast. This range and diversity is apparent in every area, be it client group, type of drug used, type of problem generated by the drug use, technique of intervention used, setting in which the intervention takes place, or aims of the counselling.

To take some examples, clients of agencies specializing in drug or alcohol problems vary along many dimensions:

(1) *age* (early teens or even younger to clients of pensionable age and considerably older);
(2) *sex* (with earlier figures of higher representation of men in both alcohol and drug agencies being superceded by far more equal representation);
(3) *who has the problem* (whether the problem is due to their own alcohol or drug use, or to someone else's – a spouse, a child, a parent, some other close relative or friend);

(4) *socio-economic status*;

(5) *type of social grouping* (glue-sniffing children, teenagers and young adults mixing amphetamines and alcohol, cannabis-smoking and LSD-using hippies, heavy drinking middle-aged businesspeople, tranquillizer using or secretly drinking housewives, elderly people on cocktails of a wide variety of prescribed drugs. Clearly these examples utilize further familiar stereotypes which surround this area, although these stereotypes are in fact based largely in reality);

(6) *type of drug used* (alcohol, solvents, prescribed drugs, and a huge range of illicit drugs including cannabis, amphetamines, cocaine, heroin, hallucinogens, and prescribed drugs sold illicitly);

(7) *method of use of the drug* (drinking, smoking, sniffing, injecting, eating);

(8) *problem areas associated with the drug use* (problems with the law, the family, other relationships, with finances, job, physical health, mental health, housing, and of course problems of addiction and dependency as well);

(9) *seriousness of alcohol or drug problem* (from mild to serious, and occasional to constant).

It is suggested that there are up to a million individuals in England and Wales with alcohol-related problems (and that around 25 per cent of British men and 8 per cent of British women, or 17 per cent of the total post-war generation, run the risk of developing an alcohol problem at some stage in their lives) (Alcohol Concern 1987). More than a million individuals have prescribed drug-related problems (Cooper 1987), and up to 100,000 individuals have illicit drug-related problems (ISDD 1984). Furthermore, each of these individuals will have contact and will influence a wide range of others: family members, friends, workmates, members of the public (who for example share the same roads as intoxicated drinkers or drug-users). The number of people who may need information, advice, and counselling related to their own or someone else's alcohol or drug problems is immense. It is also the case that not all of these people will have very serious alcohol or drug problems. Instead they fall on a continuum from early and mild problems at one end to serious and life-threatening at the other.

Yet it is not only the clients who differ to such an extent. Agencies and individual helpers will also differ in terms of their:

(1) *Philosophy and theory of the causation of problems* (alcohol or drugs – the addictive substance – is 'the problem', mentally ill people or people with inadequate or addictive personalities are 'the problem', society and its inequalities is 'the problem', the law is 'the problem', individuals' loss of religious beliefs is 'the problem');

(2) *Definition of counselling* (including peer support, behavioural orientation , psychoanalytical orientation, Rogerian, eclectic);

(3) *Techniques used to intervene* (maintenance doses of a drug to encourage

stable rather than chaotic use, gradual planned reduction of drug or alcohol use, immediate or very speedy reduction of use, withdrawal relief, relapse prevention techniques, specific techniques such as social skills or assertion training and cue exposure methods, concentration on physical-health issues, counselling individually, in groups, using existing networks such as marriages or other relationships, or families);

(4) *Setting in which the intervention takes place* (specialist drug-dependency or alcoholism-treatment unit, detoxification unit, rehabilitation-house, -hostel or -community, in-patient psychiatric or general hospital unit, out-patient clinic, community-based alcohol or drug service, local voluntary information-advice-counselling agency, self-help group); and

(5) *Aimed-for outcome of the intervention* (lifelong abstinence from the alcohol or drug, controlled or 'sensible' use of it, harm minimization, safer methods of ingestion, life-style changes, changes in social and relationship skills, increased life satisfaction).

This range and diversity means that, although there are important principles of practice which are shared by workers in this field, the first and possibly the most important point to make is that there can be no one set of key principles, methods, and techniques which will be the 'correct' one for every individual.

Nevertheless, from the examples above, three principles do emerge. The first is that the theory which a counsellor holds about the nature and cause of the problem will determine the nature of the intervention. If the counsellor believes that their clients are 'alcoholics' or 'addicts' possessing some chemical imbalance where a taste of alcohol or other drug of misuse will automatically lead to uncontrollable abuse, then their solution must be lifelong abstinence; whereas if the counsellor believes for example that the drink/drug problem is a result of faulty learning experiences or inadequate coping strategies then the solution is to re-learn or to develop more appropriate coping mechanisms.

The second principle is that dealing with individuals with alcohol or drug problems will almost invariably involve dealing with two distinct but related areas. One will concern the individual's use of drugs or drink *per se*, and the second will concern other problems which connect in some (not necessarily causal) way with this problematic use. Within the specialist field of counselling concerning alcohol or drug problems it is common to find helping agencies or individuals who argue that one or other of these areas is 'the important one' – that if one deals with the alcohol/drugs, then the other areas will fall into place; or that if one deals with the other problems (for example, housing, poverty, loneliness) the problematic alcohol/drug use will not be necessary and hence cease. In fact, both are important. In almost all cases, individuals who abuse alcohol or drugs do so for reasons which are not solely alcohol- or drug-related, and it is the task of the counsellor to explore these reasons with clients and to enable them to start to do something about them. Yet it must also be recognized that alcohol and other drugs are substances which can produce considerable dependency, and this will usually lead to difficulty in giving up or cutting down, even if the reasons for the abuse are examined and successfully tackled. Hence, it is important that both these areas are examined in counselling, and that arguments are dispensed with concerning which out of the alcohol/drug use or the other problems is 'the problem'.

The third principle is that counselling clients with alcohol or drug problems is no different to any other type of counselling. Any counsellor working in this area needs to have both good general counselling skills and specific knowledge about the area of drugs and alcohol. Clients will often present with a range of problems besides their alcohol or drug abuse, and any counsellor working in this field needs to be able to address these issues. This is no different to any other form of counselling. However, there are particular problems which the client will commonly experience which are connected with the drug/alcohol use *per se*, and concerning which a counsellor will find it useful to have some particular rather than general counselling knowledge. For example, how much alcohol or other drug is dangerous? What are the early signs of physical deterioration in a client who uses alcohol or drugs? How quickly should someone withdraw from tranquillizers? or from heroin? or from alcohol? What is the best method of preventing relapse? How does one get a client to report accurately his or her drug or alcohol use? All these and other questions will regularly confront a counsellor working in these areas; hence it is important that people who counsel clients with such problems are familiar with the information which they will need.

It is not necessary that every counsellor who works with a drug- or alcohol-related problem needs to be a specialist counsellor: indeed the numbers referred to earlier would make that an impossibility. Rather, the idea is that counsellors in the many areas in which they will come into regular contact with these problems should undergo some basic informationally orientated training to enable them to work (and feel *confident* about working) with these problems when they arise. Alcohol and drug problems do arise in a variety of counselling settings: for example, many people attempt to cope with bereavement by drinking or taking drugs, and develop some sort of problem as a result. These people may make their first contact with a bereavement counsellor. Alcohol and drugs are closely connected with marital violence and arguments; marriage-guidance counsellors may be the first to see such clients. Young people are a target for much alcohol advertising and will often be introduced to drugs, and youth counsellors may see many early problem-drinkers or drug-takers. There are more examples, but the point is that many clients want to discuss their drinking or their drug use, and the related problems; but they need counsellors to have the confidence to tackle the issue.

Issues

There are a number of current debates within the area of alcohol/drug counselling. These can be encapsulated within five main themes: aims and processes of counselling, who should do the counselling, where should counselling take place, training and skill development, and drugs and alcohol counselling and the criminal-justice system.

Aims and processes of counselling

There are a number of issues incorporated within this theme. The first relates to what is an ethically permissible aim of counselling, and as with so many ethical issues, the area is strongly bound up with philosophical stances.

Ethical aims

The field of alcohol and drug abuse has been under the influence of a medical model of addiction for a considerable period, and one of the concomitants of this model is the belief that certain people are addicts (or alcoholics) who are chemically different from 'normal' people and who must always and forever abstain from alcohol or any other drug of abuse. This has led to a very limited counselling-approach: on the one hand counselling has focused very largely on alcohol/drug use *per se* as opposed to other problem areas connected with the use; on the other hand, within this focus on alcohol/drug use, this medical model has led to a total concentration on counselling aimed at abstinence.

Over the last 20 years this model has come to be increasingly questioned. A wide variety of different models explaining the taking up and development of problematic use of alcohol or other drugs has arisen (Orford 1985). Instead of viewing the population as either 'addicts' (who have a range of problems) or 'normal people' (who have none), a view has appeared suggesting that alcohol or drug problems occur along a variety of continua: where, for example, individuals could be more or less dependent on their drug, more or less in debt, or more or less violent.

These other views have brought with them a variety of alternative aims in counselling. Hence, a focus on alcohol/drug use is now not the only or even the major preoccupation of specialist agencies: a focus on other problem areas and on life-style changes is equally important. Furthermore, within the area of counselling about drug/alcohol use itself, the focus only on abstinence has come under increasing question. In the alcohol field the idea of 'controlled drinking' has been increasingly propagated. In the drug field the idea of 'controlled drug-use' is not new: there is a long history of intervention services providing users with drugs to help stabilize their use, and this notion has been given further impetus by the AIDS issue. Attention is being increasingly placed upon the means of taking the drug (injection or not) rather than focusing solely on the issue of helping clients to stop taking it. This has led to agencies being increasingly concerned with the supply of a safe means of injecting (the needle-supply or exchange schemes). It has also raised the profile of non-drug-related aims of counselling, with agencies becoming involved in promoting harm reduction – for example, 'safer sex' by supplying condoms and information.

These changes are not occurring without conflict (Sobell and Sobell 1984). Many argue that 'allowing' clients to think that controlled use is a possibility is highly unethical. If the medical model is correct, it is not possible for an addict to control use: it is an incurable and progressive disease from this viewpoint. By mentioning controlled use a professional counsellor gives permission for the client to try it, and increases the likelihood of that client attempting control and hence relapsing.

This issue relates to that of relapse prevention (Marlatt and George 1984). It has long been recognized that problems of dependency and addiction are relapsing conditions: the difficulty is not helping clients to stop using alcohol or drugs, it is to get them to stay stopped. The argument for training in relapse prevention is that if many clients are at risk of relapse, it makes sense to warn them of the risks, to identify possible problem situations, and to get the client to work out ways of coping with relapse if it does occur. This means that any relapse should be as minor and as short-lived as possible. Again, however, this is attacked as 'unethical' on the grounds that telling clients that there is a strong risk of relapse will reduce motivation and give clients 'permission' to relapse.

Abstinence or controlled use is not only about individuals' *beliefs* as to what is ethical – evidence also exists! This evidence implies that there *are* indicators which suggest whether or not controlled use or abstinence is likely to prove more effective (Armor 1980). Hodgson *et al.* (1979), for example, show that severity of dependence is related to success in controlling alcohol use, with more severely dependent problem drinkers being more successful in abstaining and less severely dependent ones being more successful in controlling their drinking. They also show, however, that the most important concern is the clients' wishes on the matter.

Nevertheless, even the most enthusiastic proponents of 'controlled use' as an intervention aim usually accept that there is a large difference between 'controlled use' and 'normal or social use'. Someone with a serious alcohol or drugs problem will almost certainly never be able to become a 'normal', 'social' user again. Some individuals will certainly drink or take other drugs again, but drinking or other drug-taking has become, for them, a risky business, an area in which they have already experienced their behaviour getting out of control. The likelihood is that such individuals will always have to be aware of and wary about their drinking or other drug use in a way that individuals who have never developed this sort of problem do not have to be.

Success in counselling

The second issue relates to what constitutes a successful counselling intervention. First, this clearly relates to the issue previously discussed with respect to legitimate aims of counselling. A second question, however, concerns the relationship between aims and outcome. From the 1960s onwards there have been reports in the literature of individuals who have been engaged in abstinence-orientated programmes being found on follow-up to be currently controlling their drinking or drug-taking (Davies 1962). More recently there have been reports of the reverse as well: clients in controlled-use orientated programmes being found on follow-up to be abstinent (Sobell and Sobell 1984). These are cases in which the aims and the seemingly successful outcomes are different. Furthermore, what is to be concluded about success in cases where a client is still abusing alcohol or drugs, but who is managing better other aspects of his or her life such as health, employment, relationships? Do all these cases where clients change in positive directions (which may be different to or only part of the explicit aim of counselling) count as success? Furthermore, for how long does a client have to remain problem-free (or even problem-reduced) before counselling is counted as a success? This is an issue over which there is little consensus in the field.

The provision of services

A third issue relates to the process of providing, and the nature of, the intervention. There are a number of points here. The first is peculiar to the field of alcohol and drug problems. In other areas of counselling, counsellors expect clients to be currently experiencing the problem for which they are seeking help. Hence an agency which deals with depressed clients will expect clients to be depressed when they attend; an agency dealing with marital and sexual problems will expect clients to attend when they are currently experiencing marital and sexual problems. Yet agencies dealing with alcohol and drug problems often have a very different approach, only offering help if the client is no longer behaving in the way which is defining them as having a problem – i.e. no longer drinking or taking drugs. Hence, many agencies will only admit a client into their hostel, hospital ward, out-patient clinic, or counselling agency if they are currently abstaining, and will define a client's reported inability to do this as a sign of lack of motivation. Thus, for example, one local counselling agency dealing with alcohol problems which is extremely innovative in many ways still has a rule that clients who have had any alcohol at all during the day must not be seen, even if they are not at all intoxicated, and even if they are pursuing a controlled drinking goal! Although this attitude is starting to change, the majority of agencies will still only help if a client is abstinent, at least on the day of counselling. It must also be added that this issue is particularly true for alcohol-problem agencies. Many drug agencies follow a policy of insisting that clients' behaviour must be controlled when they attend, without insisting that their drug use must be controlled or absent.

The second point relates to the nature of the intervention. Over the past 10 years the linked issues of early intervention, minimal rather than maximal intervention, and of information and advice rather than 'treatment' have all become important. This is for two reasons. The first of these relates to the previous discussion of the gradual replacement of the medical model (which divided people into addicts/alcoholics versus normals) by an approach which views the use and associated problems of alcohol/drugs as falling along a continuum. As outlined earlier, using this latter approach, individuals could have a range of problems which might stretch from relatively slight to severe problems and from temporary and transient to chronic and long- term ones. This continuum concept means that services only developed to serve the chronic and massive problems of confirmed 'alcoholics' or 'addicts' were inappropriate for the large number of clients with less severe drug- or alcohol-related problems.

Early interventions using less intensive methods have become more important for a second reason as well: the previously popular intensive treatments have not proved to be very successful, even when dealing with clients at the later, more difficult and more chronic end of the continuum. Since the 1950s there has been a steady increase in the development of specialist in-patient treatment units catering for severe problem drinkers or drug-takers, although this trend has now ceased. Various evaluations of these services have shown that success rates are low (Robinson and Ettorre 1980; Thorley 1981). Much of this low success rate has been attributed to the very severe range of problems with which these specialist units have had to deal. Yet at the same time as intensive interventions were shown not to be highly successful, other studies have shown that a single session of advice and counselling can produce success rates which are at least as high, even assessed on 1- and 2-year follow-ups (Orford and Edwards 1977). Hence, these and other studies have all implied that intensive treatment is not necessarily the most efficacious method of intervention even if a client does have a severe problem; and as already discussed the majority of clients do not have problems of a severity to warrant such intensive interventions.

A third point relates to the importance of engaging clients into counselling or other forms of therapy. Recent work in the alcohol-, drug-, and family-therapy fields (Carpenter and Treacher 1983; Velleman 1984) has underlined the importance of engaging clients into counselling, and has reiterated the obvious point that this first step is the most important: unless clients can commit themselves to attending and staying in counselling, no work can be successfully performed, as the clients will not be there!

Who should do the counselling?

The second theme concerns who is the best person to do the counselling. People who counsel problem drinkers and drug-takers stand along a number of continua: those who have themselves had an alcohol/drug problem or not, those who work with this client group voluntarily or get paid for it, those who have some professional qualification or not, those who are specialist or generic workers. Hence, a counsellor of a problem drinker/drug-taker may be an untrained volunteer working in a peer-support/self-help network who has had a similar problem, or a trained volunteer counsellor working in a local counselling agency, or a professionally qualified clinical psychologist, social worker, or psychiatrist working in his or her professional department or in a specialist alcohol or drugs treatment unit or service.

Which of these individuals is the best person to counsel a client with an alcohol- or drug-related problem? People can be found who will argue that one particular combination out of the range of combinations that can be created from the four continua outlined above is the best, but there exists little evidence to advance any one claim.

Sharing the problem

Whether someone who counsels problem drinkers or drug-takers needs to have had a similar problem in order to be able to help is another issue peculiar to this field. To take the same examples used previously, few authorities would argue that a counsellor need have experienced severe depression in order to be able to counsel depressed clients, or to have experienced marital or sexual dysfunction before being able to counsel about these problems. Yet it is commonplace to find both clients and counsellors arguing that a prerequisite of helping individuals with alcohol or other drug problems is to have had such a problem oneself. Clearly, having had a similar problem can be helpful: the growth of the self-help movement internationally implies that many people find the sharing of experiences with others a helpful phenomenon. Yet no evidence exists to suggest that counsellors who have not themselves experienced alcohol or drug problems cannot as effectively help clients with these problems.

The issue here is one of empathy: the ability of the counsellor to put him- or herself in the place of the client. Having 'been there' may be very helpful, if the counsellor is able to recognize that no two situations are ever exactly the same, and that what worked for the counsellor may not be appropriate for the client. It is the experience of many agencies that counsellors who have experienced similar problems make either the best or the worst counsellors: depending on whether or not they are able to use their experiences in non-dogmatic ways where they can both empathize and yet see the client as an individual with similar but different problems and possible solutions.

Voluntary versus paid work

This issue is heavily bound up with political philosophy. On the one hand, it is argued that services which utilize volunteers (a) exploit peoples' willingness to help, (b) reduce the pressure on statutory agencies to provide paid counselling jobs which in turn both (c) deprive people of paid employment and (d) serve to reduce the professional status of counselling and counsellors. On the other hand, it is also argued that (a) using volunteer members of the general public is a way of mobilizing them, of utilizing members of the community to tackle community problems rather than simply getting outside paid helpers to do this; (b) this does not take away from the creation of paid jobs because these jobs will only be created if there is sufficient interest within the community to argue for their creation, and that using volunteers will speed up this process by augmenting that community interest; (c) there simply are not the resources to provide the number of counsellors needed in this area, so if volunteers do not perform this work no one will; and (d) the issue of *professional* status is dependent on quality of training rather than whether the job is paid or not. Certainly the issue of training and accreditation is an area over which both the national bodies in England and Wales responsible for alcohol and drug problems (Alcohol Concern and SCODA) are concerned.

Professional qualification

The term 'professional' as used here refers mainly to the 'core' mental health professions – psychology, psychiatry, and social work – although it also includes those with helping qualifications granted by any nationally recognized body such as psychiatric nurses and occupational therapists. The issue of professional qualification is very largely linked with the two previously discussed issues. Historically, in the alcohol field, professionally qualified help was almost impossible to obtain, and in the drugs field the only professional help available was for opiate addicts, and this was largely limited to the prescription of maintenance doses of morphine, heroin, or methadone. Counselling of problem drinkers and drug-takers was left almost entirely to the self-help/peer-support network of Alcoholics Anonymous and Narcotics Anonymous, or to various of the 'concept house' therapeutic community establishments based on the Synanon movement. Hence, counselling was largely offered by individuals who had themselves suffered from the problem and this counselling was largely offered voluntarily (except in the case of the private 'concept houses').

Over the years this has changed. Alcohol and drug abuse have become 'speciality' areas in their own right, with National Health Service alcoholism treatment units, drug-dependency clinics, community alcohol or drug teams, and detoxification wards, and so the issue of whether or not non-professionally qualified counsellors are competent to counsel has arisen. In some ways, of course, this is a clear case of professional imperialism, with professionals, once they have decided that the addictions are a definable speciality, attempting to annex and incorporate the area under their own professional umbrellas; yet, as will be discussed under the next theme, there are real issues of training and skill development here as well. There has been little research on the relative merits of volunteers versus professional counsellors in this field, but the weight of evidence in the counselling literature overall suggests that well-trained volunteers produce success rates which are at least equal to and often better than those produced by such professionally qualified mental health specialists as psychologists, psychiatrists, and social workers (Durlak 1979).

Specialist versus generic

'Alcoholism' and 'addiction' are regarded as difficult areas in which to work by many generic professionally qualified workers. Indeed many of these workers hold negative stereotypes about these clients: addicts/alcoholics are liars, unmotivated, untrustworthy, unpredictable. This has led to a pattern of services in which clients with these problems tend to be seen by 'specialist' addiction services: self-help groups, voluntary, or statutory agencies. Yet as specialist services have become more involved in the areas of early intervention, prevention, advice, and information as well as counselling and therapeutic interventions, so the scale of the problems has become clearer. The figures provided at the start of this chapter show that there are millions of individuals who are affected by their own or someone else's alcohol or drug use – the number of people who may need information, advice, and counselling related to this is immense. This has led to a gradual realization that specialist or expert workers in this area will never be able to deal with more than a fraction of the total number of people needing help, leading to the conclusion that generic workers must be made interested and informed so that they too can work with those with alcohol- or drug-related problems.

Where should counselling take place?

In the community or not?

Although the self-help/peer-support network has already been primarily based within the wider community, other provision has until recently been largely based outside this. Statutory provision for problem drinkers has been largely linked to in-patient, psychiatric-hospital bases. The drug rehabilitation centres (mainly private or charitable) were also often based outside the wider community because they were often sited in relatively isolated rural settings. This has meant that those requiring greater help than the peer-support network could provide needed to leave their communities in order to be helped. These individuals then usually had to return to these same communities after 'treatment' with little ongoing support. Over the last 10 years this has gradually been changing, with the increasing development of both statutory and voluntary agencies committed to providing a service within the community where people with the problems live. Thus, for example, the statutory Community Alcohol or Drug Teams and grant-supported voluntary agencies such as Local Alcohol or Drugs Advisory Services which have grown up, all provide counselling from a community base and sometimes offer community groups, domiciliary visits, and family and marital counselling.

A linked issue is whether there are any interventions for alcohol and other drug problems which require hospital as opposed to community provision. One of the areas which had been presumed usually to require hospital care was that of detoxification, but even this is increasingly being viewed as a primarily community-based need, with hospital back up being required only in an emergency (Stockwell *et al.* 1986). Nevertheless, it is still the case that even well-developed community services require some form of structured residential unit to provide a safety net for some very damaged clients (those with organic brain damage, for example).

Linked or separate services?

Another issue concerning where counselling should take place is whether alcohol and drug services should be integrated or separate. In many cases this is confounded by political power and financial concerns: if there are two agencies currently funded in any area, one offering services for drug abusers, the other for alcohol abusers, will a combined service retain the same level of resources? Who will direct the combined agency? The trend across Britain currently is for previously separate services to link up, at least informally, and many are attempting to integrate in all ways. This is often aided by existing agencies who cater for one client group expanding to cater for a second if services for this second group do not already exist. It is the case, however, that particular problems often arise when alcohol-problem agencies attempt to fit drug-users into existing routines which are inappropriate for them, such as the use of strict appointment systems.

A related issue is whether services for clients with illicit drug problems and those with prescribed drug problems should be offered from the same agency. With both this and the previous issue the concern is often that clients coming for one problem may be put off by meeting clients coming for another. In practice agencies which cater for more than one client group do not report this. Indeed the discussion in the first part of this chapter on the range of clients within any of these groups mediates against limiting access on the grounds of which drug is taken.

Counselling in the workplace

A final issue relates to the identification of and intervention with alcohol and drug abuse at work. The view is increasingly being taken that good industrial-relations practice requires employers to offer at least some assistance to employees with drink and drugs problems. The provision of counselling in the workplace is a growing area of interest (Industrial Relations Guidance Note 1986) – see Chapter 11 by Megranahan.

Training and skill development

Specialist workers

This author does not subscribe to the view discussed above that all such workers should be trained professionals – which is fortunate, because few professional-qualification training courses currently pay more than a cursory glance at the area of alcohol and drug abuse. Most training courses allocate at best an afternoon to the topic and at worst an hour's talk from a visiting 'expert', which is potentially interesting but unintegrated into the course and hence soon forgotten. This is an area in which gradual change can be perceived. The south-west office of the Central Council on Education and Training in Social Work (CCETSW) has hosted workshops on training about alcohol and other drugs in basic social-work training, and the Royal College of Physicians (1987) has argued in its recent report that 'The first group who need education on alcohol problems are medical students and young doctors' (p. 107). Psychologists are also arguing for greater emphasis in basic training (Robertson *et al.* 1984). Furthermore, in terms of more advanced training, it is now possible to attend a year's course in Alcohol Studies at Paisley College in Scotland, and the University of Kent and the Leeds Addiction Unit both have centres which regularly put on day-release or longer courses on working with clients with alcohol or drug problems. The Institute for the Study of Drug Dependence (ISDD), a library and information service, is a national research and resource centre about drugs. Nevertheless, it is still the case that most professionally qualified staff are ill-trained in this area, and that often the best trained workers with individuals with alcohol and drug problems are trained voluntary counsellors (Marshall and Velleman 1985). It is to be hoped that the drugs field will soon develop an accreditation system for their counsellors alongside or incorporating that used in the alcohol field.

Generic workers

With the discovery that the number of people with alcohol- or other drug-related problems is large has come a growing realization of the need to inform, educate, train, and support a growing number of counsellors who may not be 'specialist' alcohol or drug workers, but who, in the nature of their jobs, will make contact with many people with these problems. This move towards training and skill development has been aided in both the alcohol and the drugs area. In the alcohol field the aid came in the guise of the publication in 1976 of *Responding to Drinking Problems* (Shaw *et al.* 1976). These authors argued that the only way that services could be organized to match the needs within the population would be for the bulk of the client work to be performed by primary-care workers within the community such as voluntary agencies, general practitioners, social workers, and probation workers. As a result of their own research, however, these authors also argued that most of these workers lacked the confidence to counsel these clients, who they perceived as being difficult and unrewarding to work with. The answer, suggested Shaw *et al.*, was for specialist workers to devote most of their time not to counselling clients with these problems, but to training and supporting primary-care workers who, if they had sufficient support, would deal with all but the most difficult cases themselves. This recommendation, coupled with the growth of interest in training following the development of the network of accredited volunteer counsellors specializing in working with alcohol problems, resulted in a growth in training for generic as opposed to specialist workers.

In the drugs field the creation of the Regional Drugs Training Units has greatly helped training and skills development. The brief of these units is to promote the transmission of knowledge and skills relating to drug use to a wide professional and general audience. Furthermore, many of the growing number of Drugs Advisory Services see training of generic workers as a major part of their brief.

Training, developing the skills, and supporting generic workers is an important area which needs to be continued and extended.

Alcohol and drugs counselling and the criminal-justice system

Drug and alcohol consumption often brings people into conflict with the law. Such conflict is a major life event which can lead to a number of effects. It can lead individuals to seek help with their previously unacknowledged problems. It can lead the criminal-justice system to identify individuals as being in need of help, and so compel them to accept 'treatment'. It can lead people to be punished for their law-breaking, which can reinforce those individuals' negative self-images and so exacerbate the problem. And because of the stigmatizing aspect of criminal proceedings, it can lead to the loss of whatever gains may have been accrued through counselling, such as finding a job, improving family relationships, and finding a place to live.

This inescapable impact of the criminal-justice system on the counselling of at least some clients with alcohol and drug problems also leads to a variety of issues arising for counsellors and agencies. Thus, for example, in order to increase the accessibility of the service, do agencies involve themselves with the criminal-justice system? Alternatively, do they have little contact with clients from this source, because the issue of client 'motivation' has become obscured, due to either their compulsory treatment, or their belief that entering counselling will lead to a reduced or deferred sentence?

No counsellor working with alcohol or drug problems can consider him or herself uninfluenced by these issues. Unless the counsellor operates a very selective referral system, some clients will inevitably present themselves in conflict with the law, and this will have effects on both client and counsellor.

Future developments

There are many areas in which major changes can be predicted over the next few years; this chapter will confine itself to discussing briefly five such changes.

Integration of alcohol and drugs services

As outlined above, in many areas services for alcohol and drug problems have developed separately and often remain separate for political rather than efficiency reasons. The majority of non-aligned commentators see little reason for the continued separation of services which cater for such similar problems, and it is the prediction of this author that the gradual integration of alcohol and drugs services will continue over the next few years. If this happens it is to be hoped that the two fields will learn from the mistakes that each has made during their independent phases. It is, for example, ironic that just at a time when those in the alcohol-problems field have decided that specialist regional in-patient alcoholism treatment units are not a useful expenditure of limited resources, a policy of developing specialist regional drug-dependency units should be being pursued. It is similarly ironic that the drugs field should be moving *away* from prescribing maintenance doses to attempt to keep dependent users at a stable level, at the same time as the notion of controlled alcohol-use as a viable alternative goal of counselling is being increasingly accepted. An interesting difference between the two fields is that the clients for whom controlled drinking is recommended are the most stable ones: younger, married, with a stable job and having a shorter excessive-drinking history; whereas the clients with whom maintenance opiates are recommended are the opposite – the most chaotic users with the longest histories. The issues underlying this contrast deserve more discussion.

An issue related to this discussion is whether or not there will even be a need for specialist services in the future. The moves to train generic workers to enable them to recognize and deal with alcohol- and drug-related problems themselves, rather than refer them on to specialist workers, have been outlined above. Nevertheless, it is the view of this author that the scale of these problems in current society is so large that there will, for the foreseeable future, be a need for specialist workers. These specialists will, however, be performing a range of tasks as well as providing counselling: for example, training generic counsellors about alcohol and drugs to enable them better to retain their own clients, supporting these generic workers in dealing with the majority of cases without referral onwards, and generating innovations to counselling practice with these clients.

Controversial issues

What was controversial 10 years ago is no longer controversial: it does not take the skills of Nostradamus to predict that the current controversies – harm reduction, needle exchange, advising about safe sex, integrating alcohol, illicit and prescribed-drug services, and even the idea of controlled drinking and drug-taking in some quarters – will become less controversial. The most likely contenders for future controversial issues are: whether there will be any need for specialist services in future years, or whether all counselling will be done by generic counsellors with some extra training on alcohol and drug issues; the extent of the overlap between drugs-counselling and AIDS-counselling agencies; and the issue of privatization, both the growth of the private sector, and the possibility of central and local authorities reducing their support for local statutory and voluntary-funded services and instead buying in counselling services from the private sector.

Community-based services

Again, this is a prediction based on a prevailing national trend which far transcends the alcohol and drugs field; but it is to be expected that the current move will continue – away from large hospital-services into small community ones dealing with problems in the community in which the problems present. This move raises a number of further issues. Community-based services require accessible accommodation, usually discreetly placed yet near a city centre, and such property is hard to acquire for services catering for unpopular client groups such as those with drug and alcohol problems. Staff who have worked in hospital will often find a move to community-based work difficult, since moving from hospital treatment to community counselling requires a different training background – social work rather than nursing, for example.

At the same time as this move is apparent, it is also evident that there is a growth in private-sector provision for these client groups, and these private treatment centres are often located away from centres of population. This implies that there is still a market for such individual-centred services which attempt to 'treat the addict' rather than seeing him or her in a social and environmental context.

The family

Probably the most serious charge which can be held against the alcohol- and drugs-problems field is that disproportionate attention has been paid to the alcohol or drug-users and insufficient attention to their families. Considerable evidence exists to show that family members are often severely affected by the alcohol or other drug misuse (Orford and Harwin 1982; Dorn et al. 1987), yet it is still relatively rare for agencies to view family members as clients in their own right, or to train counsellors in family-counselling techniques as often as they train in individual counselling.

Prevention

The final area in which services will develop over the next few years will be prevention. There is a growing realization in the field that counselling on its own, without it being linked to a serious community-prevention programme (in turn linked to a realistic set of national prevention policies), can never be more than a short-term stop-gap operation which is doomed just to picking up the pieces of a continually growing problem. The current government policies of lengthening licensing hours without any serious attempt to reduce the growth in alcohol-related harm that such a move is sure to cause (Keep Alcohol Safeguards 1987) and of acting half-heartedly on international drugs-issues (Malyon 1986) do not bode well for a government-inspired prevention campaign. There is, however, evidence that in the alcohol field at least some headway is being made, with local prevention campaigns such as 'Drink Wisely North West' and the South West 'Understanding Alcohol' programme. Tether and Robinson (1986) have argued strongly that local prevention-initiatives are considerably more powerful than national ones.

While the field will change if these future developments come to fruition, will they be sufficient to turn the tide of the present degree of abuse in society, with all that this implies concerning the quality of life of abusers and those close to them such as family, friends, and colleagues? It is the impression of this author that they will not. Reducing the impact of alcohol and drugs requires a sustained campaign on two fronts: a clear commitment from central government to use its powers (taxation, licencing outlets, policing) to reduce alcohol and drug consumption, or at least keep it stable; and a national campaign to alter public attitudes to the use of mind-altering drugs such as alcohol, tranquillizers, and illicit drugs. Both these elements have occurred concerning smoking over the last decade, and their effects are being seen in a reduction in cigarette use. Neither of these elements are apparent concerning alcohol consumption; and although both are overtly present concerning illicit drugs, on neither front is the action taken at all effective. Until these elements are present, it is likely that alcohol- and drug-related problems will continue to grow.

Acknowledgements

The author thanks the editors and Gerald Conyngham, Gill Hayes, Helen Kendall, and Ian Sherwood for their useful comments on an earlier version of this chapter.

References

Alcohol Concern (1987) *The Drinking Revolution*, London: Alcohol Concern.

Armor, D. (1980) 'The Rand Reports and the analysis of relapse', in G. Edwards and M. Grant, (eds) *Alcoholism Treatment in Transition*. London: Croom Helm.

Carpenter, J. and Treacher, A. (1983) 'On the neglected but related arts of convening and engaging families and their wider systems', *Journal of Family Therapy* 5: 337–58.

Cooper, J. (1987) 'Benzodiazepine prescribing: the aftermath', *Druglink* 2(5): 8–10.

Davies, D. L. (1962) 'Normal drinking in recovered alcohol addicts', *Quarterly Journal of Studies on Alcohol* 23: 94–104.

Dorn N., Ribbens, J., and South, N. (1987) *Coping with a Nightmare: Family Feelings about Long-Term Drug Use*, London: ISDD.

Durlak, J. (1979) 'Comparative effectiveness of para-professional and professional helpers', *Psychological Bulletin* 86: 80–92.

Hodgson, R., Rankin, H., and Stockwell, T. (1979) 'Alcohol dependence and the priming effect', *Behaviour Research and Therapy* 17: 379–87.

Industrial Relations Guidance Note (1986) 'Alcohol and Drugs', *Industrial Relations Legal Information Bulletin* 315: 2–8, 21 October.

ISDD (1984) *Surveys and Statistics on Drugtaking in Britain*, London: ISDD.

Keep Alcohol Safeguards (1987) *Licencing Laws: An Essential Social Safeguard*, London: Keep Alcohol Safeguards.

Malyon, T. (1986) 'Full tilt towards a no-win 'Vietnam' war on drugs', *New Statesman*, 17 October: 7–10.

Marlatt, A. and George, W. (1984) 'Relapse prevention: introduction and overview of the model', *British Journal of Addiction* 79: 261–73.

Marshall, S. and Velleman, R. (1985) *Training Volunteers to Counsel Problem Drinkers and their Families: a Handbook*, Hull: University of Hull Addiction Research Unit.

Orford, J. (1985) *Excessive Appetites*, Chichester: Wiley.

——and Edwards, G. (1977) *Alcoholism: A Comparison of Treatment and Advice, with a Study of the Influence of Marriage*, Oxford: Oxford University Press.

——and Harwin, J. (eds) (1982) *Alcohol and the Family*, London: Croom Helm.

Robertson, I., Hodgson, R., Orford, J., and McKechnie, R. (1984) *Psychology and Problem Drinking*, Leicester: British Psychology Society.

Robinson, D. and Ettorre, B. (1980) 'Special units for common problems: Alcoholism Treatment Units in England and Wales', in G. Edwards and M. Grant (eds) *Alcoholism Treatment in Transition*, London: Croom Helm.

Royal College of Physicians (1987) *A Great and Growing Evil*, London: Tavistock.

Shaw, S., Cartwright, A., Spratley, T., and Harwin, J. (1976) *Responding to Drinking Problems*, London: Croom Helm.

Sobell, M. and Sobell, L. (1984) 'The aftermath of heresy: a response to Pendery *et al*'s (1982) critique of 'Individualised Behaviour Therapy for Alcoholics'', *Behaviour Research and Therapy* 22: 413–40.

Stockwell, T., Bolt, E., and Hooper, J. (1986) 'Detoxification from alcohol at home managed by general practitioners', *British Medical Journal* 292: 733–5.

Tether, P. and Robinson, D. (1986) *Preventing Alcohol Problems: A Guide to Local Action*, London: Tavistock.

Thorley, A. (1981) 'Longitudinal studies of drug dependence', in G. Edwards, and C. Busch (eds) *Drug Problems in Britain: A Review of Ten Years*, London: Academic Press.

Velleman, R. (1984) 'The engagement of new residents: a missing dimension in the evaluation of hostels for problem drinkers', *Journal of Studies on Alcohol* 45: 251–9.

Part five

Issues

Chapter twenty-four

Research and evaluation in counselling

Tony Bolger

Introduction

There are many difficulties in writing on research into counselling. One is the difficulty of defining 'counselling'. The term may cover a whole range of helping methods, from psychotherapy through behaviour modification, to befriending or advice-giving, and counsellors may use any or all of these methods. There is, too, a whole range of helpers involved in counselling, with workers from many different professions and volunteers in different settings. The range of clients is even greater, encompassing the whole range of humanity and its problems. Research into these helpers, their training, their agencies, their clients, and the effectiveness of their counselling is reported in a wide variety of sources: unpublished papers, theses and dissertations, counselling journals, psychological journals, medical journals, social-work journals, and other publications here and abroad. Making a choice, therefore, from among the research in this wide field is difficult and necessarily arbitrary. For the purpose of this chapter, British publications only will be considered under such headings as counselling, guidance, and psychotherapy.

When research into counselling began to be reported in British Journals in the early 1970s it reflected its origins in academic psychology. Most training courses were aimed at teachers and were situated in university departments of education. Many if not most of the trainers were educational psychologists and the research they promoted reflected their own training and the settings in which they worked. Thus, of ninety-three research papers published in the first 10 years of the British Journal of Guidance and Counselling (BJGC) (45 per cent of all published papers), twenty were concerned with testing and measurement, twenty-eight with school counselling, and thirty-five with aspects of vocational guidance (these are not discrete categories).

The journal remains the chief source of research into counselling reported in Britain and provides one index of the type of research which is currently being conducted. Editorial policy, of course, will determine the amount and kind of reported research in any particular journal, so in order to obtain an accurate picture it is necessary to consider a range of sources. These are many and varied and include the following journals: *Educational Research*, the *British Journal of Educational Psychology*, the *British Journal of Clinical Psychology*, the *British Journal of Psychiatry*, the *British Journal of Social Work*, *Counselling Psychology Quarterly*, *The Counsellor*, *New Era*, *Trends in Education*, the *Journal of the Royal College of General Practitioners*, the *Proceedings of the Royal College of Medicine*, *Vocational Education*, and *Counselling*.

In addition to academic journals, research is reported in books, reports, dissertations, and theses. Articles about counselling and counselling training, descriptions of client groups, case studies, and professional matters are much more common than research reports and many more people are prepared to write and read such articles.

Perhaps the earliest funded project in counselling in Britain was undertaken in the University of Keele in 1969 to investigate the work of some of the newly trained counsellors in secondary schools. It was funded by the Social Science Research Council (SSRC) and the report (Thompson 1971) was summarized in a brief article (Thompson and Bolger 1973). It was an ambitious project which attempted a comprehensive survey of the work of twenty-five school counsellors, assessing their effectiveness and examining their attitudes and those of their head teachers to their work. The report concluded that the school counsellors were generally perceived to be providing a necessary and effective service.

Subsequent research has followed much the same pattern, describing a particular service or agency, perhaps by means of a case study, or carrying out a survey of a particular field. Sometimes the views and reactions of clients have been sought, sometimes the attitudes of the public or different professional groups. Much research has investigated the characteristics of client groups, particularly those captive groups, students and pupils. The process of counselling has been given attention, too, as it applies to particular problems or particular techniques and there has been some evaluation of tests and other means of client assessment. Since much of the early research was carried out within training courses, either by the trainers themselves or their trainees, there has been an emphasis on the evaluation of counselling training. The evaluation of counselling itself has been attempted as a part of many of these studies. There will be an attempt to review published research on the areas just mentioned, beginning with a discussion of studies of counselling effectiveness, since such research will provide guidance into the important topic of counselling evaluation.

The evaluation of counselling

Much counselling research has originated from the natural desire of counsellors to answer the question, 'How effective is my counselling?' This would seem to be a very simple question to answer but since Eysenck's (1952) article, 'The effects of psychotherapy: an evaluation', it has been a very controversial one. Eysenck summed up contemporary research into psychotherapy as demonstrating it to be no more effective than no treatment at all. This discouraging assessment stimulated counselling research into a chain reaction of outcome studies in an attempt to disprove Eysenck's assertion. Subsequent reviews by Eysenck and his associates (Rachman 1971) culminated in the most recent study by Rachman and Wilson (1980), which goes beyond the assessment of traditional psychoanalytical psychotherapy into more familiar territory, such as client-centred and cognitive therapy, but with hardly any more encouraging results.

Conventional outcome research is very hazardous. As Maguire (1973) has pointed out, measures of effectiveness are unreliable, research design is over-simplified, and data are over-interpreted. A much more serious criticism, however, is that research is based upon a medical model of problem behaviour which assumes that such behaviour follows a course similar to that of disease, in other words it gets worse before it gets better. Maguire makes the point, however, that very little is known about the 'natural history' of behavioural disturbance and, even if the disease analogy is a useful one, we do not know how it applies to individuals, nor do we know where any one client is likely to be at any particular time in the progress of his or her disturbance. On the other hand there is no reason to suppose that emotional disturbance or behaviour problems do develop in the same way as illness. Until we have more understanding of the nature of behavioural disturbance, however, research into effectiveness is likely to remain haphazard if not hazardous and likely to produce inconclusive results in an over-simplified or over-generalized form.

In spite of these difficulties research into the outcome of counselling has continued and has produced some of the most interesting reported research. Rose and Marshall (1974) investigated counselling and school social work in a number of north-western schools and came to the cautious assessment that certain types of pupil behaviour, notably truancy and delinquency, responded favourably to counselling. Another investigation of counselling and school attendance (Connor 1979) found counselling to be effective with truants, while Lawrence (1971, 1972), in a series of studies to estimate the effect of counselling on reading retardation, demonstrated that counselling was more effective in improving the reading of slow readers than remedial reading, counselling plus remedial reading, or no treatment. The counselling approach he used was a simple version of client-centred therapy and he showed that non-professional helpers could be trained quickly to be as effective as professional helpers in improving reading through counselling. However, further studies into the effectiveness of counselling with slow learners, including a replication of Lawrence's research (Coles 1975), gave less clear-cut results. Maguire (1971), evaluating the work of several school counsellors with school children identified as 'reactively disturbed in certain specific areas', found short-term counselling to have some positive effects. Other studies which have included an evaluation of the counselling are those of Ashurst and Ward (1983) of counselling in general practice, Charlton (1980) with junior-school children, McCafferty (1977) with secondary-school boys, and Adams (1978) with undergraduates. For a review of outcome research in student counselling, see Breakwell (1987).

387

The constraints of research have caused all these studies to be of relatively short span in extent and no British study has emulated the long-term follow-up of D. P. Campbell (1965) in Minnesota, who looked at the effects of counselling after a time-gap of 25 years. Some studies of effectiveness have been carried out within the context of case studies of single services or surveys of particular fields of counselling and these sometimes use data gathered over a considerable period. There have been many examples of such surveys (for example Ness 1976; Anderson and Hasler 1979; Corney 1986) which contain some element of evaluation. The most comprehensive of these studies is the one carried out by Oldfield (1983) in the Isis Centre in Oxford. Her evaluation of the service included a follow-up for clients who were asked to give an estimate of the effectiveness of the counselling they had received.

Asking clients for their views on the effectiveness of the treatment they have received is one method which has been used to evaluate counselling. It represents the use of 'soft evidence', a term which would include all indirect measures of effectiveness such as the opinion of the client, the counsellor, or other involved person sought directly or indirectly, changes in attitudes, values, expressed interests, and so on. This may be contrasted with 'hard' evidence, which would include such data as physiological measures like galvanic skin response or blood pressure, examination or test results, attendance rates, success in finding or holding employment, medical reports, and other factual or quantifiable evidence. 'Hard' evidence is more measurable, objective, and reliable, but it may not be as valid as other, 'softer ' evidence. Thus, for example, school counselling may be evaluated by such 'hard' evidence as improvement in attendance or reduction in court appearances, but the results may not represent as useful evaluation of the counselling as the judgement of counsellors and teachers who are able to take into account the needs of particular clients and the wider aims of counselling: for example, is this particular client, whose attendance remains poor, showing more self-confidence, improved study skills, or better family relationships?

Part of the dilemma lies in the tendency of counsellors to state their goals in wide, even perhaps grandiose, terms like, for example, the achievement by the client of self-actualization or improvement in self-adjustment and, often, have been unwilling to settle for shorter-term, more limited, less ambitious goals. An exception to this has been those practising behavioural counselling, who, on principle, have worked towards the achievement of short-term, measurable goals. It is not surprising that the evidence for the effectiveness of behavioural counselling is much more impressive than for other forms of intervention (for example, see Paul 1966). An analogy may be made with education. Traditional, formal education may be evaluated by such criteria as test performance or examination results, but progressive informal education aims at wider, less quantifiable outcomes like improved adjustment, increased sensitivity, more critical awareness, and progressive teachers tend to reflect tests and examinations as inadequate or even inaccurate indicators of these qualities. While it may be true that tests necessarily over-simplify – for example, a single figure, the IQ, representing the whole complex set of skills and attitudes we call intelligence – they may provide counsellors with a means of evaluating their work which occupies a middle ground between the objectivity of hard evidence and the subjectivity of soft evidence. With the development of testing into areas such as personality, social adjustment, attitudes, and values, it is possible to move closer to the more existential aims of counselling. Some tests have been designed specifically for counsellors, the Minnesota Counseling Inventory, the Rogers Personal Adjustment Inventory, the Wrenn Study Habits Inventory, the Lewis Counselling Inventory, the Mooney Problem Check List, to name some of the better known. In addition, other testing devices such as projective tests, sentence-completion tests, sorting kits, and such like have been used to facilitate the counselling process and to evaluate its outcomes. Maguire (1971) used the MCI for these purposes while Lawrence (1971, 1972) used a reading test and the Porter and Cattell Children's Personality Questionnaire (CPQ). Much research has concerned itself with the evaluation of the measuring instruments themselves (Bolger 1973, P. P. Daws 1975, Evison and Ronaldson 1975, Bayne 1977, Nelson-Jones 1977, Janowitz and Cooper 1982, Ward 1982, Orlans and Georgiades 1983) and this is important where it produces more accurate instruments for evaluation.

It is important that counselling should be evaluated, case by case, by individual counsellors in addition to the large-scale evaluation of numbers of clients grouped according to different kinds of treatment, different kinds of problems, or different kinds of clients. All counsellors, as they evaluate the success of their own work with their own clients, should accumulate their results to give some evidence of the outcomes of counselling. Single-case research, when carried out systematically and accurately, is now an acceptable form of research (Barlow and Hersen 1984), and counsellors need not be deterred by the smallness of the scale upon which they operate. It is important, however, that certain principles of good research should be kept in mind when attempting outcome studies.

(1) *Identification of relevant variables.* These include other sources of help available to clients such as doctors, friends, the Samaritans, self-help groups, relations; environmental constraints like poor housing, lack of transport and further adverse circumstances suffered by the client. Thus, for example, in recording the outcome of counselling a pupil with reading difficulties, it would be important to report on other sources of help which are available, such as the efforts of the remedial teacher with his or her pupil, such factors as disturbed family background or the fact that the client suffered an infectious illness during the period of counselling.

(2) *Establishing the criteria of 'problem' and 'outcome'.* It is important to be clear and specific about the nature of the problem to be worked on and the expected outcome. As far as possible there should be agreement between the client and counsellor about the aims of the counselling and these should

389

be stated in terms which lend themselves to evaluation.

(3) *Accurate recording and measurement.* Different counsellors and different agencies require different forms of recording. Increasingly, summary records will be computerized and this will facilitate accumulation and cross-referencing, particularly when such matters as source of referral, presenting difficulties, personal details of clients, counselling approach used, and length of treatment are recorded. Then it is possible to calculate correlations, trends, and consistencies, and evaluate counselling ˙ accordingly. Much of the measurement used in the evaluation of counselling may be carried out by the clients themselves and the record-keeping will be an integral part of the treatment. A couple with marital problems, for example, might be set the task of recording all the helpful acts performed in the household by each of the partners. The resulting records would constitute part of the evaluation as well as much of the treatment.

(4) *Establishment of accurate controls.* For ethical and administrative reasons, it is rarely possible in counselling research to compare a treatment group with a non-treatment group as in Lawrence's (1971) research, but the setting up of clear baselines against which progress can be compared may be a partial substitute. Thus, for example, a client with study problems could provide baselines such as current academic performance, or hours of effective study, against which progress could be measured.

The suggestion here is that the methods used in the evaluation of counselling may be, at the same time, powerful ways of both helping the client and of carrying out research. If a problem-management approach to counselling is employed, as suggested by Egan (1986), then the establishment of goals and the on-going evaluation of progress will be part of the process of counselling. The matter is made clear by Sutton (1987) describing a 'goal-attainment' approach to the evaluation of counselling used in Leicester Polytechnic by herself and Professor Martin Herbert. Following a client-centred stage of relationship-building and preliminary assessment, the counsellor negotiates and agrees goals with the client. These goals are established as contracts which are then used to measure the progress of the counselling as it proceeds. Sutton suggests that this evaluation would be carried out by the clients themselves using a scale extending from +5 to -5 during each session and at a follow-up session called 2 or 3 months after the termination of counselling. These evaluations could be used either to 'shape the counselling or to evaluate its effectiveness' (Sutton 1987).

Research into therapeutic conditions and counselling training

Following the Eysenck critique mentioned earlier, research into counselling effectiveness became more sophisticated. In the USA in particular there developed a concentration upon examining the nature of the counselling process and discriminating the criteria of effective counselling (for example, Truax and Carkhuff 1967). The proliferation of such research in America was reflected in some British research (Natale 1973; Nelson-Jones and Patterson 1975; McCafferty 1977; Davies 1981; Dickson 1981). Carkhuff and his associates began by demonstrating that counselling could be for better or worse and that the main variable in its effectiveness was the counsellor him- or herself.

Effective counsellors could be differentiated from non-effective counsellors not only by the outcome of their counselling but also by the extent to which they demonstrated some 'core conditions'. Most of these conditions had already been described by Carl Rogers (1951) but what Carkhuff and his associates showed was that the conditions could be discriminated and measured. They devised scales for measuring these conditions as demonstrated by counsellors during their counselling and this encouraged further research into the nature of the conditions themselves, the relative degree to which they were possessed by particular counsellors, and the extent to which they could be learned or modified by training. This led to some varied projects. Natale (1972), for example, investigated the nature of empathy and demonstrated that it was associated with the quality of critical thinking. Law (1977a,b; 1978a,b) looked at basic attitudes underlying teacher-counsellors and discovered that they could be divided into two orientations (system orientation and client orientation) which were themselves related both to the personal characteristics of the counsellor and the nature of the training they had undertaken. Research in this area led to a movement towards 'a systematic eclectic stance' which incorporated the client-centred approach with both an older, more confrontative approach and newer behavioural aspects. More directly it produced developments in training, particularly in skill training and micro-counselling[1] which lent themselves directly to research (Nelson-Jones and Patterson 1974; Nelson-Jones 1977; Davies 1981; Dickson 1981; A. M. Daws 1982; Hargie 1984). Training has been the subject of a wide range of research studies, including descriptive surveys of a whole range of counselling training (Hughes 1974, 1977; Henstock 1977; Sutton 1987), evaluation of specific courses (Crowley 1981, Dickson 1981) or particular types of courses (Law 1977b), follow-up studies of students who had been on courses (Antonouris 1974, Connor 1987), and evaluation of particular methods and approaches (Wright 1980; Davies 1981; Connor 1987). Some of this research has given direct feedback to trainers, helping them to develop new techniques and extend their training repertoire, but much of it has languished in unpublished theses, unread by the majority of trainers. It would be of great advantage to those concerned with training to read the action research described in such theses as that of Davies (1981), in which the use of television in training was carefully monitored and evaluated; Dickson (1981), in which microskills were identified and discriminated; and Connor (1987), which was concerned with the development, the use, and the evaluation of a total training package of communication·skills for nurses.

Surveys and case studies

The advantages of research into training are that subjects are easily available and generally co-operative and the time-scale relatively short. Research into the characteristics of clients is more difficult. Chief among the difficulties in writing about it is that it may not be clearly identifiable as counselling research. Research studies of clients defined in broad groups such as pupils, students, the elderly, in terms of such problems as psychiatric disturbance, disability, or of situations such as marital breakdown, unemployment, bereavement, and victimization, are legion but are normally published in books and journals not directly associated with counselling. To take one current problem area, unemployment, research work is reported in such diverse sources as *Psychological Medicine*, the *Unemployment Unit Bulletin*, the *Employment Gazette*, and the *Psychological Bulletin*, as well as in books (Colledge and Bartholomew 1980; Warr 1982; Platt 1983; Fagin and Little 1984). Unless these studies are cross-referenced as 'counselling' they are unlikely to be included in any summary of counselling research. Among the few which may be clearly identified as such are: 'Whom are we counselling?' (Bahrami 1985) and the studies by Roberts *et al.* (1982) and Weeks (1979) of the young unemployed. Then there are studies of pupil and student perception of their problems (Alkali 1982; Baidoun 1987; Jones 1987), studies of the transfer problems of pupils (Carter 1976; James 1980), and a study of the 'one-interview client' in marriage guidance (Heisler 1980).

Information about clients appears, of course, in the effectiveness studies previously mentioned and in surveys and case studies of counselling services. In the early stages of development of any social service there is a need for descriptive surveys. Questions need to be answered: how many counsellors, how many agencies, where located, what approach, how many clients, how funded? The first target was often guidance and counselling in schools, in Scotland (Fletcher 1979; Gray 1980), in Ireland (Chamberlain and Delaney 1977), in Northern Ireland (Fulton 1975), North Wales (Rees 1977), and in colleges (Jenkin 1980; Lago 1981; Davies, 1982). While these were often factual, research into attitudes of teachers and pupils towards counselling was often undertaken (Fulton 1973; Best *et al.* 1981). At other times the interface between counselling and teaching was the subject of the survey (Farnworth 1987; Roberts 1987). Some surveys are described as pilot studies (Meacher 1976; Davies 1983), the latter being in another area which has been the subject of several surveys; that is, counselling in General Practice (Cohen 1977; Anderson and Hasler 1979; Waydenfeld and Waydenfeld 1980; Wyld 1981; Corney 1986).

Such surveys are often conducted by post in the form of questionnaires or requests for information. They sometimes include interviews and case studies. Interviews are a particularly appropriate method for counsellors and form part of many research projects (for example, Al Shawi 1986). They enable the researcher to gather much detailed information and although difficult to quantify and over-subjective, it may also be sensitive personal material which cannot be discovered easily in any other way. The case study is a popular form of research since the researchers are often enabled to investigate what concerns them more closely, their own service. Looking in detail at one agency tends to be more attractive to counsellors than more general surveys – particularly when the researcher can avoid statistics. At its best the case study of an organization can give insight into the operation of a counselling service but, at its worst, it is highly subjective and difficult to put into any wider context. Many case studies, however slight, offer the only information available about a particular aspect of counselling and even when limited in scope are valuable as pilot studies in that aspect. Examples to illustrate the scope of case studies would be 'Nightline' (Thompson and Thompson 1974) and 'The life (and death?) of a student counselling service' (Pashley 1976). There have been several detailed studies of counselling in a single organization such as a school or a college (Sheiff 1973; Thomas 1973; Cley 1976; Gordon 1978; Charlton 1980; Blomeley 1982) and these evaluate as well as describe. There have also been case studies of counselling in general practice (Marsh and Barr 1975; Meacher 1976; Cohen and Halpern 1978). Perhaps the most comprehensive research of this type is a description of the Isis Centre carried out by Oldfield (1983). This study not only describes the service and its clients but attempts, through a follow-up of clients, to evaluate their perception of the effectiveness of the services provided. Foreign students in Britain often wish to make surveys or case studies of services in their own countries (Shakir 1975; Alkali 1982; Amekudi 1982); others wish to compare clients, resources, and services there with those in this country (for example, Al Shawi 1986; Baidoun 1987). Such comparative studies are useful, not only in helping us to see ourselves as others see us but also in helping us to develop a cross-cultural perspective on counselling. Research in progress into the counselling needs of overseas students (Al Shawi 1987) suggests that such a perspective is needed in student counselling in Britain.[*]

The current situation in counselling research

Although most early counselling research emanated from the field of education, the present situation is very different. The current *Register of Educational Research in the UK* (NFER 1987) does not include 'counselling' in its index. Nor is this gap in the register filled by entries under 'pastoral care' often used as a synonym for counselling, while the term 'guidance' is mentioned only twice. On the other hand, *Current Research in Britain* (Young 1986) lists fifty-four items under 'counselling'. Of these eleven emanate from departments of education, eleven from departments of social work, sociology, and social administration, and twenty-three from departments of psychology. This represents a significant shift in the locus and nature of counselling in Britain. Parallel to the shift in the USA from educational counselling to community counselling there has been a move away from school counselling into other settings, particularly medical ones. The index includes seventeen current research projects with a medical

393

emphasis, including such topics as AIDS, alcoholism, handicap, and cancer as subjects. Thus, for example, counselling has been applied to the families of Down's Syndrome children (Brandon and Hauck 1983; Murdoch 1984), to those undergoing abortion (Ness 1976), in General Practice (Wyld 1981), and in hospital settings (Connor 1987).

Counselling continues to expand in marriage guidance, with Relate: National Marriage Guidance providing counselling for over 43,000 clients per year (Hooper 1976). Some research in this field includes Heisler's (1980) study of the one-interview client and the evaluation resulting from a follow-up of some marriage-guidance clients (Hunt 1985). Pastoral counselling continues without much evaluation since Campbell (1974) surveyed the scene, although there has been some development in training and research in bereavement care (for example, Machin 1985). Counselling in work settings and counselling for the unemployed are other development areas but while there is considerable debate about the need for staff care and for counselling as a way of dealing with 'burn-out' in the caring professions and reducing stress in work, there is only a little published research, of which the present author is aware, which looks specifically at counselling in these situations (for example, Hopson 1973; Pearson 1974; Hepworth 1980).

What I have tried to indicate in this chapter is the wide range of research activities which are relevant to counselling and the difficulties which exist in bringing these to the awareness of practising counsellors. The *British Journal of Guidance and Counselling* has provided a unique forum for the publication of research findings in counselling but has inadequately represented what has been going on in some fields, for example, medicine and social work, which have other publishing outlets. My own search for research in counselling has indicated how difficult it is to gain a whole picture and I am conscious of the inadequacy of the summary I have given here.

What has been demonstrated, I hope, is that there is a steady stream of research, mostly from sources in higher education, much of which remains unpublished. The researchers, it seems, having received their higher degrees are reluctant to publish their work in a form which would make it available to counsellors at large. Even when research is reported, the journals and books in which it appears may not always be readily available to practitioners. The result is the perpetuation of a gap between research and its utilization. This gap exists in fields other than counselling, of course, but it seems that there is a particular reason behind the slowness with which counsellors take account of research findings. The temperament and value systems of many counsellors incline them to a view of their work as an art rather than a science and to a mistrust of empirical research. Yet counselling research is important for the counselling practitioner, as Dryden (1980) has demonstrated; and, as Sutton (1987) stresses, when there are so many competing systems of counselling and psychotherapy, it is necessary for counsellors continually to evaluate their counselling. The trend towards an eclectic approach which involves goal-setting and evaluation should facilitate systematic research into the counselling process and its outcomes and encourage counsellors to become involved.

Even if this happens, however, the gap between individual evaluation, its reporting, and its implementation in training and practice will continue unless there is an improved medium for reporting small-scale research. Perhaps a central clearing-house for research notes and summaries could be set up which could publish regular reviews of research and evaluation in counselling. This might serve to stimulate the publication of research findings from theses and improve both the quality and the output of counselling research. The Counselling Research Panel of the British Association for Counselling in its second annual report (Herbert 1987) describes the production of guidelines for conducting research and a statement on the effectiveness of counselling as an immediate priority. Perhaps at some stage, the panel might be able to operate as a central clearing-house for research in the way I have suggested.

No one can be confident that all methods of counselling are equally helpful to clients, nor can anyone believe all that is claimed by some exponents of particular approaches. If counselling is to remain credible and clients are to be protected then its outcomes must be evaluated. If individual counsellors evaluate their own work, step by step as they counsel each client, and then report their findings in some widely distributed publication, then several objectives may be fulfilled. The client's interests are protected, the counsellor's personal competence is improved, and counselling, as a professional activity, will begin to come of age.

Notes

1. The discrimination and modelling of specific sub-skills.
* Editors' note: The Association of Student Counselling has commissioned research into the scope of student counselling in Britain. Part of this research focused on the needs of overseas students. At the time of writing the research report is not widely available.

References

Adams, A. (1978) 'The Perceived Effectiveness of a Form of Counselling on the Academic Progress of Undergraduates in a Large University Science Department', unpublished M.Ed. thesis, Manchester University.

Alkali, S. (1982) 'The Needs for and Provision of Guidance and Counselling Services in Secondary Schools in Niger State, Nigeria', unpublished Ph.D. thesis, University of Wales, Cardiff.

Al Shawi, R. (1986) 'Educational Counselling: A Comparative Study of Education Provision in Iraq and the UK with relation to the Selection of Subjects at First Degree Level', unpublished MA thesis, University of Keele.

——(1987) 'Guidance and counselling and the problems of overseas students', Research in progress, University of Keele.

Amekudi, O. A. (1982) 'Guidance and Counselling in Contemporary 2nd Cycle Education Institutions in Ghana', unpublished M.Ed. thesis, University of Wales, Cardiff.

Anderson, S. and Hasler, J. (1979) 'Counselling in general practice', *Journal of the Royal College of General Practitioners* 29 (203): 352–6.

Antonouris, G. (1974) 'The subsequent careers of teachers trained as counsellors', *British Journal of Guidance and Counselling* 2(2): 160–71.

Ashurst, P. M. and Ward, D. F. (1983) *'An Evaluation of Counselling in General Practice', Final Report of the Leverhulme Counselling Project (mimeo).*

Bahrami, J. (1985) 'Whom are we counselling?', *Journal of the Royal College of General Practitioners* 35 (281): 584.

Baidoun, M. (1987) 'Student Counselling: A Comparative Study of the Expressed Problems of Students in a Palestinian and British University', unpublished MA thesis, University of Keele.

Barlow, D. H. and Hersen, M. (1984) *Single Case Experimental Design; Strategies for Studying Behavior Change*, 2nd Edn., New York: Pergamon.

Bayne, R. (1977) 'The meaning and measurement of self- disclosure', *British Journal of Guidance and Counselling* 5(2): 159–66.

Best, R. E., Jarvis, C. B. Oddy, D. M., and Ribbins, P. M. (1981) 'Teacher attitudes to the school counsellor: a re-appraisal', *British Journal of Guidance and Counselling* 9(2): 159–73.

Blomeley, J. K. (1982) 'From Cathedral School to Comprehensive School: A History of Prestatyn H.S. with Special Reference to Pastoral Care, Guidance and Counselling', unpublished M.Ed. thesis, University of Wales, Bangor.

Bolger, A. W. (1973) 'KOISK: a new vocational counselling instrument', *British Journal of Guidance and Counselling* 1(2): 91–5.

Brandon, S. and Hauck, A. (1983) 'Downs Syndrome: changing patterns', *Adoption and Fostering* 7(3): 45–9.

Breakwell, G. M. (1987) 'The evaluation of student counselling: a review of the literature 1962–86', *British Journal of Guidance and Counselling* 15(2): 131–9.

Campbell, A. V. (1974) 'Research in pastoral counselling – retrospect and prospect', British Journal of Guidance and Counselling 2(1): 64–72.

Campbell, D. P. (1965) *The Results of Counseling: Twenty Five Years Later*, Philadelphia: Saunders.

Carter, R. C. (1976) 'Problems of Transfer from Primary to Secondary School', unpublished MA thesis, University of Keele.

Chamberlain, J. and Delaney, O. (1977) 'Guidance and counselling in Irish schools', *British Journal of Guidance and Counselling* 5(1): 49–55.

Charlton, A. G. (1980) 'An Evaluation of the Effects of a School-based Counselling Programme upon Locus of Control Orientation of 4th Year Junior School Children', unpublished M.Ed. thesis, University of Wales, Cardiff.

Cley, C. (1976) 'The Acceptability of Counselling in a College of Education', unpublished M.Sc. thesis, University of Salford.

Cohen, J. S. H. (1977) 'Marital counselling in general practice', *Proceedings of the Royal School of Medicine* 70: 495–6.

——and Halpern, A. (1978) 'A practice counsellor', *Journal of the Royal College of General Practice* 28 (193): 481–4.

Coles, C. M. (1975) 'A Replication and Extension of Lawrence's Work on the Effect of Counselling on Retarded Readers', unpublished M.Sc. thesis, University of Manchester.

Colledge, M. and Bartholomew, R. (1980) 'The long-term unemployed: some new evidence', *Employment Gazette* 88: 9–12.

Connor, M. P. (1979) 'School Counsellors and School Attendance: An Investigation into the Work of Counsellors with Pupils who are Poor Attenders', unpublished MA thesis, University of Keele.

——(1987) 'The Development, Implementation and Evaluation of Listening and Responding: An Approach to Teaching Communication Skills to Nurses', unpublished Ph.D. thesis, University of Keele.

Corney, R. (1986) 'Marriage guidance counselling in General Practice', *Journal of the Royal College of General Practice* (36): 424–6.

Crowley, A. D. (1981) 'Evaluating the impact of a 3rd year careers education programme', British Journal of Guidance and Counselling 9(2): 207–14.

Davies, P. G. K. (1983) 'The functioning of British counselling hot-lines: a pilot study', *British Journal of Guidance and Counselling* 10(2): 195–200.

Davies, V. P. (1981) 'Training in Counselling Skills', unpublished MA thesis, University of Keele.

Davis, P. M. (1982) 'Guidance and Counselling for Adults in Post-secondary Education', unpublished M.Phil. Thesis, University of Nottingham.

Daws, A. M. (1982) 'A Study of Eye Behaviour During Sincere and Insincere Statements', unpublished MA thesis, University of Keele.

Daws, P. P. (1975) 'The Keele Occupational Crystallisation Self-Appraisal Form', *British Journal of Guidance and Counselling* 3(1): 114–16.

Dickson, D. A. (1981) 'Microcounselling: an Evaluation Study of a Programme', unpublished Ph.D. thesis, Council for National Academic Awards, (CNAA).

Dryden, W. (1980) 'The relevance of research in counselling and psychotherapy for the counselling practitioner', *British Journal of Guidance and Counselling* 8(2): 224–32.

Egan, G. (1986) *The Skilled Helper*, 3rd edn., Monterey, CA: Brooks/Cole.

Evison, R. and Ronaldson, J. B. (1975) 'A behaviour category instrument for analysing counsellor interaction', *British Journal of Guidance and Counselling*, 3(1): 82–93.

Eysenck, H. (1952) 'The effects of psychotherapy: an evaluation', *Journal of Consulting Psychology*, 16: 319–24.

Fagin, L. and Little, M. (1984) *Forsaken Families*, Harmondsworth, Penguin.

Farnworth, P. (1987) 'Personal and Social Education: An Investigation into the Provision within a Welsh Authority', unpublished MA thesis, University of Keele.

Fletcher, A. (1979) 'Guidance and Counselling in Secondary Schools in Scotland', unpublished M.Sc. thesis, University of Strathclyde.

Fulton, J. F. (1973) 'Attitudes of secondary school teachers towards prospective school counsellors', *British Journal of Guidance and Counselling* 1(2): 86–91.

——(1975) 'Response to Change: A Study of Guidance and Counselling in Secondary and Grammar Schools and Technical Colleges in N. Ireland', unpublished Ph.D. thesis, University of Keele.

Gordon, R. B. M. (1978) 'Teacher and Pupil Attitudes to Guidance: A Study of Perth High School', unpublished M.Ed. thesis, University of Dundee.

Gray, J. (1980) 'Guidance in Scottish secondary schools: a client evaluation', *British Journal of Guidance and Counselling* 8(1): 35–44.

Hargie, O. D. W. (1984) 'Training teachers in counselling skills: the effects of microcounselling', *British Journal of Educational Psychology* 54(2): 214–20.

Heisler, J. C. (1980) 'The one-interview client', *British Journal of Guidance and Counselling* 8(1): 35–44

Henstock, M. J. (1977) 'A survey of in-service pastoral care courses for teachers', unpublished MA thesis, University of Keele.

Hepworth, S. J. (1980) 'Moderating factors of the psychological impact of unemployment', *Journal of Occupational Psychology*, 53: 139–45.

Herbert, M. (1987) 'Counselling Research Panel Report', in *BAC Eleventh Annual Report 1986–87*, Rugby: British Association for Counselling.

Hooper, D. (1976) 'Yesterday's counsellors for tomorrow's problems', *Marriage Guidance* 16(5): 147–53.

Hopson, B. (1973) 'Career development in industry: the diary of an experiment', *British Journal of Guidance and Counselling* 1(1): 51–61.

Hughes, P. M. (ed.) (1974) *Training for Counselling*, London: Standing Conference for the Advancement of Counselling.

——(1977)'Changing perspectives in full-time training', *The Counsellor* 2(2): 4–8.

Hunt, P. (1985) 'Clients' responses to marriage counselling. A report on the research project on the follow-up of marriage guidance clients', Research Report No. 3, Rugby: National Marriage Guidance Council.

James, T. (1980) 'From Primary to Secondary: A Study of the Sociometric Status and Subsequent Adjustments of an Intake of Pupils at 11+ into a Comprehensive School', unpublished MA thesis, University of Keele.

Jankowitz, A. Z. D. and Cooper, K. (1982) 'The use of repertory grids in counselling', *British Journal of Guidance and Counselling* 10(2): 136–51.

Jenkin, N. (1980) 'Pastoral Care and its Implications in the Tertiary College', unpublished M.Ed. thesis, University of Keele.

Jones, R. (1987) 'Youth in Transition: Counselling and Guidance Requirements of the 16–19 Year Olds as Observed in a VIth Form College and a Comprehensive School', unpublished MA thesis, University of Keele.

Lago, C. (1981) Establishing a counselling centre: a survey of counselling projects in their early days', *Counselling* 36: 18–24.

Law, B. (1977a) 'System orientation: a dilemma for the role conceptualization of counsellors in schools', *British Journal of Guidance and Counselling* 5(1): 129–49.

——(1977b) 'What do teachers learn from in-service guidance training?', *The Counsellor* 2(2): 8–30.

——(1978a) 'Counsellors as teachers', *British Journal of Guidance and Counselling*, 6(1): 59–75.

——(1978b) 'The concomitants of system orientation in secondary school counsellors', *British Journal of Guidance and Counselling*, 6(2): 161–75.

Lawrence, D. (1971) 'The effects of counselling on retarded readers', *Educational Research* 13(2): 119–24.

——(1972) 'Counselling of retarded readers by non-professionals', *Educational Research* 15(1): 45–51.

McCafferty, N. (1977) 'The Effect of Certain Therapeutic Conditions in Counselling upon Academic Achievement, Family Adjustment and Personality Development in 4th Year Secondary School Boys', unpublished M.Phil. thesis, New University of Ulster.

Machin, L. (1985) 'Bereavement: An Experience of Loss', unpublished MA thesis, University of Keele.

Maguire, U. (1971) 'The Effectiveness of Short-term Counselling on Secondary School Pupils', unpublished Ph.D. thesis, University of Keele.

——(1973) 'Counselling effectiveness: a critical discussion', *British Journal of Guidance and Counselling* 1(1): 38–51.

Marsh, G. N. and Barr, J. (1975) 'A marriage guidance counsellor in a General Practice', *Journal of the Royal College of General Practitioners* 25: 73–5.

Meacher, M. (1976) 'A pilot counselling scheme with GPs. Summary report', London: Mental Health Foundation.

Murdoch, J. C. (1984) 'Immediate post-natal management of the mothers of downs syndrome and spina bifida children in Scotland', *Journal of Mental Deficiency Research* 28(1): 67–72.

Natale, S. M. (1972) *An Experiment in Empathy*, London: National Foundation for Educational Research.

——(1973) 'Interpersonal counsellor qualities: their effect on client improvement',

British Journal of Guidance and Counselling 1(2): 59–66.

Nelson-Jones, R. (1977) 'A factor analysis of the counsellor attitude scale', *British Journal of Guidance and Counselling* 5(2): 185–9.

——and Patterson, C. H. (1974): 'Some effects of counsellor training', *British Journal of Guidance and Counselling* 2(2): 191–200.

——(1975): 'Measuring client-centred attitudes', *British Journal of Guidance and Counselling* 3(2): 228–36.

Ness, M. (1976) 'An appraisal of abortion counselling', *British Journal of Guidance and Counselling* 4(1): 79–87.

NFER (1987) *Register of Educational Research in the UK*, Vol. 6, 1983–86, Slough: National Foundation for Educational Research.

Oldfield, S. (1983) *The Counselling Relationship*, London: Routledge & Kegan Paul.

Orlans, V. and Georgiades, N. J. (1983) 'A study of the effects of different frames of reference on FIRO-B scores', *British Journal of Guidance and Counselling* 11(1): 86–91.

Pashley, B. W. (1976) 'The life (and death?) of a student counselling service', *British Journal of Guidance and Counselling* 4(1): 45–59.

Paul, G. L. (1966) *Insight v Desensitization in Psychotherapy; An Experiment in Anxiety Reduction*, Stanford: Stanford University Press.

Pearson, B. (1974) *An Experiment in Providing a Counselling Service in Industry'*, London: SCAC.

Platt, S. (1983) 'Unemployment and parasuicide ('attempted suicide') in Edinburgh 1968-82', *Unemployed Unit Bulletin* 10: 4–5.

Rachman, S. (1971) *The Effects of Psychotherapy*, Oxford: Pergamon.

——and Wilson, G. T. (1980) *The Effects of Psychotherapy*, 2nd enlarged edn, Oxford: Pergamon.

Rees, W. D. S. (1977) 'Counselling in colleges of education', *British Journal of Guidance and Counselling* 5(1): 65–73.

Roberts, K., Duggan, J. and Noble, M. (1982) 'Out-of-school youth in high-unemployment areas: an empirical investigation', *British Journal of Guidance and Counselling* 10(1): 1–11.

Roberts, L. (1987) 'Guidance and Curriculum in British Schools: A Survey of Innovative Practices in the Education of 14–19 Year Olds', unpublished MA thesis, University of Keele.

Rogers, C. R. (1951) *Client-Centered Therapy*, Boston: Houghton Mifflin.

Rose, G. and Marshall, T. F. (1974) *Counselling and School Social Work: An Experimental Study*, London: Wiley.

Shakir, A. (1975) 'Guidance and Counselling in the West Malaysian Education System: Need, Organisation and Teacher Attitude', unpublished MA thesis, University of Keele.

Sheiff, J. (1973) 'The Objectives, Activities and Outcomes of School Counselling', unpublished MA thesis, University of Keele.

Sutton, C. (1987) 'The evaluation of counselling: a goal attainment approach', *Counselling* 60 (May): 14–20.

Thomas, D. (1973) 'Personal Counselling in a Secondary School: Objects, Process and Outcomes', unpublished MA thesis, University of Keele.

Thompson, A. J. M. (1971) *An Investigation into the Work Performed by Some Trained Counsellors in English Secondary Schools*, Final Report to the Social Science Research Council.

——and Bolger, A. W. (1973) 'The work of the school counsellor', *Trends in Education*, 30: 47–51.

Thompson, D. and Thompson, J. (1974) 'Nightline – a student self-help organisation',

British Journal of Guidance and Counselling 2(2): 200–12.

Truax, C. B. and Carkhuff, R. R. (1967) *Towards Effective Counseling and Psychotherapy, Training and Practice*, New York: Aldine.

Ward, R. (1982) 'An assessment of the psychometric adequacy of the British adaptation of the career development inventory', *British Journal of Guidance and Counselling* 10(2): 185–95.

Warr, P. (1982) 'Psychological aspects of employment and unemployment', *Psychological Medicine* 12(1): 7–11.

Waydenfeld, D. and Waydenfeld, S. (1980) 'Counselling in General Practice', *Journal of the Royal College of General Practice* 30(22): 671–7.

Weeks, M. S. (1979) 'Unemployment and Young People: A Study of School Leavers in the Flint Area', unpublished MA thesis, University of Keele.

Wright, P. (1980) 'The use of video-tape recordings in the training of counsellors', *The New Era* 61(5): 191–5.

Wyld, K. (1981) 'Counselling in General Practice: a review', *British Journal of Guidance and Counselling* 9(2): 129–42.

Young, A. (1986) *Current Research in Britain (Social Sciences)*, Boston Spa: British Library.

Chapter twenty-five

Professional issues in counselling

David Charles-Edwards, Windy Dryden, and Ray Woolfe

Introduction

The issues

In this chapter, we look at professional issues and at some of the reasons why the very idea of professionalism is sometimes regarded with ambivalence by those involved in counselling. Concepts of professionalism applied to what are often known as 'the professions' of, for example, the law and medicine have evolved historically, and we therefore think it important to recall the relative youth of counselling when looking at its professional issues.

The professional issues considered are those which preoccupy counsellors in Britain, in particular: recognition and accreditation, standards and ethics, and training.

Professionalism

The concept of a profession refers to a field of activity characterized by an accepted method or methods of practice, based upon a clearly defined knowledge base. In well-established professions such as medicine or nursing, entry to the profession comes about through the completion of one of a limited number of approved courses of training. Once accepted into the profession, the practitioner operates within an established code of ethics, within which standards of behaviour are closely regulated. This definition of professional is a traditional one and tends to give the impression of a unitary and unchanging set of knowledge and practices. Such an impression is, however, misleading. Professions do change in response to new ideas, fashion, or discoveries. Moreover, they are often characterized by substantial differences of opinion. One development which has significance for the professional development of counselling is the concept of holism.

Holism

A major reaction to conventional orthodoxies about health and illness is to be found in the holistic approach to medicine and other helping professions. This approach perceives human beings as wholes rather than just the sum of interrelated parts. In this way it leads to a less atomized, reductionist, and mechanistic view of the human being. An illness or symptom of ill-health is seen not as an isolated phenomenon to be eliminated, but rather as having some meaning or relevance in the context of the well-being of the total organism. This results in a shift in the focus of helping people from treating the part to treating the whole; and in a corresponding shift towards maintaining good health rather than testing pathology. Medical interest in counselling is a reflection of this growing concern with holism. This is of great potential significance for achieving wider recognition, providing a more accepted place in the range of core services on offer.

Medicine, then, is not a fixed and unchanging profession and in the same way neither is counselling. Orthodox counselling therapies such as the psychodynamic and person-centred are themselves subject to examination resulting from a host of newer therapies (see Rowan and Dryden 1988). The point is that some of yesterday's promising and perhaps threatening developments eventually become today's orthodoxies and are in return replaced by newer innovative ideas and practices. It follows that in thinking about counselling as a profession and about the professional issues which characterize the field we are referring to a situation which is in a continuing state of flux.

Meanings of the term "professional"

There are a number of professional characteristics which dominate counselling. First, as a form of employment obtained after a particular education and training, professionalism represents recognition for those demonstrating high standards. But what constitutes or should constitute counselling standards, including education and training, and the recognition of those standards? These issues will be addressed later in this chapter.

A professional is also someone who earns money for what others do for pleasure, a sense of duty or its intrinsic interest. Many 'amateur' counsellors in this sense, however, will reject the implication that they lack experience, skill, or training just because they are not paid for what they do. The largest British counselling agency offering counselling, Relate: National Marriage Guidance, is based on volunteers who are carefully trained and participate in ongoing case study groups and individual supervision.

The recognition of counselling as, fundamentally, a human process used by many people in our society and potentially available to many of them can raise anxiety among paid counsellors, some of whom may fear that it could be hard to justify their salaries if it is thought that what they are doing can be done by anyone. Such professional insecurity may be expressed in the denial of counselling as a process with its roots in normal human functioning and the tendency to mystify it. The dislike of this mystification by others, because it reduces the accessibility of the process, makes them want to separate counselling as far as possible from the concept of professionalism, which can all to easily be denigrated as a polite kind of protection racket.

Recognition and accreditation

Recognition

Granting of professional status is usually dependent upon some form of certification by a professional body. For doctors, there is a statutory register operated by the General Medical Council, reflecting the established position of the profession. Counselling is, however, still in its professional infancy and without an external controlling body. Any schemes, therefore, have to be developed on a voluntary basis, as we concluded in Chapter 1. Whether or not counselling follows this kind of procedure or develops its own variations is a major issue for the future.

A number of terms are used for professional recognition, and it may be helpful to unpack some of them, so that the ideas that lie behind them are made explicit. At one end of the spectrum, the strongest form of recognition is statutory registration. At the other end is accreditation on a purely optional basis, as currently operates within the British Association for Counselling. This could be strengthened if the BAC recommended officially that its members be accredited and offered a mechanism for those for whom the scheme for general counselling is inappropriate.

A rather stronger option is that planned for the Standing Conference for Psychotherapy, in which membership will be open only to organizations satisfying entry requirements. This, as with accreditation, is likely to be related to such issues as experience, training, acceptance of a code of ethics, and ongoing supervision.

Recognition itself has several meanings, but in this context it is being used as 'admitting (someone or something) as being really (something)'. Recognition comes in many forms, from, for example, reputations informally established by word of mouth to the whole range of formal, public designation. In Britain, the process currently evolving for counselling is accreditation.

Recognition of counselling as a human process relevant to most important interpersonal relationships, at work, among friends, and within the family, is still very limited. This may change in the future as life skills and pastoral care are increasingly seen as central to education for all young people, and not just as an option for those who might be interested in it or who have special needs. Much may depend upon how the national core curriculum for schools develops. This is an issue on which two BAC Divisions, The Association for Student Counselling and Counselling in Education, have been campaigning.

Few if any of those in occupations in which counselling or interpersonal skills are required need worry at present about the issue of their skills in counselling being recognised. Their professional security and self-confidence is likely to come, for instance, from a teaching, social work, medical, or nursing qualification. The growing realization, however, that the degree to which teachers, social workers, doctors, nurses, and many others possess counselling skills (however they have been acquired) is crucial to their ability to do their job effectively may in future begin to be reflected in professional expectations and demands. This may be expressed in the inclusion of counselling skills in basic or post-basic training, and hopefully some kind of non-managerial support and supervision on an individual or group basis.

In the past, counselling has not often been seen as central to professional competence among teachers, social workers, doctors, and nurses. As long as a professional in these fields avoided behaviour so gross that it might attract allegations of misconduct leading to disciplinary action or dismissal, he or she could operate with little fear of censure.

Consumer protection has, however, been more to the fore when it comes to those who occupy roles as counsellors. Because accreditation is still in its infancy, many counsellors depend for their recognition on their reputation or on other experience or qualifications, which may not be directly related to counselling theory or practice.

Many still argue that reputation and the client's own assessment of the counsellor are the best means of recognition of competence and therefore protection of the client's interests. Counselling does not lend itself easily to objective evaluation (see Chapter 24 by Bolger), and no system of formal recognition should be regarded as conclusively indicative of a counsellor's ability. An argument against accreditation runs that a clever, manipulative, but possibly incompetent and immature counsellor may well be able to function successfully through training and achieve accreditation. The best protection against such a counsellor is for their clients to be imbued with the message that they are in charge of their own therapy. If they subsequently decide to stop counselling with a particular counsellor, that decision should be respected by the counsellor. While acknowledging this, it has also to be recognized that during counselling clients frequently experience pain, which has previously been buried, leading through sensitive counselling to a reconstruction of their self-image and their image of the world. The client wanting to terminate working with a particular counsellor has to decide whether that wish should be acted on or worked through.

Recognition does exist informally in reputations established for effective counselling. An example of this is the acceptance of some marriage-guidance counsellors as counsellors in general practice. As discussed in Chapter 8, the use of counsellors in primary-care settings, both on a paid and voluntary basis, has preceded their formal recognition within the NHS. Nevertheless, this has not inhibited the Association of Family Practitioner Committees or the British Medical Association from encouraging general practitioners to integrate counsellors into their multidisciplinary teams.

The lack of counsellor grades has also been a difficulty for the Isis Centre in Oxford, an NHS walk-in counselling service managed by the District Health Authority's Mental Illness Unit. This difficulty has not, however, prevented the Isis Centre from recognizing and employing counsellors, one way or another, since it was founded in 1971.

Industrial and commercial organizations in the public or private sectors tend to be less concerned about formal grading-systems. The decision of the Post Office, Shell, Control Data, and others to employ counsellors, in the variety of ways described in Chapter 11, is based fundamentally on short- and long-term financial judgements. The human resource is a major cost factor in any enterprise. Any cost, such as an in-company counselling project, is worth serious consideration if it can be demonstrated that it is likely to lead to significantly greater productivity than would otherwise have been the case. The recognition of counselling in industry depends upon the belief that it is cost-effective. The demonstration of this demands research drawing on subjective assessment and comparative studies of sickness absence or other relevant objective factors. There is now an increasing body of experience to tap in Britain, although company schemes were initially often American.

Accreditation

The accreditation scheme for individual counsellors was introduced by the BAC in 1983, based on training, ongoing supervision, experience, and continuing personal development. It was resolutely not academic, and its protagonists eschewed the notion that it should be used to ease counselling into a future in which it was regarded as a post-graduate activity. As Sally Aldridge (1987) reported, only 8 per cent of BAC members were accredited by 1986, but that is perhaps not surprising. As many as half of the BAC's individual members would not be eligible to apply as they are not counsellors but people using counselling skills in their work. The scheme itself was essentially experimental in its early years and required time to become widely respected. Some counsellors may have already felt adequately secure professionally speaking. The effort of applying and the fear, anxiety, and potential embarrassment of possibly being turned down are clearly disincentives for some.

Counsellors, furthermore, are generally not enamoured with authoritarian models of society, and some feel uncomfortable with the unavoidable judgemental component of accreditation. There has also been, within the BAC, a reluctance to afford respect to particularly experienced members and the concept of a distinguished British counsellor almost seems a contradiction in terms. The informal recognition of more experienced members as the natural accreditors has been slow in emerging. This is in contrast to the position in the USA, where leading counsellors appear to be given much higher professional peer regard than in Britain. This may change as accreditation becomes more securely established and as counselling supervisors become more visible and recognised.

In 1986, the accreditation scheme was reviewed by Brian Foss, then professor of psychology at the Royal Holloway and Bedford New College in the University of London, who recommended in his report that the scheme become more rigorous in several ways and that further complementary schemes be developed for accrediting supervisors, counsellor training courses, and specialist counsellors. At the time of writing, work is under way on the first two of these.

Accreditation raises almost as many questions as it resolves. The scheme has not attempted to define or assess the essential qualities to be assessed in an effective counsellor. That is left by implication to the supervisor and referee. What would they be? Listening skills and powers of observation, warmth, empathy, self-awareness, and a degree of maturity? Professor Foss on balance supported a continuation of the present 'blind' system, by which applications, at least for counsellor accreditation, are judged without any face-to-face meeting. Such a system is more manageable, and it is argued that it is more objective. That conclusion is to be reversed, however, for the supervisor and training recognition schemes, both of which are likely to have a significant element of live observation in addition to written applications.

The Association for Student Counselling introduced its specialist accreditation scheme in 1979 (Thorne 1985), 4 years before the BAC, which drew extensively on its work and that of the Association for Pastoral Care and Counselling. Other specialist accreditation remains a task for the future. One model may commend itself in which the BAC co-ordinates, monitors, and approves specialist schemes, which for the most part are developed by its divisions or organizational members. Alcohol Concern, for example, has developed a proposal for alcohol- and substance-abuse accreditation, based upon research undertaken in the Department of Social Policy and Professional Studies at the University of Hull.

If specialist accreditation is developed, its relationship with general accreditation has to be determined. Should it precede or follow general accreditation?; or should there be two versions? For example, an applicant to become recognized as a substance-abuse counsellor, who is already a generally accredited counsellor, may need to be accredited in only the specialist area. An applicant with no general counselling experience or accreditation may need some or all of the elements of the general scheme built into her or his application. In a developed series of specialist counselling options, the criteria for the different specializations will need to be examined for consistency.

It is easy to envisage a person wishing to apply for at least three kinds of specialist accreditation: as a counsellor in the NHS and/or general practice; in AIDS counselling; and in bereavement work. Another person might wish to be accredited in, for example, counselling at work; redundancy/unemployment; and substance abuse. The potential number of specialist subjects and permutations for individuals are considerable. Many of the chapter subjects in this volume are possible candidates for specialist accreditation. If the accreditation of counselling skills also develops, the relationship and possible overlap with specialist counsellor accreditation will need to be explored carefully or chaos will result.

The BAC's accreditation scheme contains one feature which differentiates it from practice in other professions. The limited 5-year period is at odds with major professional practice elsewhere. The view in medicine, social work, nursing, and psychology is that once a qualification is obtained it cannot be removed unless the ethical code is breached. Is such an approach progressive or regressive?

It could be argued that it is a highly progressive move to ask practitioners to demonstrate their competence anew after a fixed period of time. On the other hand, such an approach bears particularly hard on women, many of whom have to interrupt their careers in order to engage in child-rearing. The task of re-accreditation is then likely to be more difficult for them to achieve. Whatever view one has of these issues, however, the BAC's policy would seem to represent a departure from the usual practice of other professions.

The BAC's accreditation practice can be seen as a weak system of licensing and is typical of a profession at an early stage of its development. To practice as a doctor involves being placed on a statutory register. There is no question of voluntariness and the title doctor (of medicine) is limited to those persons on the register. An interesting intermediate position is occupied by psychologists. The British Psychological Society (BPS) was granted a Charter by the Privy Council in 1987 to establish a Register of Chartered Psychologists. To be included on this Charter an individual has to satisfy criteria laid down by the BPS. An individual not involved (or not wanting to be included on the Register) can still describe him- or herself as a Psychologist and practise as such. However, the title Chartered Psychologist will not be available to them. Here, then, we have a better established profession with a much stronger system of licensing compared to counselling, but like the latter (and unlike medicine) still employing a voluntary system.

Within psychology, a Counselling Psychology Section of the BPS was established in 1982. An interest group is defined by the BPS as a group of people concerned with a particular area of psychology, and thus they number amongst their membership all those members of the Society, irrespective of their qualification, who have an interest in scientific research relevant to the aspect of psychology covered by the section. In contrast the Society also has Divisions which are concerned with standards of professional education and knowledge, and the professional conduct of their mentors. The qualification for membership of a Division is strictly specified. The Counselling Psychology Section's aspiration to move from Sectional to Divisional status was evidenced by its application to BPS in 1988 to become a Special Group, a form of half-way house, along the road. The development of the Section both past and potential is of some significance to counsellors, as it could have major implications for the basic training of counsellors, were a basic qualification in psychology ever to become regarded as an essential matriculation requirement for further professional training in counselling. We might, in the future, conceivably have two types of people practising counselling: counsellors and counselling psychologists, the latter being a label which some psychologists are now beginning to employ.

The development of counselling psychology as a field of interest makes even more vital the task of evolving the most appropriate accreditation policy within counselling generally.

Statutory registration

For some, the ultimate form of recognition is the accolade of statutory registration, but for the present there is currently no serious movement for this in relation to either counsellors or psychotherapists.

In view of the heterogeneity of counselling and psychotherapy, this is perhaps likely to remain the position in the foreseeable future, although it does present some difficulties for some in the professions with statutory registration in recognizing those who are not as therapeutic equals. Although it is unlikely to prevail, one view put forward by some from those professions is that only psychotherapists who are already doctors, nurses, psychologists, or social workers should in future be recognized. Thus, statutory recognition might come through a primary professional qualification, irrespective of the psycho-therapeutic content in such training. This is closely related to the concept that psychotherapy should be a 'postgraduate' profession, with 'postgraduate' being defined with varying degrees of inexactitude.

Counsellors work in a wide variety of settings, as this volume describes. By contrast psychotherapists work mostly, though not exclusively, in two settings: health care and private practice. The question of statutory recognition is more pressing for those working in the NHS than, for example, in education or industry. Counsellors work in a much wider range of settings and for them statutory registration has not been on their agenda. This is partly because it is not perceived as a realistic option in the foreseeable future, nor for some counsellors critical to their recognition and acceptance, and partly because of the greater ambivalence of some counsellors towards professional aspirations than tends to exist among those who describe their work as psychotherapy.

Standards and ethics

Establishing standards

The BAC has based its efforts to establish explicit standards in counselling in Britain on the formal agreement through Annual General Meetings of a series of codes of ethics and practice. These have been achieved for counsellors in 1984, for trainers in 1985, and for supervisors in 1988. (They are reproduced as appendices to this book.) The latter was based on a consultative document for the 1987 Annual General Meeting, although any of the codes may be subject to revision through future meetings. Although the membership of the BAC is open to anyone involved in counselling without formal entry requirements, the codes are mandatory for all its members.

Violation of a code may be used as a basis for a member of the public taking up a complaint against the member through the Association's Complaints Procedure, introduced in 1983, although at the time of writing this has not occurred. The sanctions, which the Association can theoretically take, are limited, and ultimately rest on withdrawal of accreditation and possibly membership for a counsellor. This might be potentially serious, especially if the counsellor has been employed, partly at least, on the basis of her or his BAC accreditation. It is nevertheless not an absolute sanction in the sense of removal from a statutory register, and a consequent legal bar on practising.

Because the codes are written for individuals, there may be confusion about their application to agencies, for whom there is an implied requirement that their counsellors comply with their own codes or that they draw up their own code consistent with those of the BAC. To undertake the latter may be especially relevant in specialist organizations, which need codes to deal with some of their specialist issues. Perhaps this requirement should be explicit for organizational members of the Association in future.

The codes deal with responsibility, competence, the management of work, confidentiality, and advertising. They have attempted to articulate the common ground among the disparate counselling sisterhood and fraternity, while avoiding such a low common denominator that they make only a mediocre contribution to defining and establishing standards. They inevitably deal with difficult issues, some of which we shall consider further below.

Supervision and support

There is widespread acceptance that ongoing supervision is a crucial element in developing and maintaining standards in counsellors (BAC 1986, 1987a, b). The BAC Counsellor's Code puts it thus: 'Counsellors monitor their counselling work through regular supervision by professionally competent supervisors and are able to account to clients and colleagues for what they do and why.' (BAC 1984a: paragraph 3.3)

Identifying 'professionally competent supervisors' is itself an issue for two reasons. First, as we noted earlier, the Supervisor's Draft Code was only put forward first in 1987 and at the time of writing preparatory work on establishing a system for recognizing or accrediting supervisors is only beginning. For some, however, this is a rather theoretical issue as they have organized supervision for themselves with counsellors, who are also skilled and experienced supervisors, irrespective of any system of formal recognition. For others, however, the most pressing problem is finding an experienced supervisor in their localities to supervise them.

Training for counselling supervision is currently very limited outside London. The acknowledgement of the importance of supervision, which creates demand, will, we hope, lead to more training becoming available throughout Britain.

The second issue we would highlight is that of the authority and responsibility of the supervisor. In discussing confidentiality below, we refer to the exceptions allowed in the BAC Supervisors Code to the maintenance of confidentiality . The effectiveness of the supervisory relationship depends upon the build-up of trust and safety between those involved, as it does in the counselling relationship. However, the limits on confidentiality are greater in the former because the supervisor has some responsibility for competence of the counsellor. A supervisor's report, for example, may be crucial to the success of an application for accreditation or for a counsellor continuing work in a particular agency. Furthermore, a supervisor who exceptionally becomes convinced that a counsellor should not, in the short or long term, continue counselling may be in a difficult predicament, if the counsellor has not reached the same conclusion.

The supervisor has a subtle balance of accountability to both the counsellors and clients, quite apart from, in some cases, an agency or other organization. The danger of the commitment of the supervisor becoming overbalanced in the direction of the counsellor, and the relationship degenerating unwittingly into collusion, is guarded against by the edict that 'supervisors are responsible for ensuring that counsellors have a change of supervisor every 2–3 years' (BAC 1987a: paragraph 2.11). Admirable as this suggestion is, in a number of cases it may not be possible or even desirable for it to be followed rigidly.

The third professional issue we would like to highlight in relation to supervision concerns its relationship with personal counselling. There are some who regard personal counselling as an optional extra for counsellors, although even they would mostly want training to have a strong experiential component. That view is reflected in the Code of Practice for Supervision: 'If, in the course of supervision, it appears that counselling or therapy would be beneficial to the counsellor, the supervisor should discuss the issue and, if appropriate, make a suitable referral to a third party or agency.'(BAC 1987a: paragraph 1.6).

That same code, however, in its introduction on the nature of supervision acknowledges that while supervision must not be equated with counselling, nor in some circumstances can the two functions be entirely separated. The degree to which counselling may be an element in supervision will depend on the dynamics of that particular supervisory relationship. In turn this will be influenced by the counselling approaches to which both the counsellor and supervisor subscribe. These approaches may not, of course, be the same for both and a number of counsellors have deliberately chosen to switch to a supervisor from a different theoretical approach to their own training in order to broaden and deepen their counselling awareness. Thus, 'the *primary* task of supervision is neither training nor personal counselling of the counsellor, although the skills associated with these activities are central to competent supervision' (BAC 1987a: 2). For some counsellors, however, the experience of being a client is essential to their competence, and the counsellor's own therapy or counselling is the primary, although not the only, function and tool of supervision.

The last professional issue concerns the use of counselling skills and supervision or rather the frequent lack of it. Increasing numbers of people in people-oriented jobs are becoming aware of the relevance of counselling to their work. Some of them have a component in their work, in which they are expected to function as counsellors as well as using counselling skills more broadly and less explicitly.

The case for non-managerial counselling supervision and support in a form relevant to these jobs needs closer attention in the future than it has received in the past. The reasons why this kind of supervision is important if counsellors are to manage their work professionally also apply strongly to those expected to use counselling skills in their work.

Many of the benefits of supervision can be gained in joint or peer supervision and in well-led support groups, and the introduction of these in a number of settings may be an augury for the future. However, the degree to which they can offer the individual working with clients the necessary degree of rigorous supervision is an issue requiring further examination.

Confidentiality

As with other professions, those involved in counselling start with a presumption of confidentiality, which for the most part never becomes a serious issue. For some, however, questions about the limits of confidentiality can become very real. The BAC Codes for Counsellors and Supervisors are not absolute. For supervisors in particular there is an expectation that they may need to disclose confidential information, on a confidential basis, about their counsellors in the course of:

(a) evaluations of the counsellor made by trainers or training committees;
(b) recommendations concerning counsellors for professional purposes; and
(c) the pursuit of disciplinary action involving counsellors in matters
    pertaining to ethical standards (BAC 1987a: from paragraph 2.3 of the
    Code of Practice).

One of the functions of confidentiality is to create for clients a sense of psychological safety and security, necessary to fruitful and healing therapeutic relationships whether they be counselling, supervision, or training. Any limits on confidentiality may jeopardize that safety, hence the need to protect it. The Association of Sexual and Marital Therapists (ASMT) is among those who highlight the special issue of groupwork in their code: 'When (sex) therapy in a group format is offered, therapists must recognise the increased difficulty in maintaining confidentiality and discuss this with potential participants.' (paragraph 3.4 of the ASMT Code of Practice)

Only rarely does a counsellor decide that the client could cause danger to others (rather than himself): 'If counsellors believe that a client could cause danger to others, they will advise the client that they may break confidentiality and take appropriate action to warn individuals or the authorities' (BAC 1984a: from paragraph 2.3 of the Code of Practice).

The counsellor is not, however, protected by the code from having to cope with a client's suicide even after the possibility has been explored within counselling. A client who does this will often not commit suicide, but there are exceptions when a client decides, even after counselling, to end her or his life. This is an extreme emotional burden on the counsellor; however, she or he may feel legitimized in her or his silence by the code. Other organizations do not exclude the client in this context. The ASMT Code puts it thus: 'If the danger (to the life and safety of an individual) is clear and imminent, disclosure may only be made to appropriate family members, other professional workers or public authorities' (paragraph 3.5 of the ASMT Code of Practice).

Another confidentiality issue is the divided loyalty that a counsellor working within a company, university, or other organization may experience between her or his duty to the client and to the institution. Pressure is sometimes brought on the counsellor to reveal assessments or information arising out of confidential counselling to someone in managerial authority over them. There have been occasions when the counsellor's professionalism in resisting such breaches of confidence has led to an uncomfortable dispute with senior management.

The distinction between the responsibilities of the counsellor to the client and the institution is strengthened by the Supervisor's Code, which separates clearly management accountability and 'non-managerial supervision or consultative support'.

The renewed interest in business ethics may lead to an increased awareness of the need by both counsellors and their employers to strengthen the ethical compatibility of counselling and other functions, notably management of the organizations in which they work. Some tension will always be a factor of such relationships, however, as individual and corporate objectives, while having a potential for some degree of common purpose, can never coincide completely.

Sex

Sex has always provided an opportunity for controversy. The BAC Counsellors' Code (1984a) states that: 'Engaging in sexual activity with a client whilst also engaging in a therapeutic relationship is unethical.' 'It is not acceptable for a therapist to have a sexual relationship with anyone who is his or her own client' is how the Association of Sexual and Marital Therapists puts it in its code. Dr Elphis Christopher (1984), a family-planning doctor and counsellor, writing in the BAC Newsletter, expressed concern that 'there are individuals who, in the name of 'sex education' or sexual counselling seem uncertain whether there should be any boundaries or limits' (1984: 17). As discussed in Chapter 20 by Cooper, approaches to work in this field vary as do understandings of the phrase 'sexual activity'. At one extreme, the sexual attraction that not infrequently exists in a counselling relationship may be acknowledged and be the source, through resolution of transference issues, of therapeutic progress. For many, communication, verbal and non-verbal, will constitute sexual activity, even though it does not extend to physical contact.

For many counsellors, there is, however, no psychoanalytically inspired taboo on touch, and physical contact will be a legitimate and positive component of the therapeutic relationship, especially where the physical expression of feeling is a part of counselling. Such physical contact will usually have no intended sexual under- or overtones, although it is necessary that the counsellor takes responsibility for ensuring that any sexual feelings that might be stimulated through physical contact are managed therapeutically and sensitively.

Money

Counselling takes time and costs money. It has been estimated that the training, supervision, and administrative support of even unpaid counsellors costs them or their agency (at 1988 prices) £15 per hour. If clients are not to pay directly, they need to come to counselling through their employer, academic institution, the health or social services, or voluntary agencies. The latter, which can include the churches, often encourage clients to make a donation or contribution towards costs. Those working in private practice or on a freelance basis usually have a sliding scale, so that poorer clients can come on a low- or even no-fee basis. This means either charging better-off clients a subsidy component for others or having, rarely, access to Trust or some other form of funding.

There are ethical and therapeutic questions over the issue of who pays and who should pay. It is widely believed that counselling should be available to those who can benefit from it and who need it, irrespective of their ability to afford it. Each counselling setting has different financial undertones. The counsellor in private practice may believe that it is important therapeutically that clients in some way pay personally for their counselling, as this will enhance their commitment to the process and their self-respect in the therapeutic relationship.

The work counsellor, on the other hand, may advocate payment by the employer rather than the individual client. This is an expression of the company's recognition of its responsibility to its staff, even after in some cases they have left, for example in cases of redundancy. It also reflects a conviction or hope that counselling for existing staff is a sound business investment in helping to increase higher productivity or to reduce absenteeism in its various forms.

The counsellor in the NHS may have a similar but less tangible and longer-term perspective in seeing counselling as an investment by the taxpayer in a healthier, happier society. Where counselling is developed by religious groups it is seen as part of their pastoral responsibilities and service to each other and the community at large.

The underlying question for counsellors is this: Is counselling charity from the strong to the weak and inadequate; or a sound and cost-effective investment in the future health and strength of our society? According to this view, the costs will be repaid in the quality of contribution made in terms of self-motivated productivity, values, relationships, and consideration towards others.

The counsellor's experience

Whether a counsellor has had personal experience of the major or presenting problem facing the client is also an issue for specialist accreditation. Our view is that it is a counsellor's ability to empathize that is crucial, rather than shared experience. Indeed, counsellors need to be wary of equating the experience of their clients to their own. They may both have experienced, for example, the death of a partner and there may be common elements in those experiences, but it is dangerous to make such assumptions. To do so may lead counsellors to identify so closely, and possibly inaccurately, with clients that they may not be able to relate to clients as they really are. Typically, therefore, the marriage counsellor is not necessarily required to be married or the AIDS counsellor to be HIV positive.

Nevertheless, some common experience may be invaluable in building client confidence in the counsellor's level of understanding: consequently, most marriage counsellors have been or are married. This is sometimes taken further. Some outplacement agencies, for example, will only employ people as counsellors who have had the experience of unemployment. It helps reinforce the probability that the counsellor will have adequate comprehension of clients' experiences; and clients will be less likely to feel they will be regarded as inferior by the counsellor because they are unemployed.

This will continue to be an issue for the future, although the development of specialist accreditation may make it easier for those relying on direct experience of the presenting problem, such as unemployment, to replace it by recognition of the counsellor's ability to empathize, linked to any necessary training or knowledge that is needed for particular kinds of counselling.

Power and oppression

In Chapter 13 by Lago and Thompson, the implications of a particular kind of experience, that of racial identity, for the counselling relationship were examined. There are, however, a number of other ways in which one individual is likely to be in a more powerful position within society, psychologically and economically, simply through membership of a particular group. The professional issue is how counsellors can work ethically and effectively, if at all, across these barriers. How can they ensure that, even if it is not always possible to turn such barriers into bridges, they are at least not obstacles to the effectiveness of counselling? Many women may not only feel safer with a female counsellor, but work more effectively with one too. The counsellor is in a powerful role and the very fact that a woman's counsellor is male may reinforce an experience of being relatively powerless with men. When this is coupled with a male counsellor, who may himself be relatively unaware of the subtleties of his unconscious, as well as conscious, conditioning, clients may end up with an experience of counselling that reinforces oppression rather than helps them become liberated from at least its psychological effects.

The Oppressive Role	The Oppressed Role	Nature of Primary Oppression
'White'	'Black'	Racism
Male	Female	Sexism
Upper/middle	Middle/working	Classism
Middle-aged or young	Older/child	Ageism
Heterosexual	Lesbian/gay	Homophobia
Gentile	Jew	Anti-Semitism
British	Irish	Anti-Irish
Rich	Poor	Financial
Employed	Unemployed	

Fig. 25.1 Kinds of oppression

If counselling is to be experienced as empowering, counsellors who by the accident of their birth find themselves in any of the culturally oppressive roles listed above need to pause. One view that can be adopted is to avoid working with clients in oppressed groups, but that may be neither practical nor necessary, although there are some who advocate this. For those not taking this view, there are two questions. Do counsellors working with clients from oppressed groups have an adequate understanding of what it is like to be a member of those groups on a day-to-day basis, quite apart from living with what is often a painful collective as well as individual history? Second, have such counsellors worked experientially, as clients or trainees, on their own conscious and unconscious culturally specific conditioning that may make them feel superior to people from some other groups? Such work should be designed so that it does not build up self-hatred or just reinforce guilt, but helps the counsellor work through it. The guilt of belonging to a group whose power and prosperity is, even partly, derived from historically oppressing other human beings is a burden that becomes heavier with awareness. For those in such positions, their effectiveness as counsellors depends upon their ability to put that burden down, so that maximum free attention is available for the client.

While the types of oppression set out in Figure 25.1 are some of the typical British oppressive influences, which often come in clusters in particular relationships, it is not an exhaustive list. Nor should it be assumed that those who fit into the first column of Figure 25.1 have not themselves been oppressed. Indeed, a potent method of training people to become oppressors is to oppress them, for example in the training of torturers and some military personnel. It can also be seen in the past traditions and customs of some English boys' public schools.

The issue for counselling training is whether it adequately reflects a societal as well as an individual dimension. If it does, it will contain a significant component of work on oppression and liberation. This need not be seen as politically controversial, as people in Britain of all political persuasions, except neo-fascist groups, at least pay lip-service to equal opportunity. What is being addressed is its application to counselling practice.

An issue for those involved in counselling is also whether they can, in their training and practice, sufficiently transcend any party-political or tribal allegiances they may have to allow the societal components of a client's experience to be faced. Carl Rogers has given a graphic account of how he helped Protestants and Catholics in a group from Belfast work with and through bitterness, which involved questions of economic, religious, and cultural hatred. Although some would say he was over-optimistic, one of his conclusions is that

> even in the space of 16 hours, centuries-old feuds can be modified and reduced....One striking outcome was that even in this short space of time people could move so far from their own constituency, from the beliefs of their own group, that their lives may have been endangered. This is a problem which needs to be recognised.
>
> (Rogers and Ryback 1985: 7)

Equally counsellors need themselves, and not just in Northern Ireland, to be able to move beyond their own cultural, conceptual prison so that they can effectively help individuals – working on a one-to-one basis, in relationships, or in groups – move through and beyond the cultural limitations in their thinking and feeling.

Of course, counsellors are human and fallible, and cannot wait until their personal nirvana has been achieved before beginning to work with clients. One way forward is, perhaps unconsciously, to choose a setting in which the challenge of confronting one's own societal prejudices is likely to be largely absent. So counsellors with a right- or left-wing orientation may gravitate to agencies or client groups in which collusion with their own conditioning will be quietly prevalent.

Where this does not happen, the sparks are likely to fly and it is important that the agency has external supervision or consultancy to help those involved to work through their distress, in such a way that the group does not become stuck in patterns of destructive scapegoating and projection within the agency.

There are, however, limits. Counselling is usually a client-centred, non-judgemental process, but this does not mean, despite some assertions to the contrary, that counselling is value free. The values may be implied and not imposed, but they are present. They are, as described elsewhere by one of us (Charles-Edwards 1988: 10):

> a commitment to encouraging individual and group growth and autonomy within a wider framework; to goal setting and output as well as process; to prioritising and making decisions; to thinking things through and being open; to liberation from oppression and elitism; to supporting and valuing the kind of leadership that facilitates leadership and empowering in others; to cherishing and respecting each other.

Such values make it unethical for counselling to be used legitimately to support clients in being oppressive, although the process may well require clients to have the opportunity to explore, express, and discharge within counselling their oppressive feelings towards others.

Training

Common Standards in training?

Counselling training involves potentially four components:

(a) theory,
(b) skills practice,
(c) counselling under supervision, and
(d) personal-development activities, including experience of being a client.

The concept of a trained counsellor or a person trained in counselling skills suggests that such individuals have been through a similar experience, which though not identical will have a substantial element in common. In practice, training varies in length, depth, and breadth, from full-time to half-day introductions within some professional or management courses. The theoretical base will also determine the content, although there appears to be an increasing tendency to make courses to some degree eclectic. The *Directory of Training in Counselling* (BAC 1984b), which briefly lists courses in Britain, is consistently the BAC's most popular publication, reflecting the expansion of such training with demand.

The degree to which those trained in counselling do have some basic standards in common, if any, is not known with any degree of certainty. The accreditation route represents an effort to identify such standards across different agencies and approaches to training.

417

Accreditation and training

When, in 1983, the scheme for accrediting counsellors was first introduced by the BAC, applicants were expected to have received 'recognized training' or had additional experience under supervision to compensate for the lack of formal training. In the revision of the scheme, introduced in 1987, the requirements were more specific and explicit in terms of the number of hours:

> the successful applicant will be one who has undertaken a total of 900 hours of training and practice, comprising three elements:

(a) 250 hours of theory
(b) 200 hours of skills development, supervision and case discussion
(c) 450 hours of counselling practice with clients under supervision over a minimum period of three years.

Alternatively, 'those with no formal training in counselling will be considered for accreditation after 10 years experience in counselling with a minimum of 150 hours a year counselling practice under supervision'.

The word 'recognized' had been dropped, because no national system of recognition existed, although, also in 1987, a scheme for recognizing counsellor training courses was accepted by the BAC in principle. This is not, however, intended to be applicable to the many courses providing training in counselling skills for the much wider group of those jobs in education, health and social services, industry, and so on for which such skills are deemed to be relevant. The priority given to extending the scheme or developing new arrangements for these courses is a professional issue, although the Royal Society of Arts has introduced a degree of accreditation of its own for counselling-skills training initiated especially in the education sector.

Informed consensus and national guidelines

Accreditation on a national basis is likely to be a slow and relatively expensive process. Meanwhile, training is being started or revised constantly in a wide variety of settings and organizations. The case has therefore been argued for establishing national guidelines at three levels (for counsellors, counselling skills used in related roles, and basic support and helping skills), and also for the training of supervisors. These were indeed the first priorities agreed for the BAC Training Committee in 1987. The Committee also aims to study the feasibility and desirability of the BAC offering a training resource service incorporating consultancy, advanced or pilot training, and training material.

Brigid Proctor (1978), now convenor of that committee, endorsed in the introduction to her book *Counselling Shop* the suggestion in 1977 of a BAC working party on training: 'one of the best ways of creating and maintaining standards of counselling training was to create informed consumers' (p. 12).

National guidelines on training could play a useful part in helping to inform consumers of training of what they can hope to expect. In turn, guidelines, if adequately publicized, will also contribute to informing consumers of counselling about what they might look for in a trained counsellor. This issue is addressed in the introduction to the *Counselling and Psychotherapy Resources Directory* (BAC 1988a) in the section 'How to choose the right person for you'. Individual counsellors in the Directory are required to be explicit about their qualifications and training, their personal therapy, their supervision, and their theoretical approach. In addition to the BAC, the Consumers Association, MIND, the Mental Health Foundation, Broadcasting Support Services, and a number of series or features in the national press, radio, and television have all contributed to educating the general public about the nature and availability of counselling.

Training and a common language

The need for some common standards in counselling training on a multidisciplinary basis is a professional issue which will be easier to resolve the sooner it is tackled. There is an increasing acceptance, as many of the chapters in this Handbook illustrate, that counselling skills are relevant to the performance of certain roles in a variety of professions. In some cases, that realization is beginning to be expressed by including some work on counselling in basic or post-basic training, even if it is at first only a nominal half-day. Such training may contribute significantly to or, equally unintentionally, undermine the kind of team work which may be professionally crucial to effectiveness. Hospital patients, for example, depend for the quality of their recovery in many instances on the degree to which some combination of doctors, nurses, social workers, chaplains, therapists, and perhaps psychologists work together. It is possible that each of those groups has received some introduction to counselling in their own professional training. If they possess a common language across the professions about this aspect of their work, they will be able to communicate with each other more clearly and perhaps at greater depth as a consequence. If they do not share counselling concepts, there is a danger of it being marginalized in their professional interactions.

Many professionals receive their training on a multidisciplinary basis, but that does not necessarily lead to a common language of counselling, unless all the training is with agencies with similar approaches. Without wanting to seek to impose a rigid straight-jacket on such training, there is a need to develop some common approach not only to the concepts of counselling but to the term itself, which can jockey for position with, for instance, communications skills, interpersonal skills, care, human relations, and so on.

National guidelines, supported by key professional bodies, could help remove interdisciplinary confusion about counselling. They would also act as a counterweight to the enthusiastic and enterprising consultant re-inventing wheels by inventing new terminology, if not new theories, in the interest of establishing a sharp market profile. Even though the content of such guidelines is likely to reflect what is already available, for example from Francesca Inskipp (1985), their influence and authority would be greater than anything put forward by a single individual or organization.

Criteria for counsellor training-course recognition

The Accreditation process is itself one means of establishing guidelines for others to follow, including some who may have no wish to seek accreditation. Thus, the criteria for the BAC scheme to provide the recognition of counsellor training-courses represent a significant pointer. It may be useful, therefore, to consider some of these proposals in detail (BAC 1988b).

The selection process should be designed so that those selected show evidence of the following attributes or the potential for developing them:

— self-awareness, maturity and stability;
— the ability to make use of and reflect upon life experience;
— the capacity to cope with the emotional and intellectual demands of the course;
— the ability to form a helping relationship;
— the ability to be self-critical.

Selection for counsellor training in some instances means that, if the course is completed successfully, the trainee will have the opportunity to become a counsellor in the agency which organized the training. The selection process for training can, therefore, in effect be the first step to a form of accreditation.

Choosing attributes as a basis for selection involves facing the issue of subjectivity. Qualities such as maturity and stability are notoriously difficult to assess in objective, behavioural terms, but to choose to omit them for that reason from explicit consideration in selection means leaving out factors at the heart of effective counselling. That the word 'emotional' precedes 'intellectual' in the criteria reflects the view that such training should not be primarily academic, nor that a person's intellectual development be the primary consideration in selecting a potential counsellor.

In the operational stage of training, a balance is advocated between work on self and with clients. Courses should provide:

— 'Regular and systematic approaches to self-awareness work which is congruent with the course rationale;
— A balance between individual growth work, group interpersonal experience and community meeting interaction;
— Experience of being in the client role.'

In practice, training has varied considerably in the degree to which the last of these points is included, although for many some form of personal therapy is a crucial counselling qualification.

The criteria also specify 'substantial and regular counselling practice with more than one client during the course' and 'regular supervision for the students' counselling work consistent with the course rationale, design and philosophy'. The skills-training component, and the content and method of teaching and learning, need to reflect work on self and with clients, and also on the cultural, social, and political contexts in which counselling takes place. The latter can be seen in three ways:

(a) The 'social, cultural, ethnic, philosophical, ethical, and political issues' affecting the systems in which we live;
(b) The work of 'other professionals in the mental health field';
(c) The world of counselling itself, including the BAC Code of Ethics and Practice and its implications for counsellors, and the Code for Trainers.

Training in counselling skills and supervision

The length and depth of counselling training appears at times to be infinitely variable, and this in itself is not an issue. A well-constructed half or full day can provide a useful introduction to counselling skills. However, what so often generates controversy are the claims, real or assumed, arising from training. 'He had a session on counselling in his management course and now thinks that he is a trained counsellor.' That he may have also had a session on budgetary control on the same course, without claiming as a consequence to be an accountant, points up the uncertainty about what different kinds of counselling training mean at present.

Although in the past, the initiatives in identifying criteria and recognition arrangements in training have tended to focus on counsellor training, the need to balance that in the future by attention to counselling skills is well recognized. The energy for this work is likely to come mainly from the trainers rather than the practitioners themselves, for whom counselling is not (as with counsellors) their primary professional interest. It is often seen as secondary to, for example, nursing or social work. This is consistent with counselling being regarded as an extra, added on to the essential elements of a job, at worst a work hobby for a few enthusiasts. This may change, however, if and when counselling comes to be seen as a core activity for a particular role, in which case it would deserve to attract the same degree of seriousness and rigour from within the profession as do other core activities.

Conclusion

While this chapter has concentrated on 'professional issues' it is still a truism

421

about counselling, as Bolger (1978) noted, that it has become in recent years both more professional and more amateur. In his inaugural address to the Standing Conference for the Advancement of Counselling, Sutherland (1971: 14), formerly director of the Tavistock Clinic, suggested that the needs of our future society would be 'to have all individuals realise to the full their potential', and this would require counselling services to be widely available

> for all stages of the life-cycle and at the same time, a constant scrutiny of the fit between our institutions and the kind of person we want them to produce. Thus we have to ask what kind of schools and further education establishments will equip people to make this new society, in which the price of permissiveness is inevitably greater responsibility and concern for each other?

He spoke then with the optimistic vision associated with the much-maligned 1960s.

While counselling often still reflects those values, it also has transcended them, and the increasing recognition of its relevance to human development and relationships comes from a very wide cross-section of organizations and individuals. In a world in which human beings have never been more in danger of alienation from each other and their own humanity, counselling has and will have a crucial role in helping people remain human.

References

Aldridge, S. (1987) 'The role of accreditation within BAC', *Counselling* 61 (August): 24–8.

BAC (1984a) *Codes of Ethics and Practice for Counsellors*, Rugby: BAC.

——(1984b) *A Directory of Training in Counselling*, with 1988 update, Rugby: BAC.

——(1986) Information Sheet, 'Identifying appropriate supervision', Rugby: BAC.

——(1987a) *Draft Code of Ethics and Practice for the Supervision of Counsellors*, Rugby: BAC.

——(1987b) Information Sheet, 'Supervision of counselling, Rugby: BAC.

——(1988a) *Counselling and Psychotherapy Resources Directory*, Rugby: BAC.

——(1988b) *Recognition of Counsellor Training Courses*, Rugby: BAC.

Bolger, A. W. (1978) 'Systematic desensitisation as a counselling procedure', *British Journal of Guidance and Counselling* 6 (1): 45–53.

Charles-Edwards, D. M. (1988) 'Counselling, management and BAC', *Counselling* 63 (February): 10.

Christopher, E. (1984) 'Some thoughts and personal views on codes of ethics', *BAC Newsletter* 24 (February).

Inskipp, F. (1985) *A Manual for Trainers*, Cambridge: Alexia Publications, later National Extension College.

Proctor, B. (1978) *Counselling Shop: An Introduction to the Theories and Techniques of Ten Approaches to Counselling*, London: Burnett Books.

Rogers, C. R. and Ryback, D. (1985) 'The alternative to nuclear planetary suicide', *Counselling* 52 (May): 1–17.

Rowan, J. and Dryden, W. (eds) (1988) *Innovative Therapy in Britain*, Milton Keynes: Open University Press.

Sutherland, J. D. (1971) 'Some reflections on the development of counselling services', London: The National Council of Social Services (now National Council for Voluntary Organisations).

Thorne, B. J. (1985) 'Guidance and counselling in further and higher education', *British Journal of Guidance and Counselling* 13 (1): 22–34.

The British Association for Counselling's Code of Ethics and Practice for Counsellors

A. CODE OF ETHICS

Introduction

The purpose of this Code of Ethics is to establish and maintain standards for counsellors and to inform and protect members of the public seeking their services.

Ethical standards comprise such values as integrity, competence, confidentiality, and responsibility. Members of this Association, in assenting to this Code, accept their responsibility to clients, colleagues, this Association, their agencies and society. The client's interest is paramount, but where counsellors have a conflict of responsibilities they have to use their considered judgement. Therefore the Code of Ethics is a framework within which to work – more a set of instruments than a set of instructions.

In pursuit of these principles counsellors subscribe to standards in the following areas:

   1. The Nature of Counselling
   2. Issues of Responsibility
   3. Issues of Competence

1. The Nature of Counselling

1.1 The term 'counselling' includes work with individuals and with relationships which may be developmental, crisis support, psychotherapeutic, guiding or problem solving. It may be practised within a counselling or other professional work setting, or in private practice on a paid or voluntary basis. People working as 'carers', 'counsellors', or 'befrienders' will also find much of this code relevant to their work.

1.2 The task of counselling is to give the 'client' an opportunity to explore, discover, and clarify ways of living more satisfyingly and resourcefully. Maintaining good standards of counselling involves continuing self-monitoring and self-development on the part of the counsellor.

1.3 The counselling relationship by its nature is confidential.

2. *Issues of Responsibility*

2.1 Counselling is a deliberately undertaken responsibility.

2.2 Counsellors are responsible for the observation of the principles embodied in this Code of Ethics.

2.3 Counsellors respect the dignity and worth of every human being and their ultimate right to self-determination, whilst having due regard for the interests of others. Counsellors accept a responsibility to encourage and facilitate the self-development of the client within the client's network of relationships.

2.4 Counsellors are responsible for setting and monitoring the boundaries between a working relationship and friendship, and for making the boundaries as explicit as possible to the client.

2.5 Counsellors respect clients as human beings working towards autonomy, able to make their decisions and changes in the light of their own beliefs and values.

2.6 Counsellors are responsible for ensuring that the satisfaction of their own emotional needs is not dependent upon relationships with their clients.

2.7 Engaging in sexual activity with a client whilst also engaging in a therapeutic relationship is unethical.

3. *Issues of Competence*

3.1 Counsellors commit themselves to a basic training course in counselling and undertake further training at intervals.

3.2 Counsellors seek ways of increasing their professional development and self-awareness.

3.3 Counsellors monitor their counselling work through regular supervision by professionally competent supervisors and are able to account to clients and colleagues for what they do and why.

3.4 Counsellors monitor the limits of their competence.

3.5 Counsellors, with their employers or agencies, have a responsibility to themselves and their clients to maintain their own effectiveness, resilience and ability to help clients, and to know when their personal resources are so depleted as to make it necessary for them to seek help and/or withdraw from counselling, whether temporarily or permanently.

B. CODE OF PRACTICE

Introduction

This Code of Practice is intended to provide more specific information and guidance in the implementation of the principles embodied in the Code of Ethics.

1. Management of the Work

1.1 Counsellors should inform clients as appropriate about their training and qualifications, and the methods they use.

1.2 Counsellors should clarify with clients the number and duration of sessions, fees, if any, and method of payment; they should also explore with clients, the client's expectations of what is involved in counselling.

1.3 Counsellors have a responsibility to confirm with clients what other therapeutic or helping relationships are current. Counsellors should gain the client's permission before conferring with other professional workers.

1.4 Counsellors who become aware of a conflict between their obligation to a client and their obligation to an agency or organization employing them will make explicit the nature of the loyalties and responsibilities involved.

1.5 Counsellors take account of the limitations of their competence, and make an appropriate referral when necessary. It is their responsibility, as far as possible, to verify the competence and integrity of the person to whom they refer a client.

1.6 Counsellors work with clients to terminate counselling when the clients have received the help they sought, or when it is apparent that counselling is no longer helping them.

2 Confidentiality

2.1 Counsellors treat with confidence personal information about clients, whether obtained directly or indirectly or by inference. Such information includes name, address, biographical details, and other descriptions of the client's life and circumstances which might result in identification of the client.

2.2 'Treating with confidence' means not revealing any of the information noted above to any other person or through any public medium, except to those to whom counsellors owe accountability for counselling work (in the case of those working within an agency or organizational setting) or on whom counsellors rely for support and supervision.

2.3 Notwithstanding the above sections 2.1 and 2.2, if counsellors believe that a client could cause danger to others, they will advise the client that they may break confidentiality and take appropriate action to warn individuals or the authorities.

2.4 Information about specific clients is only used for publication in appropriate journals or meetings with the client's permission and with anonymity preserved when the client specifies.

2.5 Counsellors' discussion of the clients with professional colleagues should be purposeful and not trivialising.

3 Advertising/Public Statements

3.1 When announcing counselling services, counsellors limit the information to name, relevant qualifications, address, telephone, hours available and a brief listing of the services offered. Such statements are descriptive but not evaluative as to their quality or uniqueness.

3.2 Counsellors do not display an affiliation with an organization in a manner that falsely implies the sponsorship or verification of that organization.

©BAC 1984

The British Association for Counselling's Code of Ethics and Practice for the Supervision of Counsellors

A. INTRODUCTION

A.1 The purpose of this Code of Ethics is to establish standards for Supervisors in their supervision work with Counsellors, and to inform and protect Counsellors seeking supervision.

A.2 Ethical standards comprise such values as integrity, competence, confidentiality and responsibility.

A.3 This document should be seen in relation to the Code of Ethics and Practice for Counsellors.

A.4 Members of this Association, in assenting to this Code, accept their responsibilities to counsellors and their clients, their agencies, to colleagues, and this Association.

A.5 There are various models of supervision. The Code applies to all Supervision arrangements.

The Code of Ethics has three sections:

1. The Nature of Supervision
2. Issues of Responsibility
3. Issues of Competence

The Code of Practice has two sections:

1. The management of the supervision work
2. Confidentiality

The Appendix describes different models of Supervision, and comments on issues that may be relevant to particular models.

B. CODE OF ETHICS

B.1 *The Nature of Supervision*

1.1 The primary purpose of supervision is to ensure that the counsellor is addressing the needs of the client.

1.2 Supervision is a formal collaborative process. The term 'Supervision' encompasses a number of functions concerned with monitoring, developing, and supporting individuals in their counselling role. [This process is sometimes known as 'non-managerial supervision' or 'consultative support'].

1.3 To this end supervision is concerned with:
   a) the relationship between counsellor and client, to enhance its therapeutic effectiveness.
   b) monitoring and supporting the counsellor in the counselling role.
   c) the relationship between the counsellor and the supervisor, in order to enable the counsellor to develop his/her professional identity through reflection on the work, in the context of this relationship, which will be both critical and supportive.
   d) clarifying the relationships between counsellor, client, supervisor, and (if any) the organisation(s) involved.
   e) ensuring that ethical standards are maintained throughout the counselling work.

1.4 Supervision is therefore not primarily concerned with:
   a) training
   b) personal counselling of the counsellor
   c) line management.
   However, the skills associated with these activities are central to competent supervision.

1.5 The supervisory relationship must by its nature be confidential.

1.6 A counsellor should not work without regular supervision.

B.2 *Issues of Responsibility*

2.1 Given that the primary purpose of supervision is to ensure that the counsellor is addressing the needs of the client:
   a) Counsellors are responsible for their work with the client, and for presenting and exploring as honestly as possible that work with the supervisor.
   b) Supervisors are responsible for helping counsellors reflect critically upon that work.
   It is important that both parties are able to work together effectively. (See C.2.1 to C.2.4).

2.2 Supervisors are responsible with counsellors for ensuring that they make best use of the supervision time.

2.3 Supervisors and counsellors are both responsible for setting and maintaining clear boundaries between working relationships and friendships or other relationships, and making explicit the boundaries between supervision, consultancy, therapy and training.

2.4 Supervisors and counsellors must distinguish between supervising and counselling the counsellor. They would not normally expect to mix the two. On the rare occasions when the supervisor might engage in counselling with the counsellor, a clear contract must be negotiated, and any counselling done must not be at the expense of the supervision time.

2.5 Supervisors are responsible for the observation of the principles embodied in this Code of Ethics & Practice for the Supervision of Counsellors, and the Code of Ethics & Practice for Counsellors.

2.6 Supervisors must recognize the value and dignity of counsellors as people, irrespective of origin, status, sex, sexual orientation, age, belief or contribution to society.

2.7 Supervisors are responsible for encouraging and facilitating the self-development of counsellors, whilst also establishing clear working agreements which indicate the responsibility of counsellors for their own continued learning and self-monitoring.

2.8 Both are responsible for regularly reviewing the effectiveness of the supervision arrangement, and considering when it is appropriate to change it.

2.9 Supervisors are responsible for ensuring that the satisfaction of their own needs is not dependent upon the supervisory relationship, and they should not exploit this relationship.

2.10 The supervisor and counsellor should both consider their respective legal liabilities to each other, the employing organisation, if any, and the client.

B.3 *Issues of Competence*

3.1 Supervisors should continually seek ways of increasing their own professional development, including, wherever possible, specific training in the development of supervision skills.

3.2 Supervisors must monitor their supervision work and be prepared to account to their counsellors and colleagues for the work they do.

3.3 Supervisors must monitor the limits of their competence.

3.4 Supervisors are strongly encouraged to make arrangements for their own consultancy and support to help them evaluate their supervision work.

3.5 Supervisors have a responsibility to monitor and maintain their own effectiveness. There may be a need to seek help and/or withdraw from the practice of supervision, whether temporarily or permanently.

3.6 Counsellors should consider carefully the implications of choosing a supervisor who is not a practising counsellor. This applies especially to inexperienced counsellors.

C. CODE OF PRACTICE

C.1 *Introduction*

This Code of Practice is intended to give more specific information and guidance regarding the implementation of the principles embodied in the

Code of Ethics for the Supervision of Counsellors.

C.2 *The Management of the Supervision Work*

In order to establish an effective supervision contract, the following points should be considered:

2.1 Supervisors should inform counsellors as appropriate about their own training, philosophy and theoretical approach, qualifications, and the methods they use.

2.2 Supervisors should be explicit regarding practical arrangements for supervision, paying particular regard to the length of contact time, the frequency of contact and the privacy of the venue.

2.3 Fees required should be arranged in advance.

2.4 Supervisors and counsellors should make explicit the expectations and requirements they have of each other, and each party should assess the value of working with the other.

2.5 Before embarking on a supervision contract, supervisors should ascertain what, if any, therapeutic or helping relationships the counsellor has had, or is currently engaged in. This is in order to establish any effect this may have on the counsellor's counselling work.

2.6 If, in the course of supervision, it appears that counselling or therapy would be beneficial to a counsellor, the supervisor should discuss the issue and, if appropriate, make a suitable referral to a third party or agency.

2.7 Supervisors should ensure that counsellors are given regular opportunities to discuss and evaluate their experiences of supervision.

2.8 Supervisors should regularly review how the counsellor engages in self-assessment and self-evaluation of their work.

2.9 Supervisors should ensure that counsellors understand the importance of further training experiences, and encourage the counsellor's professional development in this way.

2.10 Supervisors must ensure that counsellors are made aware of the distinction between counselling, accountability to management, consultancy, support, supervision and training.

2.11 Because there is a distinction between line management and counselling supervision, where a counsellor works in an organisation or agency, the lines of accountability and responsibility need to be clearly defined, between: counsellor/client; supervisor/counsellor; organisation/client; organisation/supervisor; organisation/counsellor; supervisor/client.

2.12 Supervisors who become aware of a conflict between their obligation to a counsellor and their obligation to an employing organisation will make explicit to the counsellor the nature of the loyalties and responsibilities involved.

2.13 Where personal disagreements cannot be resolved by discussion between supervisor and counsellor, the supervisor should consult with a fellow professional and, if appropriate, offer to refer the counsellor to another supervisor.

2.14 In addition to the routine self-monitoring of their work, supervisors are strongly encouraged to arrange for regular evaluation of their work by an appropriately experienced consultant.

2.15 Supervisors should, whenever possible, seek further training experience that is relevant to their supervision work.

2.16 Supervisors should take account of the limitations of their competence, and arrange consultations or referrals when appropriate.

C.3 *Confidentiality*

3.1 As a general principle, supervisors must maintain confidentiality with regard to information about counsellors or clients, with the exceptions cited in C.3.2, C.3.3 and C.3.4.

3.2 Supervisors must not reveal confidential information concerning counsellors or clients to any other person or through any public medium, unless:
   a) It is clearly stated in the supervision contract that this is acceptable to both parties, or
   b) When the supervisor considers it is necessary to prevent serious emotional or physical damage to the client.
   When the initial contract is being made, agreement about the people to whom a supervisor may speak must include the people on whom the supervisor relies for support, supervision or consultancy. There must also be clarity at this stage about the boundaries of confidentiality regarding people (other than the counsellor) to whom the supervisor may be accountable.

3.3 Confidentiality does not preclude the disclosure of confidential information relating to counsellors when relevant to the following:
   a) Recommendations concerning counsellors for professional purposes.
   b) Pursuit of disciplinary action involving counsellors in matters pertaining to ethical standards.

3.4 Information about specific counsellors may only be used for publication in journals or meetings with the counsellor's permission, and with anonymity preserved when the counsellor so specifies.

3.5 Discussion by supervisors of counsellors with professional colleagues should be purposeful and not trivialising.

D. APPENDIX

D.1 *Models of Supervision*

1.1 There are different models of supervision. This appendix outlines the particular features of some of these models.

1.2 One-to-one: Supervisor-Counsellor:
This involves a single supervisor providing supervision for one other counsellor, who is usually less experienced than themselves in counselling. This is still the most widely used method of supervision. Its long history means that most of the issues requiring the supervisor's and counsellor's consideration are well understood, and these are included within the Code of Practice above.

1.3 One-to-one: Co-supervision:
This involves two participants providing supervision for each other by alternating the roles of supervisor and counsellor. Typically, the time available for a supervision session is divided equally between them.

1.4 Group supervision with identified supervisor(s):
There are a range of ways of providing this form of supervision. At one end of the spectrum the supervisor, acting as the leader, will take responsibility for apportioning the time between the counsellors, and then concentrating on the work of individuals in turn. At the other end of the range, the counsellors will allocate supervision time between themselves, using the supervisor as a technical resource. There are many different ways of working between these two alternatives.

1.5 Peer group supervision:
This takes place when three or more counsellors share the responsibility for providing each others' supervision within a group context. Typically, they will consider themselves to be of broadly equivalent status, training and/or experience.

1.6 Eclectic methods of supervision:
Some counsellors use combinations of the above models for their supervision.

D.2 *Points requiring additional consideration*

2.1 Certain models require the consideration of some of the points listed below, that are additional to the contents of the Code of Practice.

TYPES OF SUPERVISION (See below D.2)	POINTS FOR CONSIDERATION							
	2	3	4	5	6	7	8	9
D1.2 One-to-one: Supervisor-counsellor	X							
D1.3 One-to-one Co-supervision	X	X	X	X				
D1.4 Group supervision with identified supervisors	X	X	X	X	X			
D1.5 Peer group supervision	X	X	X	X	–	X	X	X
D1.6 Eclectic model	All relevant points.							

2.2 All the points contained elsewhere within the Code of Practice should be considered.

2.3 Sufficient time must be allocated to each counsellor to ensure adequate supervision of the counselling work.

2.4 This method is unlikely to be suitable for newly trained or inexperienced counsellors, because of the importance of supervisors being experienced in counselling.

2.5 Care needs to be taken to develop an atmosphere conducive to sharing, questioning and challenging each others' practice in a constructive way.

2.6 As well as having a background in counselling work, supervisors should have appropriate groupwork experience in order to facilitate this kind of group.

2.7 All the participants should have sufficient groupwork experience to be able to engage the group process in ways in which facilitate effective supervision.

2.8 Explicit consideration should be given to deciding who is responsible for providing the supervision, and how the task of supervision will be carried out.

2.9 It is desirable that these groups are visited from time to time by a consultant to observe the group process and monitor the quality of the supervision.

©BAC 1988

The British Association for Counselling's Code of Ethics and Practice for Trainers

A. CODE OF ETHICS: TRAINERS

Introduction

The purpose of this Code of Ethics is to establish and maintain standards for trainers and to inform and protect members of the public seeking counselling training.

This document should be seen in relation to the Code of Ethics and Practice for Counsellors.

Ethical standards comprise such values as integrity, competence, confidentiality and responsibility. Members of this Association, in assenting to this Code, accept their responsibilities to trainees, colleagues and clients, this Association, their agencies and society. Trainers are those who train people to become counsellors or who train people in counselling skills.

The relationship between trainers and trainees is similar in some respects to that between counsellors and clients. Trainees, during some of this training, may find themselves in a vulnerable situation with regard to a trainer where painful and potentially damaging material may be revealed which needs to be handled in a sensitive and caring manner. In other respects, the relationship is different. Trainees are adult learners who bring to the training their prior experience and personal style. This should be respected by trainers and only challenged in relation to the stated objectives of the particular training.

Trainers need to be guided by this ethical code so that they can maintain the highest standards of responsibility towards trainees. Therefore this Code of Ethics is a framework within which to work – more a set of instruments than a set of instructions.

1. Issues of Responsibility
2. Issues of Competence

1. Issues of Responsibility

1.1   Training a person as a counsellor in counselling skills is a deliberately undertaken responsibility.

1.2   Trainers are responsible for the observance of the principles embodied in this Code of Ethics and Practice for Trainers and the Code of Ethics for Counsellors.

1.3   Trainers must recognise the value and dignity of trainees irrespective of origin, status, sex, sexual orientation, age, belief or contribution to society.

1.4   Trainers accept a responsibility to encourage and facilitate the self-development of trainees whilst also establishing clear working agreements which indicate the responsibility of trainees for their own continued learning and self-monitoring.

1.5   Trainers are responsible for setting and monitoring the boundaries between working relationships and friendships or other relationships, and for making boundaries between therapy, consultancy, supervision and training explicit to trainees.

1.6   Trainers are responsible for ensuring that the satisfaction of their own emotional needs is not dependent upon relationships with their trainees.

1.7   Trainers should not engage in sexual activity with their trainees whilst also engaging in a training relationship.

1.8   Trainers should not accept their own trainees for treatment or individual therapy for personal or sexual difficulties should these arise or be revealed during the programme of training. Trainees should be referred to an appropriate individual or agency.

2. Issues of Competence

2.1   Trainers, having undertaken a basic course in counselling training, should commit themselves to undertake further training as trainers at regular intervals thereafter and consistently seek ways of increasing their professional development and self- awareness.

2.2   Trainers must monitor their training work and be able to account to trainees and colleagues for what they do and why.

2.3   Trainers should monitor the limits of their competence.

2.4   Trainers have a responsibility to themselves and to their trainees to maintain their own effectiveness, resilience, and ability to help trainees, and to know when their personal resources are so depleted as to make it necessary for them to seek help and/or withdraw from counselling training whether temporarily or permanently.

B.CODE OF PRACTICE: TRAINERS

Introduction:

This Code of Practice is intended to provide more specific information and guidance regarding the implementation of the principles embodied in the Code of Ethics for Trainers.

1. Management of the training work:

1.1 Trainers should inform trainees as appropriate about their own training, philosophy and theoretical approach, qualifications, and the methods they use.

1.2 Trainers should be explicit regarding the training programmes and courses offered and what is involved. It is desirable that there should be some consistency between the theoretical orientation of the course and the teaching methods used on it e.g. client-centred courses will tend to be trainee-centred.

1.3 Any fees required should be disclosed before courses begin.

1.4 Trainers should be open with intending trainees regarding potential suitability for training and make clear what selection procedures are involved.

1.5 Trainers have a responsibility to confirm with trainees what therapeutic or helping relationships are in existence before the course begins, and enable trainees to consider their own needs for personal therapy outside the course and the contribution it might make to their work during their training programme.

1.6 Trainers should ensure that practical experience of counselling under regular supervision should be part of counselling training.

1.7 Trainers should arrange for initial, continuous, and final assessments of trainees' work and their continuing fitness for the course. Trainers should make trainees aware of this process.

1.8 Trainers should provide opportunities for trainees to work with self individually, and in groups, so that trainees may learn to integrate professional practice and personal insights.

1.9 Trainers should ensure that trainees are given the opportunity to discuss their experience of the course in groups, individually or both.

1.10 Trainers should encourage self-assessment and peer assessment amongst their trainees.

1.11 Trainers are to ensure that their trainees are made aware of the distinctions between counselling, managerial, and consultancy tasks and roles in training and supervision.

1.12 Trainers who become aware of a conflict between their obligation to a trainee and their obligation to an agency or organization employing them will make explicit to the trainee the nature of the loyalties involved.

1.13 Where personal differences cannot be resolved the trainer will consult with and where appropriate refer to another colleague.

1.14 Trainers should arrange for regular evaluation and assessment of their work by a professional supervisor or consultant and should ask for full and prompt information of the results.

1.15 Trainers should take account of the limitations of their competence and make appropriate arrangements when necessary.

2. Confidentiality

2.1 Confidentiality must be maintained with regard to information of a personal or sexual nature obtained by the trainer.

2.2 Trainers may not reveal confidential information concerning trainees to any other person or through any public medium except to those to whom trainers owe accountability for training work (in the case of those working within an agency or organizational setting) or on whom trainers rely for support and supervision.

2.3 Confidentiality does not preclude the disclosure of confidential information relating to trainees when relevant to the following:
   a. evaluation of the trainee by trainers or training committee.
   b. recommendations concerning trainees for professional purposes.
   c. pursuit of disciplinary action involving trainees in matters pertaining to ethical standards.
   d. selection procedures.

2.4 Information about specific trainees may only be used for publication in appropriate journals or meetings with the trainee's permission and with anonymity preserved when the trainee so specifies.

2.5 Discussion by trainers of their trainees with professional colleagues should be purposeful and not trivialising.

©BAC 1985

Author Index

Subject Index

accreditation 13, 15, 20; alcohol- and substance-abuse 406; argument against 404; and the BAC 13, 15, 20, 146, 294, 403, 405–8, 418; for 'medical' counselling 132; for pastoral counselling 260; and redundancy counselling 294; specialist 406–7; and training 418

Age Concern: and disability 342

ageing 28–9; and chance 30; and personal identity 29–30

AIDS: see counselling and HIV/AIDS

Alcohol Concern: and accreditation 406

alcohol/drug counselling 364–81; in the community 374, 378–9; and controlled use 369; counsellor identity in 371–4; criminal-justice system and 377; early intervention in 370–1; empathy in 372; and Employee Assistance Programmes 181–2; ethical aims of 368–9; and the family 379; future developments in 377–80; generic 373–4, 376–7; integrated vs. separate 375; prevention and 379–80; principles of 364–7; professional qualification in 373; Regional Drugs Training Units 376; service integration in 377–8; and service provision 370–1; specialist vs. generic 373–4, 376–7; success in 369–70, 371, 373; training/skills development in 375–7; voluntary vs. paid 372–3; in the workplace 180–1, 375

Alcoholics Anonymous 373

anger: of dying patients 298; expressed in groupwork 97

anxiety attacks: and gender in counselling 232

ARC (AIDS-related Complex) 348; see also counselling and HIV/AIDS

assertiveness training 93, 235

Association of Black Counsellors 208

Association of Sexual and Marital Therapists: and confidentiality 411–12; and sex in counselling 412

astrology: and gender-specific images 229

Barclay Report (1982) 110, 111

behavioural approaches: to children's problems 86, 145; in co-therapy 68; in couples counselling 68; evaluation of 388; to family relations 75–6; to sexual dysfunctions 323, 326; see also behaviourism, cognitive-behavioural approaches

behaviourism 11–12

bereavement: see counselling and death and bereavement

Biestek, Felix: and casework principles 108–9

body awareness 224–5, 230

British Association of Cancer United Patients (BACUP) 21

British Association of Counselling 13, 16, 17–20; and accreditation 13, 15, 20, 146, 294, 403, 405–8; and AIDS counselling 347; aims of xii; Association for Pastoral Care and Counselling 18, 255, 260, 406; Association for Student Counselling 155–6, 162, 395, 404, 406; Code of Ethics (counsellors) 294, 424–5; Code of Ethics (supervision) 428–30; Code of Ethics (trainers) 435–6; Code of Practice (counsellors) 426–7; Code of Practice (supervision) 430–2; Code of

dying 299; normal and abnormal 304;
of parents 305; as a process 303–5
passim; varieties of 304–5; *see also*
counselling and death and bereavement
groupwork: conflict in all-female 225; in
higher education 153, 159–60; and
sexual dysfunctions 324; for staff
support 345; *see also* counselling in
groups

HIV infection: *see* counselling and
HIV/AIDS
Homestart Scheme 193
homosexuality: origins of 246; *see also*
counselling and sexual orientation
humanistic psychology 10, 44–5; and
counsellor–client relationships 52; in
groupwork 91; in social-work
counselling 109–10

individual counselling 43–57;
confidentiality in 43, 51;
contraindications for 49–50; in
different arenas 50–1; eclecticism in
53–4; effectiveness of 46, 48; Egan on
48–9, 56n; explanatory frameworks in
46–8; future developments in 53–6;
holistic focus in 46; ineffective 47;
integration in 53–4; and marital
problems 61; modality focus in 51–2;
the relationship in 43, 45, 48–9, 52;
and relationships 44; specialized vs.
generalized 55; and supervision 410;
tasks in 47–8; therapeutic approaches
to 44–5, 52, 52–3; therapeutic merits of
43–4; time/space focus in 52–3; and
training choice 51
Institute of Marital Studies 58, 59, 71
Institute for the Study of Drug
Dependence 376
Isis Centre (Oxford) 21, 124, 388; and
counsellor grades 405; and service
evaluation 393

Jung, C. G.: and religion 254, 263

Kelly, George 25
Kleinian approaches: to disability 329

Lake, Frank: and psychological-religious
insights 258
Leeds Addiction Unit 376

lesbianism and counselling: *see*
counselling and sexual orientation
life cycle (the) 28–40; and ageing 28–30;
and counselling intervention 34–9; and
developmental counselling 37–8; of the
family 33–4, 74–5, 78; life events in
36–7; marker points in 30–1; and
redundancy counselling 292; and stage
theories of development 31–3
Lloyd, G. 362n
logotherapy 25

marital therapy: *see* couples counselling,
family counselling
marriage enrichment 70
Moreno, J. L.: and psychodrama 93
multiple sclerosis: and counselling 342

Narcotics Anonymous 373
National Association for Pastoral Care in
Education 136
National Marriage Guidance Council: *see*
Relate: National Marriage Guidance
National Training Laboratory (Bethel,
Maine): and groupwork 91
neurolinguistic programming: and
computerized counselling 293

Open University: counselling in the 152,
158; and disability 342

pastoral care: defined 253; in higher
education 151; and pastoral counselling
254, 259; in schools 136–8, 143,
145–6; *see also* pastoral counselling
pastoral counselling 252–65; and
accreditation 260; ambience of 253–5;
and the BAC 255, 260; case-studies in
255–7; defined 252, 253–4; evangelical
255; and faith–psychology issues
257–9; and Freud 254; functions of
253; future developments in 261–4;
international 260; and Jung 254; and
Church liberalization 259; and matters
of faith 257; in a multifaith society
261–2; organizations 255; and pastoral
care 254, 259; and the peace movement
259; and political issues 263; research
into 394; the story in 262; *see also*
pastoral care, Westminster Pastoral
Foundation
person-centred (Rogerian) counselling